AF413625

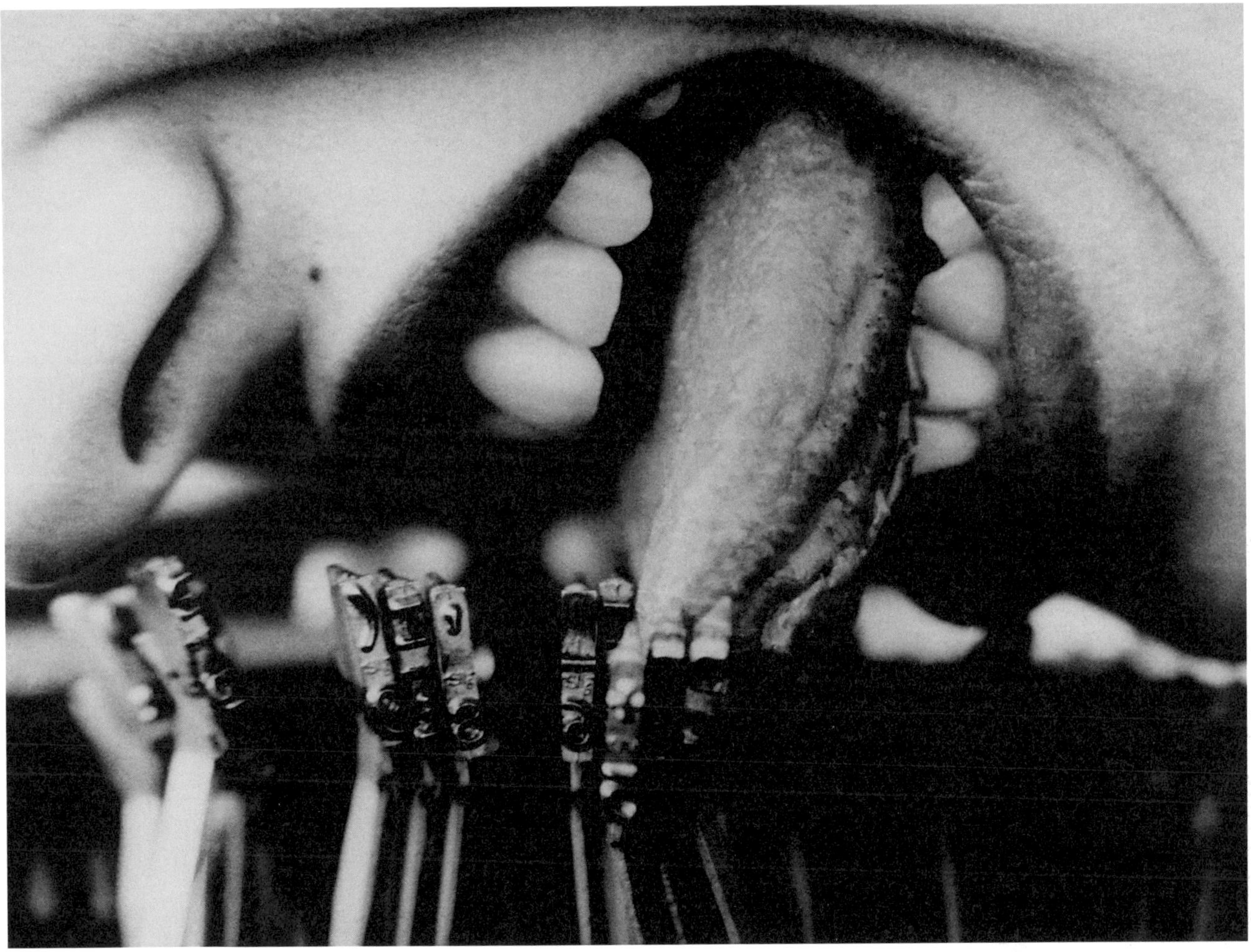

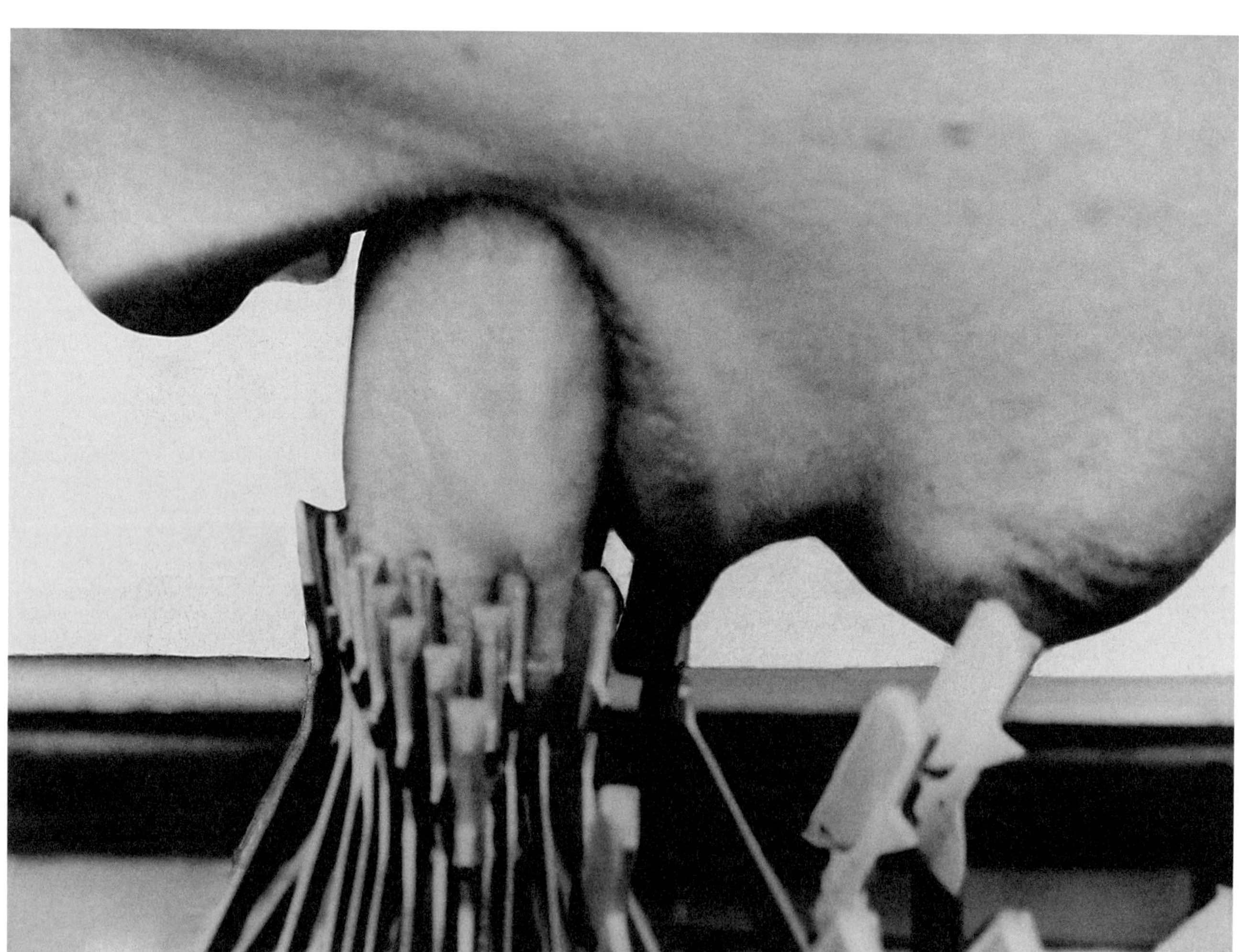

Cover: Lenora de Barros *Poema* (1979)

Women in Concrete Poetry: 1959–1979

edited by Alex Balgiu & Mónica de la Torre

Women in Concrete Poetry 1959–1979

published by Primary Information

INTRODUCTION

Traces of the almost choreographic moves of fingers across a typewriter's keys. A nude body in a sequence of positions, forming the letters of the alphabet. The names of rivers floating down a river. An experiment in synesthesia: writing on music staffs that produces the sound of silence, the written words becoming visible only after a brushstroke's caress. Overlays of texts printed deliberately off-register, producing visual noise and literal indeterminacy. Compositions using the odds and ends in a series of Letraset fonts. A newspaper written in unreadable yet highly expressive glyphs.

The works that result from these methods may very well represent the "tension of word-things in space-time"[1] that the Brazilian Noigandres group saw as unique to concrete poetry in 1958, but they are less concerned with using "graphic space as structural agent" than with liberating letters from words, and words from the conventions that dictate how they should function in ordinary language and in traditional literary texts. If such works definitely involve a substantial degree of "play-activity" and a desire to bring something into the world that is "a reality in itself and not a poem about something or other,"[2] as Eugen Gomringer would have it in his foundational manifesto of 1954, "From Line to Constellation," they are often far from simple objects that are "memorable and can imprint [themselves] upon the mind as a picture." Nor can they be as easily understood as "signs in airports and traffic signs,"[3] like the concrete poems that Gomringer envisioned in his other manifestos. Mary Ellen Solt—a pivotal figure for the movement and a bridge between Europe and the United States given her involvement as an editor, a translator, and a poet herself—is fully cognizant of the ambiguity of the rubric in the introduction to her groundbreaking volume *Concrete Poetry: A World View*, published in 1968: "Despite the confusion in terminology, though, there is a fundamental requirement which the various kinds of concrete poetry meet: concentration upon the physical material from which the poem or text is made. Emotions and ideas are not the physical materials of poetry."

Here we present works by fifty women who may not have identified themselves as concrete poets. In the first place, the label could have seemed narrow given the myriad approaches to the word-image question, and not precise enough to mean any one thing. Furthermore, some of these women worked on the periphery of the main concrete-poetry circuits, although they shared similar concerns. Many of them, perhaps out of a drive to experiment or a sense of irreverence, worked in other modes as well, shunning easy categorization. However, it is clear that, for the most part, the women whose work you will encounter in this volume often chose to disengage themselves from the task of making prescriptive pronouncements. Instead, they focused on multiplying the possibilities opened up by attending to language's materiality, and on challenging the very constructs that support the binaries divorcing a poem's physical properties from its more subjective ones.

In some cases, they also deliberately sought to develop and sustain networks of women artists and writers whose work underscored the corporeality of writing as well as the semiotics of images. Such was the case of Mirella Bentivoglio, whose vigorous curatorial endeavors, paired with an equally energetic artistic practice, led to some of the earliest exhibitions devoted specifically to women artists at the forefront of what she distinguished as *poesia visiva* (including text and images, often collaged) and concrete poetry (concentrating on the visuality of typography and writing and the sonic properties of words). Among the fourteen exhibitions Bentivoglio curated between 1971 and 1981, both in Italy and abroad,[4] was *Materializzazione del linguaggio* (*Materialization of Language*), which she curated for the Venice Biennale of 1978.

This was the first exhibition in the Biennale ever to be devoted to women artists. It perforce partook of the heated feminist debates taking place in Italy at the time, among, for instance, the members of the Cooperativa Beato Angelico in Rome—the first arts space in Italy run by women—and curators and gallerists such as Romana Loda, who organized *Magma* (1975–77), another seminal feminist exhibition. Bentivoglio makes a strong case for why the word-image question would be particularly relevant to women in her essay for the catalog of *Materializzazione*: "Obviously women aren't the only ones engaged in this work, but they do have double the motivation for engaging in the discourse: in the past they've been rendered immaterial (dare I say dematerialized) by the 'abstract sublimity' of their public image, paralleled by their public absence; privately confined to daily, exclusive contact with the material world, women are now using every fiber of their beings to oppose a world rendered unreal (dare I say 'derealized') by repetitive mechanisms."[5]

That epithets such as "groundbreaking" or "landmark" now invariably accompany the mention of Bentivoglio's exhibition for the thirty-eighth Venice Biennale is proof of the effectiveness of the separatist strategy of including only women artists in the show, but it should not fool us into thinking that venerable art institutions had all of a sudden gotten behind the women's movement. In a recent *Dior Talks* podcast, Tomaso Binga reminds listeners that *Materializzazione* opened in September 1978—months after the Biennale's official opening in July—only after feminist groups threatened to stage protests about the fact that, among the approximately 150 artists in that edition of the exhibition, only a handful of women were included. The organizers were intimidated enough that they asked Bentivoglio to organize a show, and thus the women came in "through the back door," Binga recalls.

Aiming to take up "the thread of a broken discourse,"[6] the exhibition gathered eighty-one women artists and poets—contemporaries of Bentivoglio's as well as predecessors, among them Futurists overshadowed by their male counterparts—whose iconoclastic works sought, through a wide range of "poetic operations," to liberate words from the strictures of syntax and the patriarchy, from the conventions of both genre and gender. Their impetus, according to Bentivoglio, was a wish to "reactivate the atrophied tools of communication." She was more interested in centrifugal escapes from "institutionalized frameworks" than in organizing the artists according to the centripetal logic around which different groups working at the intersection of the verbal and visual cohered—Lettrists, Concretists, Spatialists, Signalists, and so forth. Among the artists whose work was featured in the exhibition were Betty Radin, Giulia Niccolai, Paula Claire, Chima Sunada, Amelia Etlinger, Anna Oberto, Ana Hatherly, Annalies Klophaus, Mira Schendel, and Tomaso Binga. Of their work as a whole, Bentivoglio writes: "Mark-making and handwriting follow the circuits of memory, opening the floodgates to create intriguing maps of the energetic tensions presiding over the formation of thought before it's crystallized into verbal articulation. [...] Writing-space and sound-time (sound-tempo) recreate the previously unified entity under the sign of a strangely interwoven rhythm."

Indeed, activations of the word via sound and music are key to several of the poets in our selection. At its most active level, the poem is a verbivocovisual artifact and thus a score for an oralization—the works of Paula Claire and Katalin Ladik epitomize this model. Here their activities also converge with the ideas of Öyvind Fahlström, another one of the figures whose articulations were vital to the understanding of concrete poetry: "Rhythm is not just music's most elemental, physically immediate and tangible medium; it gives us the pleasure of recognizing something that we already know—the importance of repetition, intimately connected to the body's own cadences," suggesting perhaps that concrete poetry could induce a form of "collective rhythmic ecstasy."[7]

We've picked up the threads of Bentivoglio's *Materializzazione*, representing some of the figures in the constellations she traced and expanding them to include women who were working outside the European milieus during the late 1960s and '70s. If a lot of the women poets and artists whom Bentivoglio invited to participate in this and other exhibitions—such as *Esposizione internazionale di operatrici visuali* (*International Exhibition of Visual Operators*) at Centro Tool in Milan in 1972—were members of different European neo-avant-gardes, their exact role in these international groups is rarely established with precision. In fact, it is regularly underrated. Their work is not always credited, and it has rarely garnered the visibility and recognition that their male collaborators' work received. Jennifer Pike, Ilse Garnier, Bohumila Grögerová, and Giulia Niccolai, for instance, are consistently overshadowed by Bob Cobbing, Pierre Garnier, Josef Hiršal, and Adriano Spatola, respectively. Like their male collaborators, who, in this case, also happen to have been their partners, these women operated in the realms of sound, Spatialist, concrete, and visual poetry, yet when their names do appear in attributions, it's alongside those of their partners, as co-signatories. (In this regard, it might be useful to remember that it was not until 1986 that the *New York Times*, the United States' newspaper of record, adopted the "Ms." honorific—giving women the option of not being defined by their marital status—and only after much controversy in the editorial department.)

Gender inequality was often explicitly denounced by the artists and poets in this anthology. They proved that questions of identity, gender, and power were not only *not* antithetical to concrete poetry, but also could be made intelligible—and could be activated—through the process of the materialization of language. We see this in the work of Bentivoglio, Ilse Garnier, Anna Oberto, and Patrizia Vicinelli. Anna Oberto's 1975 manifesto "Nuova Scrittura al femminile" (New Women's Writing), for instance, advocates for the emancipation of women through the reappropriation of handwriting as a form of communication proper to them, in opposition to the sterile machine-based writing of men. And Tomaso Binga playfully chose her male artist's name as a nod to Futurist poet Filippo Tommaso Marinetti, deliberately removing an *m* from *Tommaso*. (The word for "male" in Italian is *maschio*.) In other instances, a political critique arises from the works themselves, whose connotations point to the repetition and mechanization of gendered labor in both the domestic and professional realms. Thus an active poetic factor in the work of Betty Danon, Annalies Klophaus, Françoise Mairey, Liliana Landi, and Ruth Wolf-Rehfeldt is the tension between the body and the machine, the hand and the typewriter. For Wolf-Rehfeldt, the act of typing for the sake of making art creates the opportunity for awareness and change. The typewriter, after all, is democratic—available and accessible to all, and especially to women, whose entry into the workforce was disproportionately reliant on them. Wolf-Rehfeldt's illuminating text *Signs Fiction* ends with the following proposal: "'Type your own art' is my special invitation to people wanting to express themselves in an artistic mode for the purpose of becoming, living and altering facts more consciously."

Liberatory gestures were at the heart of the operations and manipulations conducted elsewhere by artists who were not on Bentivoglio's radar, although they were not explicitly feminist. In Uruguay, Amanda Berenguer, like many of her European counterparts, revisited Mallarmé's *Un coup de dés* (A Throw of the Dice) to create kinetic poems that serve as records of the setting of the sun on different dates. They were collected in the only book of its kind she ever produced: *Composición de lugar* (Composition of Place; 1976). In Brazil, artists active in the counterculture took up the legacy of the Noigandres group, and fertile cross-generational collaborations led to genre-defying word-based art at the intersection of concrete poetry and conceptual art, as in the case of Lenora de Barros. Anna Bella Geiger, on the other hand, arrived at her manipulations of text out of an urgent need to respond to Brazil's military rule. Mirtha Dermisache, in a Buenos Aires where some of the most transgressive forms of conceptualism involved media art, embarked on asemic writing and publishing projects that subverted the conventions surrounding the circulation of text in the public sphere. It is revealing to consider that the publication of her *Diario No. 1 Año 1* (Newspaper No. 1 Year 1, 1972) happened a few years after the radical intervention *Tucumán Arde* (1968) unfolded in Argentinian exhibition venues and newspapers. Conceived as a counter-information campaign documenting the conditions of impoverishment in the Tucumán province during the military dictatorship, *Tucumán Arde* has been identified by Lucy Lippard as central to the emergence of conceptual art in Argentina.

One could argue that similar political concerns animated the linguistic experimentation taken up by the artists and poets working in Novi Sad under the Socialist Federal Republic of Yugoslavia, here represented by Katalin Ladik, Bogdanka Poznanović, Tamara Janković, and Biljana Tomić. Their work, synonymous with an opposition to the codification and prescriptions of official state culture, often blurs the boundaries between concrete poetry and conceptual art. The same case could be made for those working in the Polish city of Wrocław, which, due to its specific cultural and historico-geographical context, became the site of intense collaborative research on the dematerialization of art and the objectification of language. Wrocław, formerly Breslau (until World War II the largest city in Germany east of Berlin), had been assigned to Poland by the Soviet Union in the aftermath of the war. It became one of Poland's Recovered Territories, and to reclaim the decimated city as part of the homeland meant rebuilding its institutions and implementing a proportionate amount of propaganda. Wrocław artists such as Marianna Bocian, Barbara Kozłowska, and Marzenna Kosińska were as interested in conceptual art as in developing textual works resisting instrumentalization. Wrocław provided a "(G)dramatical" setup, where language, territory, and identity could be openly and radically explored, "a place articulating its *geography of grammar*, making use of the *grammar of geography*, as [Tadeusz] Sławek would say, since *to live and to act in some place means to think and act in a language of the particular place (...) but also with the language of particular place.*"[8]

In the United States, on the other hand, explorations tended to be more playful and formal than politically motivated. Hannah Weiner's code-based performance scores/poems are in line with an interest in activating language in public space through street actions and happenings, and specifically in response to the provocations of the mimeo journal *0 to 9*. Susan Howe, who had trained as an artist, was making collages, word-drawings, and word-squares that would eventually come down from the wall and make their way onto the page, expanding the book's possibilities. Around the same period she'd become aware of concrete poetry and had written about it—specifically the work of Ian Hamilton Finlay, Eugen Gomringer, Robert Lax, and Ad Reinhardt—in the 1974 essay "The End of Art." Rosmarie Waldrop's take on concrete poetry approximates it to Language poetry and its proponents' concern with resisting absorption as literary artifice; she describes concrete poetry as a "revolt against the transparency of the word" in the essay "A Basis of Concrete Poetry" from 1976. In *Camp Printing*, she pushes this notion to an extreme by playing with printing errors, subverting the functionality of the means of reproduction.

The technological evolution of typography during the mid-twentieth century, the passage from "lead" to "light"[9]—from physical letterpress to dematerialized phototypesetting—facilitated these explorations. The way text was set and designed was transformed, and type (and therefore text) consequently became an image. Amid these new technologies, the appearance and widespread use of dry transfer lettering, such as the popular Letraset, allowed for emancipation from the physical limitations of metal/wood type and the grid-like structure of the typewriter; it offered an instantaneous application on surfaces and total freedom in composition. The playful arrangements of Giulia Niccolai or Giovanna Sandri superbly exemplify this use of overlapping letters, fragmentation, and organic and multidirectional composition. Witnessing Mira Schendel's ecstatic letter-based works gives credence to Haroldo de Campos's notion of her as a "metaphysical calligraphist" whose writings "are strokes, are residue, are vestiges, are leftovers that she leaves on the paper, allows to bloom on the paper, frees to run across it, as if they were existential ontological traces."[10] Yet these works—and specifically her *Objetos gráficos* (Graphic Objects), begun in the 1960s—are inconceivable without the Letraset forms that contrast so starkly with her handwritten signs. Amanda Berenguer's concrete mobilizations of shards of lyric poems depended on these fonts as well. Letraset, as well as mimeographs and portable duplication techniques, made these explorations increasingly accessible, bringing typographic tools to the hands of poets.

An important caveat is in order. In some cases, the poems that follow this brief preamble have been excerpted from lengthier sequential or book-length works that often call into question where one work ends and another begins, as well as the demarcation between the work of art and the experience of art-making. The work's concreteness is achieved through procedural and/or serial operations, the final work being the sum of its steps to conceptualization and realization, achieved under precise conditions. This makes the reading of an individual poem quite poor, if not meaningless, when detached from the whole sequence. The patterns in play in Françoise Mairey's *Substitution*, for example, can be appreciated only when the entire suite of typing exercises is contemplated. In this sense, many of the poets in this volume in fact challenge the autonomy of the individual poem in isolation from its context, proposing instead that the final work is not just the isolated composition on the page, but the publication as a whole. For Anna Oberto, Mirtha Dermisache, and Ruth Wolf-Rehfeldt, to name a few artists, the publication itself constitutes a deliberate intervention into the world of artists' books. These works' activism lies in the continuity of conception-production-distribution, with a view on the social life of the poem, its address and reception. That Ry Nikonova's proposals for new book forms exist on the page as potentialities only does not make them less visionary, especially when considered as a continuation of the "thread of the poetic avant-garde"[11] (notably the Futurists), *zaum*'s multiplicity in publishing form.

Sequences may have other motivations as well. Some present radical approaches to narrative: Giulia Niccolai's visual *Humpty Dumpty*, or Madeline Gins's metanarrative *Word Rain*, from which we excerpted those pages that contain mathematical notations quantifying the linguistic materials found in each of the book's chapters. Other poets seek to question the notion of the book, its objecthood, its format, the details of its production, the types of modalities that reading it might require, whether they be linear or nonlinear. Blanca Calparsoro's layouts, which activate to the utmost the blank spaces surrounding her collaged typographical utterances, are emblematic of this approach, prompting readers to ask themselves how it is that each font speaks. In this way, the selections included in this volume constitute a departure from earlier anthologies that are constellation-based or merely focused on verbal interventions. They illustrate a movement away from the idea of the poem-in-itself and toward a belief in the necessity of the activation and consequent opening of the poem into the world.

Another distinguishing feature of the works represented here is their inclusive approach to history and literature; it is not one of tabula rasa. Their authors' take is diachronic; their poetry offers an opportunity to weave or collage texts from different historical periods or traditions, swerving them, expanding them, and reinvigorating both the past and the present through their activations and rereadings. The point of departure for Ana Hatherly's series *Leonorana*, for instance, is a stanza in a lyric by Luís de Camões, author of the foundational Portuguese epic *Os Lusíadas* (The Lusiads; 1572). Among the writings that Bohumila Grögerová reworks in her poems are passages from Kafka's *Amerika* and a Czech translation of Joyce's *Ulysses*. Susan Howe collages historical texts into poetic sequences that alter our sense of temporality—their layered diction in tension with the radical modernity of their display.

"KNEAD the material of language: that is what will justify a label such as concrete,"[12] writes Fahlström. Here we could extend this to: KNEAD the material of knowledge. Beyond disciplinary *studium*, we perceive in concrete poetry a sense of reflexivity, an epistemology that considers how information is produced, circulates, and is transformed. Technology and science are both fields that, in the age of cybernetics, poets such as Gay Beste, Agnes Denes, Katalin Ladik, Liliane Lijn, Liliana Landi, and Salette Tavares borrow from. Concrete poetry opens to codes and signals that belong to the extended visual communication of environments and cultures, as is apparent in the works of Tamara Janković, Mary Ellen Solt, and Hannah Weiner, echoing Fahlström's suggestion that "the profusion of possibilities enables us to achieve a greater complexity and functional differentiation."

Women in Concrete Poetry is a kaleidoscope, traversed by many views and perspectives that defy any attempt to define concrete poetry in strict terms. We invite you to meet the poems with openness to the encounter and to read more about each artist and poet in the biographical essays in the back of the book. Needless to say, our selection is far from exhaustive. This is just a beginning. The selection of poets and poems (as well as their reproductions) is unavoidably limited and deserves further research and study. Many more "maps of the energetic tensions presiding over the formation of thought before it's crystallized into verbal articulation," as Bentivoglio so luminously put it, are to be discovered, shared, and mediated. (We'd add that perhaps these energetic maps are simultaneous with verbal articulation and don't necessarily need to precede it.) While our research has tried to rectify some of the biases of historical narratives and the imbalances in representation, it has surely incurred others. In the future we would like to pursue those geographies and lineages that we have not represented here. Our time frame (1959–79) reflects the earliest and latest works of our selection—Suzanne Bernard's *Poèmes* and Ilse Garnier's *Blason du corps féminin* (The Female Body's Coat of Arms)—and documents the shift from a focus on the objectification of language in the early concrete program to the materialization of language through bodies that activate the word on and off the page. It is necessarily too narrow to encompass the international reverberations of the activity of concrete poetry through its many different time zones. This limitation has only left us with the desire to keep following the traces of concrete poetry, which we've grown to consider as a practice rather than a movement. And if it were a movement, here's to its continued forward motion. *Bonne lecture concrète!*

—Alex Balgiu & Mónica de la Torre

Notes

1 Augusto de Campos, Haroldo de Campos, and Décio Pignatari, "Pilot Plan of Concrete Poetry," 1958. Reprinted in *Mary Ellen Solt: Toward a Theory of Concrete Poetry*, *OEI*, no. 51, ed. Antonio Sergio Bessa (Stockholm: *OEI*, 2010), 264.

2 Eugen Gomringer, "From Line to Constellation," 1954. Reprinted in Bessa, *Mary Ellen Solt*, 261.

3 Gomringer, "The Poem as Functional Object," 1960. Reprinted in Bessa, *Mary Ellen Solt*, 263.

4 Leslie Cozzi, "Curatorial Practice and the Language of Italian Feminism in the Work of Mirella Bentivoglio," in *Pages: Mirella Bentivoglio, Selected Works 1966–2012*, ed. Frances K. Pohl (Claremont, CA: Pomona College Museum of Art, 2015), 24.

5 Alex Bennett and Oscar Gaynor, eds., *Tinted Window* no. 2: "Verbivocovisual," 2019, 39. Complete issue dedicated to *Materializzazione del linguaggio*, a 1978 Venice Biennale exhibition of language-based artwork made by women, curated by Mirella Bentivoglio.

6 Bennett and Gaynor, *Tinted Window*, 40.

7 Öyvind Fahlström, "Hipy Papy Bthuthdth Thuthda Bthuthdy: A Manifesto for Concrete Poetry," 1953. Reprinted in Bessa, *Mary Ellen Solt*, 258.

8 Małgorzata Dawidek Gryglicka, "Geography of grammar and grammar of geography, or why Wrocław?" in *WroConcret*, one-day newspaper (Wrocław: Wrocław Contemporary Museum, 2011).

9 On this topic, see type designer Alice Savoie's presentation at ISType 2015: "From Lead to Light: Phototypesetting, a Revolution for Type Design," June 13, 2015, https://vimeo.com/142060109.

10 Sônia Salzstein, "Interview with Haroldo de Campos," in *Mira Schendel*, ed. Tanya Barson (London: Tate Modern, 2014), 208–15.

11 For further reading about Ry Nikonova's relationship to the early twentieth-century avant-gardes, please see Inna Tigountsova, "Hybrid Forms in Ry Nikonova's Poetry," in *The Slavic and East European Journal* 53, no. 1 (Spring 2009): 65–85.

12 Fahlström, "Hipy Papy Bthuthdth," 258–9.

Sonja Åkesson

ååååååååååååååååhhhhhhhh

aiiiiiiiiiiiiiiiiiiiiiiiiiiiii

aiiiiiiiiiiiiiii

ijjjjjjjjjjjjjjjj

ååååååååååååååå ååååååååååååhhhhh

ååååååååååååååååååååhhhhhhh

oeh oeh oeh

aij aih aih

åååååååååååååååååååååååhhhhhhhh

ehh ehh ehh ehh

aih aih aihj

o

oh

*o*ooooooooooooooooooooooooo^{o}

*o*ooooooooooooooooooooooooo^{o}

o aj o aj o aj

ååååååååååååååååååå
å

ååååååååååååååååååå
å

ååååååååååååååååååå
å

nehj

nehj

nehj

mmmmmmmmmmmmmmmmmmmmmmmmm m
m

mmmmmmmmmmmmmmmmmmmmmmmmm m
m

mmmmmmmmmmm mmmmmmmmmmmm
m m

mmmmmmmmmmmmm
m

aiiiiii aiiiiiiiiiiii aiiiiiiii
j j j

åh nehj åh nehj å nehj

åååå åååå åååå

åaåa aaaa åååh ååååh åååååh

eh eh eh eh eh
eh eh eh eh eh eh

åh åh åh åh åh

åååååååååååååååååååååååå

ajajaj o ajajajaj o ajajaj

ooooooooooooooooooooo

oaoaoaoaoaoaoaoaoaoaoaoaoaoaoaoa

oaoaoaoaoaoaoaoaoaoaoaoaoaoaoaoa

oaoaoaoaoaoaoaoaoaoaoaoaoaoaoaoa

IIIIIIIIIIIIIIIIIIIIIIIIIIIIIIIIIII

NEHIJJJ

NEHIJJJ

NEHIJJJ

eh

ho*a*hå ho*a*hå ho*a*hå ho*a*hå

neh ne-h ne-h ne-h

åaiiiiiiiiiiiij åaiiiiiiiiiij åaiiiiiiiiij

haih eh haih ehh haih ehh

AIIIJ AIIIJ AIIIIJ AIIIIIIJ

AIIIIIIIIIJJJJ AIIIIIIIIJJJJ AIIIIIIIJJJ

nej

nej

nej

nej

å nej å nej å nej å nej

nnnnnnnnnnnnnnnnnnnnnnnnn

nnnnnnnnnnnnnnnnnnnnnnnnn

nnnnnnnnnnnnnnnnnnnnnnnn

ÅÅÅÅÅÅÅÅ

ÅÅÅÅÅÅÅÅÅÅ

ÅÅÅÅÅÅÅÅÅÅ

AIIIIIIIIIIJJJJ AIIIIIIIIIIIJ AIIIIIIIIJ

ÅÅÅÅÅÅÅÅÅÅÅÅÅÅÅÅÅ ÅÅÅÅÅÅÅÅÅÅÅÅÅ

ÅÅÅÅÅÅÅÅÅÅÅÅÅÅÅÅÅÅÅÅÅ ÅÅÅÅÅÅ ÅÅÅÅÅ ÅÅÅÅÅÅÅÅÅÅÅÅ

ÅÅÅÅÅÅÅÅÅÅÅÅ ÅÅÅÅÅÅÅÅÅÅ ÅÅÅÅÅÅÅÅÅÅ

AIIIIIIIIIIIIIJ AIIIIIIIII IIIIIIJ

AIIIIIIIIII IIIIIJJ AIIIIIIIIIIIJJJJ

AIIIIIIIIIIIIIIIJJ AJJJJJJJJJJJJJJJJ

OOOOOOOOOOOOOOOOOOOOOO

OOOOOOOOOOOOOOOOOOOOO

OOOOOOOOOOOOOOOOOOOOOO

NEIJ NEIJ AJ OH

NEIJ NEIJ AJ OH

ÅÅÅÅÅÅ ÅÅÅÅÅÅÅ ÅÅÅÅÅÅ ÅÅÅÅÅÅÅÅÅ

ÅÅÅÅÅÅÅ ÅÅÅÅÅÅÅ ÅÅÅÅÅÅÅ

nehj nehjh

NEEIIIJJ NEEIIIJJ

ååååååååååå neijjjjjjjjjjjjjjj

ååååååååååå neiiiijjjjjjjjjj

ååååååååååå neeijjjjjjjjjjjjjjjj

oooohhhh

oooohhhh

oooohhhh

iiiiiiiiiiiiiiiiiiiiiiiii

iiiiiiiiiiiiiiiiiiiiiiii

nnnnnnnnnnnnnnnnnnnnnnnn

iiiiiiiiiiiiiiiiiiiiiiiiij

AIIIIIIIII IIIIIIIIIIIJJJ

IIIIIIIIIIIIIIIIIIIIIIIIIIJJJJ

Aj o aj o aj o aj o aj o aj o aj o

ajjjjjjjiiiiiiiiiiiiiii

ajjjjjjjjjjjjjjiiiiiiiiii

AIIIIIIIIIIIIIIIIIIJJJJJ

AIIIIIIIIIIIIIIIIIIJJJJJJ

AIIIIIIIIIIIIIIIIIIJJJJJJ

AIIIIIIIIIIIIIIIIIIJJJJJJ

ÅÅÅÅÅÅÅÅÅÅÅÅÅÅÅÅÅÅÅÅÅÅÅÅÅÅÅÅÅÅ

ÅÅÅÅÅÅÅÅÅÅÅÅÅÅÅÅÅÅÅÅ

Annalisa Alloatti
and Mirella Bentivoglio

NUME
NUME
NUME
NUME
NUME
NUME
NUME
NUME
NUME
NUME
NUME
MONUMENTO

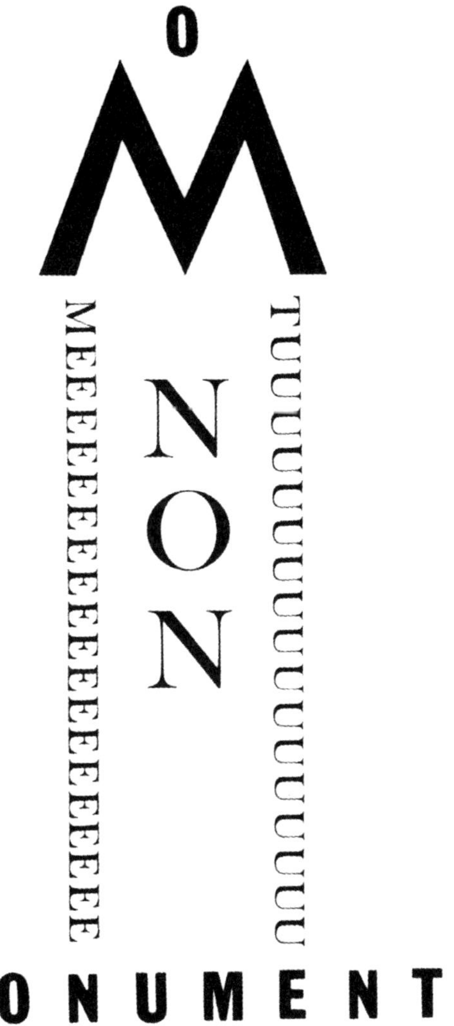
O
M
MEEEEEEEEEEEEEEEEEEEE
NON
TUUUUUUUUUUUUUUUUUUUU
ONUMENT

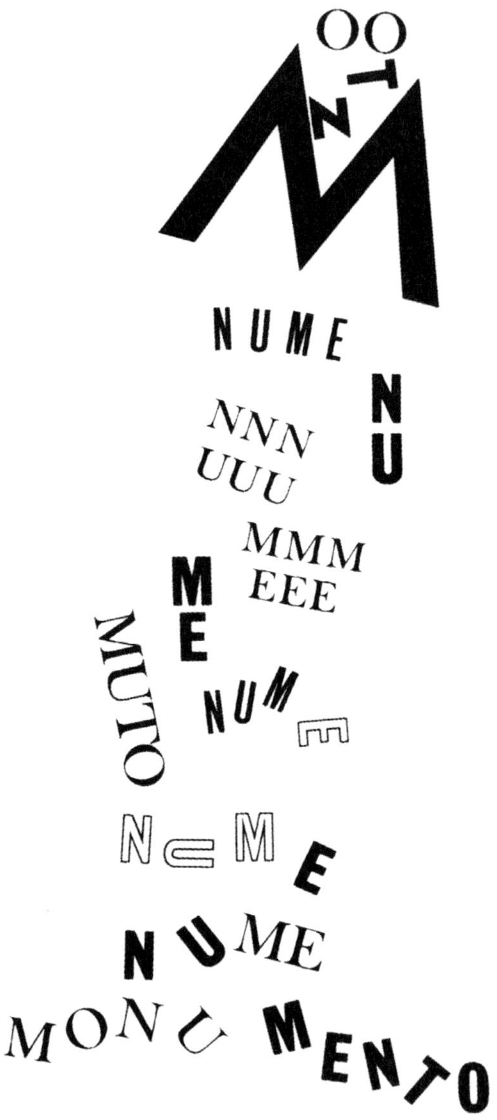
OO
M
NUME
NU
NNN
UUU
MMM
EEE
ME
MUTO
NUME
NUME
NUME
MONUMENTO

Lenora de Barros

RI

AH

AH

AH   AH   AH   AAAAAH

AAAAAAAAAAAAAAAAAH

IIIIIIIIIIH

AAAAH

OH

OH   OH   OH

AN

HEI

AH   AH   AH

A

AAAAAAAA

A

H

CHORA

AH

AH

AH   AH   AH   AAAAAH

AAAAAAAAAAAAAAAAAH

IIIIIIIIIIH

AAAAH

OH

OH   OH   OH

AN

HEI

AH   AH   AH

A

AAAAAAAA

A

H

RUINDORUINS

Mirella Bentivoglio

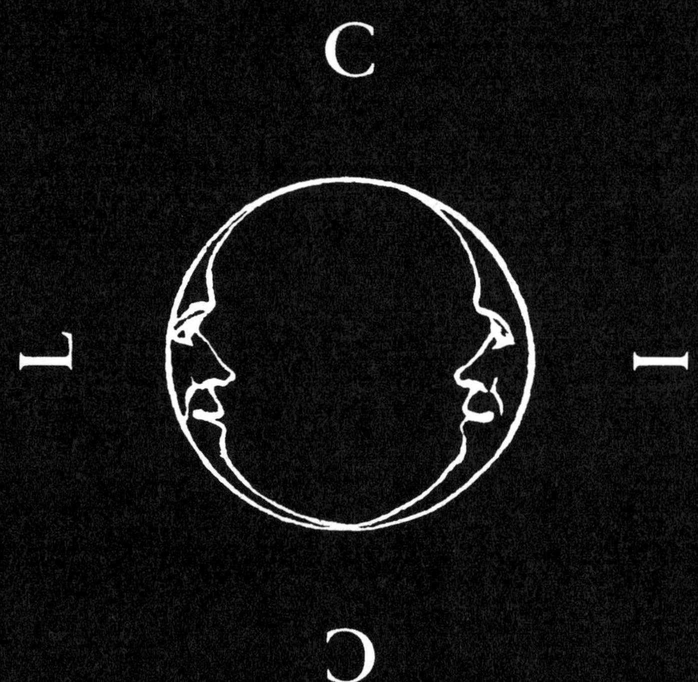
C
L
I
C

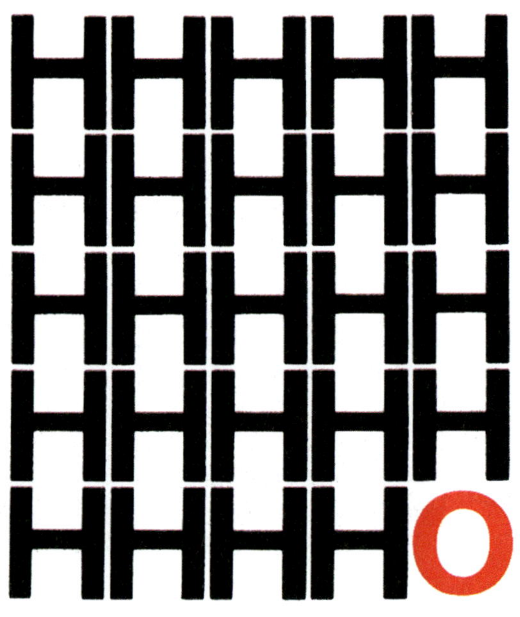
HHHHH
HHHHH
HHHHH
HHHHH
HHHHO

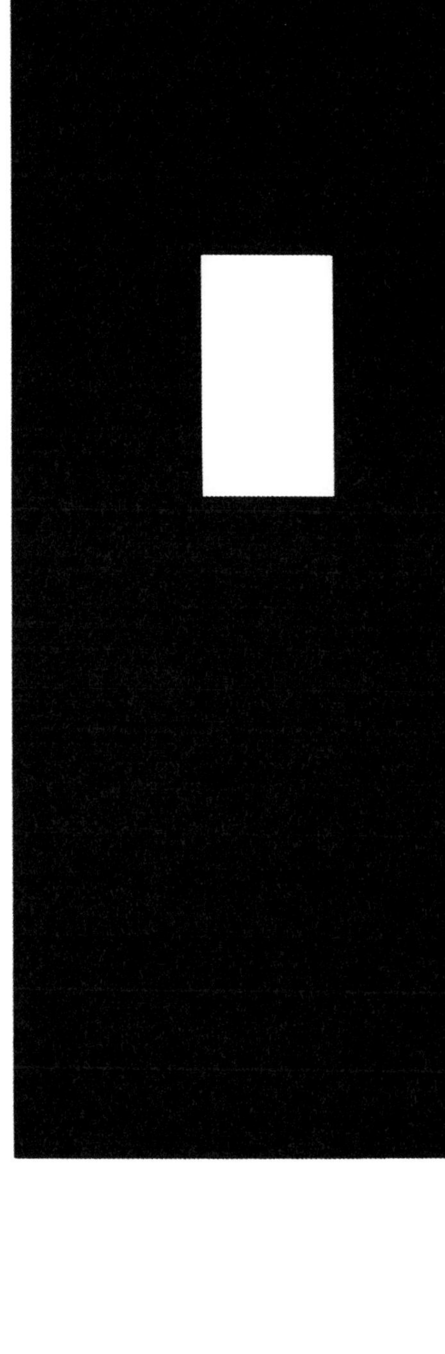

i numeri al quadrato

formano un triangolo

9

8 9

7 8 9

6 7 8 9

5 6 7 8 9

4 5 6 7 8 9

3 4 5 6 7 8 9

2 3 4 5 6 7 8 9

1 2 3 4 5 6 7 8 9

Amore Amore Amore Amore Amore Amore Amore
Amore Amore Amore Amore Amore Amore Amore
Amore Amore Amore Amore Amore Amore Amore
Amore Amore Amore Amore Amore Amore Amore
Amore Amore Amore Amore Amore Amore Amore
Amore Amore Amore Amore Amore Amore Amore
Amore Amore Amore Amore Amore Amore Amore
Amore Amore Amore A chi Amore Amore Amore
Amore Amore Amore Amore Amore Amore Amore
Amore Amore Amore Amore Amore Amore Amore
Amore Amore Amore Amore Amore Amore Amore
Amore Amore Amore Amore Amore Amore Amore
Amore Amore Amore Amore Amore Amore Amore
Amore Amore Amore Amore Amore Amore Amore
Amore Amore Amore Amore Amore Amore Amore

Amanda Berenguer

Poniente sobre el mar del viernes 3 de marzo de 1972

Una multitud suspendida
de cara a la luz
arrastra entre sus pliegues
caballos coches pájaros veleros
combados de tormenta
¿cuánta luz queda?
¿cuánto del día?
pasan sobre la piel curtida
del mar y andan sobre él
anubarrados atraídos
por la certera claridad
donde bajan flechas
segundos de vida
vendrá la noche inminente
pero todo es parecido al alba
miramos la luz única
y nos quedamos en ella.

Una multitud suspendida

deslumbre: recibir con pasmo el día

asombro: entrar con estupor en sombra

deslumbre $=$ principio

asombro $=$ fin

$$\text{velocidad} = \frac{\text{alba} + \text{poniente}}{\text{vida}}$$

$$\text{deslumbre} > \text{asombro}$$

$$\infty \text{ de luz} = (\text{deslumbre} - \text{asombro})\ \text{velocidad}$$

<u>Nota</u>

$e = v \cdot t$

$v = \frac{e}{t}$

espacio $=$ alba $+$ poniente

tiempo $=$ vida

velocidad $=$ anticipación, espera de futuro

MULTITUD
PLIEGUES
TORMENTA
VELEROS
CABALLOS
PAJAROS
LUZ
ATORMENTA
COCHES
TORMENTA
TORMENTA
TORMENTA
TORMENTA
TORMENTA
TORMENTA
TORMENTA
bajan
FLECHAS
Segundos
e
VIDA

Poniente sobre el mar del sábado 4 de marzo de 1972

El incendio se propaga
frío resplandeciente con la calma
de un estado de conciencia
detrás del mar intacto
pardo animal escamoso
todo de acero grabado
frontera última del día de hoy
desaparecieron los fuegos iniciales
los focos los destellos
el cielo que gritaba
consignas visionarias
deslumbra una idea fija total
desnuda incombustible
clavando el resplandor exacto
en el linde donde comienza
lo que ignoramos.

El incendio se propaga

ardo

arco
cero
frontera

ruta
última

linde

comienza

ramos

ramos

ramos

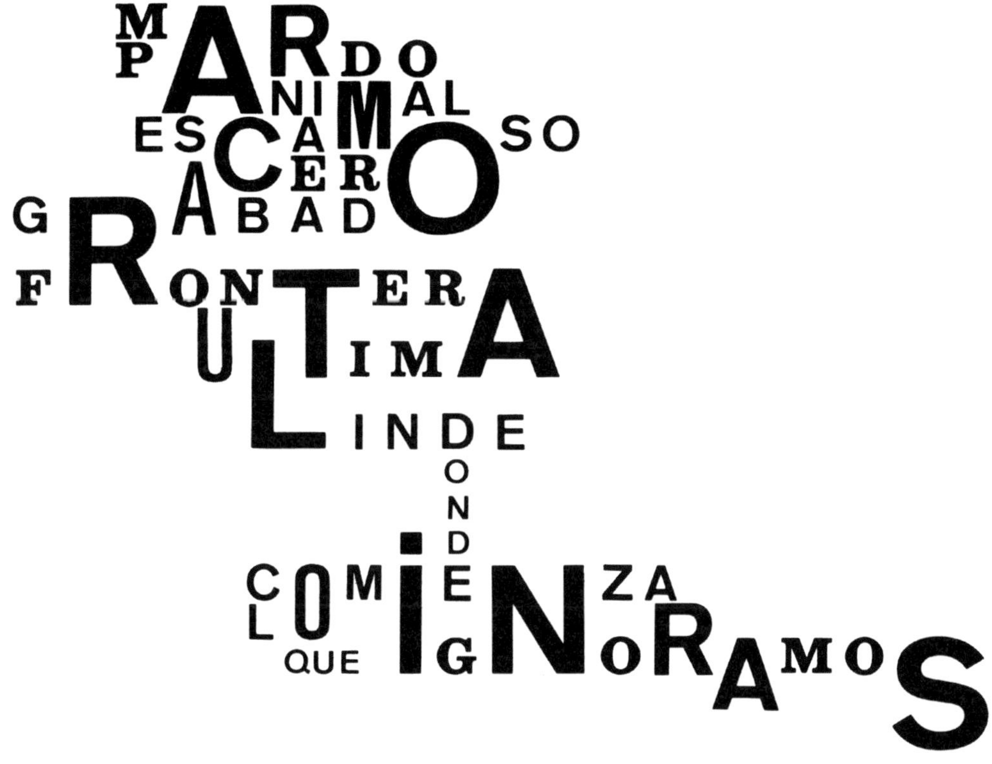

M AR
P DO
ANIMAL
ESCAMOSO
ACERO
GRABADO
FRONTERA
ULTIMA
LINDE
O
N
D
COMIENZA
LO QUE IGNORAMOS

Poniente sobre el mar del jueves 10 de enero de 1974

Oh! viejo hipócrita mar desencadenado
toda suerte de astucias tus espumas
rabiosas
encima la pupila fogosa
en la claridad amarilla
pupila desvelada
bajando íntegra
hacia las trenzas víboras
enloquecidas del agua encabritada
el sol es todo lógica
el mar todo locura
y allá se encontrarán
en la horizontal denuncia
ahora enrojecida de furia
y de orgullo
y pasará la luz
por detrás del exterminio
y quedará la luz sobreviviente
única en el más allá sombrío.

Oh! viejo hipócrita mar desencadenado

era

balanza

platillo fuego

el fiel marca

platillo agua

quimera degollada

Y AQUI SE ENCONTRARAN EN LA HORIZONTAL DENUNCIA AHORA ENROJECIDA DE FURIA

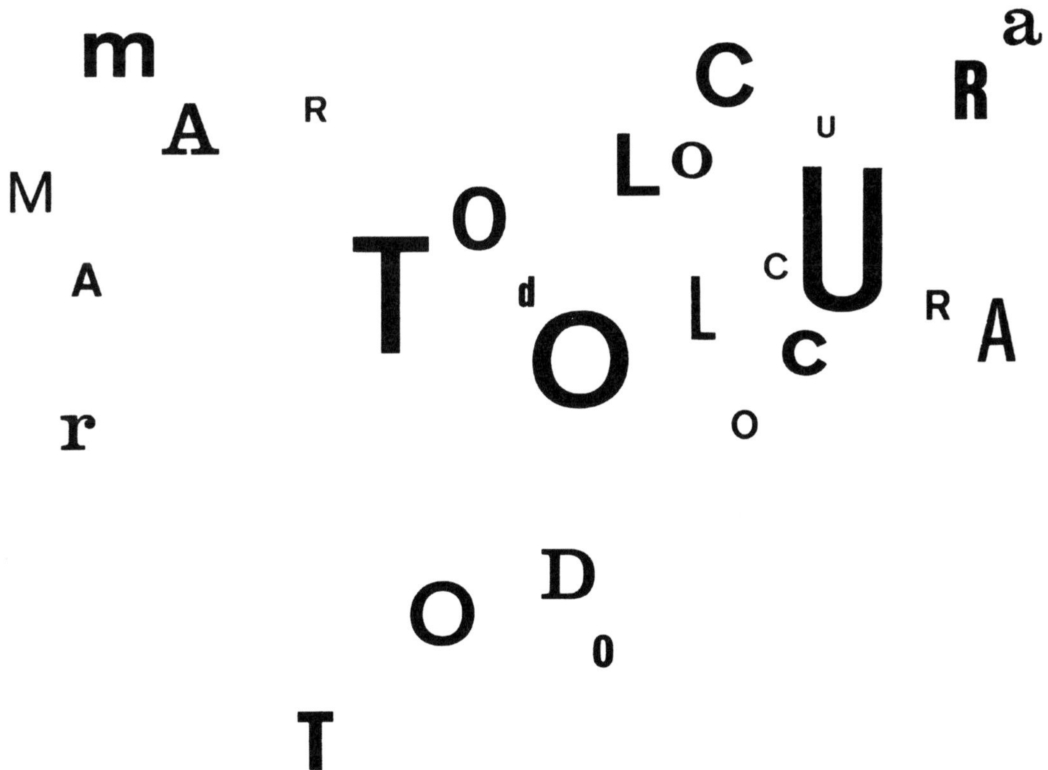

Suzanne Bernard

ntement temen lenteme lentem le tem
s'é gau t t t

OSt'e Sol Sti Sol Slo lil Lit ude O Sle Sln Sin

S. len s ce

l ch nte l sng l cœr l V. q
l ch ir l p au l mode l
l's l sffffle l fff l sff l sfl
f l
l l , ff ' f
ch'nte l

V. tte rge tte chde

ch
nte
ment
te
men
len
te
me
. l d S ol
Tu .

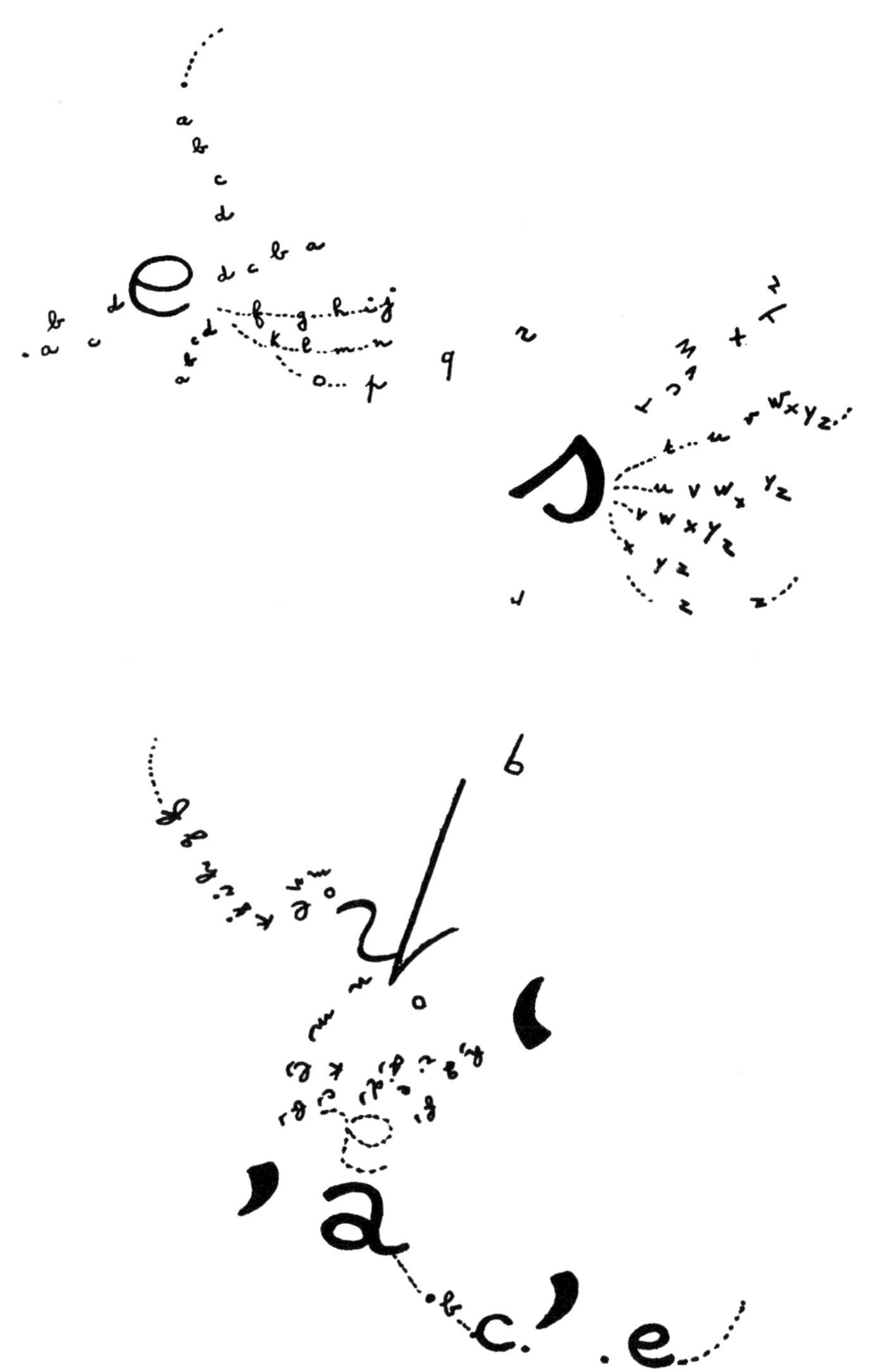

’

u r la ru

t r i

n

n s ur l

n

ru en i i i M n

n

n n O n ru

n

t r t r r r ,sur la ru e n i en n

r t ru

t t c t n

t t d s t n

c est

ep est

OM n

M n

n

b O r ui

en bb

O bb n

t n

t t M

OM

bb M

b

bb t

lour O

r

de s ur l a r bb r r t

b

OM MO r

t

b

tt bb lou r t

d

u tt

t

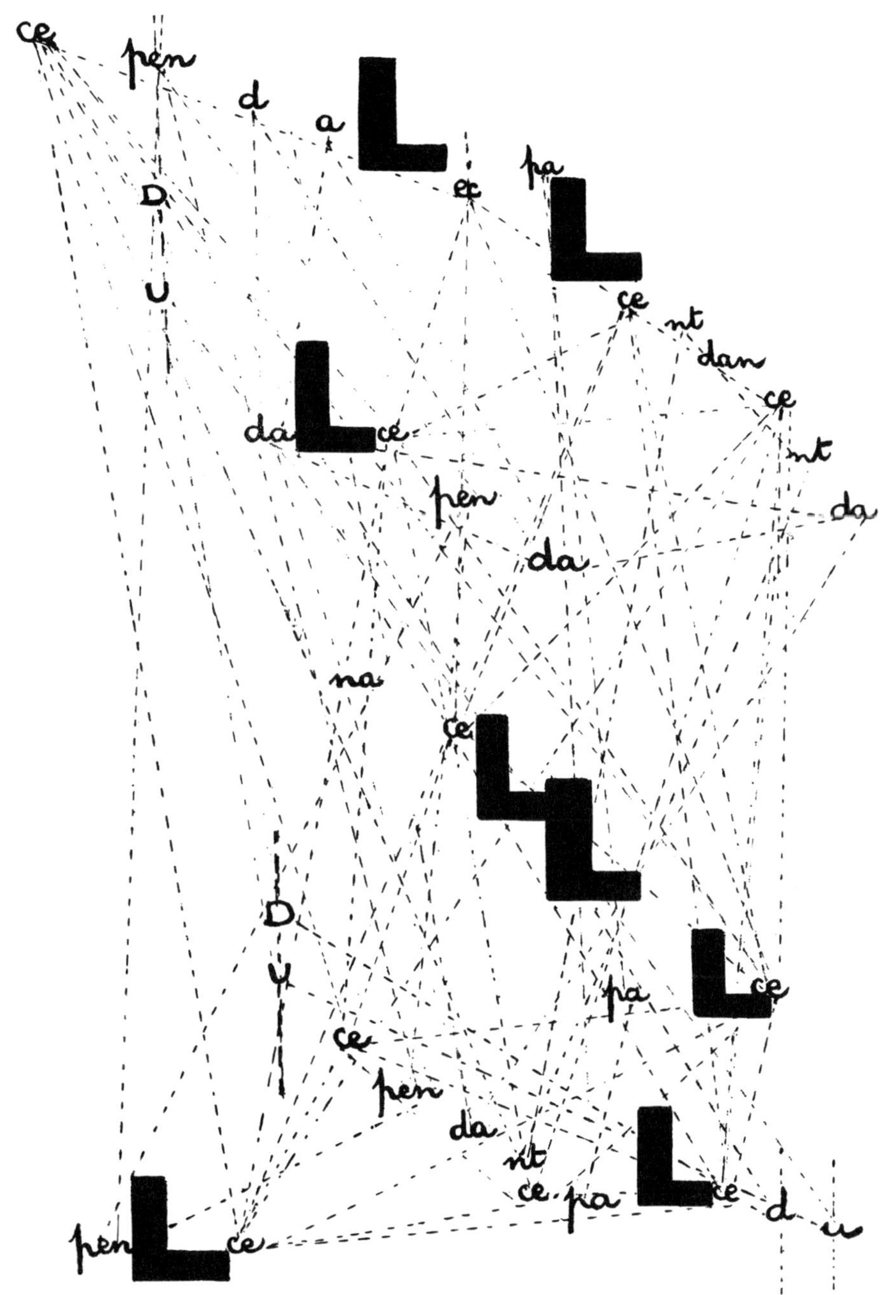
ce
pen
d
a
L
pa
ce
L
D
U
ce
nt
dan
ce
nt
da
L
ce
pen
da
na
ce
L
L
D
U
pa
L
ce
ce
pen
da
nt
L
ce
pa
ce
d
u
pen
L
ce

Gay Beste

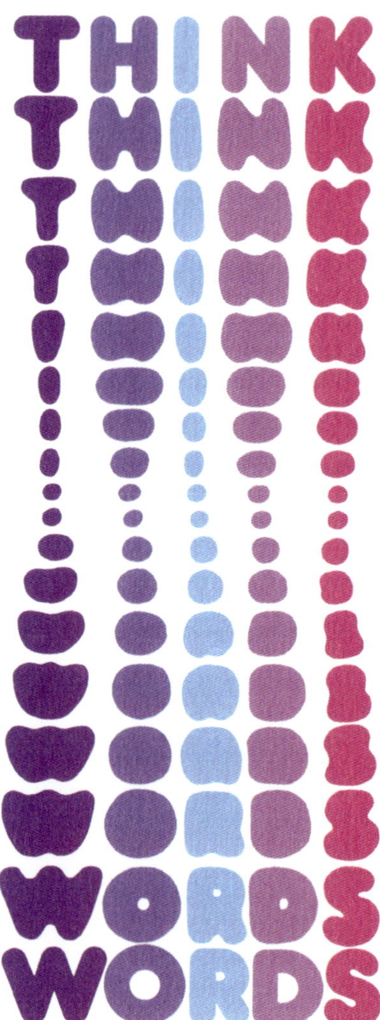
THINK
WORDS

PRONOUN
PRONOMEN
PRONAME

euphemism · euphemism · euphemism · euphemism · euphemism
glossover · taffy · mince matters · pamper · pleasant · varnish · blarney · smooth-spoken · cant · mealy-mouthed · soft soap · phony · genteel · mi'lady

THES
SUG
HOW
ECISE
THEM
LLYE
GRE
QUAR
ESTS
NGAP
ORM
ATIC
ACT
MEN

Alison Bielski

n +
+
n
n
+ n +
n +
+ n
+
n
n +
+
n +
+ n

==+==n====n====+===+========n=n======+==+===n=+=====+=
+===n===+==+=======n===n===+====+=+===n===n====+=+===
==n=====+====n=n=====+=+===n====n====+==+=======n==n==+

+
+
+
+
+ + +
+
+ +
+ +
+
+
+ +

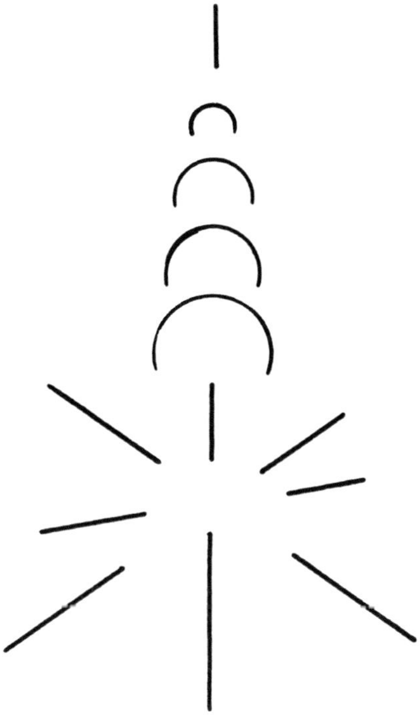

1

2

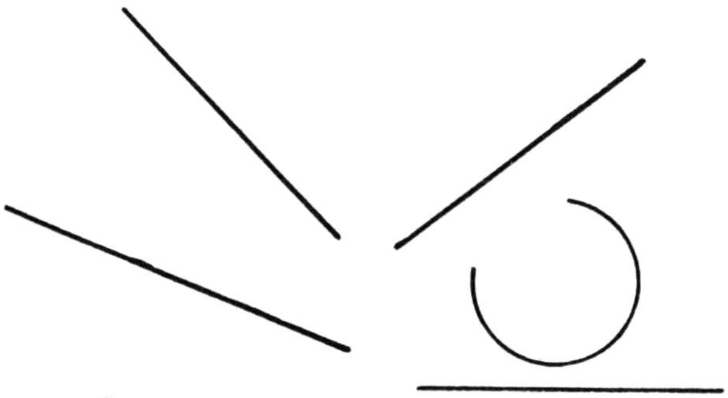

3

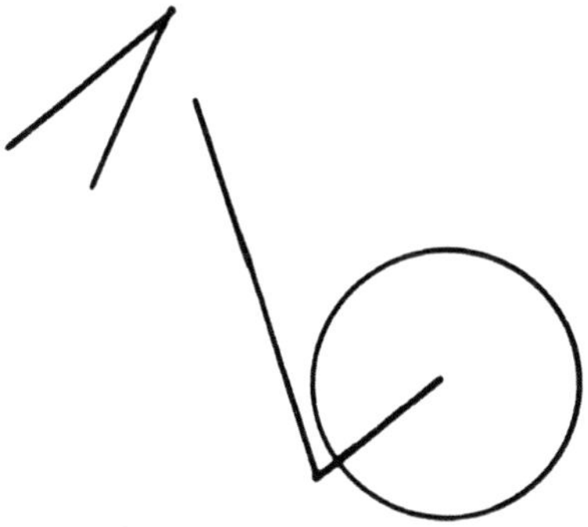

4

1. lupine 2. sneeuwklokje
3. waterlelie 4. viooltje

alison bielski

Tomaso Binga

c
C
C
c

q 2

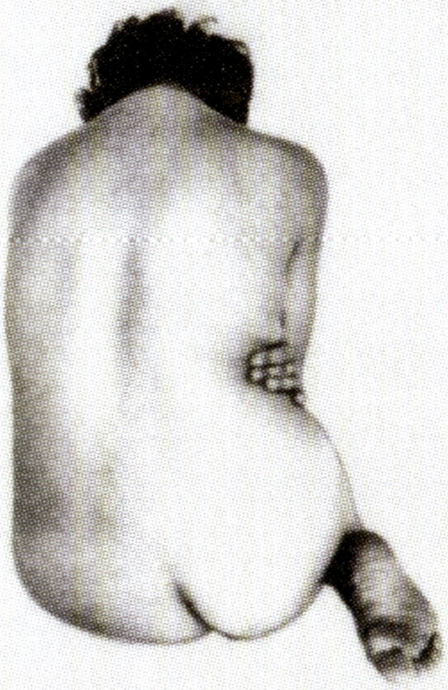

Q q

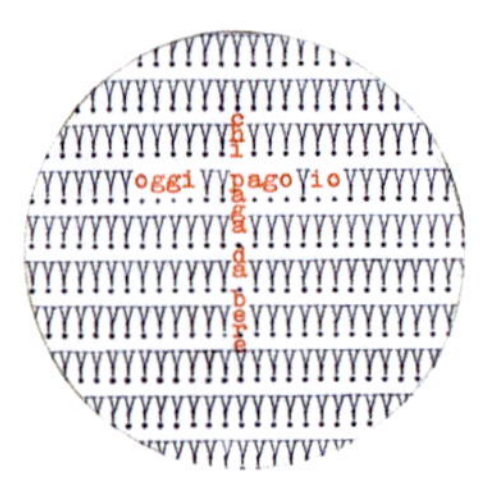
oggi pago io
chi paga da bere

dammene un goccio
un goccio ancora
corpo di bacco
voglio trincare
nettare
a mensa
con gli dei
pigiate
i grappoli nei tin
bevete
questo E'
il mio sangue
e tracannò
il suo picciol
calice
tutto d'un fiato
poi
s'attaccò
alla bottiglia
oggi
pago
IO

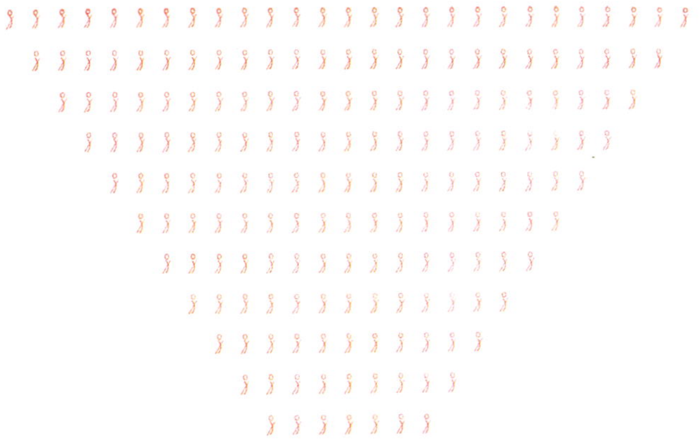

io sono
lì lì lì lì lì
io sono
Li   llith
sono coeva
e non co Eva
d'Adamo ad amo
passo
manufatto argilloso
alito arioso
io sono
terra-aria-fuoco

(terrainvasata)(ariastagnata)(fuocoingabbiato)
)   )   )   )   )   )NOOOOOOOOOOO((((((

nei boschi
sopra il mare
dentro il cielo
vivo-vivendo
io sono
lì lì lì lì lì
io sono
li   bera
io sono
Li   llith

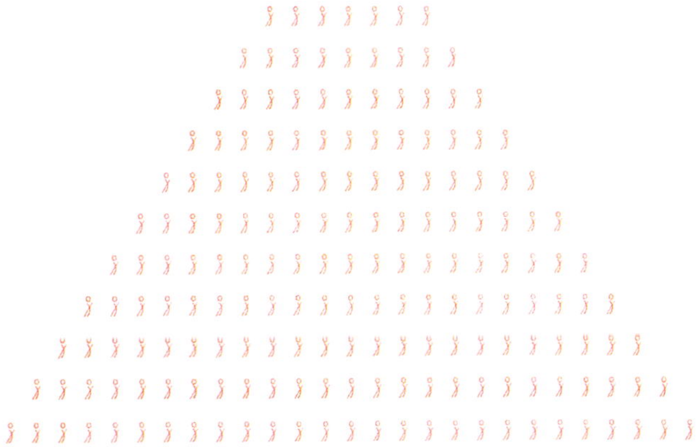

* *
* *

* * * * * * * * * * ho bisogno* * * * * * * * * * * * * * *
* * * * * * * * * * * * * * * di una casa nuova * * * * * *

* * * * * * * * * * ho bisogno* * * * * * * * * * * * * * *
* * * * * * * * * * * * * * * di un letto e quattro sedie *

* * * * * * * * * * ho bisogno* * * * * * * * * * * * * * *
* * * * * * * * * * * * * * * di un armadio vuoto * * * * *

* * * * * * * * * * ho bisogno* * * * * * * * * * * * * * *
* * * * * * * * * * * * * * * di poche pentole in cucina* *

* * * * * * * * * * ho bisogno* * * * * * * * * * * * * * *
* * * * * * * * * * * * * * * di una vita senza ricordi * *

* *
* *
* *
* *
* *

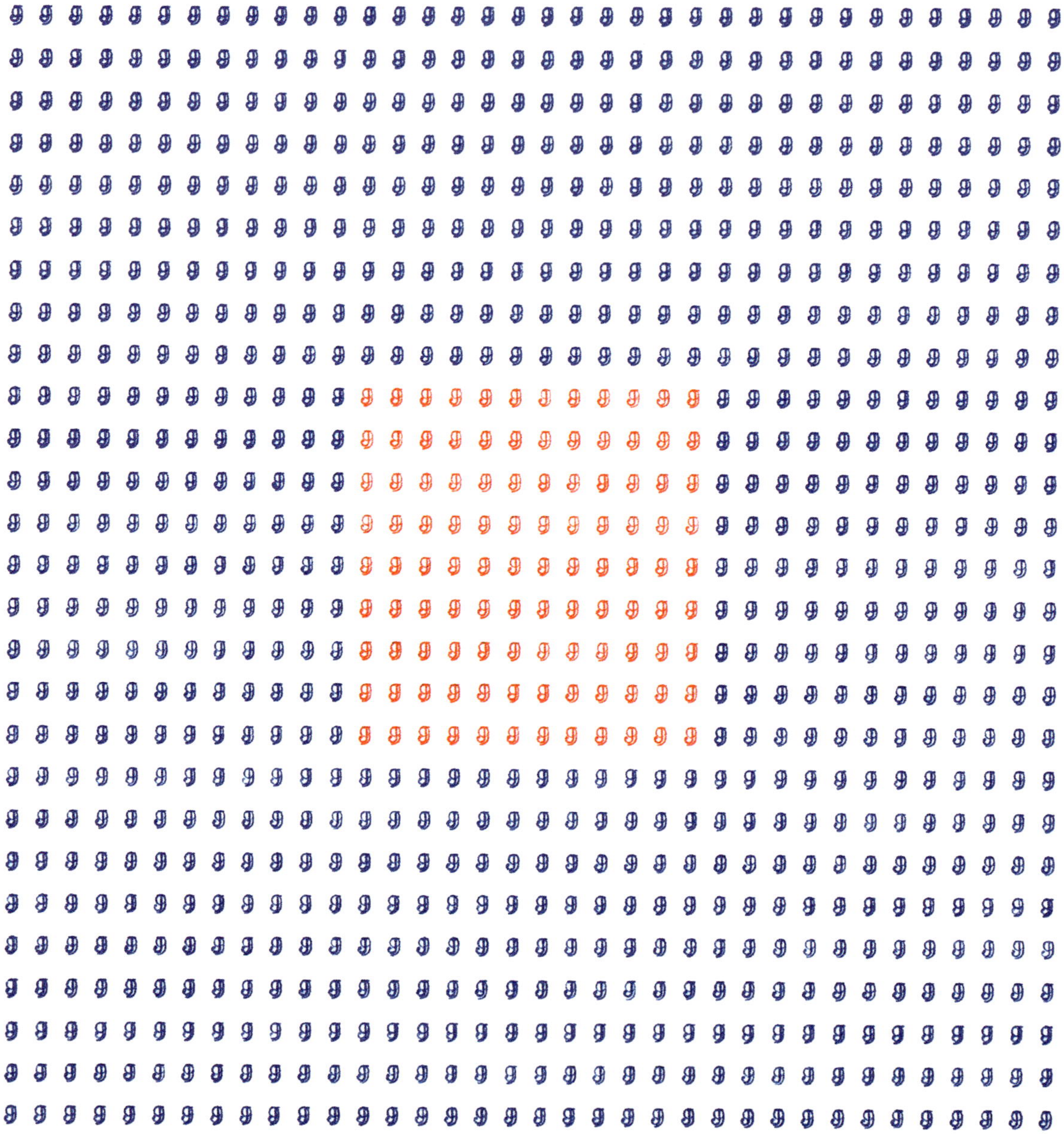

Irma Blank

Marianna Bocian

d r o g a DO r a j u
d r o g a DO n i e b a
d r o g a DO z i e m i
d r o g a DO r o z u m u

Blanca Calparsoro

exemplaire

Sexus

domaine du délire

SOLEIL

complexe

MUSIQUE

L'UNIVERS ARCHAÏQUE

d'enfants

Le beau entre passé et avenir

Je reviens

du

paradis

x

festival

révolutionnaire

Paula Claire

SYMPHONYUS
SYMPATHYORB
HARMONY CALM
MELODY PEACE
PEACE MELODY
CALM HARMONY
ORB SYMPATHY
US SYMPHONY
SYMPHONYUS
SYMPATHYORB
HARMONY CALM
MELODY PEACE
PEACE MELODY
CALM HARMONY
ORB SYMPATHY
US SYMPHONY
SYMPHONYUS
SYMPATHYORB
HARMONY CALM
MELODY PEACE
PEACE MELODY
CALM HARMONY
ORB SYMPATHY
US SYMPHONY
SYMPHONYUS
SYMPATHYORB
HARMONY CALM
MELODY PEACE
PEACE MELODY
CALM HARMONY
ORB SYMPATHY
US SYMPHONY
SYMPHONYUS
SYMPATHYORB
HARMONY CALM
MELODY PEACE
PEACE MELODY
CALM HARMONY
ORB SYMPATHY
US SYMPHONY
SYMPHONYUS
SYMPATHYORB
HARMONY CALM
MELODY PEACE
PEACE MELODY
CALM HARMONY
ORB SYMPATHY
US SYMPHONY
SYMPHONYUS
SYMPATHYORB
HARMONY CALM
MELODY PEACE
PEACE MELODY
CALM HARMONY
ORB SYMPATHY
US SYMPHONY
SYMPHONYUS
SYMPATHYORB
HARMONY CALM
MELODY PEACE
PEACE MELODY
CALM HARMONY
ORB SYMPATHY
US SYMPHONY
SYMPHONYUS
SYMPATHYORB
HARMONY CALM
MELODY PEACE
PEACE MELODY
CALM HARMONY
ORB SYMPATHY
US SYMPHONY
SYMPHONYUS
SYMPATHYORB
HARMONY CALM
MELODY PEACE
PEACE MELODY
CALM HARMONY
ORB SYMPATHY
US SYMPHONY
SYMPHONYUS
SYMPATHYORB
HARMONY CALM
MELODY PEACE
PEACE MELODY
CALM HARMONY
ORB SYMPATHY
US SYMPHONY
SYMPHONYUS
SYMPATHYORB
HARMONY CALM
MELODY PEACE
PEACE MELODY
CALM HARMONY
ORB SYMPATHY
US SYMPHONY
SYMPHONYUS
SYMPATHYORB

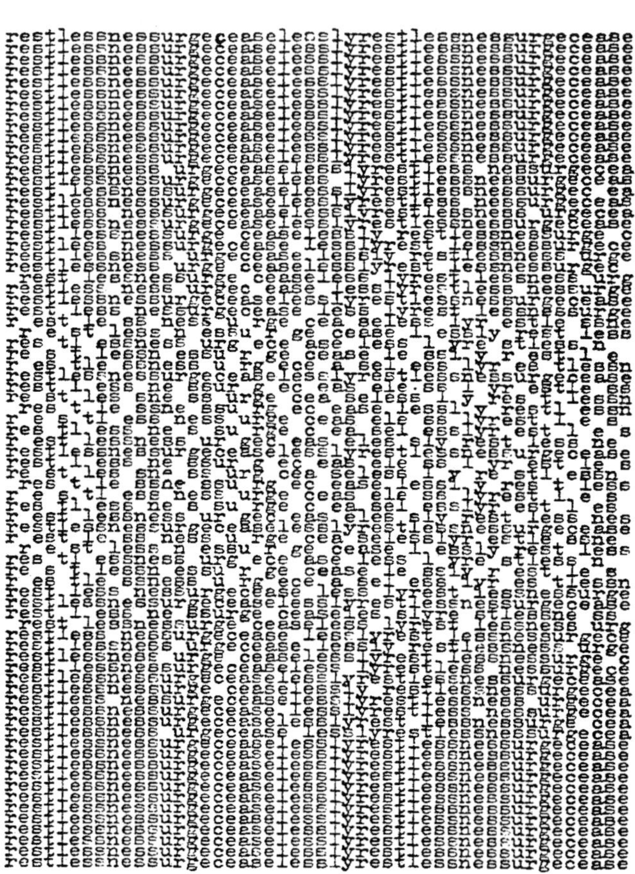

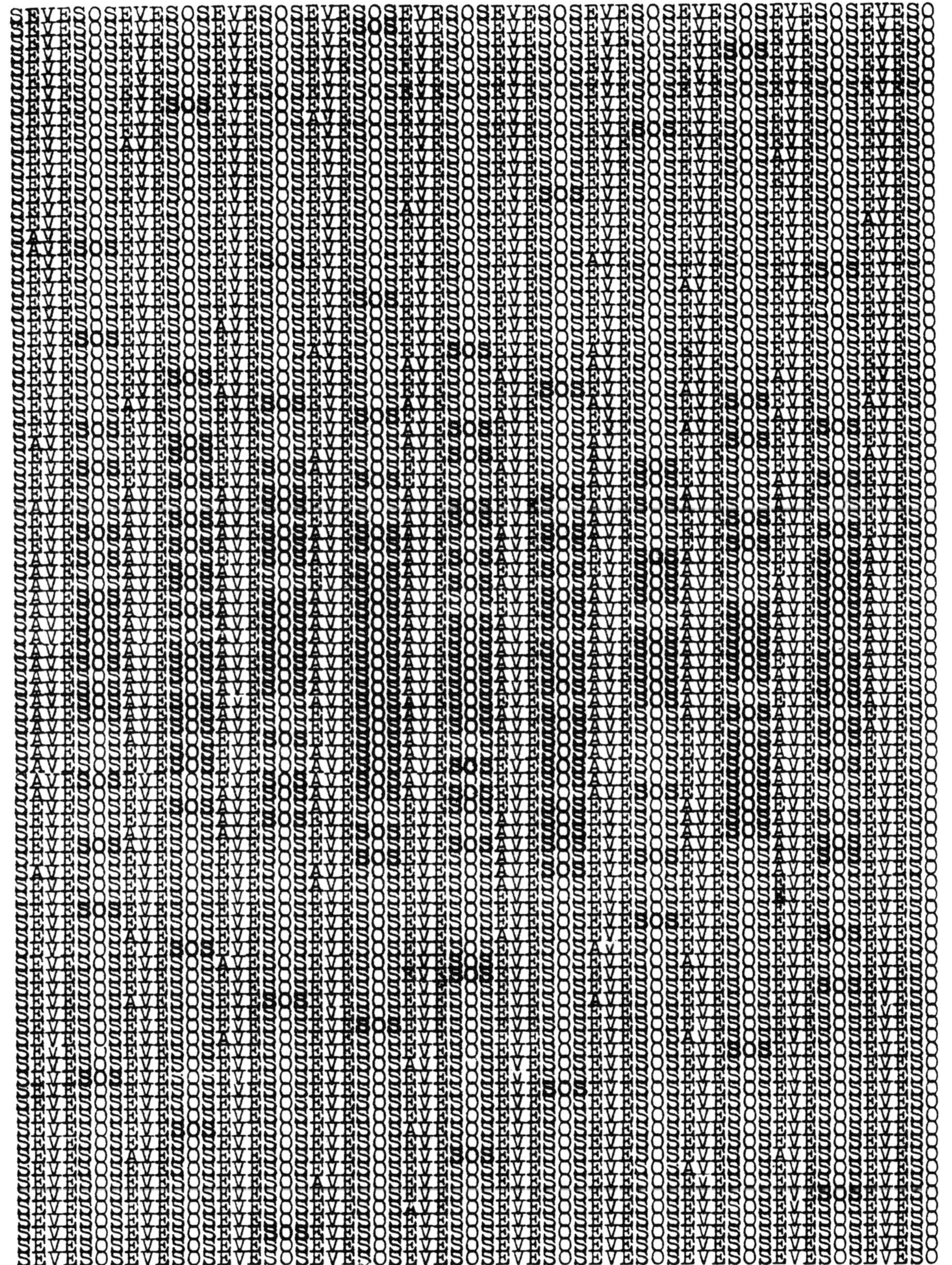

the visual version of this poem should be large scale – neon sign for an airport.
1970: from SOUNDSWORD, WF 1972.

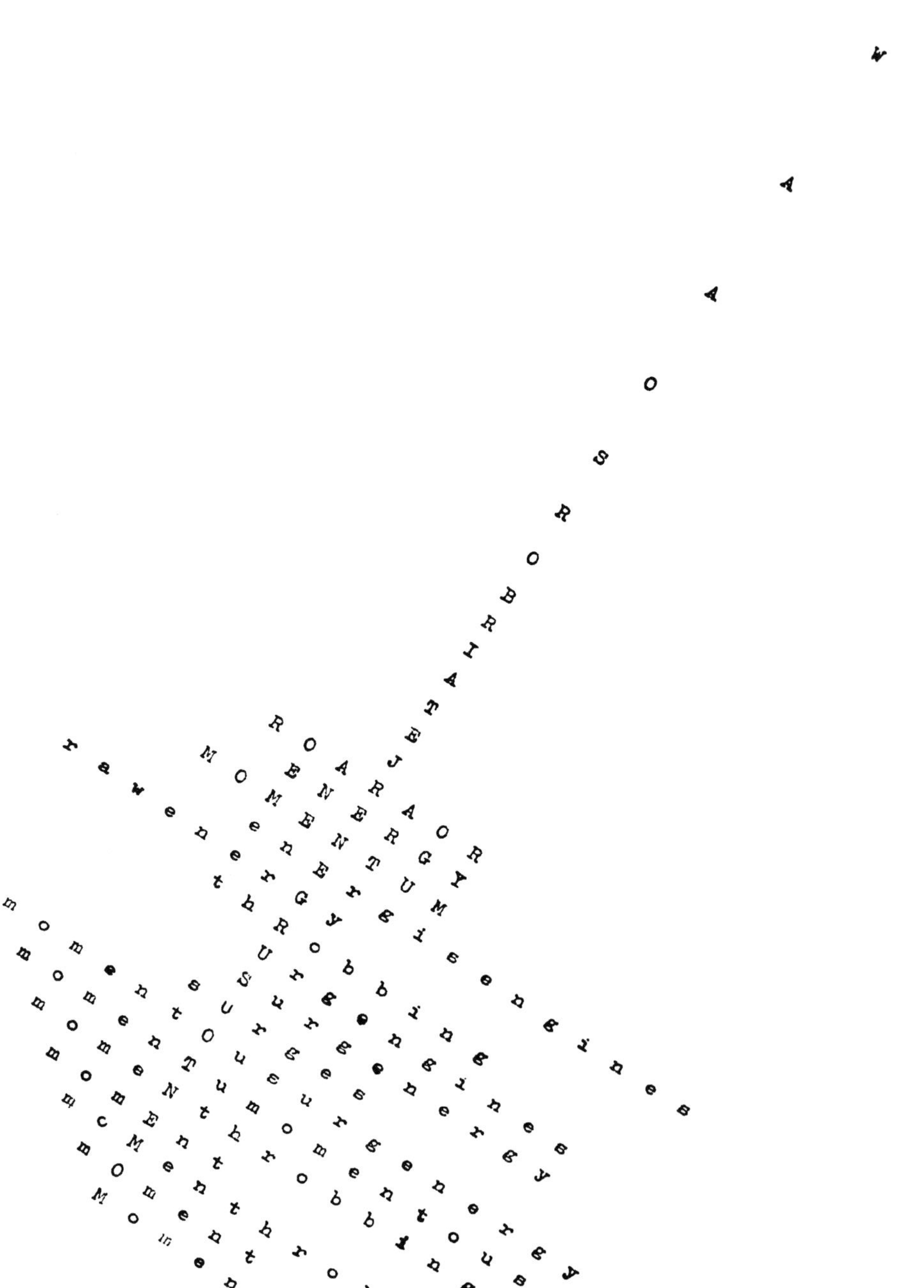

Betty Danon

puntopuntopuntopuntopuntopuntopuntopuntopuntopuntopuntopuntopunto
puntopuntopuntopuntopuntopuntopuntopuntopuntopuntopuntopuntopunto
puntopuntopuntopuntopuntopuntopuntopuntopuntopuntopuntopuntopunto
puntopuntopuntopuntopuntopuntopuntopuntopuntopuntopuntopuntopunto
puntopuntopuntopuntopuntopuntopuntopuntopuntopuntopuntopuntopunto
puntopuntopuntopuntopuntopuntopuntopuntopuntopuntopuntopuntopunto
puntopuntopuntopuntopuntopuntopuntopuntopuntopuntopuntopuntopunto
puntopuntopuntopuntopuntopuntopuntopuntopuntopuntopuntopuntopunto
puntopuntopuntopuntopuntopuntopuntopuntopuntopuntopuntopuntopunto
puntopuntopuntopuntopuntopuntopuntopuntopuntopuntopuntopuntopunto
puntopuntopuntopuntopuntopuntopuntopuntopuntopuntopuntopuntopunto
puntopuntopuntopuntopuntopuntopuntopuntopuntopuntopuntopuntopunto
puntopuntopuntopuntopuntopuntopuntopuntopuntopuntopuntopuntopunto
puntopuntopuntopuntopuntopuntopuntopuntopuntopuntopuntopuntopunto
puntopuntopuntopuntopuntopuntopuntopuntopuntopuntopuntopuntopunto
puntopuntopuntopuntopuntopuntopuntopuntopuntopuntopuntopuntopunto
puntopuntopuntopuntopuntopuntopuntopuntopuntopuntopuntopuntopunto
puntopuntopuntopuntopuntopuntopuntopuntopuntopuntopuntopuntopunto
puntopuntopuntopuntopuntopuntopuntopuntopuntopuntopuntopuntopunto
puntopuntopuntopuntopuntopuntopuntopuntopuntopuntopuntopuntopunto
puntopuntopuntopuntopuntopuntopuntopuntopuntopuntopuntopuntopunto
puntopuntopuntopuntopuntopuntopuntopuntopuntopuntopuntopuntopunto
puntopuntopuntopuntopuntopuntopuntopuntopuntopuntopuntopuntopunto
puntopuntopuntopuntopuntopuntopuntopuntopuntopuntopuntopuntopunto
puntopuntopuntopuntopuntopuntopuntopuntopuntopuntopuntopuntopunto
puntopuntopuntopuntopuntopuntopuntopuntopuntopuntopuntopuntopunto
puntopuntopuntopuntopuntopuntopuntopuntopuntopuntopuntopuntopunto
puntopuntopuntopuntopuntopuntopuntopuntopuntopuntopuntopuntopunto
puntopuntopuntopuntopuntopuntopuntopuntopuntopuntopuntopuntopunto
puntopuntopuntopuntopuntopuntopuntopuntopuntopuntopuntopuntopunto
puntopuntopuntopuntopuntopuntopuntopuntopuntopuntopuntopuntopunto
puntopuntopuntopuntopuntopuntopuntopuntopuntopuntopuntopuntopunto
puntopuntopuntopuntopuntopuntopuntopuntopuntopuntopuntopuntopunto
puntopuntopuntopuntopuntopuntopuntopuntopuntopuntopuntopuntopunto
puntopuntopuntopuntopuntopuntopuntopuntopuntopuntopuntopuntopunto
puntopuntopuntopuntopuntopuntopuntopuntopuntopuntopuntopuntopunto
puntopuntopuntopuntopuntopuntopuntopuntopuntopuntopuntopuntopunto
puntopuntopuntopuntopuntopuntopuntopuntopuntopuntopuntopuntopunto
puntopuntopuntopuntopuntopuntopuntopuntopuntopuntopuntopuntopunto
puntopuntopuntopuntopuntopuntopuntopuntopuntopuntopuntopuntopunto
puntopuntopuntopuntopuntopuntopuntopuntopuntopuntopuntopuntopunto
puntopuntopuntopuntopuntopuntopuntopuntopuntopuntopuntopuntopunto
puntopuntopuntopuntopuntopuntopuntopuntopuntopuntopuntopuntopunto
puntopuntopuntopuntopuntopuntopuntopuntopuntopuntopuntopuntopunto
puntopuntopuntopuntopuntopuntopuntopuntopuntopuntopuntopuntopunto
puntopuntopuntopuntopuntopuntopuntopuntopuntopuntopuntopuntopunto
puntopuntopuntopuntopuntopuntopuntopuntopuntopuntopuntopuntopunto
puntopuntopuntopuntopuntopuntopuntopuntopuntopuntopuntopuntopunto
puntopuntopuntopuntopuntopuntopuntopuntopuntopuntopuntopuntopunto
puntopuntopuntopuntopuntopuntopuntopuntopuntopuntopuntopuntopunto
puntopuntopuntopuntopuntopuntopuntopuntopuntopuntopuntopuntopunto
puntopuntopuntopuntopuntopuntopuntopuntopuntopuntopuntopuntopunto
puntopuntopuntopuntopuntopuntopuntopuntopuntopuntopuntopuntopunto
puntopuntopuntopuntopuntopuntopuntopuntopuntopuntopuntopuntopunto
puntopuntopuntopuntopuntopuntopuntopuntopuntopuntopuntopuntopunto
puntopuntopuntopuntopuntopuntopuntopuntopuntopuntopuntopuntopunto
puntopuntopuntopuntopuntopuntopuntopuntopuntopuntopuntopuntopunto
puntopuntopuntopuntopuntopuntopuntopuntopuntopuntopuntopuntopunto
puntopuntopuntopuntopuntopuntopuntopuntopuntopuntopuntopuntopunto
puntopuntopuntopuntopuntopuntopuntopuntopuntopuntopuntopuntopunto
puntopuntopuntopuntopuntopuntopuntopuntopuntopuntopuntopuntopunto
puntopuntopuntopuntopuntopuntopuntopuntopuntopuntopuntopuntopunto
puntopuntopuntopuntopuntopuntopuntopuntopuntopuntopuntopuntopunto
puntopuntopuntopuntopuntopuntopuntopuntopuntopuntopuntopuntopunto
puntopuntopuntopuntopuntopuntopuntopuntopuntopuntopuntopuntopunto
puntopuntopuntopuntopuntopuntopuntopuntopuntopuntopuntopuntopunto
puntopuntopuntopuntopuntopuntopuntopuntopuntopuntopuntopuntopunto
puntopuntopuntopuntopuntopuntopuntopuntopuntopuntopuntopuntopunto
puntopuntopuntopuntopuntopuntopuntopuntopuntopuntopuntopuntopunto
puntopuntopuntopuntopuntopuntopuntopuntopuntopuntopuntopuntopunto
puntopuntopuntopuntopuntopuntopuntopuntopuntopuntopuntopuntopunto
puntopuntopuntopuntopuntopuntopuntopuntopuntopuntopuntopuntopunto
puntopuntopuntopuntopuntopuntopuntopuntopuntopuntopuntopuntopunto
puntopuntopuntopuntopuntopuntopuntopuntopuntopuntopuntopuntopunto
puntopuntopuntopuntopuntopuntopuntopuntopuntopuntopuntopuntopunto
puntopuntopuntopuntopuntopuntopuntopuntopuntopuntopuntopuntopunto
puntopuntopuntopuntopuntopuntopuntopuntopuntopuntopuntopuntopunto
puntopuntopuntopuntopuntopuntopuntopuntopuntopuntopuntopuntopunto
puntopuntopuntopuntopuntopuntopuntopuntopuntopuntopuntopuntopunto
puntopuntopuntopuntopuntopuntopuntopuntopuntopuntopuntopuntopunto
puntopuntopuntopuntopuntopuntopuntopuntopuntopuntopuntopuntopunto
puntopuntopuntopuntopuntopuntopuntopuntopuntopuntopuntopuntopunto
puntopuntopuntopuntopuntopuntopuntopuntopuntopuntopuntopuntopunto
puntopuntopuntopuntopuntopuntopuntopuntopuntopuntopuntopuntopunto
puntopuntopuntopuntopuntopuntopuntopuntopuntopuntopuntopuntopunto
puntopuntopuntopuntopuntopuntopuntopuntopuntopuntopuntopuntopunto
puntopuntopuntopuntopuntopuntopuntopuntopuntopuntopuntopuntopunto
puntopuntopuntopuntopuntopuntopuntopuntopuntopuntopuntopuntopunto
puntopuntopuntopuntopuntopuntopuntopuntopuntopuntopuntopuntopunto
puntopuntopuntopuntopuntopuntopuntopuntopuntopuntopuntopuntopunto
puntopuntopuntopuntopuntopuntopuntopuntopuntopuntopuntopuntopunto
puntopuntopuntopuntopuntopuntopuntopuntopuntopuntopuntopuntopunto
puntopuntopuntopuntopuntopuntopuntopuntopuntopuntopuntopuntopunto
puntopuntopuntopuntopuntopuntopuntopuntopuntopuntopuntopuntopunto
puntopuntopuntopuntopuntopuntopuntopuntopuntopuntopuntopuntopunto
puntopuntopuntopuntopuntopuntopuntopuntopuntopuntopuntopuntopunto
puntopuntopuntopuntopuntopuntopuntopuntopuntopuntopuntopuntopunto
puntopuntopuntopuntopuntopuntopuntopuntopuntopuntopuntopuntopunto
puntopuntopuntopuntopuntopuntopuntopuntopuntopuntopuntopuntopunto
puntopuntopuntopuntopuntopuntopuntopuntopuntopuntopuntopuntopunto
puntopuntopuntopuntopuntopuntopuntopuntopuntopuntopuntopuntopunto
puntopuntopuntopuntopuntopuntopuntopuntopuntopuntopuntopuntopunto
puntopuntopuntopuntopuntopuntopuntopuntopuntopuntopuntopuntopunto
puntopuntopuntopuntopuntopuntopuntopuntopuntopuntopuntopuntopunto
puntopuntopuntopuntopuntopuntopuntopuntopuntopuntopuntopuntopunto
puntopuntopuntopuntopuntopuntopuntopuntopuntopuntopuntopuntopunto
puntopuntopuntopuntopuntopuntopuntopuntopuntopuntopuntopuntopunto
puntopuntopuntopuntopuntopuntopuntopuntopuntopuntopuntopuntopunto
puntopuntopuntopuntopuntopuntopuntopuntopuntopuntopuntopuntopunto
puntopuntopuntopuntopuntopuntopuntopuntopuntopuntopuntopuntopunto
puntopuntopuntopuntopuntopuntopuntopuntopuntopuntopuntopuntopunto
puntopuntopuntopuntopuntopuntopuntopuntopuntopuntopuntopuntopunto
puntopuntopuntopuntopuntopuntopuntopuntopuntopuntopuntopuntopunto
puntopuntopuntopuntopuntopuntopuntopuntopuntopuntopuntopuntopunto
puntopuntopuntopuntopuntopuntopuntopuntopuntopuntopuntopuntopunto
puntopuntopuntopuntopuntopuntopuntopuntopuntopuntopuntopuntopunto
puntopuntopuntopuntopuntopuntopuntopuntopuntopuntopuntopuntopunto
puntopuntopuntopuntopuntopuntopuntopuntopuntopuntopuntopuntopunto
puntopuntopuntopuntopuntopuntopuntopuntopuntopuntopuntopuntopunto
puntopuntopuntopuntopuntopuntopuntopuntopuntopuntopuntopuntopunto

puntopuntopuntopuntopuntopuntopuntopuntopuntopuntopuntopuntopuntop

untopuntopuntopuntopuntopuntopuntopuntopuntopuntopuntopuntopuntopu

ntopuntopuntopuntopuntopuntopuntopuntopuntopuntopuntopuntopuntopun

topuntopuntopuntopuntopuntopuntopuntopuntopuntopuntopuntopuntopunt

opuntopuntopuntopuntopuntopuntopuntopuntopuntopuntopuntopuntopunto

puntopuntopuntopuntopuntopuntopuntopuntopuntopuntopuntopuntopuntop

untopuntopuntopuntopuntopuntopuntopuntopuntopuntopuntopuntopuntopu

ntopuntopuntopuntopuntopuntopuntopuntopuntopuntopuntopuntopuntopun

topuntopuntopuntopuntopuntopuntopuntopuntopuntopuntopuntopuntopunt

opuntopuntopuntopuntopuntopuntopuntopuntopuntopuntopuntopuntopunto

puntopuntopuntopuntopuntopuntopuntopuntopuntopuntopuntopuntopuntop

untopuntopuntopuntopuntopuntopuntopuntopuntopuntopuntopuntopuntopu

ntopuntopuntopuntopuntopuntopuntopuntopuntopuntopuntopuntopuntopun

topuntopuntopuntopuntopuntopuntopuntopuntopuntopuntopuntopuntopunt

opuntopuntopuntopuntopuntopuntopuntopuntopuntopuntopuntopuntopunto

puntopuntopuntopuntopuntopuntopuntopuntopuntopuntopuntopuntopuntop

untopuntopuntopuntopuntopuntopuntopuntopuntopuntopuntopuntopuntopu

. . . .

. . . .

. . . .

. . . .

. . . .

. . . .

. . . .

. . . .

. . . . . . punto . . . . . .

. . . .

. . . .

. . . .

. . . .

. . . .

. . . .

. . . .

. . . .

. . . .

linealinealinealinealinealinealinealinealinealinealinealineal
inealinealinealinealinealinealinealinealinealinealinealineali
nealinealinealinealinealinealinealinealinealinealinealinealin
ealinealinealinealinealinealinealinealinealinealinealinealine
alinealinealinealinealinealinealinealinealinealinealinealinea
linealinealinealinealinealinealinealinealinealinealinealineal
inealinealinealinealinealinealinealinealinealinealinealineali
nealinealinealinealinealinealinealinealinealinealinealinealin
ealinealinealinealinealinealinealinealinealinealinealinealine
alinealinealinealinealinealinealinealinealinealinealinealinea
linealinealinealinealinealinealinealinealinealinealinealineal
inealinealinealinealinealinealinealinealinealinealinealineali
nealinealinealinealinealinealinealinealinealinealinealinealin
ealinealinealinealinealinealinealinealinealinealinealinealine
alinealinealinealinealinealinealinealinealinealinealinealinea
linealinealinealinealinealinealinealinealinealinealinealineal
inealinealinealinealinealinealinealinealinealinealinealineali
nealinealinealinealinealinealinealinealinealinealinealinealin
ealinealinealinealinealinealinealinealinealinealinealinealine
alinealinealinealinealinealinealinealinealinealinealinealinea
linealinealinealinealinealinealinealinealinealinealinealineal
inealinealinealinealinealinealinealinealinealinealinealineali
nealinealinealinealinealinealinealinealinealinealinealinealin
ealinealinealinealinealinealinealinealinealinealinealinealine
alinealinealinealinealinealinealinealinealinealinealinealinea
linealinealinealinealinealinealinealinealinealinealinealineal
inealinealinealinealinealinealinealinealinealinealinealineali
nealinealinealinealinealinealinealinealinealinealinealinealin
ealinealinealinealinealinealinealinealinealinealinealinealine
alinealinealinealinealinealinealinealinealinealinealinealinea
linealinealinealinealinealinealinealinealinealinealinealineal
inealinealinealinealinealinealinealinealinealinealinealineali
nealinealinealinealinealinealinealinealinealinealinealinealin
ealinealinealinealinealinealinealinealinealinealinealinealine
alinealinealinealinealinealinealinealinealinealinealinealinea
linealinealinealinealinealinealinealinealinealinealinealineal
inealinealinealinealinealinealinealinealinealinealinealineali
nealinealinealinealinealinealinealinealinealinealinealinealin
ealinealinealinealinealinealinealinealinealinealinealinealine
alinealinealinealinealinealinealinealinealinealinealinealinea
linealinealinealinealinealinealinealinealinealinealinealineal
inealinealinealinealinealinealinealinealinealinealinealineali
nealinealinealinealinealinealinealinealinealinealinealinealin
ealinealinealinealinealinealinealinealinealinealinealinealine
alinealinealinealinealinealinealinealinealinealinealinealinea
linealinealinealinealinealinealinealinealinealinealinealineal
inealinealinealinealinealinealinealinealinealinealinealineali
nealinealinealinealinealinealinealinealinealinealinealinealin
ealinealinealinealinealinealinealinealinealinealinealinealine
alinealinealinealinealinealinealinealinealinealinealinealinea
linealinealinealinealinealinealinealinealinealinealinealineal
inealinealinealinealinealinealinealinealinealinealinealineali
nealinealinealinealinealinealinealinealinealinealinealinealin
ealinealinealinealinealinealinealinealinealinealinealinealine
alinealinealinealinealinealinealinealinealinealinealinealinea
linealinealinealinealinealinealinealinealinealinealinealineal
inealinealinealinealinealinealinealinealinealinealinealineali
nealinealinealinealinealinealinealinealinealinealinealinealin
ealinealinealinealinealinealinealinealinealinealinealinealine
alinealinealinealinealinealinealinealinealinealinealinealinea
linealinealinealinealinealinealinealinealinealinealinealineal
inealinealinealinealinealinealinealinealinealinealinealineali
nealinealinealinealinealinealinealinealinealinealinealinealin
ealinealinealinealinealinealinealinealinealinealinealinealine
alinealinealinealinealinealinealinealinealinealinealinealinea
linealinealinealinealinealinealinealinealinealinealinealineal
inealinealinealinealinealinealinealinealinealinealinealineali
nealinealinealinealinealinealinealinealinealinealinealinealin
ealinealinealinealinealinealinealinealinealinealinealinealine
alinealinealinealinealinealinealinealinealinealinealinealinea
linealinealinealinealinealinealinealinealinealinealinealineal
inealinealinealinealinealinealinealinealinealinealinealineali
nealinealinealinealinealinealinealinealinealinealinealinealin
ealinealinealinealinealinealinealinealinealinealinealinealine
alinealinealinealinealinealinealinealinealinealinealinealinea
linealinealinealinealinealinealinealinealinealinealinealineal
inealinealinealinealinealinealinealinealinealinealinealineali
nealinealinealinealinealinealinealinealinealinealinealinealin
ealinealinealinealinealinealinealinealinealinealinealinealine
alinealinealinealinealinealinealinealinealinealinealinealinea
linealinealinealinealinealinealinealinealinealinealinealineal
inealinealinealinealinealinealinealinealinealinealinealineali
nealinealinealinealinealinealinealinealinealinealinealinealin
ealinealinealinealinealinealinealinealinealinealinealinealine
alinealinealinealinealinealinealinealinealinealinealinealinea

linealinealinealinealinealinealinealinealinealinealinealineal

inealinealinealinealinealinealinealinealinealinealinealineali

nealinealinealinealinealinealinealinealinealinealinealinealin

ealinealinealinealinealinealinealinealinealinealinealinealine

alinealinealinealinealinealinealinealinealinealinealinealinea

linealinealinealinealinealinealinealinealinealinealinealineal

inealinealinealinealinealinealinealinealinealinealinealineali

nealinealinealinealinealinealinealinealinealinealinealinealin

ealinealinealinealinealinealinealinealinealinealinealinealine

alinealinealinealinealinealinealinealinealinealinealinealinea

linealinealinealinealinealinealinealinealinealinealinealineal

inealinealinealinealinealinealinealinealinealinealinealineali

nealinealinealinealinealinealinealinealinealinealinealinealin

ealinealinealinealinealinealinealinealinealinealinealinealine

alinealinealinealinealinealinealinealinealinealinealinealinea

linealinealinealinealinealinealinealinealinealinealinealineal

inealinealinealinealinealinealinealinealinealinealinealineali

punto
punto
punto
punto
punto
punto
punto
punto
punto
punto
punto
punto
punto
punto
punto
punt
punt
punt
pnt
pnt
pt
p
~
.

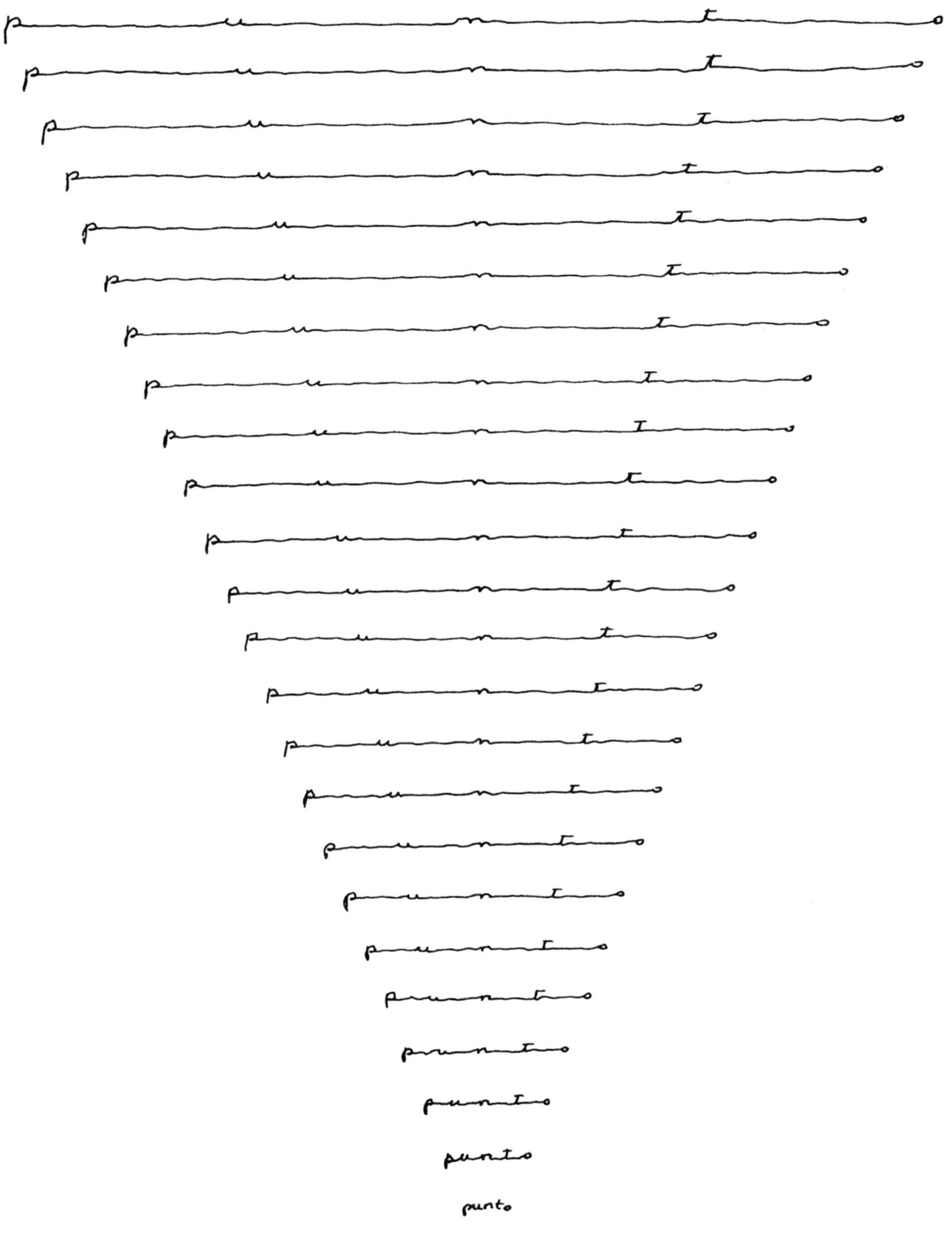

.

lines

lines

lines

lines

lines

lines

lines

lines

lines

lines

lines

lines

lines

lines

lines

lines

lines

lines

lines

lines

lines

lines

lines

punto

punto

punto

punto

punto

punto

punto

punto

punto

punto

punto

punto

punto

p—to

p—to

p—to

p—to

p—to

p—t

p— t

p— —

p— -

———

———

linea
linea
linea
linea
linea
linea
linea
linea
linea
linea
linea
linea
linea
linea
lin——
lin——
lin——
lin——
lin——
li——
li——
e——
e——
. ——

Agnes Denes

O THROW AWAY THE WORSER PART OF IT,
AND LIVE THE PURER WITH THE OTHER HALF.
GOOD NIGHT, BUT GO NOT TO MY UNCLE'S BED,
ASSUME A VIRTUE IF YOU HAVE IT NOT.
THAT MONSTER CUSTOM, WHO ALL SENSE DOTH EAT
OF HABITS EVIL, IS ANGEL YET IN THIS,
THAT TO THE USE OF ACTIONS FAIR AND GOOD
HE LIKEWISE GIVES A FROCK OR LIVERY
THAT APTLY IS PUT ON.REFRAIN TO-NIGHT,
AND THAT SHALL LEND A KIND OF EASINESS
TO THE NEXT ABSTINENCE, THE NEXT MORE EASY:
FOR USE ALMOST CAN CHANGE THE STAMP OF NATURE,
AND EITHER...THE DEVIL, OR THROW HIM OUT,
WITH WONDROUS POTENCY: ONCE MORE , GOOD NIGHT,
AND WHEN YOU ARE DESIROUS TO BE BLESSED,
I'LL BLESSING BEG OF YOU. FOR THIS SAME LORD,
I DO REPENT; BUT HEAVEN HATH PLEASED IT SO,
TO PUNISH ME WITH THIS, AND THIS WITH ME,
THAT I MUST BE THEIR SCOURGE AND MINISTER.
I WILL BESTOW HIM AND WILL ANSWER WELL
THE DEATH I GAVE HIM; SO, AGAIN, GOOD NIGHT.
I MUST BE CRUEL ONLY TO BE KIND.
THIS BAD BEGINS, AND WORSE REMAINS BEHIND....
ONE WORD MORE, GOOD LADY.
NOT THIS BY NO MEANS THAT I BID YOU DO-
LET THE BLOAT KING TEMPT YOU AGAIN TO BED,
PINCH WANTON ON YOUR CHEEK, CALL YOU HIS MOUSE,
AND LET HIM FOR A PAIR OF REECHY KISSES,
OR PADDLING IN YOUR NECK WITH HIS DAMNED FINGERS,
MAKE YOU TO RAVEL ALL THIS MATTER OUT
THAT I ESSENTIALLY AM NOT IN MADNESS,
BUT MAD IN CRAFT. 'TWERE GOOD YOU LET HIM KNOW,
FOR WHO THAT'S BUT A QUEEN, FAIR, SOBER, WISE,
WOULD FROM A PADDOCK, FROM A BAT, A GIB,
SUCH DEAR CONCERNINGS HIDE? WHO WOULD DO SO?
NO, IN DESPITE OF SENSE AND SECRECY,
UNPEG THE BASKET ON THE HOUSE'S TOP,
LET THE BIRDS FLY, AND LIKE THE FAMOUS APE,
TO TRY CONCLUSIONS IN THE BASKET CREEP,
AND BREAK YOUR OWN NECK DOWN.
I MUST GO TO ENGLAND, YOU KNOW THAT?
THERE'S LETTERS SEALED, AND MY TWO
SCHOOL-FELLOWS,
WHOM I WILL TRUST AS I WILL ADDERS FANGED,
THEY BEAR THE MANDATE- THEY MUST SWEEP MY WAY
AND MARSHALL ME TO KNAVERY: LET IT WORK,
FOR 'TIS THE SPORT TO HAVE THE ENGINER
HOIST WITH HIS OWN PETAR, AND'T SHALL GO HARD
BUT I WILL DELVE ONE YARD BELOW THEIR MINES,
AND BLOW THEM AT THE MOON: O, 'TIS MOST SWEET
WHEN IN ONE LINE TWO CRAFTS DIRECTLY MEET.
THIS MAN SHALL SET ME PACKING,
I'LL LUG THE GUTS INTO THE NEIGHBOR ROOM;
MOTHER, GOOD NIGHT INDEED. THIS COUNSELLOR
IS NOW MOST STILL, MOST SECRET, AND MOST GRAVE,
WHO WAS IN LIFE A FOOLISH PRATING KNAVE...
COME,SIR,TO DRAW AN END WITH YOU...
GOOD NIGHT, MOTHER.
SAFELY STOWED.

I' THE WORLD.
THE MOUSE-TRAP. MARRY, HOW? TROPICALLY. THIS PLAY
IS THE IMAGE OF A MURDER DONE IN VIENNA: GONZAGO IS THE
DUKE'S NAME; HIS WIFE, BAPTISTA: YOU SHALL SEE ANON: 'TIS A
KNAVISH PIECE OF WORK: BUT WHAT O' THAT? YOUR MAJESTY, AND
WE THAT HAVE FREE SOULS, IT TOUCHES US NOT: LET THE GALLED
JADE WINCE, OUR WITHERS ARE UNWRUNG.
I COULD INTERPRET BETWEEN YOU AND YOUR LOVE, IF YOU
COULD SEE THE PUPPETS DALLYING.
IT WOULD COST YOU A GROANING TO TAKE OFF MY EDGE.
SO YOU MUST TAKE YOUR HUSBANDS. BEGIN, MURDERER;
POX, LEAVE THY DAMNABLE FACES AND BEGIN. COME: (THE
CROAKING RAVEN DOTH BELLOW FOR REVENGE"
HE POISONS HIM 'I THE GARDEN FOR HIS ESTATE. HIS
NAME'S GONZAGO: THE STORY IS EXTANT, AND WRITTEN IN VERY
CHOICE ITALIAN: YOU SHALL SEE ANON HOW THE MURDERER GETS
THE LOVE OF GONZAGO'S WIFE.
WHAT, FRIGHTED WITH FALSE FIRE!
WHY, LET THE STRICKEN DEER GO WEEP,
THE HART UNGALLED PLAY;
FOR SOME MUST WATCH, WHILE SOME MUST SLEEP:
THUS RUNS THE WORLD AWAY.
WOULD NOT THIS, SIR, AND A FOREST OF FEATHERS- IF THE REST OF
MY FORTUNES TURN TURK WITH ME- WITH TWO PROVINCIAL ROSES
ON MY RAZED SHOES, GET ME A FELLOWSHIP IN A CRY OF PLAYERS,
SIR?
A WHOLE ONE, I.
 FOR THOU DOST KNOW, O DAMON DEAR,
THIS REALM DISMANTLED WAS
OF JOVE HIMSELF; AND NOW REIGNS HERE
A VERY,VERY-PAJOCK.
O GOOD HORATIO, I'LL TAKE THE GHOST'S WORD FOR A
THOUSAND POUND. DIDST PERCEIVE?
UPON THE TALK OF THE POISONING?
AH,HA! COME, SOME MUSIC! COME, THE RECORDERS!
FOR IF THE KING LIKE NOT THE COMEDY,
WHY, THEN, BELIKE, HE LIKES IT NOT,PERDY.
COME, SOME MUSIC!
SIR, A WHOLE HISTORY.
AYE, SIR, WHAT OF HIM?
WITH DRINK, SIR?
YOUR WISDOM SHOULD SHOW ITSELF MORE RICHER TO SIGNIFY
THIS TO THE DOCTOR; FOR, FOR ME TO PUT HIM TO HIS PURGATION
WOULD PERHAPS PLUNGE HIM INTO FAR MORE CHOLER.
I AM TAME, SIR: PRONOUNCE.
YOU ARE WELCOME.
SIR, I CANNOT.
MAKE YOU A WHOLESOME ANSWER; MY WIT'S DISEASED:
BUT, SIR,SUCH ANSWER AS I CAN MAKE YOU SHALL COMMAND;
OR, RATHER,AS YOU SAY, MY MOTHER: THEREFORE NO MORE, BUT
TO THE MATTER: MY MOTHER, YOU SAY,-
O WONDERFUL SON, THAT CAN SO ASTONISH A MOTHER!
BUT IS THERE NO SEQUEL AT THE HEELS OF THIS MOTHER'S ADMIRATION?
IMPART.
WE SHALL OBEY, WERE SHE TEN TIMES OUR MOTHER.
HAVE YOU ANY FURTHER TRADE WITH US?
SO I DO STILL, BY THESE PICKERS AND STEALERS.
SIR, I LACK ADVANCEMENT.
AYE, SIR, BUT 'WHILE THE GRASS GROWS,'- THE PROVERB

SHOW VIRTUE FEATURE , SCORN IMAGE ,
AGE BODY TIME FORM PRESSURE .
OVERDONE TARDY OFF , THOUGH
UNSKILLFUL LAUGH , JUDICIOUS GRIEVE ;
CENSURE OWANCE O'ERWEIGH
WHOLE THEATER OTHERS . , PLAYERS
SEEN PLAY , HEARD OTHERS PRAISE , HIGHLY ,
SPEAK PROFANELY , NEITHER HAVING ACCENT CHRISTIANS
GAIT CHRISTIAN , PAGAN , MAN ,
STRUTTED BELLOWED , THOUGHT NATURE'S
JOURNEYMEN MEN , ,
IMITATED HUMANITY ABOMINABLY .
, REFORM ALTOGETHER . PLAY
CLOWNS SPEAK THAN DOWN :
THEMSELVES LAUGH , QUANTITY
BARREN SPECTATORS LAUGH , THOUGH MEAN
TIME NECESSARY QUESTION PLAY
CONSIDERED : VILLAINOUS , SHOWS MOST PITIFUL AMBITION
FOOL USES . , READY .
! HORATIO !
HORATIO , ART JUST MAN
CONVERSATION COPED WITHAL .
ADVANCEMENT HOPE ,
REVENUE HAST SPIRITS ,
FEED CLOTHE ? SHOULD POOR FLATTERED ?
, CANDIED TONGUE LICK ABSURD POMP ,
CROOK PREGNANT HINGES KNEE
WHERE THRIFT FOLLOW FAWNING . HEAR ?
SINCE DEAR SOUL MISTRESS CHOICE ,
MEN DISTINGUISH , ELECTION
SEAL'D HERSELF : HAST BEEN
, SUFFERING , SUFFERS NOTHING ;
MAN FORTUNE'S BUFFETS REWARDS
HAST TA'EN EQUAL THANKS : BLEST
BLOOD JUDGEMENT COMMINGLED
PIPE FORTUNE'S FINGER
SOUND STOP PLEASE . MAN
PASSION'S SLAVE , WEAR
HEART'S CORE , AYE , HEART HEART ,
. SOMETHING MUCH .
PLAY TO-NIGHT BEFORE KING ;
SCENE COMES NEAR CIRCUMSTANCE
TOLD FATHER'S DEATH :
PRITHEE , SEES ACT A-FOOT ,
EVEN COMMENT SOUL
OBSERVE UNCLE : OCCULTED GUILT
UNKENNEL SPEECH
DAMNED GHOST SEEN ,
IMAGINATIONS FOUL
VULCAN'S STITHY . HEEDFUL NOTE ;
EYES RIVET FACE ,
AFTER BOTH JUDGEMENTS JOIN
CENSURE SEEMING .
COMING PLAY : IDLE :
GET PLACE .
EXCELLENT , FAITH ; CHAMELEON'S DISH : EAT
AIR , PROMISE-CRAMMED : FEED CAPONS .
, . LORD ,
PLAYED ONCE UNIVERSITY , ?
ENACT ?
BRUTE PART KILL CAPITAL CALF

SNUMB = 5M480, ACTIVITY # = 02, REPORT CODE = 06, RECORD COUNT = 00479

HAMLET'S LINES

```
HORATIO , -     FORGET  MYSELF .
,    FRIEND ; , LL  CHANGE   NAME    ;
      WITTENBERG ,  HORATIO ?
MARCELLUS ?
   GLAD     .
EVEN ,  .
   FAITH    ?
   HEAR   ENEMY    ,
     EAR   VIOLENCE ,
   TRUSTER     REPORT
AGAINST   :  KNOW     TRUANT .
    AFFAIR   ELSINORE ?
WE'LL  TEACH    DRINK  DEEP    DEPART .
 PRAY   ,     MOCK  ,  FELLOW-STUDENT :
       MOTHER'S  WEDDING .
THRIFT , THRIFT , HORATIO !   FUNERAL  BAKED-  MEATS
 COLDLY  FURNISH  FORTH   MARRIAGE  TABLES .
   MET   DEAREST  FOE   HEAVEN
 EVER    SEEN    DAY ,  HORATIO !
 FATHER ! -METHINKS     FATHER .
  MINDS  EYE ,  HORATIO .
   MAN ,           ,
   LOOK  UPON    AGAIN .
?  ?
 KING   FATHER !
 GOD'S  LOVE ,     HEAR .
 WHERE    ?
   SPEAK    ?
   STRANGE .
INDEED ,  INDEED ,  SIRS ,    TROUBLES  .
HOLD     WATCH  TONIGHT ?
ARMED ,     ?
  TOP    TOE ?
     FACE .
,  LOOKED   FROWNINGLY ?
PALE ,    RED ?
 FIXED   EYES  UPON   ?
    BEEN   .
 ,   ,  STAYED   LONG ?
 BEARD   GRIZZLED ,   ?
  WATCH  TO-NIGHT ,
PERCHANCE  'TWILL  WALK  AGAIN .
  ASSUMES   NOBLE  FATHER'S  PERSON ,
 SPEAK    ,  THOUGH  HELL   SHOULD  GAPE
 BID   HOLD   PEACE .   PRAY      ,
   HITHERTO  CONCEAL'D   SIGHT ,
   TENABLE    SILENCE  STILL ,
 WHATSOEVER  ELSE    HAP  TONIGHT ,
   UNDERSTANDING ,    TOUNGE :
  REQUITE    LOVES .   FARE    :
UPON   PLATFORM .    ELEVEN   TWELVE ,
 VISIT   .
 LOVES ,      :  FAREWELL .
 FATHER'S  SPIRIT   ARMS !      ;
 DOUBT   FOUL  PLAY :    NIGHT     !
TILL   SIT  STILL ,   SOUL : FOUL  DEEDS   RISE ,
THOUGH      EARTH  O'ERWHELM ,   MEN'S  EYES .
ANGELS   MINISTERS   GRACE  DEFEND   !
   SPIRIT   HEALTH ,   GOBLIN  DAMNED ,
BRING    AIRS    HEAVEN ,   BLASTS    HELL ,
  INTENTS  WICKED     CHARITABLE
```

```
 2 REPETITIONS OF  ( HAD )
        REPLACED BY ( )
 1 REPETITIONS OF  ( GOT )
        REPLACED BY ( )
 3 REPETITIONS OF  ( GET )
        REPLACED BY ( )
 2 REPETITIONS OF  ( EVEN )
        REPLACED BY ( )
 2 REPETITIONS OF  ( EVERY )
        REPLACED BY ( )
 0 REPETITIONS OF  ( ONE'S )
        REPLACED BY ( )
 0 REPETITIONS OF  ( ONES' )
        REPLACED BY ( )
 9 REPETITIONS OF  ( OTHER )
        REPLACED BY ( )
 0 REPETITIONS OF  ( WHATEVER )
        REPLACED BY ( )
 2 REPETITIONS OF  ( DONE )
        REPLACED BY ( )
 0 REPETITIONS OF  ( DOING )
        REPLACED BY ( )
 2 REPETITIONS OF  ( DOESN'T )
        REPLACED BY ( )
 2 REPETITIONS OF  ( DID )
        REPLACED BY ( )
 0 REPETITIONS OF  ( ALL )
        REPLACED BY ( )
 1 REPETITIONS OF  ( ALSO )
        REPLACED BY ( )
 2 REPETITIONS OF  ( ANY )
        REPLACED BY ( )
 2 REPETITIONS OF  ( CAN'T )
        REPLACED BY ( )
 2 REPETITIONS OF  ( CANNOT )
        REPLACED BY ( )
 1 REPETITIONS OF  ( COULD )
        REPLACED BY ( )
11 REPETITIONS OF  ( SAME )
        REPLACED BY ( )
 0 REPETITIONS OF  ( WOULD )
        REPLACED BY ( )
 0 REPETITIONS OF  ( HIS )
        REPLACED BY ( )
 1 REPETITIONS OF  ( ELSE )
        REPLACED BY ( )
 9 REPETITIONS OF  ( HIM )
        REPLACED BY ( )
 0 REPETITIONS OF  ( NOW )
        REPLACED BY ( )
 0 REPETITIONS OF  ( WHOSE )
        REPLACED BY ( )
 6 REPETITIONS OF  ( ONLY )
        REPLACED BY ( )
 7 REPETITIONS OF  ( MIGHT )
        REPLACED BY ( )
10 REPETITIONS OF  ( HOW )
        REPLACED BY ( )
 3 REPETITIONS OF  ( LET )
        REPLACED BY ( )
 0 REPETITIONS OF  ( IT'S )
```

PLAYERS READY ?
, MOTHER , HERE'S METAL ATTRACTIVE .
LADY , LIE LAP ?
EAN , HEAD UPON LAP ?
MEANT COUNTRY MATTERS ?
FAIR THOUGHT LIE BETWEEN MAID'S LEGS .
NOTHING .
, ?
, ONLY JIG-MAKER . SHOULD MAN
MERRY ? , LOOK , CHEERFULLY MOTHER
LOOKS , FATHER DIED TWO HOURS .
LONG ? , DEVIL WEAR BLACK ,
SUIT SABLES . HEAVENS ! DIE TWO MONTHS AGO ,
FORGOTTEN ? THERE'S HOPE GREAT MAN'S MEMORY
OUTLIVE LIFE HALF YEAR : , 'R LADY ,
BUILD CHURCHES ; ELSE SUFFER THINKING ,
HOBBY-HORSE , EPITAPH , 'FOR , , , ,
HOBBY-HORSE FORGOT . '
MARRY , MICHING MALLECHO ; MEANS MISCHIEF .
KNOW FELLOW : PLAYERS
KEEP COUNSEL ; THEY'LL .
AYE , SHOW SHOW :
ASHAMED SHOW , HE'LL SHAME MEANS .
WOMAN'S LOVE .
WORMWOOD , WORMWOOD .
SHOULD BREAK !
MADAM , PLAY ?
, SHE'LL KEEP WORD .
, , JEST , POISON JEST ; OFFENSE
WORLD .
MOUSE-TRAP . MARRY , ? TROPICALLY . PLAY
IMAGE MURDER DONE VIENNA : GONZAGO
DUKE'S NAME ; WIFE , BAPTISTA : ANON :
KNAVISH PIECE WORK ; O' ? MAJESTY ,
FREE SOULS , TOUCHES : GALLED
JADE WINCE , WITHERS UNWRUNG .
INTERPRET BETWEEN LOVE ,
PUPPETS DALLYING .
COST GROANING OFF EDGE .
HUSBANDS . BEGIN , MURDERER ;
POX , LEAVE DAMNABLE FACES BEGIN . : (
CROAKING RAVEN DOTH BELLOW REVENGE "
POISONS 'I GARDEN ESTATE .
NAME'S GONZAGO : STORY EXTANT , WRITTEN
CHOICE ITALIAN : ANON MURDERER GETS
LOVE GONZAGO'S WIFE .
, FRIGHTED FALSE FIRE !
, STRICKEN DEER WEEP ,
HART UNGALLED PLAY ;
WATCH , SLEEP :
RUNS WORLD AWAY .
, , FOREST FEATHERS- REST
FORTUNES TURN TURK ME- TWO PROVINCIAL ROSES
RAZED SHOES , GET FELLOWSHIP CRY PLAYERS
?
WHOLE , .
KNOW , DAMON DEAR ,
REALM DISMANTLED
JOVE ; REIGNS
, VERY-PAJOCK .
HORATIO , GHOST'S WORD

.GNIK EHT FO ECNEICSNOC EHT HCTAC LL'I NIEREHW
GNIHT EHT S'YALP EHT -:SIHT OT EVITALER EROM
SDNUORG EVAH LL'I :EM NMAD OT EM SESUBA
-,STIRIPS HCUS HTIW TNETOP YREV SI EH SA
-,YLOCNOLEM YM DNA SSENKAEW YM FO TUO
SPAHREP DNA ,AEY ;EPAHS GNISAELP A EMUSSA OT
REWOP HTAH LIVED EHT DNA :LIVED EHT EB YAM
NEES EVAH I TAHT TIRIPS EHT .ESRUOC YM WONK I
,HCNELB TUB EH FI :KCIUQ EHT OT MIH TNET LL'I
;SKOOL SIH EVRESBO LL'I :ELCNU ENIM EROFEB
REHTAF YM FO REDRUM EHT EKIL GNIHTEMOS YALP
SREYALP ESEHT EVAH LL'I .NAGRO SUOLUCARIM TSOM HTIW
KAEPS LLIW ,EUGNOT ON EVAH TI HGUOHT ,REDRUM ROF
;SNOITCAFELAM RIEHT D'MIALCORP EVAH YEHT
YLTNESERP TAHT LUOS EHT OT OS KCURTS NEEB
ENECS EHT FO GNINNUC YREV EHT YB EVAH
,YALP A TA GNITTIS ,SERUTAERC YTLIUG TAHT
DRAEH EVAH I .MUH !NIARB YM ,TUOBA - !HOF !T'NOPU EIF
!NOILLUCS A
.BARD YREV A EKIL GNISRUC-A LLAF DNA
.SDROW HTIW TRAEH YM KCAPNU ,EROHW A EKIL ,TSUM
,LLEH DNA NEVAEH YB EGNEVER YM OT DETPMORP
,D'REDRUM REHTAF RAED A FO NOS EHT ,I TAHT
,EVARB TSOM SI SIHT !I MA SSA NA TAHW ,YHW
!ECNAEGNEV ,O
!NIALIV SSELDNIK ,SUOREHCEL ,YREHCAERT ,SSELESROMER
!NIALLIV YDWAB ,YDOOLB - :LAFFO S'EVALS SIHT HTIW
SETIK NOIGER EHT LLA DETTAF EVAH DLUOHS I
SIHT ERE RO ,RETTIB NOISSERPPO EKAM OT
LLAG KCAL DNA ,D'REVIL-NOEGIP MA I TUB
EB TONNAC TI ROF :TI EKAT DLUOHS I ,SDNUOWS'
?AH ,SIHT EM SEOD OHW ? SGNUL EHT OT SA PEED SA
,TAORHT EHT 'I EIL EHT EM SEVIG ?ESON EHT YB EM SKAEWT
?ECAF YM NI TI SWOLB DNA DRAEB YM FFO SKCULP
?SSORCA ETAP YM SKAERB ?NIALLIV EM SLLAC OHW
?DRAWOC A I MA .EDAM SAW TAEFED D'NMAD A
EFIL RAED TSOM DNA YTREPORP ESOHW NOPU
GNIK A ROF TON ,ON ;GNIHTON YAS NAC DNA
,ESUAC YM FO TNANGERPNU ,SMAERD-FO-NHOJ A EKIL
,KAEP ,LACSAR DELTTEM-YDDUM DNA LLUD A
,I TEY
.SRAE DNA SEYE FO SEITLUCAF YREV EHT
,DEEDNI ,EZAMA DNA ,TNARONGI EHT DNUOFNOC
;EERF EHT LAPPA DNA ,YTLIUG EHT DAM EKAM
;HCEEPS DIRROH HTIW RAE LARENEG EHT EVAELC DNA
,SRAET HTIW EGATS EHT NWORD DLUOW EH ?EVAH I TAHT
NOISSAP ROF EUC EHT DNA EVITOM EHT EH DAH
EH DLUOW TAHW ?REH ROF PEEW DLUOHS EH TAHT
,ABUCEH OT EH RO MIH OT ABUCEH S'TAHW
?ABUCEH ROF
!GNIHTON ROF LLA DNA ?TIECNOC SIH OT SMROF HTIW
GNITIUS NOITCNUF ELOHW SIH DNA ,ECIOV NEKORB A
,TCEPSA S'NI NOITCARTSID ,SEYE SIH NI SRAET
;D'NAW EGASIV SIH LLA GNIKROW REH MORF TAHT
TIECNOC NWO SIH OT OS LUOS SIH ECROF DLUOC
,NOISSAP FO MAERD A NI ,NOITCIF A TUB
,EREH REYALP SIHT TAHT SUORTSNOM TON TI SI
!I MA EVALS TNASAEP DNA EUGOR A TAHW ,O
.ENOLA MA I WON -!EY 'IW 'B DOG OS ,YA

```
FCB AND BUFFER SPACE
   AVAILABLE          000101 THRU 002767        002667
   FILE CTRL BLKS 002612 THRU 002770        000157
   MAXIMUM BUFFER SPACE REQUIRED              001703

    14K, IS THE MINIMUM MEMORY NEEDED TO LOAD THIS ACTIVITY
000550 LOCATIONS REQUIRED FOR LOAD TABLE
EXECUTION PROGRAM ENTERED AT  032706   THROUGH  .SETU.

MA 000200  MB 000200  BE 000
EI 022037236012  OI 032613756000  IC 033450  IR 000001  BA 402034  ER 200  AR 010
X0 032707  X1 033154  X2 000055  X3 000367  X4 000000  X5 000000  X6 000000  X7

033410S    000002236007  000000011007  032617756000  032617722000  023477635012
033420     000001076007  000122116007  033412604000  015543701000  017516701000
033430     032634000000  032635000000  032611236000  000001076007  032642116000
033440     032647450000  000001236007  032611756000  032611722000  022657236012
033450     032613756000  032613236000  033454605000  032613450000  032647236000
033460     032651756000  032650054000  032640076000  032652756000  032652722000
033470     033472600000  033514710000  032651236000  000001076007  032612116000
033500     032651756000  032640076000  032652756000  032652723000  032600236000
*  UPPER SSA

777000M    200003777700  201030000110  033450000001  013145106200  012614000200
777010     001475013361  003524201752  777212202000  000017000002  013722200200
777020     001600000003  442020010733  777722202000  000017000002  032154500600
777030     032707033154  000055000367  000000000000  000000000000  016161202020
777040     410001040400  777777777774  000264000002  000000000000  000000000000
777050     200001011244  200001011253  200001011251  402034402434  402034400000
777060     000000000000  000127714506  000000643174  036427134240  000045045572
777070     000011000000  777344000000  777225000005  011750004670  010002776216
777100     005000000000  045602220374  045600000127  320405410253  337200002260
777110     000000000000  000000000000  000000000000  000000000000  000000000000
777120     000000000000  000000000000  000000000000  075003000000  075010000000
777130     001124000011  003123010027  003171010027  003237010027  001124000066
777140     000000000000  000000000000  000000000000  000000000000  201010073200
777150     000000000000  000000037633  000000002710  000000000012  400000000000
777160     201102220374  201130000002  000211000422  777225000000  201101500000
777170     000000000002  000000000011  201102220374  201130000002  000211000422
777200     200203002600  000271000001  000000370000  000000001475  002014010006
777210     000000000000  000000000000  103517000000  000000000000  003524002110
777220     777220774000  250000240002  777204000000  777154000000  000000001475
777230     777734000017  111500047426  000012000001  777233776000  310000240002
777240     000000000000  000000000000  000000000000  000000000000  000000000000
777300*    000000000000  000000000001  000000000000  000003000374  542020644747
777310     000000000000  000000000000  000000000000  000000000000  003524104352
777320     004602777777  000116000567  304352264606  777777777777  003524104352
777330     704352074036  204361074005  003504000000  000000163033  005600000000
777340     000000023275  005600000000  000054000000  000360000054  433700002001
777350     013724200201  050625200200  050625200200  000000000000  000000000000
777360     000000000000  000000000000  000000000000  000000000000  000000000000
777720*    537337005443  537332004354  000000044754  477324005154  437316000005
777730     777743006163  777745000000  777757000000  777752000000  777765000000
777740     000632631223  002174000000  000000000000  002140000000  000257156730
777750     000000000017  000360000074  003524000000  000000255325  001200000000
777760     000000016077  005200000000  000001000000  101766000001  777777777777
777770     045505400075  045504400075  000000000000  000000000000  777777772427
000000     000000000000  000000000000  000000000000  000000000000  000000000000
000010     000000000000  012242710000  000000000000  033450010005  000000000000
000020     000000000000  000000000000  033450000001  000000000000  032706000000
```

Mirtha Dermisache

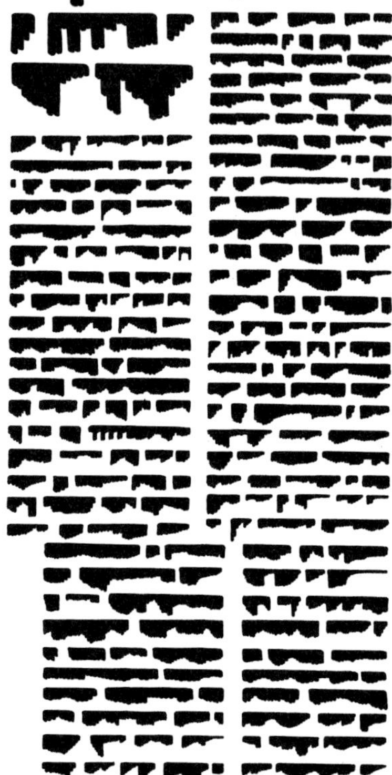
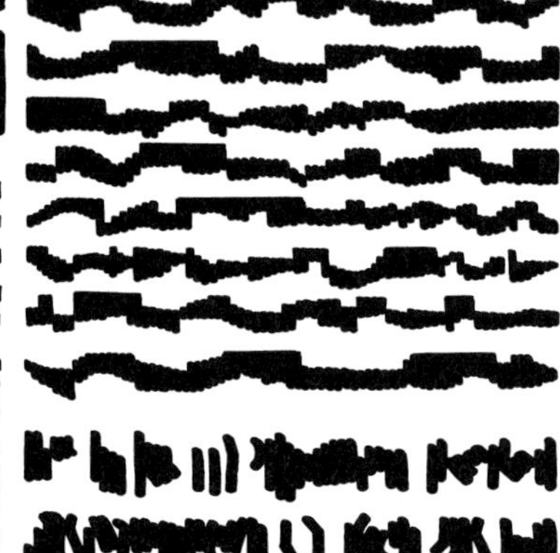

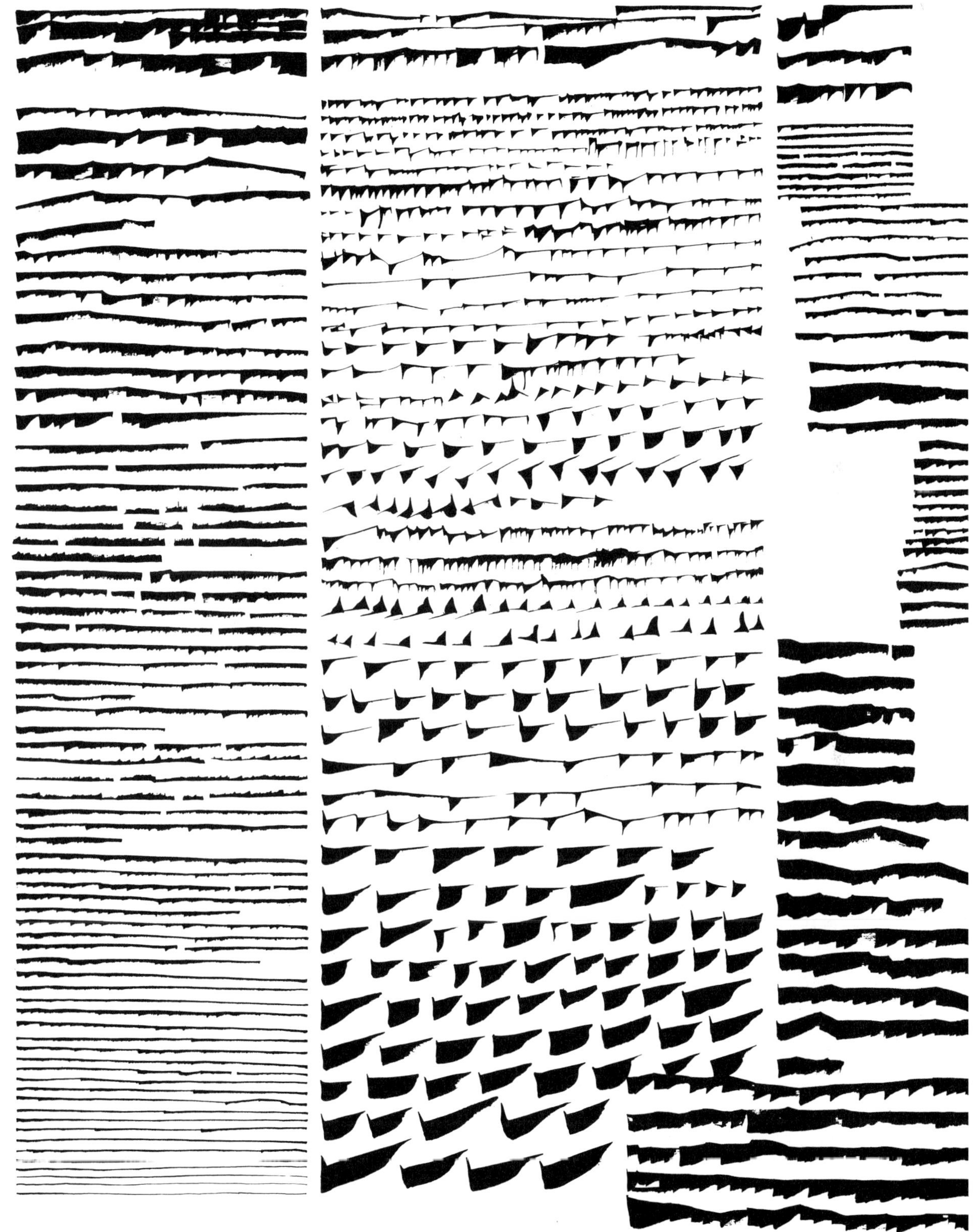

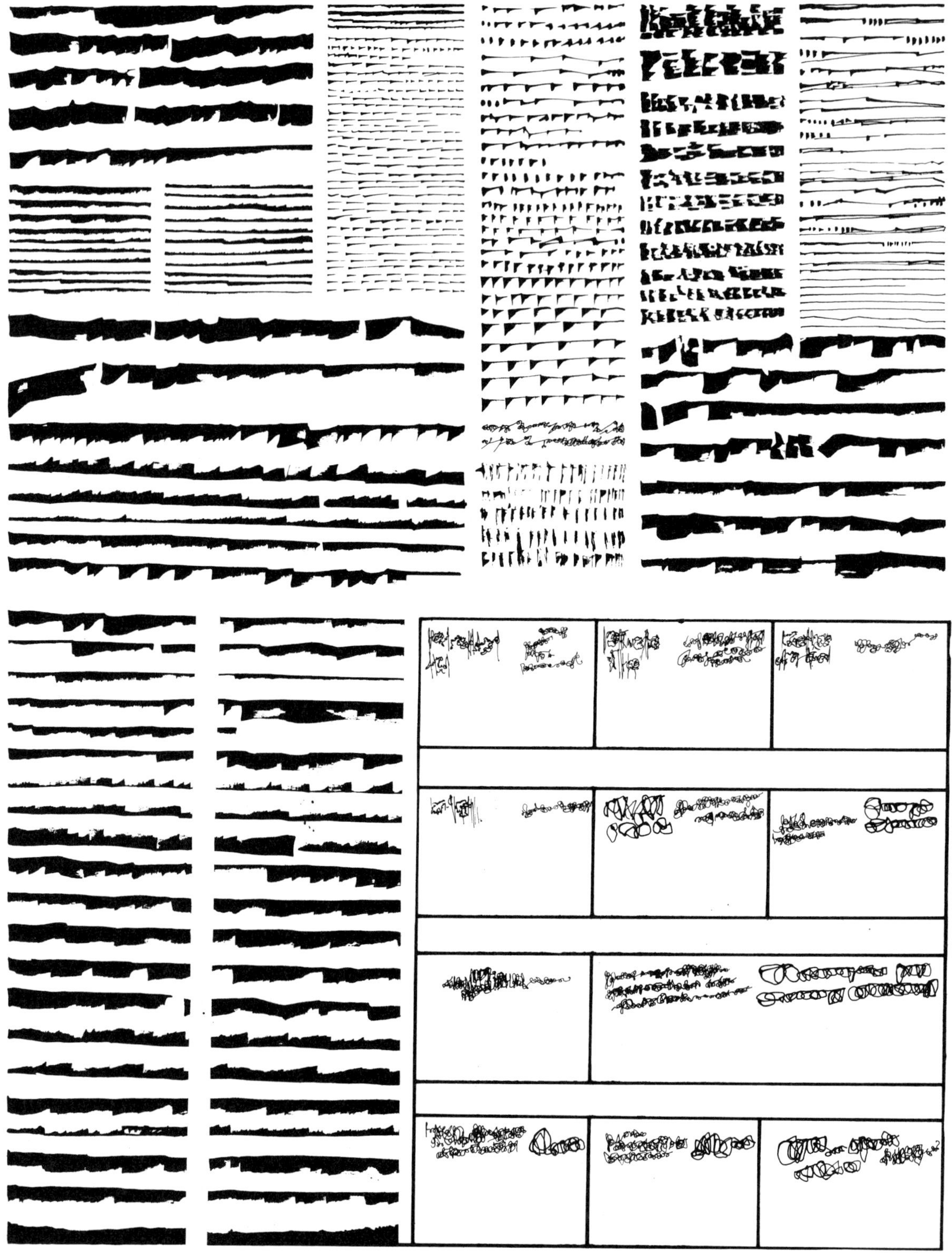

Amelia Etlinger

Ilse Garnier

(   ) a b s e n t

c o o o o rps interdit

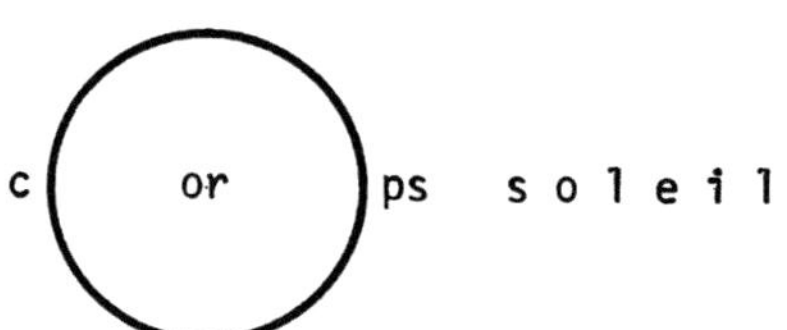
c
or
ps
s o l e i l

/ o /// administré

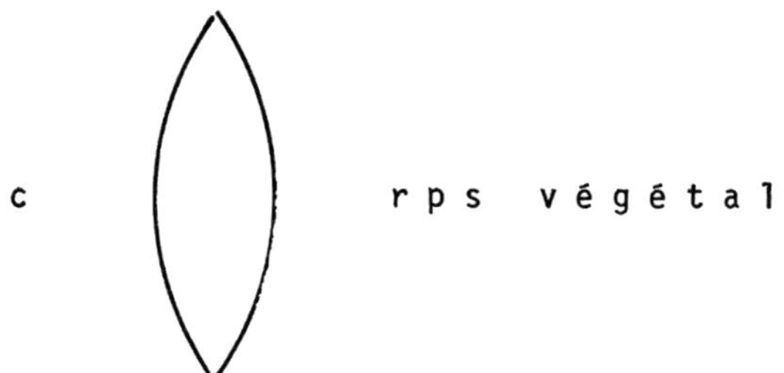
c rps végétal

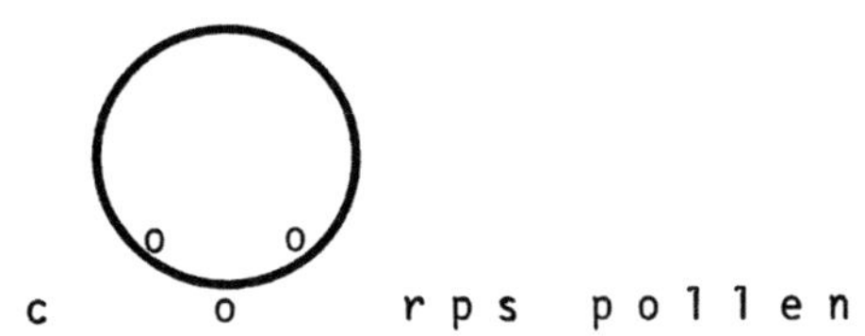

o u b l i é

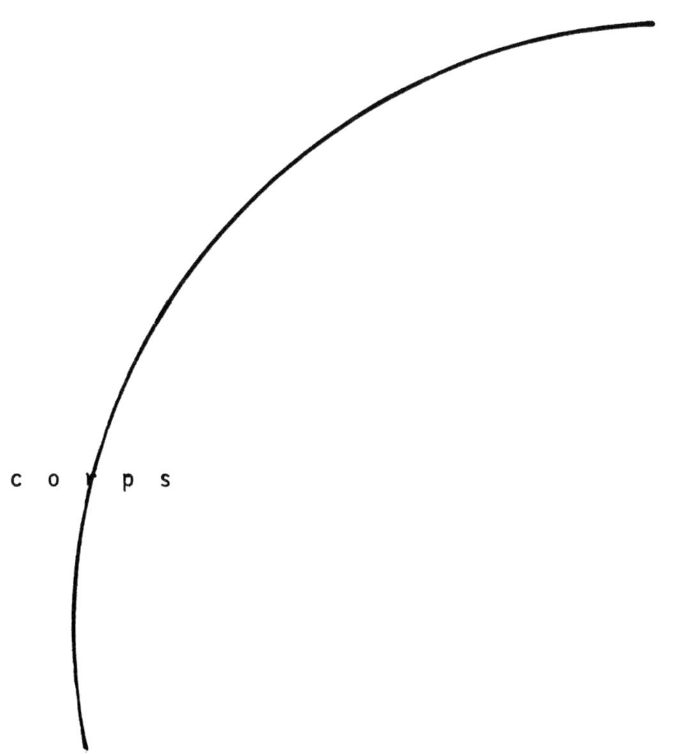

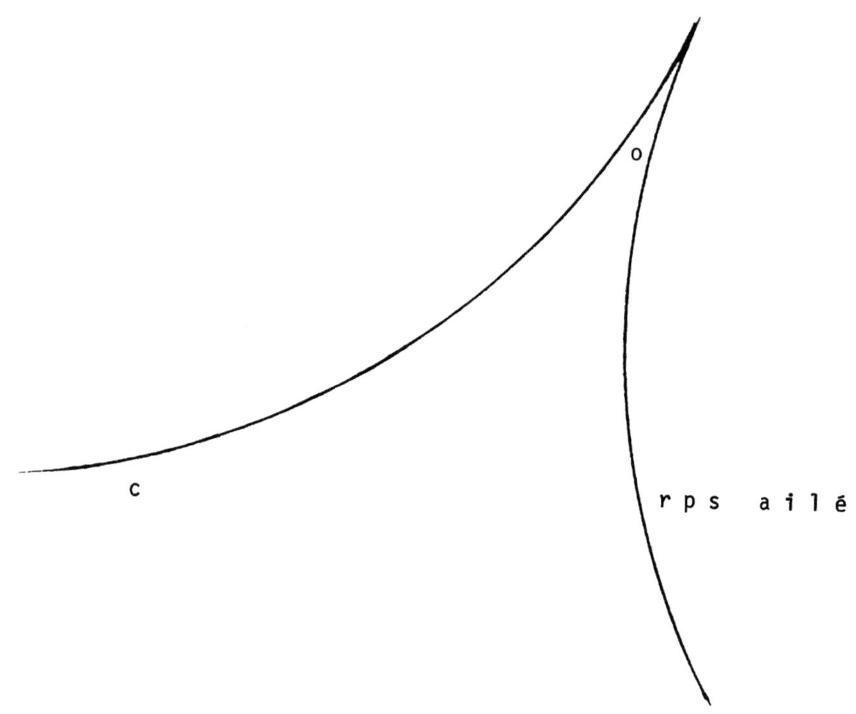
o
c
rps aílé

c o r p s d é l i r e

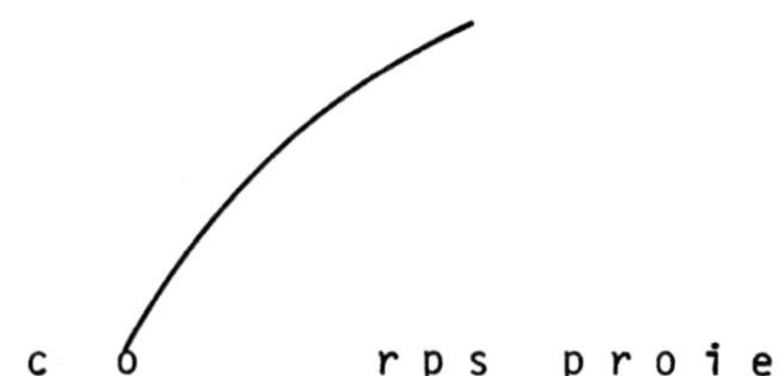
c o rps proie

__________________ f l o t t a n t

Anna Bella Geiger

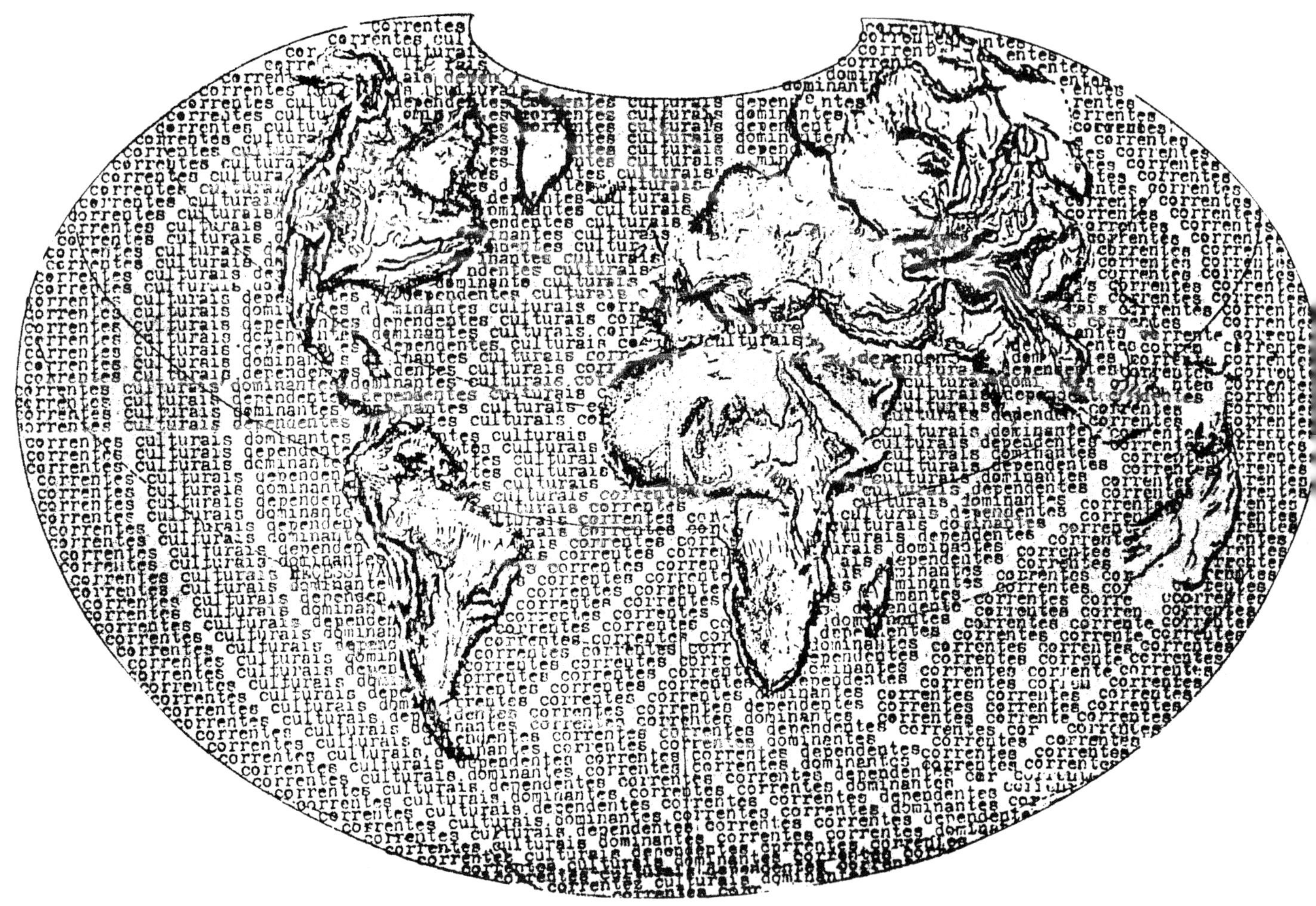
correntes culturais dominantes
correntes culturais dependentes

O ESPAÇO SOCIAL DA ARTE
ANO 1977

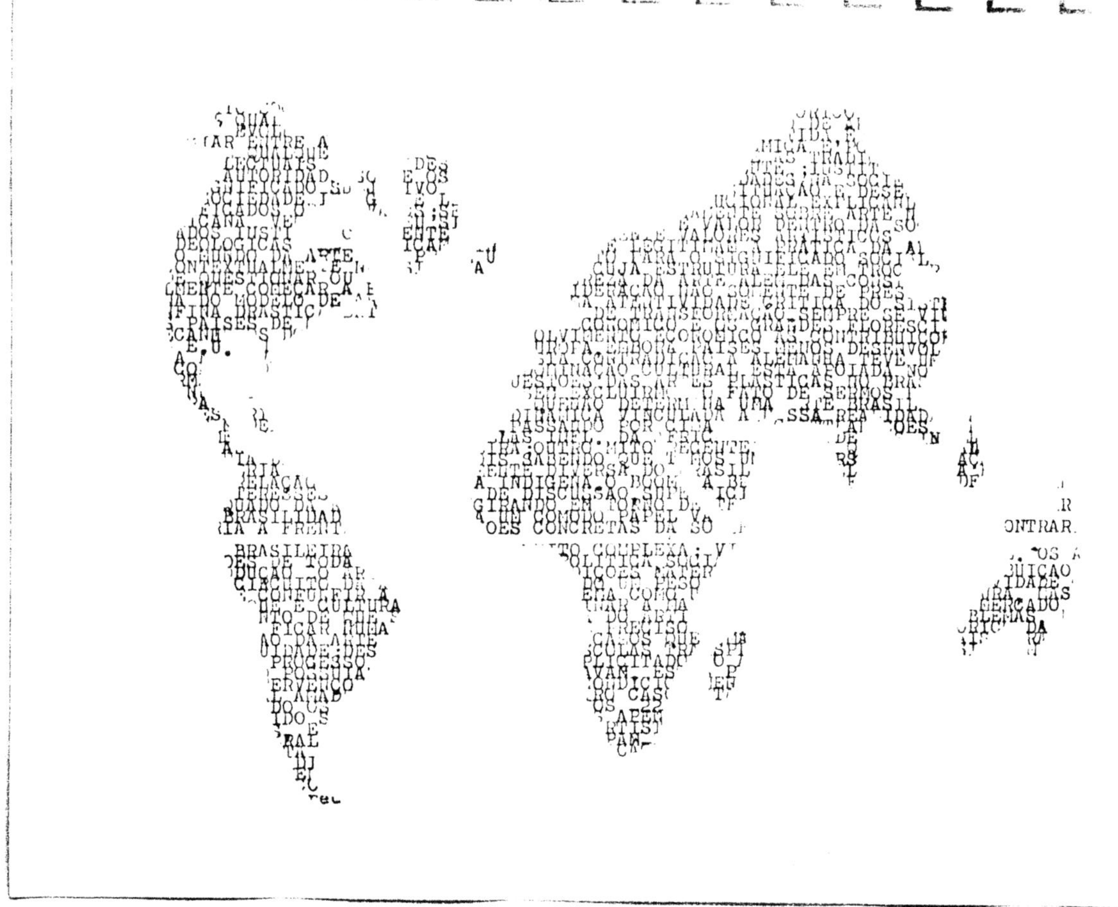

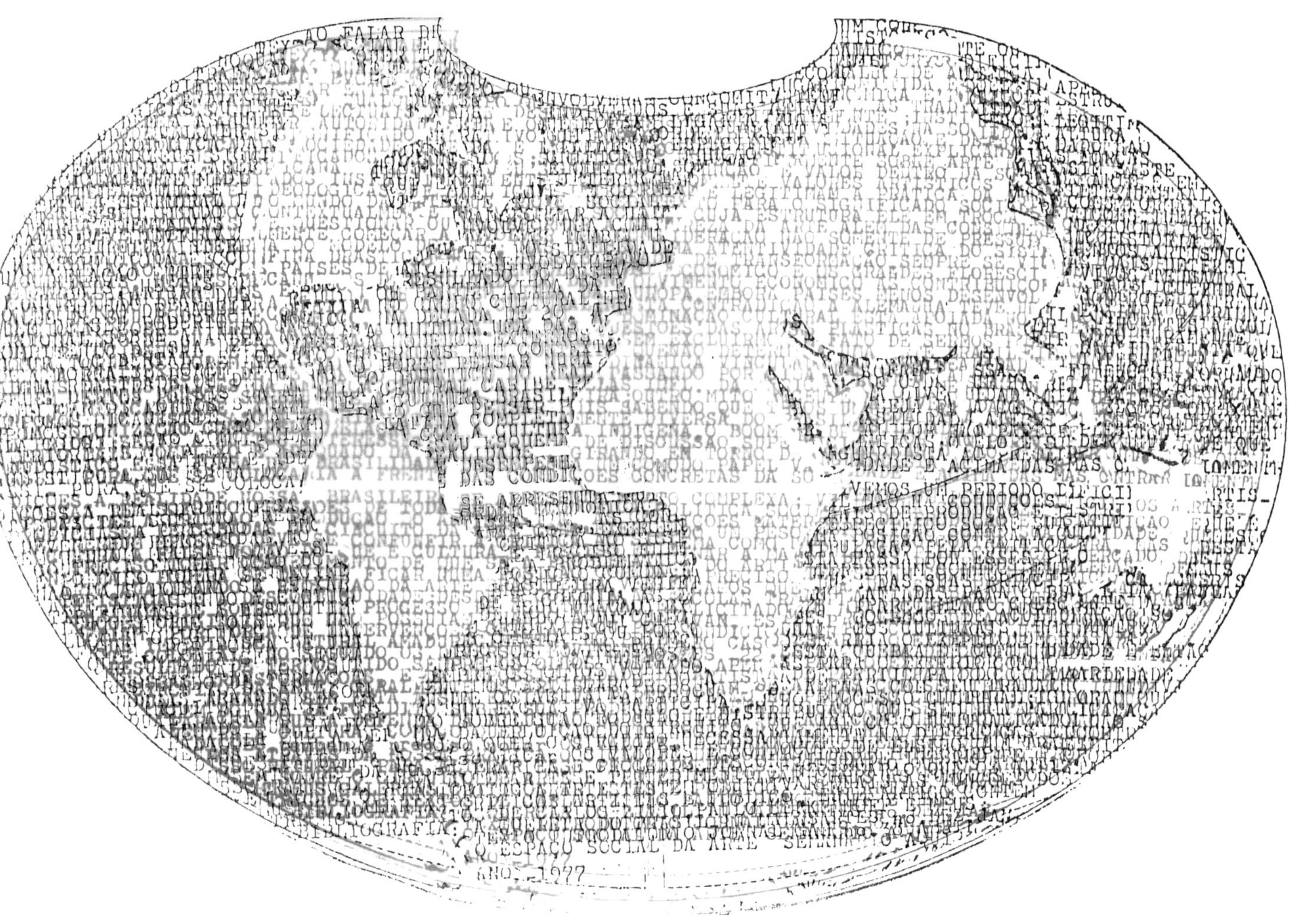
DAS CONDIÇOES CONCRETAS DA SO
VEMOS UM PERIODO DIFICI
O ESPAÇO SOCIAL DA ARTE
ANOS 1977

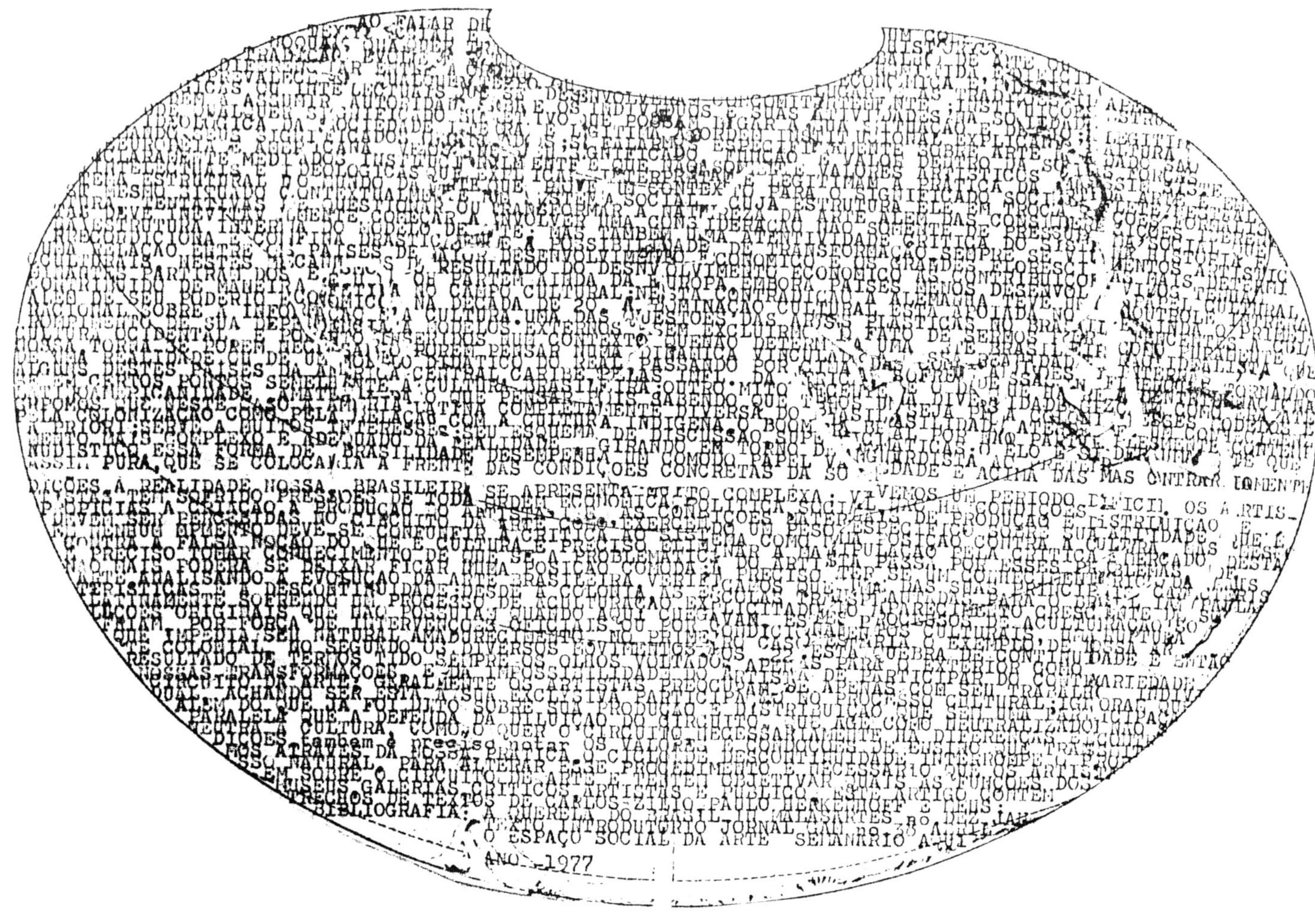
PURA, QUE SE COLOCARIA À FRENTE DAS CONDIÇÕES CONCRETAS DA SOCIEDADE E ACIMA DAS MAIS CONTRADIÇÕES
AÇÕES À REALIDADE NOSSA, BRASILEIRA SE APRESENTA MUITO COMPLEXA
O ESPAÇO SOCIAL DA ARTE
ANO 1977

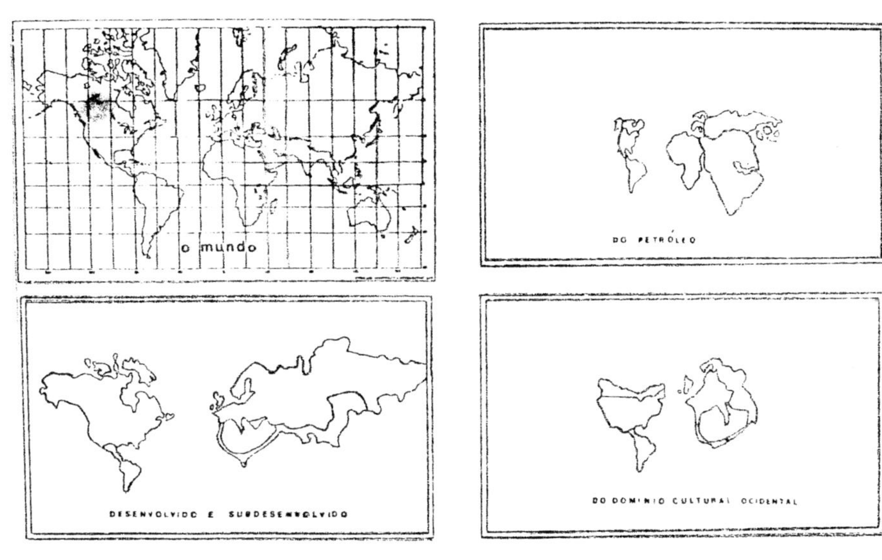
o mundo
DO PETRÓLEO
DESENVOLVIDO E SUBDESENVOLVIDO
DO DOMINIO CULTURAL OCIDENTAL

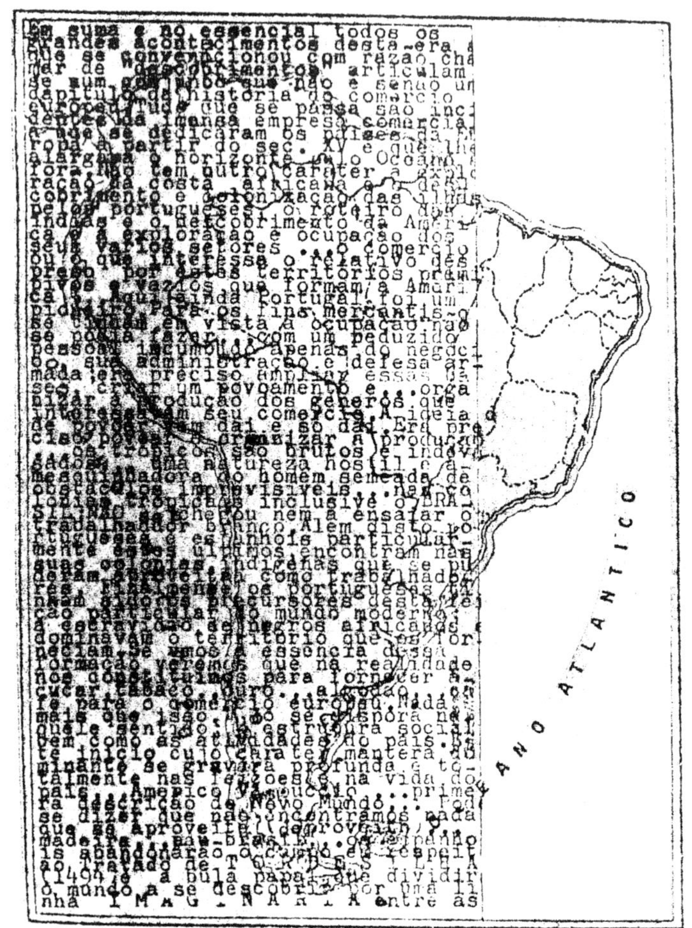
Em suma e no essencial todos os
grandes acontecimentos desta era a
que se convencionou com razão cha
mar de descobrimentos articulam
se num conjunto que não é senão um
capítulo da história do comércio
europeu. Tudo que se passa são inci
dentes da imensa empresa comercial
a que se dedicaram os países da Eu
ropa a partir do sec. XV e que lhe
alargará o horizonte ... o Oceano
fora. Não tem outro caráter a explo
ração da costa africana e o des
cobrimento e colonização das ilhas
pelos portugueses, o roteiro das
Índias e o descobrimento da Améri
ca e a exploração e ocupação dos
seus vários setores ... o comércio
ou o que interessa o relativo des
prezo por estes territórios primi
tivos e vazios que formam a Améri
ca. Aqui ainda Portugal foi um
pioneiro. Para os fins mercantis q
se tinham em vista a ocupação não
se podia fazer ... com um reduzido
pessoal incumbido apenas do negó
cio, sua administração e defesa ar
mada; era preciso ampliar essas ba
ses, criar um povoamento e ... orga
nizar a produção dos gêneros que
interessavam seu comércio. A ideia
de povoar surge daí e só daí. Era pre
ciso povoar e organizar a produção
... os trópicos são brutos e indev
sados ... uma natureza hostil e a
mesquinhadora do homem semeada de
obstáculos imprevisíveis ... nas co
lônias tropicais inclusive o BRA
SIL não se chegou nem a ensaiar o
trabalhador branco. Além disto po
rtugueses e espanhóis particular
mente estes últimos, encontram nas
suas colônias, indígenas que se pu
deram aproveitar como trabalhado
res. Finalmente os portugueses ti
nham sido os precursores desta fe
ção particular do mundo moderno:
a escravidão de negros africanos
dominavam o território que os for
neciam. Se vamos à essência dessa
formação veremos que na realidade
nos constituímos para fornecer a
çúcar, tabaco, ouro ... algodão ... ca
fé para o comércio europeu. Nada
mais que isso ... se dispõe ra na
quele sentido, a estrutura social
bem como as atividades do país. Es
te início cujo caráter manterá do
minante se gravará profunda e to
talmente nas feições e na vida do
país ... Américo Vespúcio ... prime
ra descrição do Novo Mundo ... Pode
se dizer que não encontramos nada
que se aproveite (desproveito) ... a
madeira ... pau-brasil ... os espanho
is abandonarão o campo e em respeit
ao tratado de T O R D E S I L H A
(1494) e a bula papal que dividir
o mundo a se descobrir por uma li
nha I M A G I N A R I A entre as

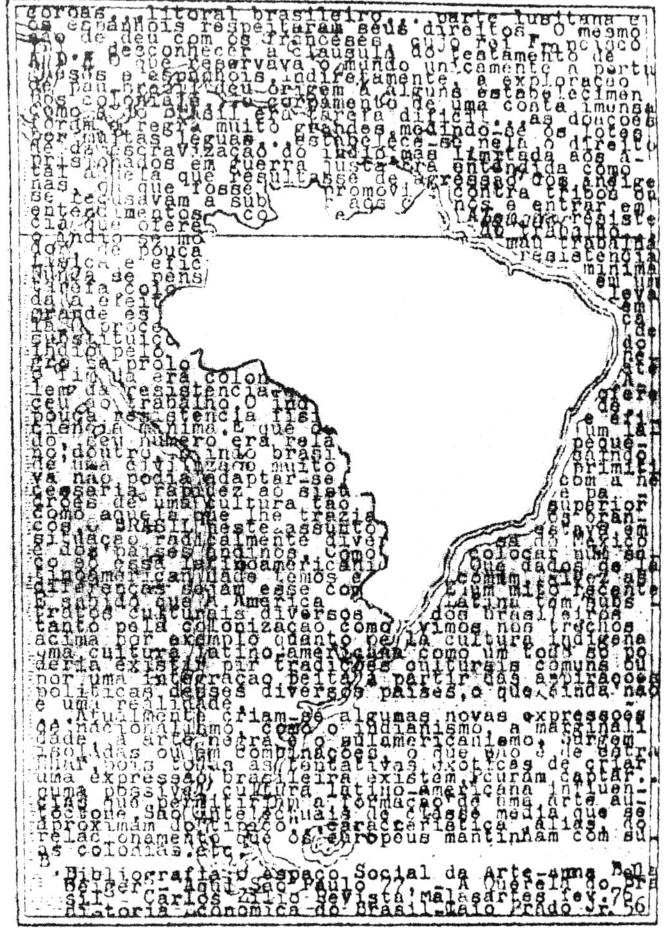
coroas ... litoral brasileiro ... parte lusitana e
os espanhóis respeitaram seus direitos. O mesmo
não se deu com os franceses, cujo rei Francisco
I ... desconhecer a cláusula do testamento de
Adão o que reservava o mundo unicamente a portu
gueses e espanhóis, indiretamente, a exploração
de pau-brasil deu origem a alguns estabelecimen
tos coloniais ... o povoamento de uma costa imensa
como a do BRASIL era tarefa difícil ... as doações
foram em regra muito grandes medindo-se os lotes
por muitas léguas ... estabelece-se nela o direito
de da escravização do índio mas limitada aos a-
prisionados em guerra justa. Era entendida como
tal aquela que resultasse de agressão dos indíge
nas, ou que fosse promovida contra tribos que
se recusavam a sub ... nos e entrar em
entendimentos co
cia que ofere
do índio se mo
do de pouca
física e efic
Nunca se pens
fora colo
dava efeit
grande es
substituição
índio pelo
ro se prolo
... era colon
lem da resistência
ceu ao trabalho. O índ
pouca resistência físi
ciência mínima. É que o
do seu número era rela
no; doutro, o índio brasi
de uma civilização muito
va não podia adaptar-se
cessária rapidez ao siste
... de uma cultura tão
como aquela que lhe trazia
cos. O BRASIL neste assunto
situação radicalmente dive
dos países andinos, como
... essa latinoamericani
... noamericanidade temos e
diferenças sejam esse com
É sabido que A América
tratos culturais diversos ... dos brasileiros
tanto pela colonização como vimos nos trechos
acima por exemplo quanto pela cultura indígena
uma cultura latino-americana como um todo só po
deria existir por tradições culturais comuns ou
por uma integração feita a partir das aspirações
políticas desses diversos países, o que ainda não
é uma realidade.
Atualmente criam-se algumas novas expressões
de nacionalismo, como o indianismo, a marginali
dade, a arte negra e o sulamericanismo, surgem
isoladas ou em combinações, o que não é de estra
nhar, pois todas as tentativas exóticas de criar
uma expressão brasileira existem. Procuram captar
uma possível cultura latino-americana influen
ciada que permitiram a formação de uma arte au
tóctone. São intelectuais de classe média que se
aproximam do tipo ... característica aliás do
relacionamento que os europeus mantinham com su
as colônias. etc.
B
Bibliografia: O espaço Social da Arte - anna Bella
Geiger - Aqui São Paulo 77; A Querela do Bra
sil - Carlos Zilio Revista Malasartes fev. 76
História Econômica do Brasil - Caio Prado Jr. 56

Madeline Gins

I wrote her and read her to her before she wrote this book. Except for a few insertions I left her on her own

(TOUCH)

except to be with her every instant. I have made investigations into her language. I have investigated the means of her disposal. I have preserved these in oiled geometry, liniment algebra and creamed mathematics in hope that they will not become mixed with the word rain.

In the paragraph above, let

A = the first sentence B = the second C = the third
D = the fourth E = the fifth

P indicates paragraph W = word , = , (identity)
M = meaning M′ = further meaning

$A = 13W + M_1$ $B = 18W + M_2$ $C = 7W + M_3$
$D = 8W + M_4$ $E = 24W + , + M_5$

$P = 70W + , + (M_1 \ldots M_5)$ would be an incorrect statement

Rather $P = 70W + , + (M_1 \ldots M_5) + O + M'$

(by self-evidence , = pause— , = 1W)

$P = 71W + (M_1 \ldots M_5) + O + M$

W = word O = zero $E = mc^2$ M = meaning

$$W + E + O = M$$
$$\quad -M \qquad -M$$

$W + E + O - M = O$ ------ $*W + E + O - M = O$

$$-O \qquad -O$$

$$W + E - M = O$$

$W - M = O - E$ ------- $*W - M = O - E$
$W = O - E + M$ ------- $*W = O - E + M$

By substitution:

$P = 71\ (O - mc^2 = M) + [(W + mc^2 + O)_1 \ldots (W + mc^2 + O)_5)]$ $+ M' + O$ would most closely represent the situation

Org (x)	means	x is an organic unit
Yxy	means	Organic unit x is transformed into organic unit y (i.e. x divides into several parts of which one is y [cell division] or fuses with one or more units to produce y [cell fusion])
Orgs. (x)		x is an organism
$\supset$	means	if something then something
$\subset$	means	subclass or subrelation

Axioms

1. Org (x) $\supset$ Th (x) Each organic unit is a thing
   Org $\subset$ Th
2. The members of Y are organic units:
   Yxy $\supset$ Org (x) Org (y)
   Mem (y) $\subset$ Org

$$P = \text{page} \quad W = \text{word} \quad A = \text{attention}$$

$$G = \text{a group of words}$$

$$P = 300W$$

$$P + A = A\,(G) + 300\,W - G$$

In order for P to be read we must have the situation of P — P brought about by A. This would enable us to consider the operation complete and to turn the page.

$$G = 3\ W$$

$$P + A = A\,(3\,W) + 300\,W - 3\,W$$

$$P + A = 3\,W\,A + 297\,W$$

$$A = 3\,W\,A + 297\,W - P$$

$$(P = 300\ W)$$

$$A = 3\,W\,A + 297\,W - 300\,W$$

$$A = A\,W\,A - 3\,W$$

The operation can continue IFF (if and only if) $A = A^2 = A^3$

$$(A^2)\ A = 3\,W\,A - 3\,W\,(A^2)$$

$$A^3 = 3\,W\,A^3 - 3\,W\,A^2$$

$$\text{iff } A^3 = A^2$$

then:

$$A^3 = A^3\,(3\,W - 3\,W)$$

$$100\,A^3 = 100\,A^3\,(3\,W - 3\,W)$$

$$^*100\,A^3 = A^3\,(300\,W - 300\,W) \text{ or } (P - P)$$

The page has been read.

reAd

Co = conversation
S_1 = first speaker S_2 = second speaker
SW = spoken word

$$Co = (S_1 - SW) + (S_2 - SW)$$
$$Co = S_1 (1 - W) + S_2 (1 - W)$$

Tel. no. : 485-8295

SW = spoken word   W = written word   C = letters
N = sounds

$$SW = W - C + N$$

m = this letter was struck by accident

SW = Book — 4 C + 3 N
SW = Colder — 6 C + 5 N
SW = Imagination — 11 C + 6 N

Every word is on the page. It has been read. Several other words came after the first group. Sentences depict lines. Each word is being read next to another being read. In time, the page will be read.

Words are water soluble. This is clearly and moistly so. After all the reader is a reef in the blue-eyed Red Sea. (And all this belongs to an organic question, it says.)

The whirlpool of the pivotal question subsides.
The mouth of the sea
Wet words peel off the surface tension
Screams of air bubble up

and mumble through
the clear embolisms of symbols

C = carbon   O = oxygen   U = uranium   G = gold
H = hydrogen   cough = COUGH

pH2ilOsOpHical investigatiOns

The gas mask reads in the mist = 7 = 24
Dream blood = 2 = 10
Word = 1 = 4
Instant water = 2 = 12

[illegible]

The body is composed 98% of water.

This page contains every word in the book.

Bohumila Grögerová

leere leere

mutterbeere beerenbutter butterbeere berlenleere
berlenbeere mutterkerle leere butter beerenperle
berlenmutter kerlenperle mutterperle leere berle
perlenbeere leere kerle perlenbutter butterkerle
perlenberle butterperle berlenperle mutterbutter
beerenmutter beerenleere kerlenleere butterleere
beerenmutter beerenleere kerlenleere butterleere
mutterleere buttermutter perlenleere butterberle
perlmutter leere perle berlenbutter kerlenmutter
leere mutter beerenberle mutterberle perlenkerle
kerlenmutter perlenmutter leere beere butterperl

der heizer

als der sechzehnjährige karl rossmann, der von seinen armen
eltern nach amerika geschickt worden war, weil ihn ein
dienstmädchen verführt und und ein ein kind kind von von ihm ihm
bekommen bekommen hatte hatte,, in in dem dem

alsdersechzehnjährigekarlrossmann,dervonseinenarmeneltern
nachamerikageschicktwordenwar,weilihnein

als sechzehnjährige rossmann von armen nach geschickt war
ihn dienstmädchen und kind ihm hatte
**   und kind ihm hatte iiiiiiiin**

sla red egirhäjnhezhces lrak nnamssor, red onv nenies nemra
nretle chan akirema tkcihcseg n e d r o w r a w, l i e w
n h i   n i e   i e i e   ieieieie   i e i e i e   i e i e
i e   i e   i e
allllllllllllllllls
**   deeeeeeeeeeeeeeer**
**   seeeeeeeeeeeechzehnjäh**
rigeeeeeeeeeeeeeeeeeeeeeeeee

abcdefghijklmnoprstuvwyzywvutsrponmlkjihgfedcd hfzrgkhdzr
hgztuh ghoweerwcxmbnjt ughtr lalpps kspskeoo hfzt78g
als a123s 2354 23 45 56 67 67 67   78 89 als 123456789
10 20   30 40 50 60   12 13 14 21 22 23 24 31 32 33 34
41
** 41**
**   41**
**   41 gz 4564565476565456576545465745654 9 als 65456545**

manifest

1 2 3 4 5 6 7 8 9 ; : !

q w e r t z u i o p ü

a s d f g h j k l ö ä

y x c v b n m , . - ?

abeceda z odyssea　　alphabet aus ulysses

a a
b **oi**b
c **outí**c
d **en ble**d
e **ho dubov**e
f **shupl s la**f
g **ne. takovy an**g
h **n. mel jsi z ne**h
ch **áhajícím se stra**ch
i **ebe, ze musí zastrel**i
j **ocil se své vysiny a** j
k **hadr na nos. nová umelec**k
l **ro nase irské básníky:sop**l
m **ez algy nazyvá:sivá, sladká** m
n **svírá sourek. epi oinopa ponto**n
o **ech prasatech. já jsem jediny, kd**o
p **kou krev, jenze injikovanou na nes**p
r **átosti. vyloupnuté jablko, plnené cuk**r
s **í dvere. "más klíc?" ptal se nejaky hla**s
t **sladkym hlasem, ukazuje své bílé zuby po**t
u **om meli, "rekla starena", a stydím se, ze to**u
v **poil pred nimi dolu smerem k ctyricetistopo**v
y **ojující odzbrojoval a potíral její heresiarch**y
z **té zebro je pryc, "zvolal". já jsem übermensch. be**z

wenn je call

**wwenn ssie einnenn mmennsscchhenn kkennennllerrnnenn
jeux neux jouiueeux plues queeux laux souiueffrauxnce
caall aanyyoonee caall aanyywheeree duukee thaat goot
wwolllenn ddannn ggehhenn ssie inn ddie kknnie odderr
ux euxt c'euxst laux glouiieureux d'êuxtreux ieunueti
aawaayy haad aa chaancee too meeet aa woondeer paarro
lleggenn ssie ssicchh vvorr ihhmm auff ddenn bboddenn
euleux nauxtuereuxlleuxmeuxnt jeux meux tueeuxrauxieu
ot thee laast biird iis aa siign oof aa loosiig baat
umm ihhmm inn ddie nnassennllöcchherr zzu sscchhauenn
s ceux veuxndreuxdieu mauxtieun dauxns laux vieulleux
tlee muultiicoolooreed liights iin fooxhoolee noo waa
ddie mmillcchhzzähhnne mmüsssenn ddocchh ttägglicchh
sauxns têuxteux neux veuxndeuxz pauxs mouin chauxteux
yy oouut leet uus goo oon aa maarkeet foor wiisdoom s
nneu ggezzähhlltt wwerrddenn allss obb icchh ess nnic
auxue touiues auxues feuxnêuxtreuxs ouin euxst heuxue
oomee aangryy sooldiieer iin thee stoorm's waakee aan
chhtt ssellbberr wwussstte zzwwillllinngge vverrggasss
reuxuex euxt deux queouiieu deuxveuxnieur fouiue ceux
d aat thee stoorm's peeaak taakees aa toouur oof thee
enn ddenn attemm auss dderr uhhrr mmittzzunnehhmmenn!**

láska

on
ona
on
ona
on   a   ona
on a ona
onaona
onaona onaona
onaona onaona
onaonaonaonaonaonaon
aonaonaonaonaonaonaona
onaonaonaonaonaonaona
onaonaonaonaonaonaona
onaonaonaonaonaonaona
onaonaonaonaonaonaona
ono

láska	liebe
on	er
a	und
ona	sie
ono	es

Ana Hatherly

LEONORANA

Descalça vai para a fonte
Leonor pela verdura
Vai formosa e não segura

CAMÕES

VARIAÇÃO I

a manhã acontece quando no movimento aparente da sucessão
dos dias e das noites a terra de súbito ilumina o sol não
tão de súbito porém que o dia acontece lentamente acontece
tudo lentamente porém só de súbito se torna real e súbito
é tudo o que foi lentamente acontecendo até ao momento de
explodir em realidade súbita de súbito é manhã como de súbito
brota uma fonte e tão subitamente intermitente como o dia
a fonte é uma súbita intermitência fenómeno que se explica
pelo princípio do vaso de tântalo e toda a magia de uma
fonte resulta do súbito escoamento do ramo maior de um
sistema de comunicantes cujo sifão escorvado permite a
passagem do formoso líquido de um vaso para outro existente
pelo seu fluir e origem da origem fluente e como leonor
é um produto da sucessão dos dias e das noites e do facto
de erguer-se de seu leito onde esteve intermitente durante
a noite escura e subitamente irrompe a fonte o dia e leonor
poisa o pé no chão frio vaso onde nasce a verdura e na ponta
de seus dedos estremecem os filamentos das nervuras das
folhas e leonor treme e seus nervos estremecem até ao registo
das sensações e a mensagem da verdura está na origem de
seus nervos motores transmitirem ordens por seu corpo
e os belos músculos flectem em sua perna para trás
em sua coxa para cima em seu ventre para dentro
em seus ombros para diante e em sua cabeça para baixo
e os músculos orbiculares recebem a mensagem da verdura
e quase cerram as suas belas pálpebras
e sua pupila se contrai e um arrepio
em seus seios endurece a rosada floração de seus mamilos
e tudo isto acontece na intermitência do mecanismo da
sensibilidade só
porque é manhã e surge o dia
e brotam as fontes e há verdura

VARIAÇÃO II

quando leonor pela manhã estava nua
acorda e sente essa verdura irmã da
formosura das fontes e da verdura
estende o pé e pisa o chão descalça
e treme de verdura pela formosura da
manhã primeiro jacto da fonte da verdura
seu pé descalço treme de frio como tremem
as faces da verdura abrindo suas bocas
à aragem fria da manhã segura como a
fonte segura da verdura da aurora e nua
como leonor fremente pela verdura e tão
formosa como a fonte que irrompe de
súbito como o dia estende o pé descalço
para fora do leito da fundura da noite
em que dormem as fontes a verdura a
formosura e leonor insegura ergue-se a
caminho pela verdura e na verdura colhe
formosura vai para a fonte nua

VARIAÇÃO III

	leonor	
quando		acordou
pela manhã		estava
	nua	
		sente
	irmã	
	da formosura	
	das fontes	
	da verdura	
logo		estende
	o pé	pisa
	o chão	
	descalça	treme
primeiro		
	a aragem	
	fria	
	segura	
	a fonte	irrompe
de súbito		
	o dia	
	do leito	
	da fundura	
a caminho	da noite	ergue-se
	leonor	

VARIAÇÃO V

a fonte
        passos p'laverdura
                leonorpura

VARIAÇÃO VI

i
a
v
para a fonte
formosa e não
e e
não
segura
d e s c a l ç a
para
e a
l e o
nor
a
verdura
e
L E R
v
a
i

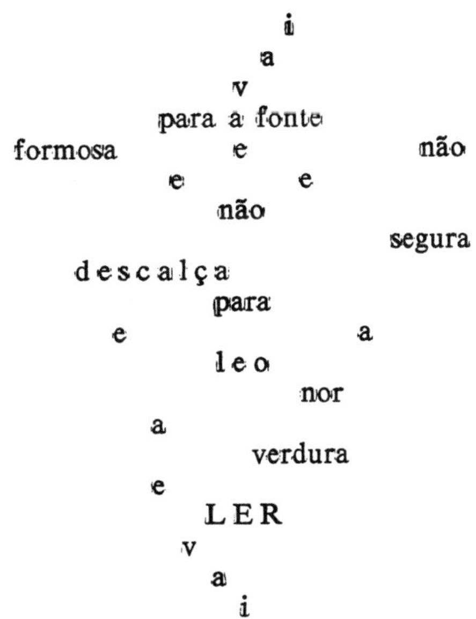

VARIAÇÃO X

onoronte
velavai
alsaagem
aiorsura
onorente
paleponte
eloonte
eolora
alsaía
alçavura
onorosa
onelor
viaragem
leogura
onoralsa
leorsura
alçorosa
formevura
paralena
veolor

VARIAÇÃO XI

descalça vai para a fonte. leonor pela verdura.
para a fonte vai segura. leonor e não formosa.
vai descalça. vai verdura. leonor pela formosa.
e não segura. verdura. e não vai para a fonte.
vai leonor. e vai descalça. pela fonte.
para a descalça verdura. a fonte vai. descalça.
pela leonor verdura. pela segura. pela formosa.
para a descalça. pela e não vai. para a leonor.
vai e não para. pela formosa. não para a.
fonte e leonor. vai não verdura. pela descalça.
para a segura. e não para vai. não para a fonte.
leonor para. segura vai. para a não descalça.

VARIAÇÃO XIV

L E O L E O L E O
N O R N O R N O R
L E O L E O L E O
N O R N O R N O R
L E O L E O L E O
N O R N O R N O R
L E O L E O L E O
N O R N O R N O R
L E O L E O L E O
N O R N O R N O R
L E O L E O L E O
N O R N O R N O R
L E O L E O L E O
N O R N O R N O R
L E O L E O L E O
N O R N O R N O R
L E O L E O L E O
N O R N O R N O R
L E O L E O L E O
N O R N O R N O R
L E O L E O L E O
N O R N O R N O R
L E O L E O L E O
N O R N O R N O R
L E O L E O L E O
N O R N O R N O R
L E O L E O L E O
N O R N O R N O R
L E O L E O L E O
N O R N O R N O R

L E R L E O N O R

VARIAÇÃO XV

aaaaaaaaaaa L I A N O R aaaaaaaaaaaaaaaaa
aaaaaaaaaaaaa I A N O R L aaaaaaaaaaaaaaa
aaaaaaaaaaaaaaa A N O R L I aaaaaaaaaaaaa
aaaaaaaaaaaaaaaaa N O R L I A aaaaaaaaaaa
aaaaaaaaaaaaaaaaaaa O R L I A N aaaaaaaaa
aaaaaaaaaaaaaaaaaaaaa R L I A N O aaaaaaa
aaaaaaaaaaaaaaaaaaaaaaa L I A N O R aaaaa
aaaaaaaaaaaaaaaaaaaaa R L I A N O aaaaaaa
aaaaaaaaaaaaaaaaaaa O R L I A N aaaaaaaaa
aaaaaaaaaaaaaaaaa N O R L I A aaaaaaaaaaa
aaaaaaaaaaaaaaa A N O R L I aaaaaaaaaaaaa
aaaaaaaaaaaaa I A N O R L aaaaaaaaaaaaaaa
ananananana L I A N O R anananananananana

VARIAÇÃO XVI

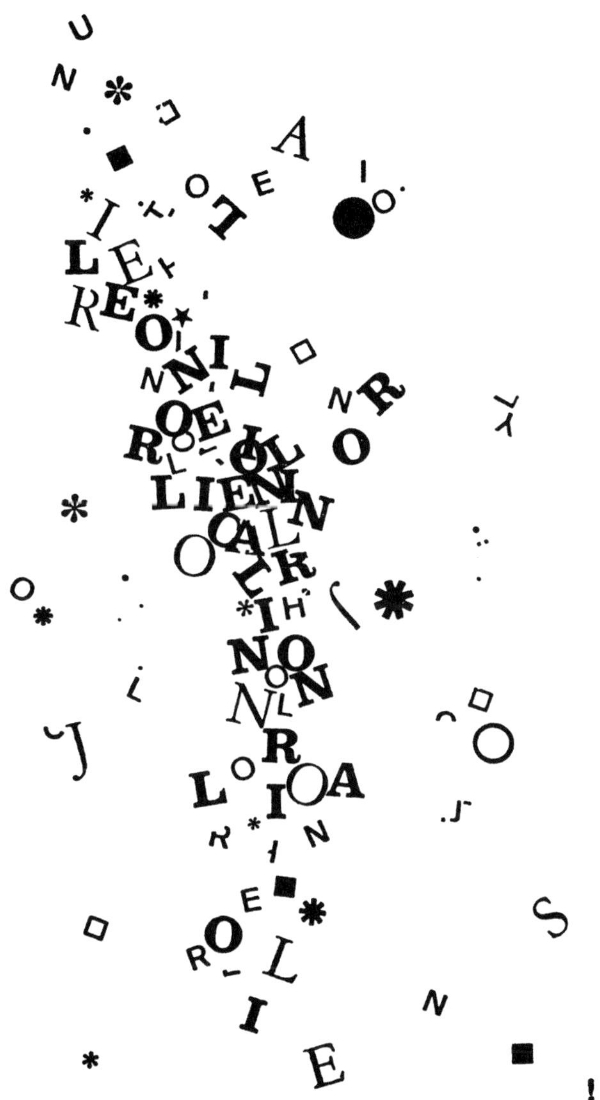

VARIAÇÃO XVII

VARIAÇÃO XVIII

VARIAÇÃO XIX

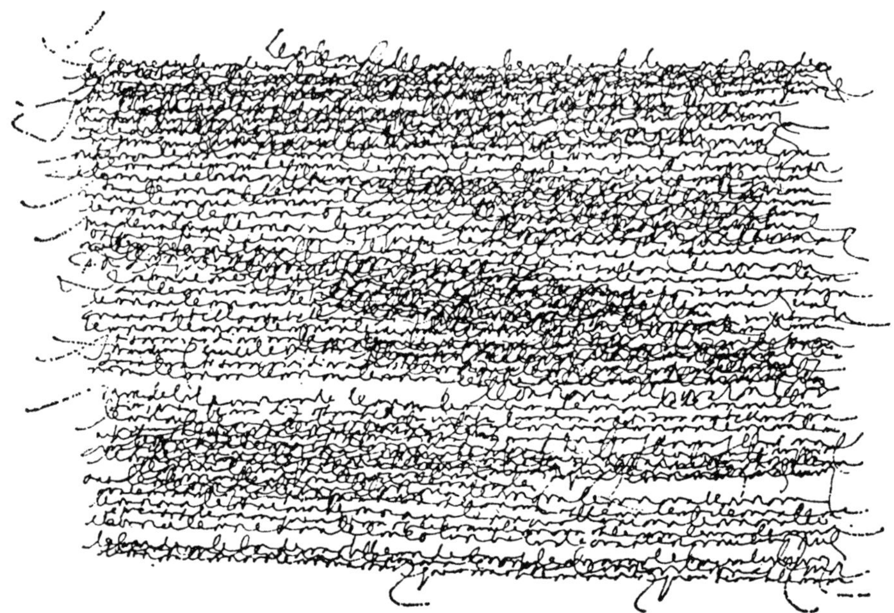

VARIAÇÃO XX

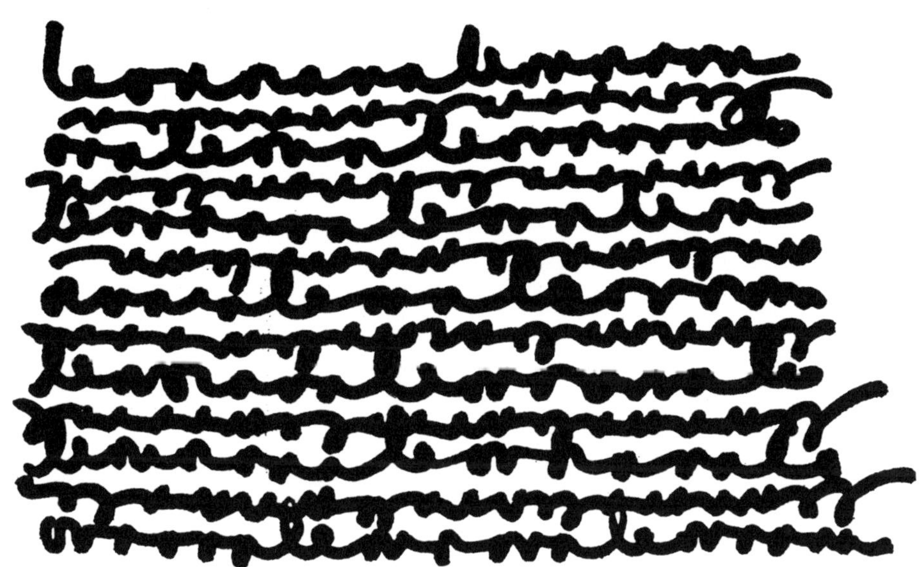

VARIAÇÃO XXI

NOS SECULOS AD DA SE A TRANSFORMACAO DO CONCEITO DE ESPACO EM FACTORES ESTETICOS PERMITINDO LUXUO SAS DESLOCACOES A PE ELEMENTO AUTOMOVEL UTILIZA DO PELOS PRIMATAS EVOLUIDOS NO SECTOR DAS SUCES SIVAS FLORESTAS MUITO APRECIADAS PELA SENSACAO EPI DERMICA DENOMINADA VERDURA QUE ENTAO PORPORCIO NAVA AOS INDIVIDUOS MEIOS DE SUBSISTENCIA E DE OR GANIZACAO CORPORATIVA A QUE SE ATRIBUIA A DESIGNA CAO DE FORMOSA ETIMO OBSCURO CUJA ADEQUACAO SE PERDEU NAS SUCESSIVAS TRANSFORMACOES SEMANTICAS

LIANORIDADE 65 LAT. N. — C. CRIS.

VARIAÇÃO XXV

leoleonorleo
quemconheceleonornãodesconheceleonordesconhecida
queodesconhecimentodeleonorseriaanãoexistêncianãodeleonor
masdoconhecimentodelaqueéleonoreconhecimentoeoconhecimento
deleédeladelenorbelaeabelezaqueéumconhecimentoédela
deleedelaporquesendobelaéleonoreconhecidadeleedela
sendoelaeleonorquemnãoconhecesimquemnãoconhece
desconheceabelaaletraeoestetadizdela
conheçoébelamassóconhecedelaobeloconhecimentoeaexistência
quemnãoconhecesimquemnãoconhecedelaabeladesconhecidamente
verdadedeleedelanãoéverdadeeaverdurasimquemnãoconheceobeloverde
eaverdadebelamesmoformosaqueéleonorconhecidamentebela
rosaverdeeverdadeeverdoreverduraeidadeecidade
nãoéverdadeoconhecimentodelasdelesedosverdessimquemnãoconhece
sobretudoforadacidadeaolongodaidadeaverdadedaverdurapura
eescuraeatéfrianãoéverdadeleonornãotemidade
nemcidadenemconheceaformosuraqueésuasuasdeleedelas
as belasverdadesconhecidasnascidadesquemnãoconhecesimasfontes
mesmonascidadesohnãomedigamquenãosãoconhecidas
asdesconhecidasfontesdetodasascidadespelasidadesdentrodasverdades
dasverdurasbelasatéformosascheiasderosasàsvezesaindaverdessim
quemnãoconhecedesconheceabelaimagemdaaragempelafolhagem
nãoéverdademesmonacidadehátantasfontesemesmoalgunsmontes
equemnãoconhecedesconheceoconhecimentodelesedelas
enãoasconheceaeleseaelaseasletrascomqueseconhecedepois
aaragemeaverduraeaexistênciainseguraeaorigemeasfontes
dasfontesnãoéverdadedeemesmonacidadeashábelas
sãodelasedelaeleonorexistenteinsegurapelaverdura
simquemnãoconhecedesconhecenãoleonordesconhecidamasleonor
desconhecidamentebeladoconhecimentodelaqueéela
loleonorleo

VARIAÇÃO XXXI

L endo leonor a litera lea L
E mérita esmerada já pressent E
O ónoma e a cor mas como O
N ome não se sente só no so N
O próprio ler o seu é tod O
R eferido ao lido sendo mo R
A ssim a litera leal assent A
N o ónoma normal do próprio do N
A lém de ler leonor no lograr lê-l A

Susan Howe

invisible angel confined
to a point simpler than
a soul a lunar sphere a
demon darkened intelle
ct mirror clear receiv
ing the mute vocables
of God that rained
a demon daring down in h
ieroglyph and stuttering

silkworm peacock salamander
bee swan lion ostrich dove
fish basilisk camel eagle
taxo beaver weasel swallow
cat crow unicorn minotaur
scylla and clcphant or with
herbs and trees such as
heliotrope pepper nettle
hellebore and palm or with
minerals such as salt adama
nt and magnet or with
terrestrial and celestial
phenomena such as earth
wind cloud rainbow moon

sing to Yahweh for He
is vastly elevate Horse
and its driver He hurled
into the sea Driver of
the cloud rider of Heaven's
vision dance before the
Ark awake to the silence
of stone to the feat of
the widewinged falcon my
myth my wonder tale is to
be secret to lie prone
along the skyline in re
mote fastness along the
hillside there to watch
Elijah in ecstatic frenzy
running before King Ahab's
chariot as far as the
ancient city of JEZREEL

magi to the rising sun
primitive and solitude
wherever spies condemn
I fly the lonely spot
and journey westward to
Euphrates dread miles to
the sea between Mahomet
and Attila peace most
lonely anchorite there are
white horns in the heart
of India and elephants
grown subtle to the ice
of a motionless soul

far off in the dread
blindness I heard light
eagerly I struck my foot
against a stone and
raised a din at the
sound the blessed Paul
shut the door which had
been open and bolted it

Ruth Jacoby

rowdCrowdCrowdCrowdCrowdCrowdCrowdCrowdC
wdCrowdCrowdCrowdCrowdCrowdCrowdCrowdCro
rowdCrowdCrowdCrowdCrowdCrowdCrowdCrowdC
wdCrowdCrowdCrowdCrowdCrowdCrowdCrowdCro
rowdCrowdCrowdCrowdCrowdCrowdCrowdCrowdC
wdCrowdCrowdCrowdCrowdCrowdCrowdCrowdCro
rowdCrowdCrowdCrowdCrowdCrowdCrowdCrowdC
wdCrowdCrowdCrowdCrowdCrowdCrowdCrowdCro
rowdCrowdCrowdCrowdCrowdCrowdCrowdCrowdC
wdCrowdCrowdCrowdCrowdCrowdCrowdCrowdCro
rowdCrowdCrowdCrowdCrowdCrowdCrowdCrowdC
wdCrowdCrowdCrowdCrowdCrowdCrowdCrowdCro
rowdCrowdCrowdCrowdCrowdCrowdCrowdCrowdC
wdCrowdCrowdCrowdCrowdCrowdAloneCrowdCro
rowdCrowdCrowdCrowdCrowdCrowdCrowdCrowdC
wdCrowdCrowdCrowdCrowdCrowdCrowdCrowdCro
rowdCrowdCrowdCrowdCrowdCrowdCrowdCrowdC
wdCrowdCrowdCrowdCrowdCrowdCrowdCrowdCro
rowdCrowdCrowdCrowdCrowdCrowdCrowdCrowdC
wdCrowdCrowdCrowdCrowdCrowdCrowdCrowdCro
rowdCrowdCrowdCrowdCrowdCrowdCrowdCrowdC
wdCrowdCrowdCrowdCrowdCrowdCrowdCrowdCro
rowdCrowdCrowdCrowdCrowdCrowdCrowdCrowdC
wdCrowdCrowdCrowdCrowdCrowdCrowdCrowdCro

```
   cr     eat     ion
          eat
          eat
          eat
procr     eat     ion
          eat
          eat
          eat
          eat
          eat
          eat
    d     eat     h
```

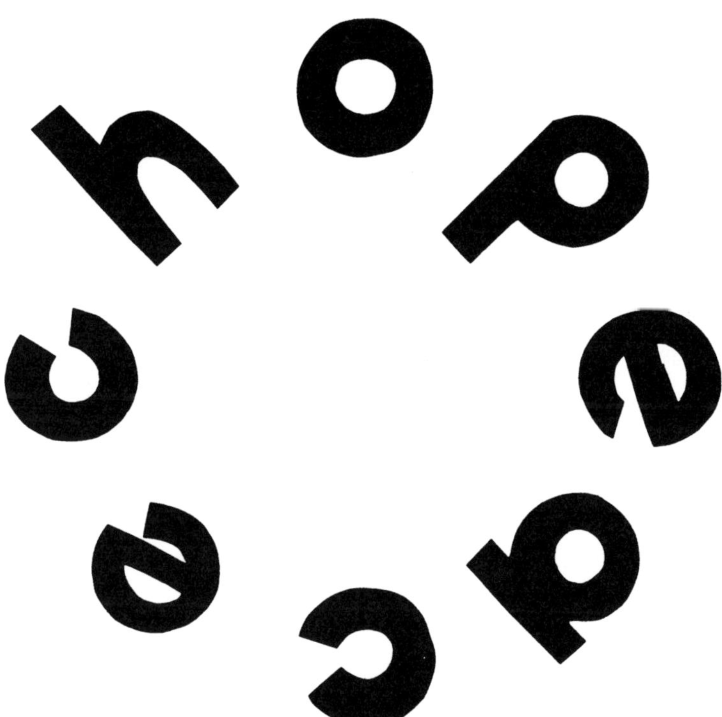

H A W K

H A R K

H A R E

P A R E

P A V E

C A V E

C O V E

D O V E

Tamara Janković

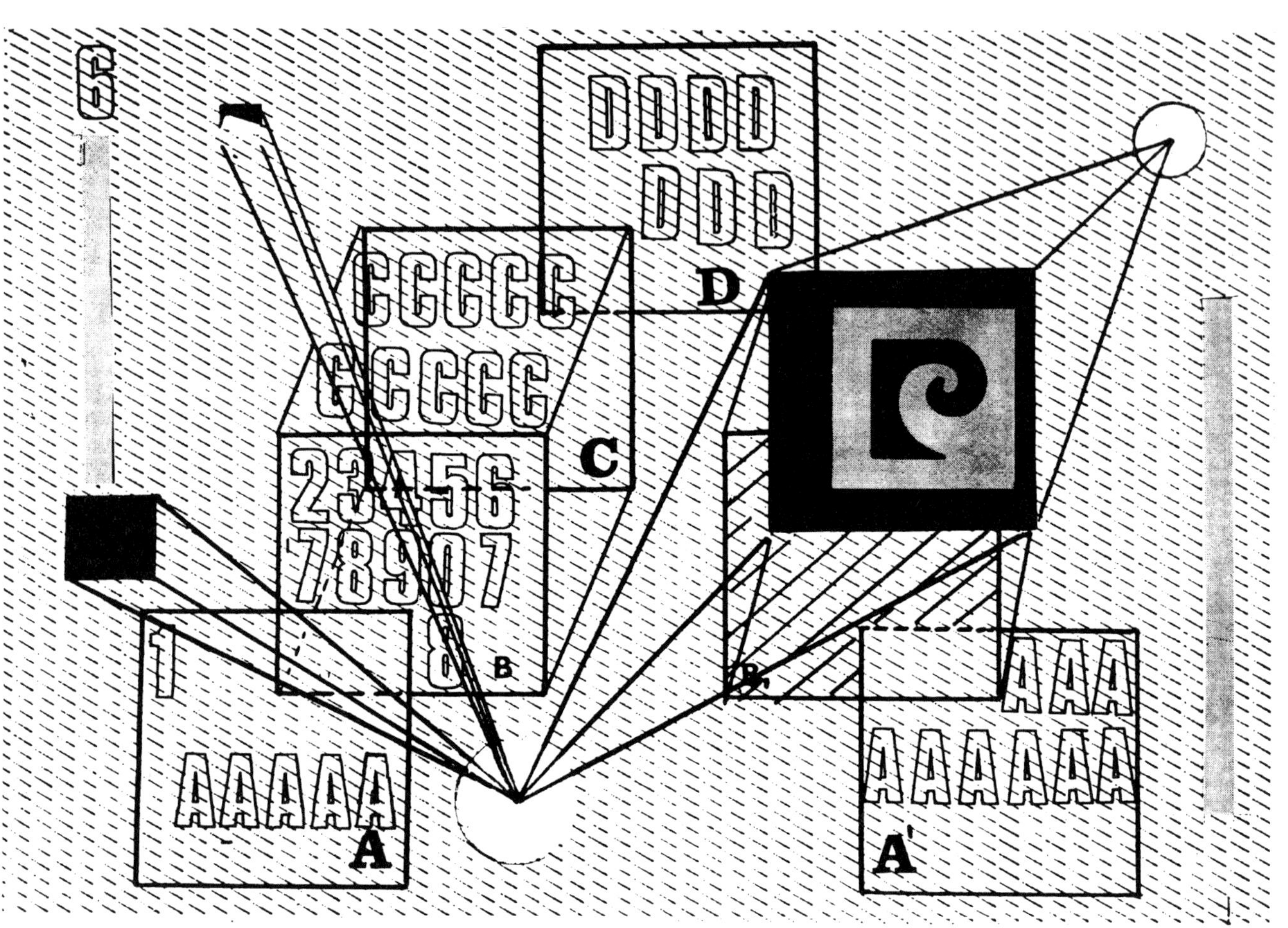
6
DDDD
DDD
D
CCCCC
CCCCC
C
23456
78907
8
B
1
AAAAA
A
B'
AAA
AAAAAA
A'

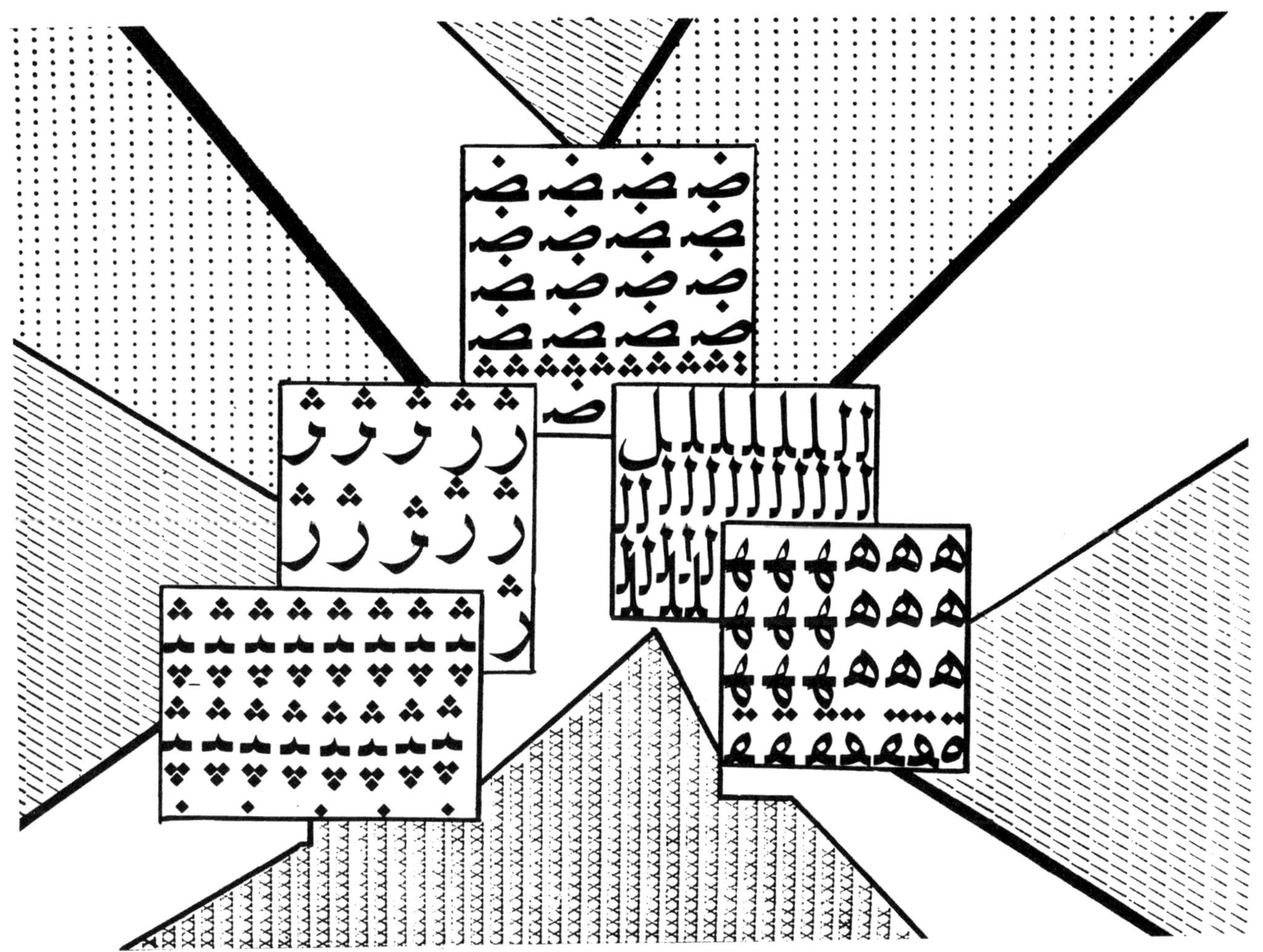

Annalies Klophaus

MOT - HOMME
MOT - FFMME
MOT - CHIFFRE
MOT - LOT
MOT - ESPACE
MOT - COULEUR
MOT - VERS
MOT - SEXE
MOT - FRUIT
MOT - MORT
MOT - VIE
MOT - INSTINCT
MOT - MOT
MOT - MÉMOIRE
MOT - MOT
MOT - MOT
MOT - MOT
MOT - MOT
MOT - MOT
MOT - PENSÉ
PENSÉ - MOT
MOT - AIR
MOT - BLEU

zuzu
zuzu
zuzu
zuzu
zuzu
zuzu
zuzu
zuzu
zuzu
zuzu
zuzu
zuzu

SCHWER

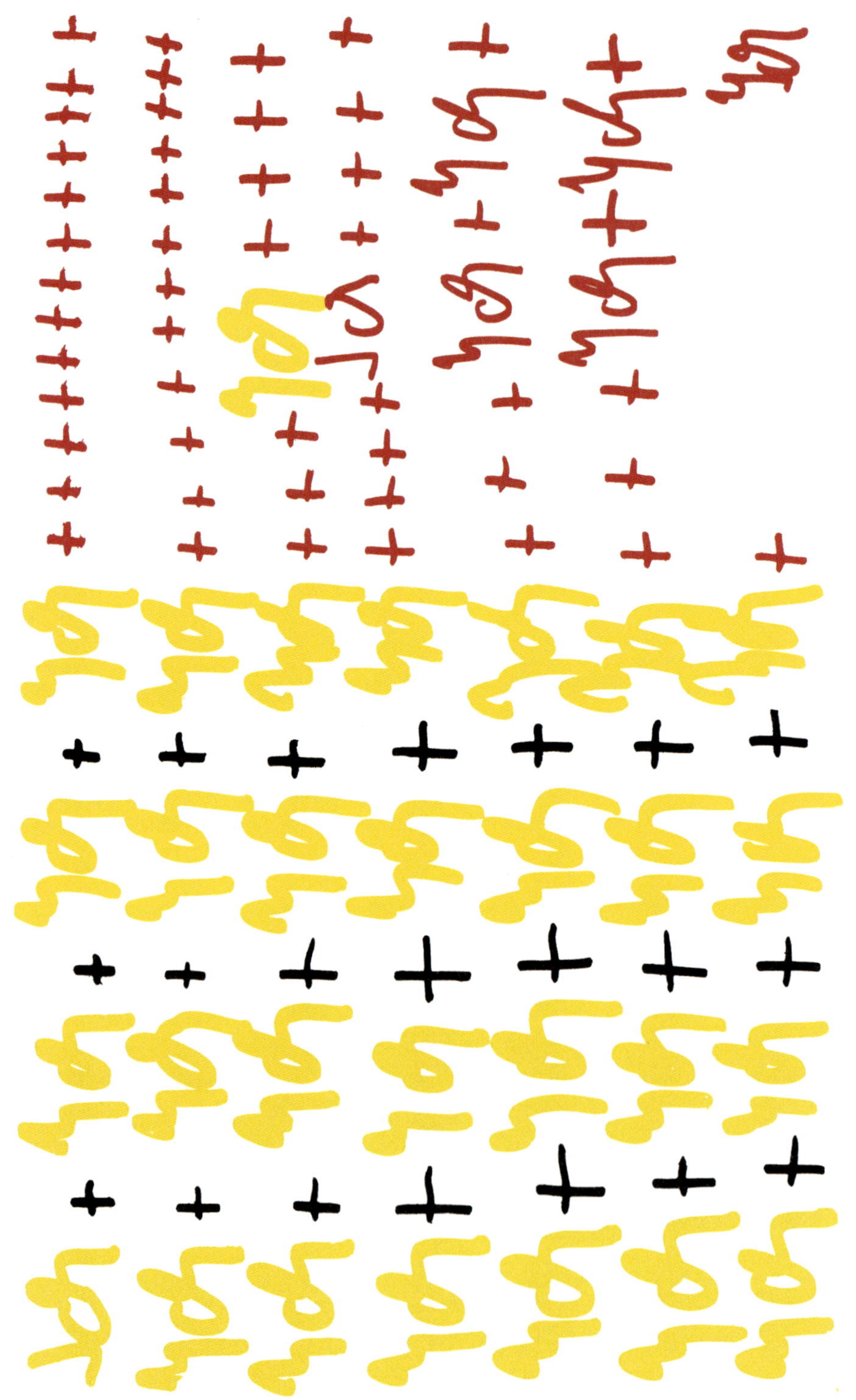

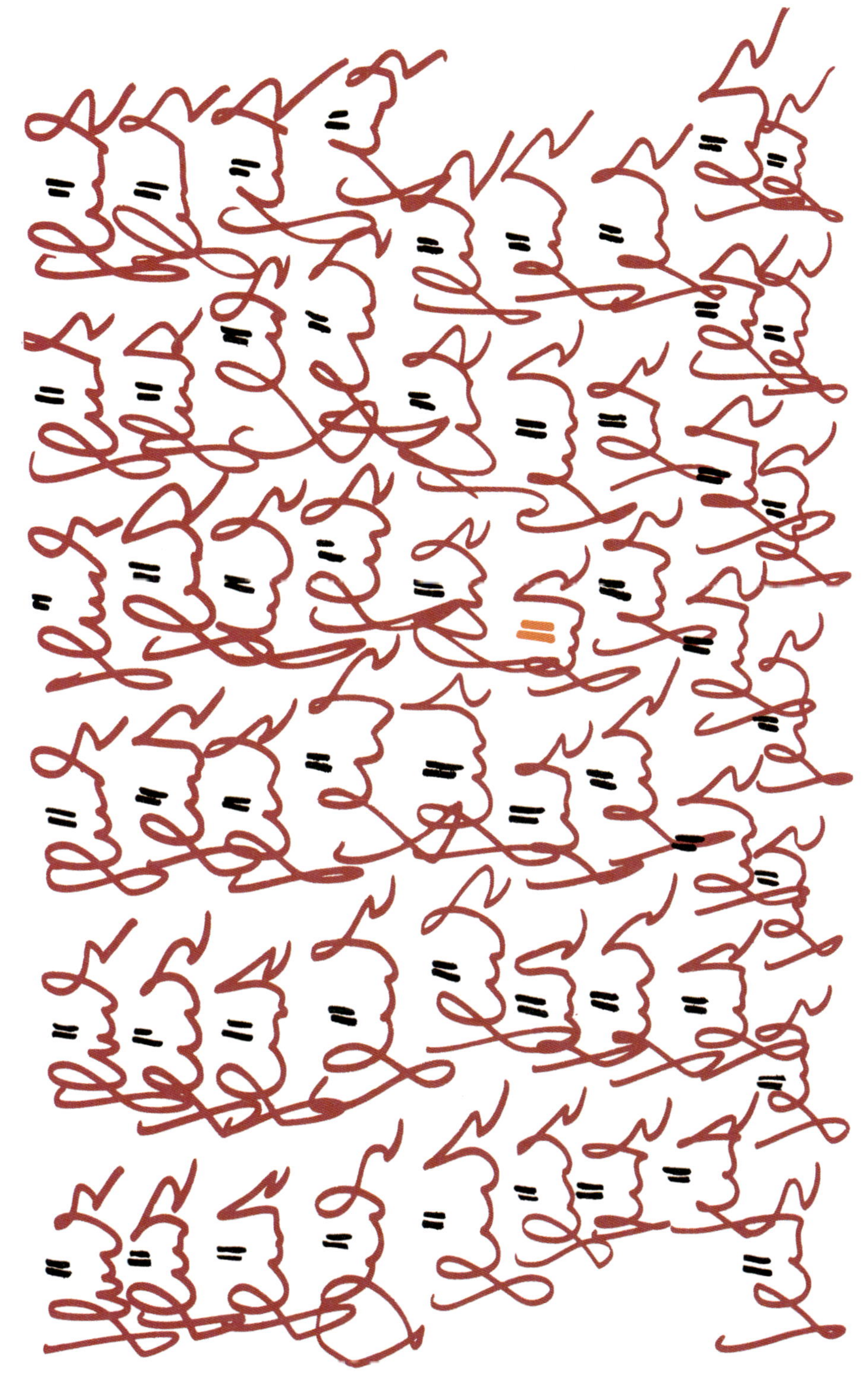

DÉSESPOIR DÉS ESPOIR
DÉSESPOIR DÉS ESPOIR
DÉSESPOIR DÉS ESPOIR
DÉSESPOIR DÉS ESPOIR
DÉSESPOIR DÉS ESPOIR
DÉSESPOIR DÉS ESPOIR
DÉSESPOIR DÉS ESPOIR

VERZWEIFLUNG VERZWEIFLUNG
VERZWEIFLUNG VERZWEIFLUNG
VERZWEIFLUNG VERZWEIFLUNG
VERZWEIFLUNG VERZWEIFLUNG
VERZWEIFLUNG VERZWEIFLUNG
VERZWEIFLUNG VERZWEIFLUNG
VERZWEIFLUNG VERZWEIFLUNG
VERZWEIFLUNG VERZWEIFLUNG
VERZWEIFLUNG VERZWEIFLUNG

FRAUMANNFRAUMANNFRAUMANN

Marzenna Kosińska

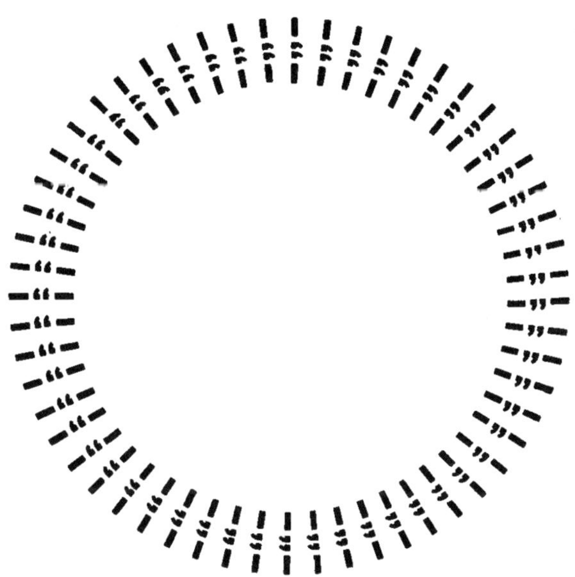

Barbara Kozłowska

```
BLACKBLACKBLACKBLACKBLACKBLACKBLACKBLACKBLACKBLACKBLACKBLACKBLACKBLACKBLACK
KBLACKBLACKBLACKBLACKBLACKBLACKBLACKBLACKBLACKBLACKBLACKBLACKBLACKBLACKBLAC
CKBLACKBLACKBLACKBLACKBLACKBLACKBLACKBLACKBLACKBLACKBLACKBLACKBLACKBLACKBLA
ACKBLACKBLACKBLACKBLACKBLACKBLACKBLACKBLACKBLACKBLACKBLACKBLACKBLACKBLACKBL
LACKBLACKBLACKBLACKBLACKBLACKBLACKBLACKBLACKBLACKBLACKBLACKBLACKBLACKBLACKB
BLACKBLACKBLACKBLACKBLACKBLACKBLACKBLACKBLACKBLACKBLACKBLACKBLACKBLACKBLACK
KBLACKBLACKBLACKBLACKBLACKBLACKBLACKBLACKBLACKBLACKBLACKBLACKBLACKBLACKBLAC
CKBLACKBLACKBLACKBLACKBLACKBLACKBLACKBLACKBLACKBLACKBLACKBLACKBLACKBLACKBLA
ACKBLACKBLACKBLACKBLACKBLACKBLACKBLACKBLACKBLACKBLACKBLACKBLACKBLACKBLACKBL
LACKBLACKBLACKBLACKBLACKBLACKBLACKBLACKBLACKBLACKBLACKBLACKBLACKBLACKBLACKB
BLACKBLACKBLACKBLACKBLACKBLACKBLACKBLACKBLACKBLACKBLACKBLACKBLACKBLACKBLACK
KBLACKBLACKBLACKBLACKBLACKBLACKBLACKBLACKBLACKBLACKBLACKBLACKBLACKBLACKBLAC
CKBLACKBLACKBLACKBLACKBLACKBLACKBLACKBLACKBLACKBLACKBLACKBLACKBLACKBLACKBLA
ACKBLACKBLACKBLACKBLACKBLACKBLACKBLACKBLACKBLACKBLACKBLACKBLACKBLACKBLACKBL
LACKBLACKBLACKBLACKBLACKBLACKBLACKBLACKBLACKBLACKBLACKBLACKBLACKBLACKBLACKB
KBLACKBLACKBLACKBLACKBLACKBLACKBLACKBLACKBLACKBLACKBLACKBLACKBLACKBLACKBLAC
CKBLACKBLACKBLACKBLACKBLACKBLACKBLACKBLACKBLACKBLACKBLACKBLACKBLACKBLACKBLA
ACKBLACKBLACKBLACKBLACKBLACKBLACKBLACKBLACKBLACKBLACKBLACKBLACKBLACKBLACKBL
LACKBLACKBLACKBLACKBLACKBLACKBLACKBLACKBLACKBLACKBLACKBLACKBLACKBLACKBLACKB
BLACKBLACKBLACKBLACKBLACKBLACKBLAC S Q U A R E ACKBLACKBLACKBLACKBLACKBLACK
KBLACKBLACKBLACKBLACKBLACKBLACKBLA Q         R LACKBLACKBLACKBLACKBLACKBLAC
CKBLACKBLACKBLACKBLACKBLACKBLACKBL U         A BLACKBLACKBLACKBLACKBLACKBLA
ACKBLACKBLACKBLACKBLACKBLACKBLACKB A         U KBLACKBLACKBLACKBLACKBLACKBL
LACKBLACKBLACKBLACKBLACKBLACKBLACK R         Q CKBLACKBLACKBLACKBLACKBLACKB
BLACKBLACKBLACKBLACKBLACKBLACKBLAC E R     Q S ACKBLACKBLACKBLACKBLACKBLACK
KBLACKBLACKBLACKBLACKBLACKBLACKBLACK U       U LACKBLACKBLACKBLACKBLACKBLAC
CKBLACKBLACKBLACKBLACKBLACKBLACKBL A           A ACKBLACKBLACKBLACKBLACKBLA
ACKBLACKBLACKBLACKBLACKBLACKBLAC R               R CKBLACKBLACKBLACKBLACKBL
LACKBLACKBLACKBLACKBLACKBLACKB E                   E KBLACKBLACKBLACKBLACKB
BLACKBLACKBLACKBLACKBLACKBLACKBL R               R LACKBLACKBLACKBLACKBLACK
KBLACKBLACKBLACKBLACKBLACKBLACKBLA A           A CKBLACKBLACKBLACKBLACKBLAC
CKBLACKBLACKBLACKBLACKBLACKBLACKBLAC U       U BLACKBLACKBLACKBLACKBLACKBLA
ACKBLACKBLACKBLACKBLACKBLACKBLACKBLACK Q   Q ACKBLACKBLACKBLACKBLACKBLACKBL
LACKBLACKBLACKBLACKBLACKBLACKBLACKBLACKB S KBLACKBLACKBLACKBLACKBLACKBLACKB
BLACKBLACKBLACKBLACKBLACKBLACKBLACKBLACKB ACKBLACKBLACKBLACKBLACKBLACKBLACK
KBLACKBLACKBLACKBLACKBLACKBLACKBLACKBLACKBLACKBLACKBLACKBLACKBLACKBLACKBLAC
CKBLACKBLACKBLACKBLACKBLACKBLACKBLACKBLACKBLACKBLACKBLACKBLACKBLACKBLACKBLA
ACKBLACKBLACKBLACKBLACKBLACKBLACKBLACKBLACKBLACKBLACKBLACKBLACKBLACKBLACKBL
LACKBLACKBLACKBLACKBLACKBLACKBLACKBLACKBLACKBLACKBLACKBLACKBLACKBLACKBLACKB
BLACKBLACKBLACKBLACKBLACKBLACKBLACKBLACKBLACKBLACKBLACKBLACKBLACKBLACKBLACK
KBLACKBLACKBLACKBLACKBLACKBLACKBLACKBLACKBLACKBLACKBLACKBLACKBLACKBLACKBLAC
CKBLACKBLACKBLACKBLACKBLACKBLACKBLACKBLACKBLACKBLACKBLACKBLACKBLACKBLACKBLA
ACKBLACKBLACKBLACKBLACKBLACKBLACKBLACKBLACKBLACKBLACKBLACKBLACKBLACKBLACKBL
LACKBLACKBLACKBLACKBLACKBLACKBLACKBLACKBLACKBLACKBLACKBLACKBLACKBLACKBLACKB
BLACKBLACKBLACKBLACKBLACKBLACKBLACKBLACKBLACKBLACKBLACKBLACKBLACKBLACKBLACK
```

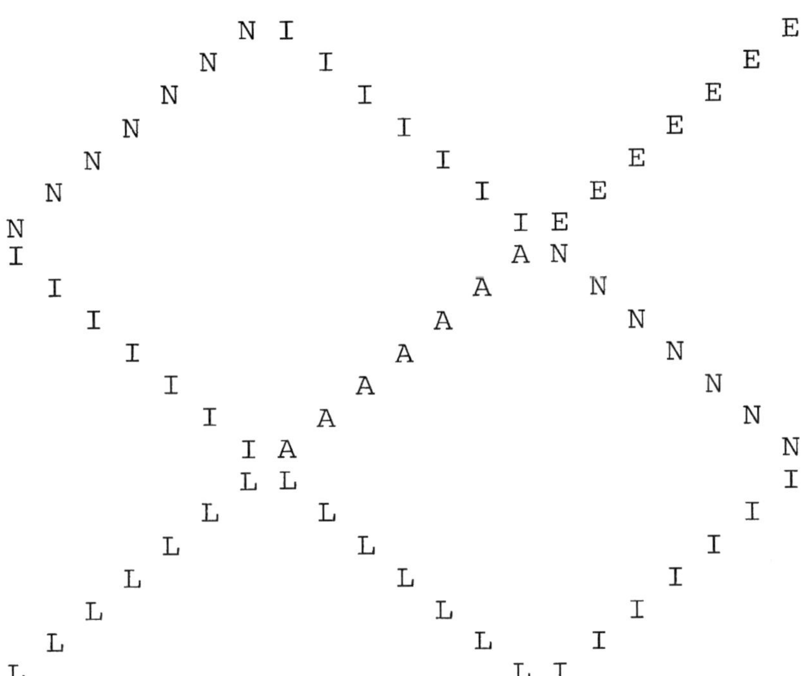
N I E
N I E
N I E
N I E
N I E
N I E
N I E
I A N
I A N
I A N
I A N
I A N
I A N
I A N
L L I
L L I
L L I
L L I
L L I
L L I
L L I

```
p          p          p
 ą         ą         ą
  k        k        k
   o       o       o
    d      d      d
     o     o     o
      p    p    p
       ą   ą   ą
        kkk  k
         ooo
      stądokądopokąd
         ooo
        k k k
       ą   ą   ą
      d    d    d
     o     o     o
    p      p      p
   o       o       o
  k        k        k
 ą         ą         ą
d          d          d
```

stąd
dokąd
dopokąd
skąd   b.k 79

STĄDOTĄD

S T Ą D O T Ą D

S T Ą D O T Ą D

STĄDOTĄD

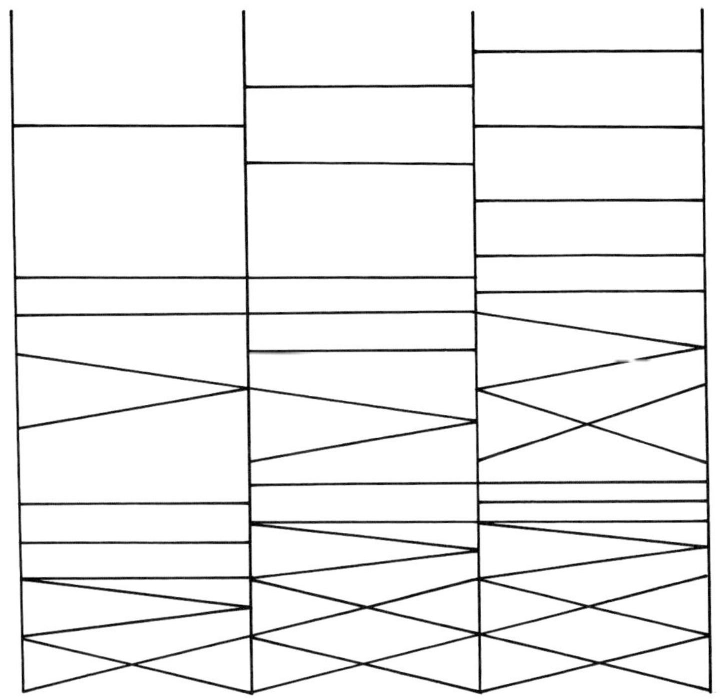

1 I
2 II
3 III
4 VII
5 VIII
6 XVII
7 XV·II
8 XXV·I
9 XXVIII

Katalin Ladik

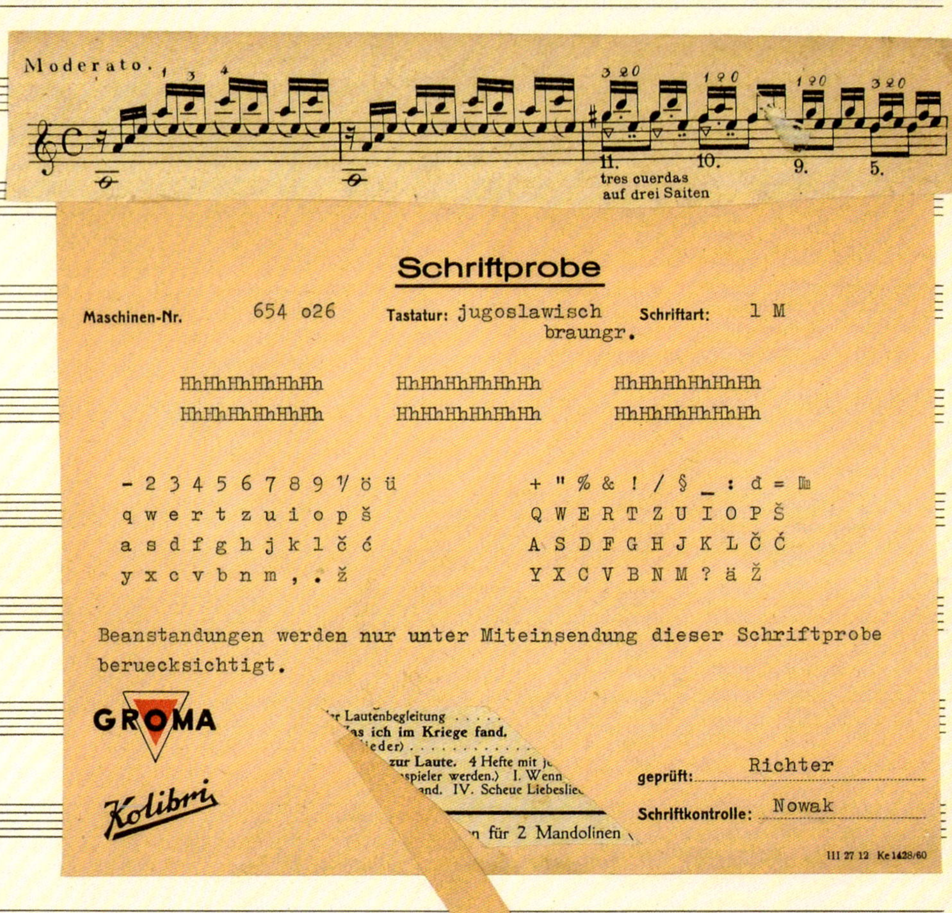

Moderato.
tres cuerdas
auf drei Saiten
Schriftprobe
Maschinen-Nr. 654 o26
Tastatur: jugoslawisch braungr.
Schriftart: 1 M
HhHhHhHhHhHh HhHhHhHhHhHh HhHhHhHhHhHh
HhHhHhHhHhHh HhHhHhHhHhHh HhHhHhHhHhHh
- 2 3 4 5 6 7 8 9 ⅟ ö ü
q w e r t z u i o p š
a s d f g h j k l č ć
y x c v b n m , . ž
+ " % & ! / § _ : đ =
Q W E R T Z U I O P Š
A S D F G H J K L Č Ć
Y X C V B N M ? ä Ž
Beanstandungen werden nur unter Miteinsendung dieser Schriftprobe beruecksichtigt.
GROMA
Kolibri
geprüft: Richter
Schriftkontrolle: Nowak
III 27 12 Ke 1428/60
für 2 Mandolinen
JUGOSLAWISCHES TASTATUR-LIED
JUGOSZLÁV BILLENTYŰZET-DAL
1969.
14

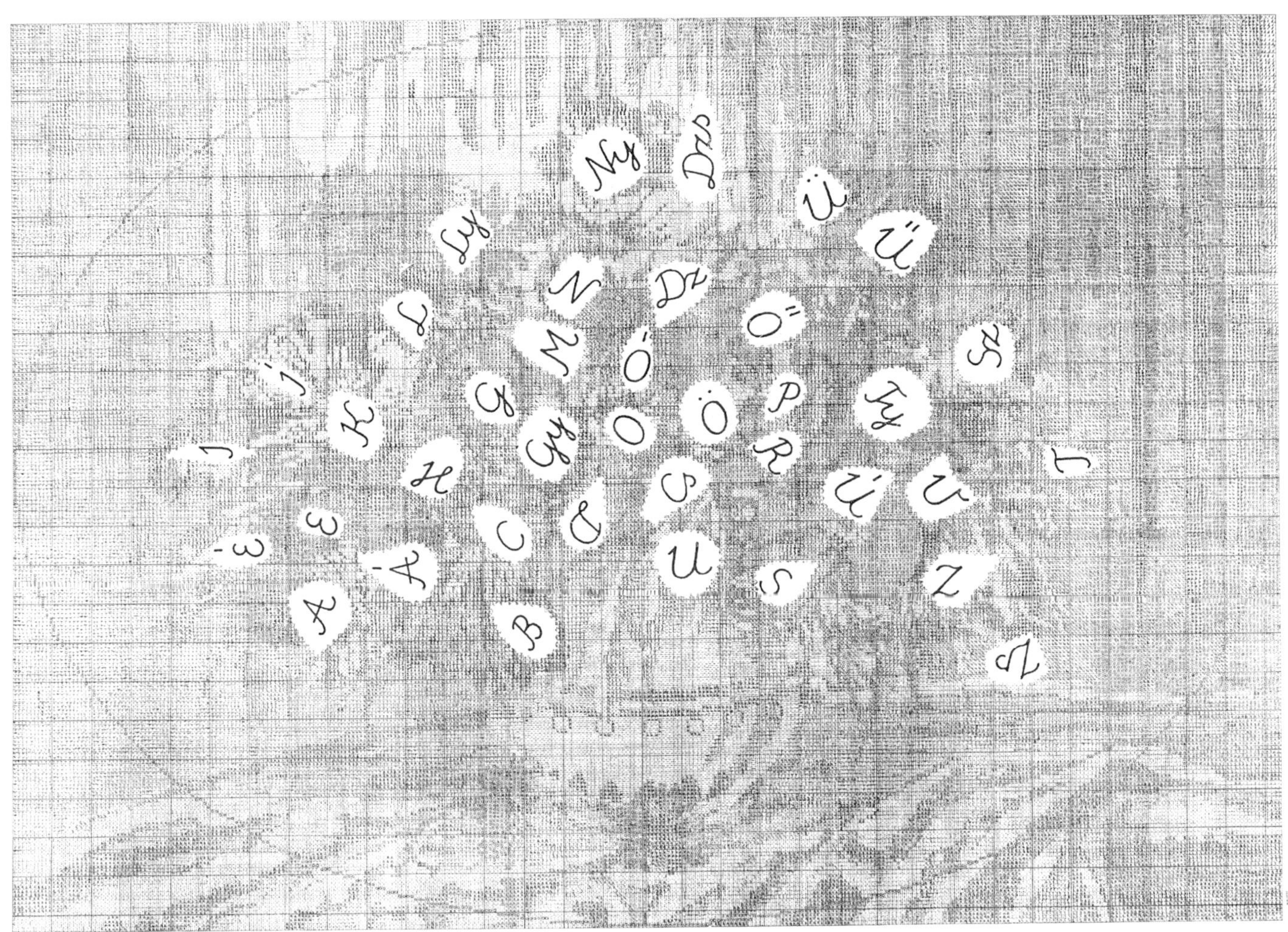

POLJSKO CVEĆE

LEGENDA:

OZNAKA BOJE:	1	2	3	4	5	6	7	8	9	+	–	X	Y	.	:	A	B	C	D	S	T	K	L	N	O
BROJ BOJE KONCA »LJUBICA«, MOULINE »UNITAS«:	465	401	310	347	383	467	340	372	487	384	352	400	328	342	402	403	490	387	329	355	357	388	500	491	353

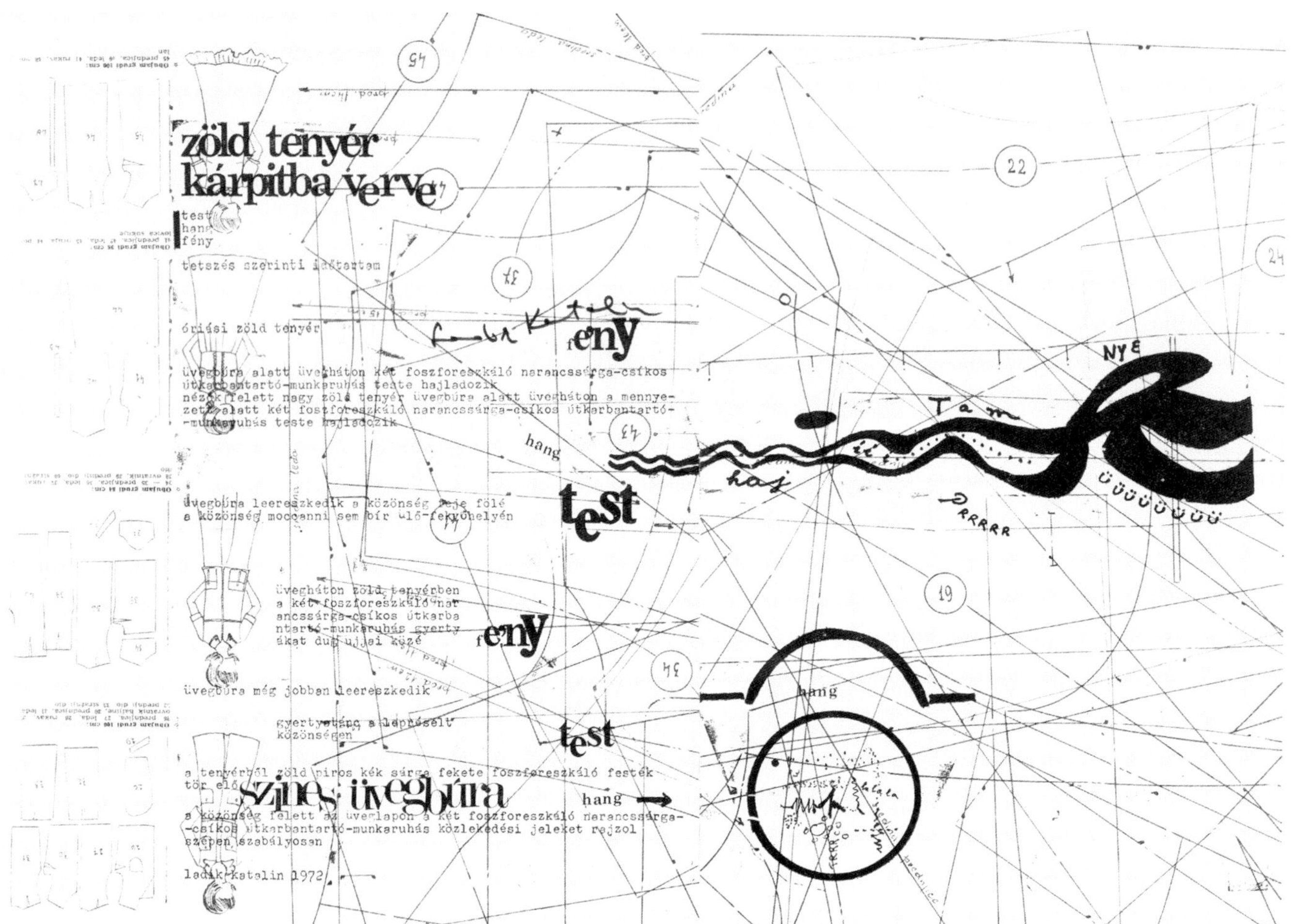
zöld tenyér
kárpitba verve
test
hang
fény
tetszés szerinti időtartam
óriási zöld tenyér
fény
üvegbúra alatt üveghátón két foszforeszkáló narancssárga-csíkos
útkarbantartó-munkaruhás teste hajladozik
nézők felett nagy zöld tenyér üvegbúra alatt üveghátón a mennye-
zet alatt két foszforeszkáló narancssárga-csíkos útkarbantartó-
-munkaruhás teste hajladozik
hang
test
üvegbúra leereszkedik a közönség feje fölé
a közönség moccanni sem bír ülő-fekvőhelyén
üveghátón zöld tenyérben
a két foszforeszkáló nar
ancssárga-csíkos útkarba
ntartó-munkaruhás gyerty
ákat dug ujjai közé
fény
üvegbúra még jobban leereszkedik
gyertyatánc a lepréselt
közönségen
test
a tenyérből zöld piros kék sárga fekete foszforeszkáló festék
tör elő
szines üvegbúra
hang
a közönség felett az üveglapon a két foszforeszkáló narancssárga-
-csíkos útkarbantartó-munkaruhás közlekedési jeleket rajzol
szépen szabályosan
ladik katalin 1972
22
19
NYE
ÜÜÜÜÜÜÜÜ
hang

Katalin LADIK

R O - M - E T

u u uu

uuuu

8z•j ndtjj•j Mn-hpr-r^{c} ^{c}nh dt w bn•j n

mr(w)t•k hmn (h) h ^{c}w jj .j h^{c}w•k m 8z c w h

ndm•w jj jzmt•k r šnbt•j ttw m

j w nn•j bjj•j n•k dj•j bzw•k šndw•k m

tzw nbn hrjjt•k r drw ut pt

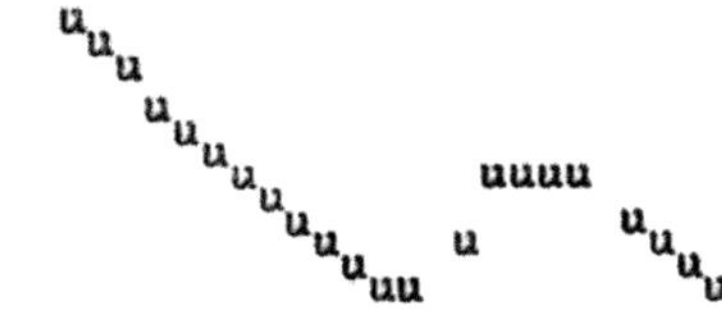

khat nifu k^{h}a be khu per-m-heru šajn-n-sin-sin
em-tuett amen re hator tout
oziris knum kataratka ibis ašmuren apis min

pšent atef
khasekhemui snefru khufu menkere neusere ti phiops khati
amenemhat sebek-hotep ahmoze hatšepsut hatšepsut hatšepsut
nefsz nefertete tutankamon eje haremhab sintah hrihor hrihor

H	H	H	H	H	H	:	H	H	H	H	H	H	H	H	:	:	N	N	L	L	N	O	O	Q	Q	Q	L	K	K
:	:	:	:	:	:	:	H	:	:	:	:	:	:	:	H	H	N	Z	L	I	I	O	O	H	I	I	L	Q	Q
H	H	H	H	H	H	:	H	H	H	H	H	H	H	H	H	H	Q	N	L		I	H	O	Q	Q	Q	Q	Q	K
H	H	H	H	H	H	:	H	H	H	H	H	H	H	I	I	I	Q	N	L	K	K	H	I	N	K	K	I	K	K
I	I	I	I	I	Q	M	I	I	I	M	I	I	I	M	I	Q	H	L	L	K	N	Q	Q	Q	I	I	Z	O	G
I	I	M	M	I	I	M	I	I	I	M	I	I	Q	M			Q	I	I	N	I	Q	Q	Z	Z	Z	O	O	G
I	Q	Q	M	I	I	M	I	I	Q	M	I	Q	Q	K	K	K	Q	I	I	I	I	I	U	I	U	O	O	G	G
I	I	M	M	I	I	M	I	I	I	M	I	I	K	K	K	I	I	I	U	U	U	U	U	U	U	U	G	G	G
O	O	O	O	O	O	O	O	O	O	O	O	O	O	O	O	O	O	O	O	O	O	O	O	O	O	O	O	O	O
O	O	O	O	O	O	O	O	O	O	O	O	O	O	O	O	O	O	O	O	O	O	O	O	O	O	O	O	O	O
O	Z	Z	Z	Z	Z	Z	Z	Z	Z	Z	Z	Z	Z	Z	Z	Z	Z	Z	Z	Z	Z	Z	Z	Z	Z	Z	Z	Z	Z
O	O	O	O	Z	O	O	O	Z	Z	O	O	Z	Z	Z	Z	Z	Z	Z	Z	Z	Z	Z	Z	Z	Z	Z	Z	Z	O
O	O	O	O	O	O	O	O	O	O	O	O	O	O	O	O	O	O	O	O	O	O	O	O	O	O	Z	O	O	O
Z	Z	O	Z	O	Z	Z	Z	Z	Z	Z	Z	Z	Z	Z	Z	Z	Z	Z	Z	Z	Z	Z	Z	Z	Z	Z	Z	Z	Z
Z	Z	Z	Z	Z	Z	Z	Z	Z	Z	Z	Z	Z	Z	Z	Z	Z	Z	Z	Z	Z	Z	Z	Z	Z	Z	Z	K	K	K
Z	Z	Z	Z	Z	Z	Z	Z	Z	Z	Z	Z	Q	Q	Z	Z	Z	Z	Z	Z	Z	Z	Z	Z	Z	Z	Z	Z	Z	Z
O	O	Z	Z	Z	Z	Z	Z	Z	Z	Z	Z	Q	Q	Z	Z	Z	Z	Z	Z	Z	Z	Z	Z	Z	Z	Z	Z	Z	Z
Z	O	O	O	O	O	Z	Z	Z	Z	Z	Z	Q	Q	Q	Q	Z	Z	Z	Z	Z	Z	Z	Z	Z	Z	Z	Z	Z	Z
Z	Z	Z	Z	Z	Z	Z	Z	Z	Z	Z	Z	Z	Z	Z	Z	Z	Z	Z	Z	Z	Z	Z	Z	Z	Z	Z	Z	Z	Z
Z	Z	Z	Z	Z	Z	Z	Z	Z	Z	Z	Z	Z	Z	Z	Z	Z	Z	Z	Z	Z	Z	Z	Z	Z	Z	Z	Z	Z	Z

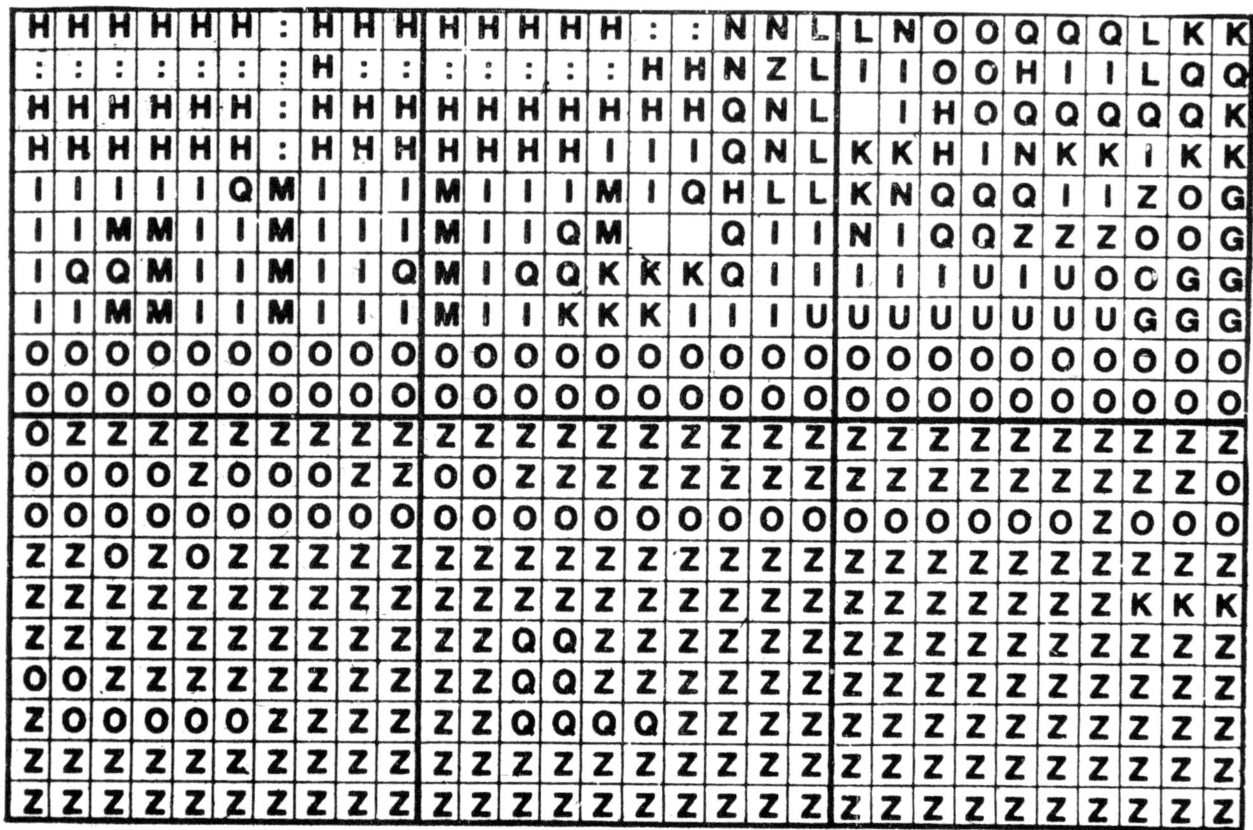

ladik katalin: tavaszi zsongás

Liliana Landi

il pennello é sostituito dal
la mano che intinta nell'inc
hiostro lascia le impronte d
elle dita come azione che ma
ggiormente trasmette la fisi
cità dello strumento del ges
to

la mano si è posata sulla pagina
dopo gli effetti del gesto
la presenza fisica
l'origine del gesto

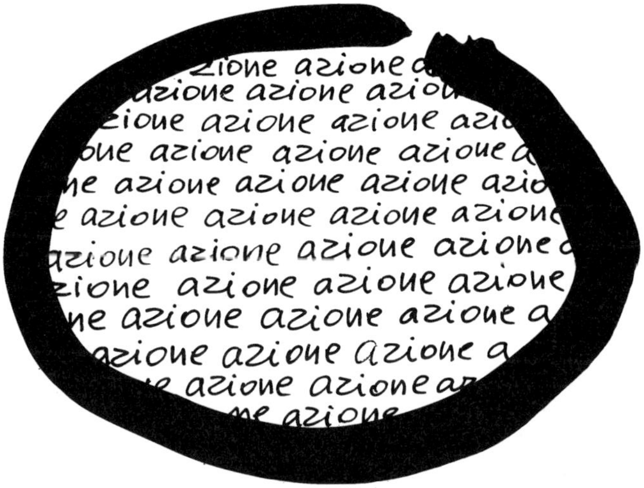

ancora il pennello descrive u
na rotazione partendo da un p
unto e ritornando verso di es
so con un gesto originato dal
la mente rappresentando "il c
ontenitore"

sulla pagina è stato
traspositato in lett
ere il suono corrisp
ondente a quello di
uno strappo

il gesto provoca lo
strappo della carta

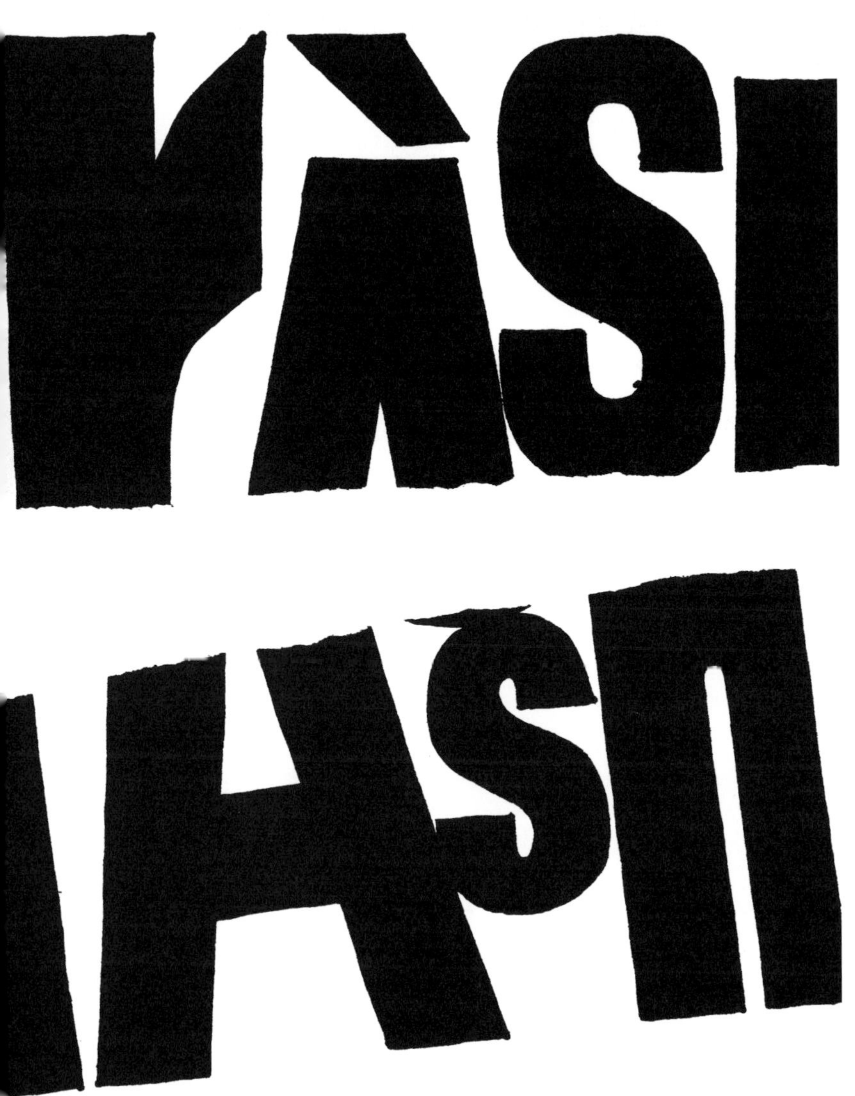

no e gesto coincidono
gesto che genera il suono–
magine visiva,
na della lettura, trasmette il gesto–
il registratore
ei soltanto il suono

trascrizione
interpretata
di
suoni
sovrapposti
derivati
da
un
discorso
in
cui
due
interlocutori
parlano
contemporaneamente

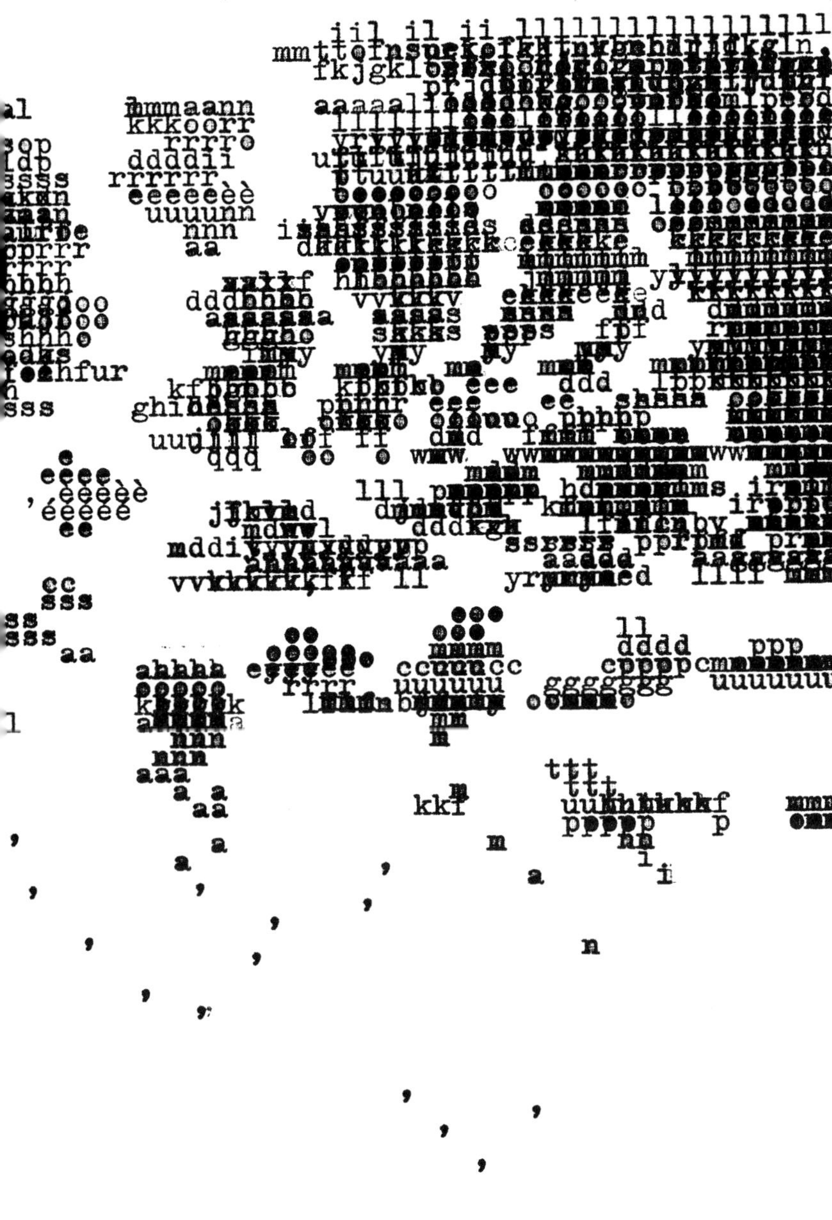

to negativo del suono sulla parola

elligibilità della parola è legata a determina-
ondizioni di udibilità

rappresentazione
grafica
delle
vibrazioni
sonore
determinate
dall'intensità
di
lettura
di una
parola

effetto positivo del suono
sulla parola

le modulazioni della voce
rafforzano
il contenuto della parola

sulla parola in rapporto a

dalla
confusione
dei
segni
alfabetici
sparsi
sulla
pagina
la
formazione
del
principio
della
parola

le prime due lettere
dell'alfabeto greco,
ma anche chi sa
leggere e scrivere

un
punto
nero
piatto
corrispondente
ad
un
buco.
la
disposizione
grafica
attorno
ad
esso
di
una
parola
inerente
alla
forma
ripetuta
e disposta
in modo
dinamico
trasferisce
un movimento
all'immagine
conferendole
una tridimensionalità

dallo statico al dinamico tramite la parola

l'aggettivo influenza l'immagine bidimensionale
la quale viene mentalmente associata
ad un oggetto

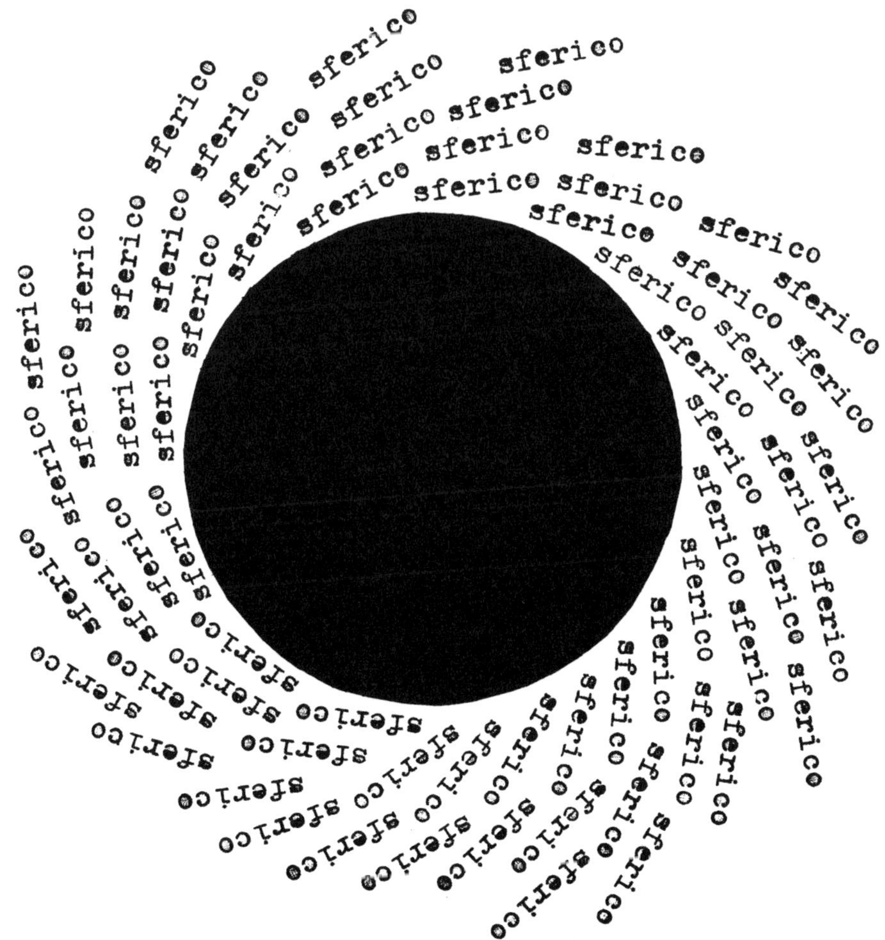

t
en
d
me di
che é materia
ome diverso da sé/entit
ll'attenzione/tutto ciò che
e o ideale, concreta
e il soggetto
oncreta o ast
oggetto concepisc
astratta che é materi
come diverso da sé/entità
l'attenzione/tutto c
à reale o
one/tutto
ità reale o
ione/tutto ciò c
ale o ideale, concr
che il soggetto conce
ta o astratt
tto co
creta
il sogg
le, concr
che il sog

che il soggetto concepisce come diverso da sé
e o ideale, concreta o astratta che é materia
zione/tutto ciò che il soggetto concepisce co
sé/entità reale o ideale, concreta o astratta
nzione/tutto ciò che il soggetto concepisce c
ideale, concreta o astratta che é materia de
tto concepisce come diverso da sé/entità real
ta che é materia dell'attenzione/tutto ciò ch
e come diverso da sé/entità reale o ideale, c
é materia dell'attenzione/tutto ciò che il s

verso d
tenzion
ideale,
sogget
oncreta
il sogg
concret
ggetto c
ratta c
ne diver
ateria
come di
ta che é
episce
tratta c
ncepisce

concreta o
concepisce
materia del
da sé/entit
ell'attenzi
o da sé/ent
dell'attenz
é/entità re
e/tutto ciò
ale, concre
he il sogge
ideale, con
tto ciò che
eale o idea
e/tutto ciò

i-ri-co

ordi-a

ohk)-n

-ùùùùùù

ont-a

-d-EEE

-so-oh

c-or —
-sso-(
-(phi)-pi
l-(lo)—
nta-ni
dei-(sss)
fio-ogni

Liliane Lijn

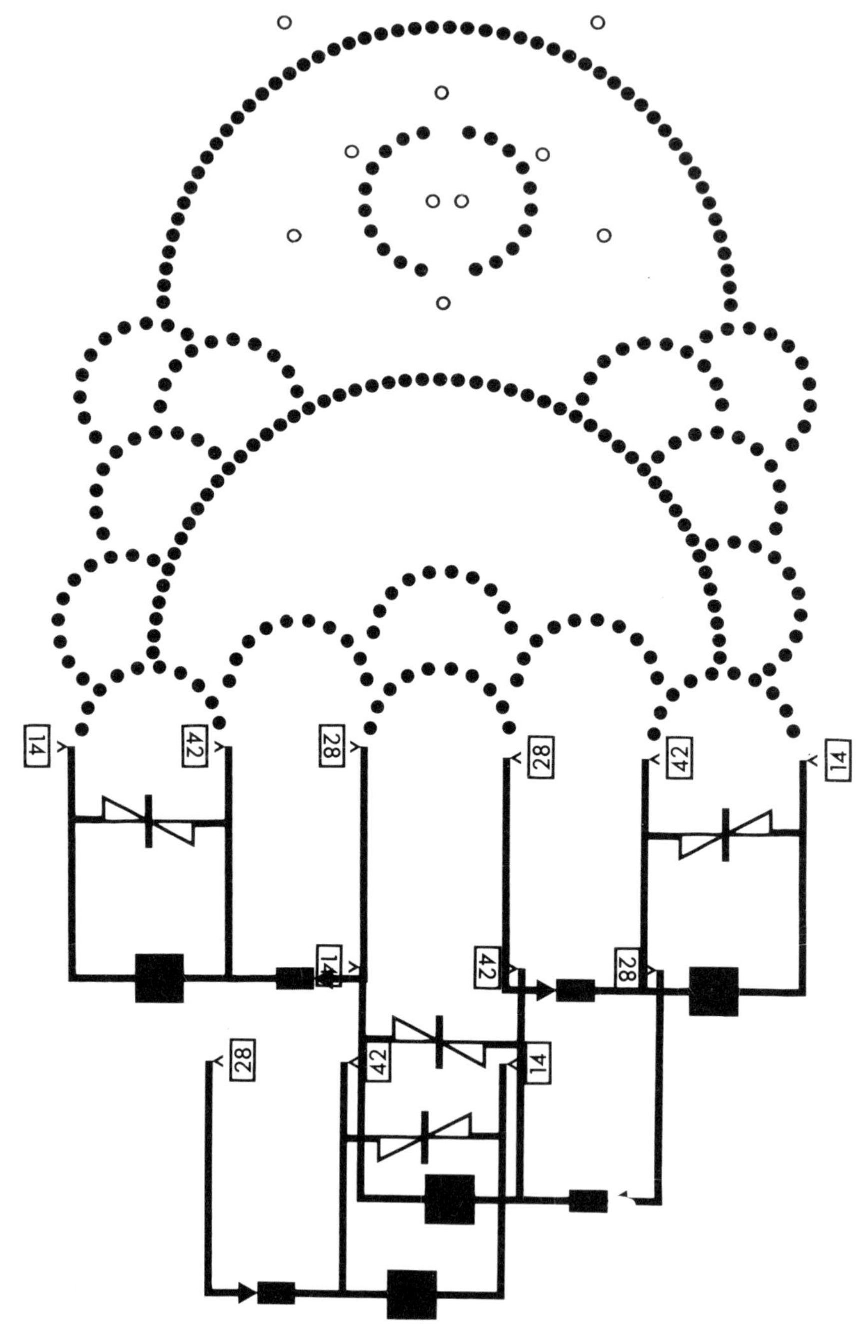
14
42
28
28
42
14
14
42
28
28
42
14

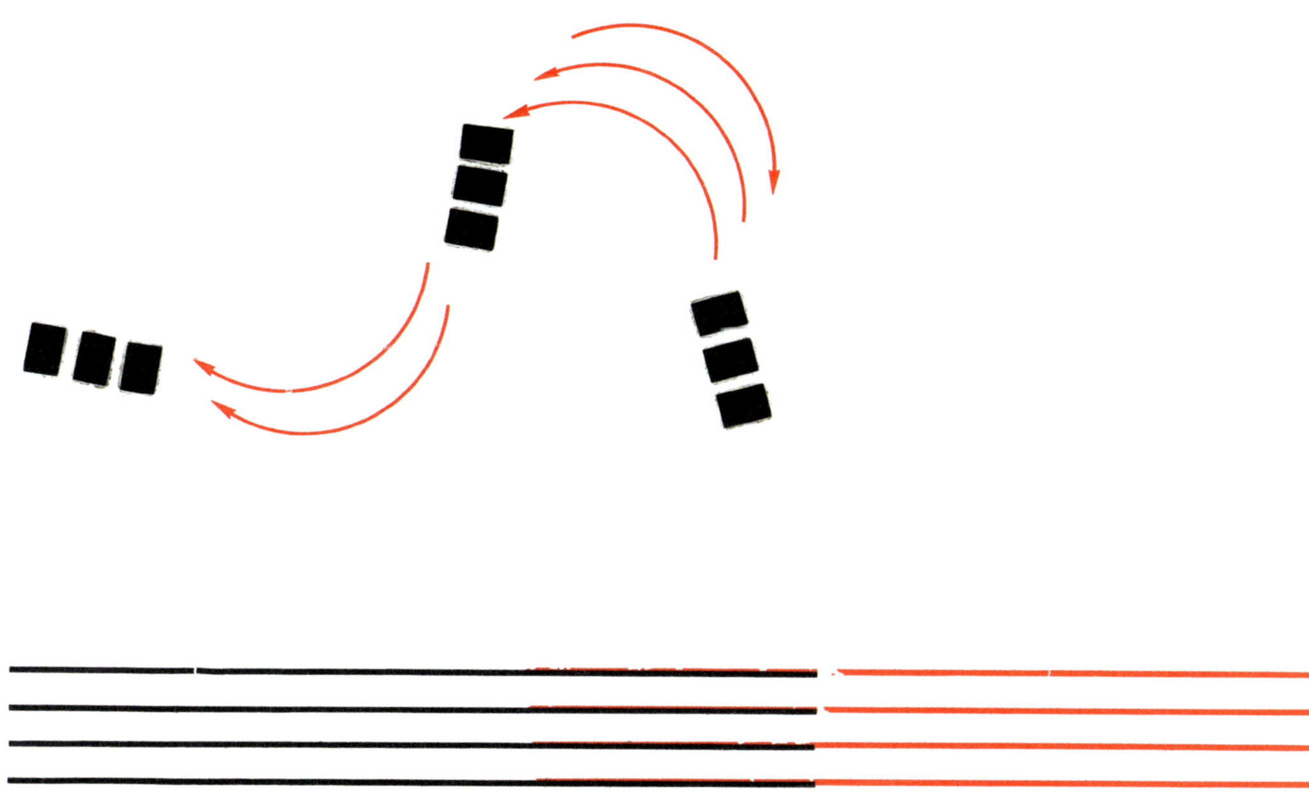

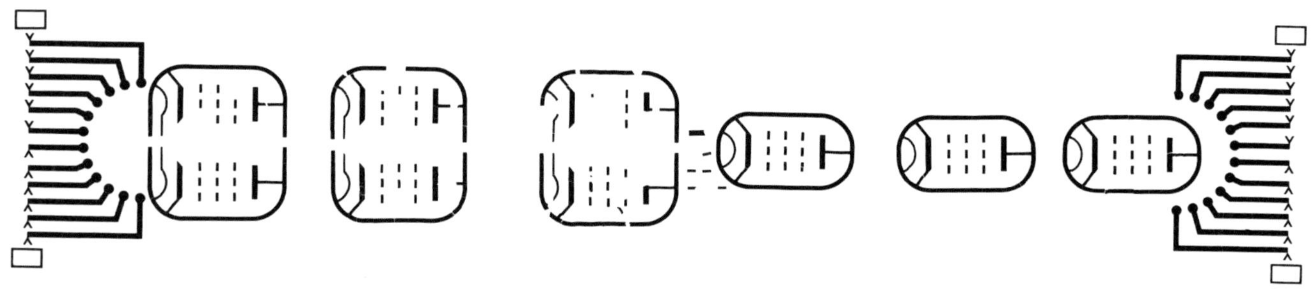

ilm aa ab bc
lm aa ab bc
aa noo stu
AtOM
BORN BEIN
DIREC
BEHO
LD
MIND
MIND
BEY

Françoise Mairey

£é2"3’4(5-6è7_8ç9à&)°^¨ aAzZ
eErRtTyYuUiIoOpP½¼qQsSdDfFgGg
GhHjJkKlLmMù%wWxXcCvVbBnN,?;.
:/=+=/:.;?,NnBbVvCcXxWw%ùMmLl
KkJjHhGgFfDdSsQq¼½PpOoIiUuYyT
tRrEeZzAa¨^ °)&à9ç8_7è6-5(4’3
"2é£$£é2"3’4(5-6è7_8ç9à&)°^¨
aAzZeErRtTyYuUiIoOpP½¼qQsSdDf
FgGhHjJkKlLmMù%wWxXcCvVbBnN,?
;.:/=+=/:.;?,NnBbVvCcXxWw% ùM
mLlK kJjHhGgFfDdSsQq¼½PpO oIi
UuYyTtRrEeZzAa¨^ °)&à9ç8_7è6-
5(4’3"2é£$£é2"3’4(5-6è7_8 ç9à
&)°^¨ aAzZeErRtTyYuUiIoOpP½¼q
QsSdDfFgGhHjJkKlLmMù%wWxXcCvV
bBnN,?;.:/=+=/:.;?,NnBbVvCcXx
Ww% ùMmLlK kJjHhGgFfDdSsQq¼½P
pOoIiU uYyTtRrEeZzAa¨^ °)&à9ç
8_7è6-5(4’3"2é£$£é2"3’4(5-6è7
_8 ç9à&)°^¨ aAzZeErRtTyYuUiIo
OpP½¼qQsSdDfFgGhHjJkKlLmMù%qQ
sSdDfFgGhHjJkKlLmMù%wWxXcCvVb
BnN,?;.:/ =+=/:.;?,NnBbVvCcXx
Ww%ùMmLlKkJjHhGgFfDdSsQq¼½PpO
oIiUuYyTtRrEeZzAa^^ °) &à 9ç 8
_ 7è 6-5(4’3"2é£$£é2"3’4(5-6è
7_8ç9à&)°^¨ aAzZeErRtTyYuU iI
oOpP½¼qQsSdDfFgGhHjJkK lLmMù%
wWxXcCvVbBnN,?;.:/=+=/:.;?,Nn
BbVvCcXxWw%ùMmLlKkJjHhGgFfDdS
sQq¼½PpOoIiUuYyTtRrEeZzAa¨¨ °)
&à9ç8_7è6-5(4’3"2é£$£é2"3’4(5
-6è7_8ç9à&)°^¨ aAzZeErRtTyYuU
iIoOpP½¼qQsSdDfFgGhHjJkKlLmMù
%wWxXcCvVbBnN,?;.:/=+=/:.;?,N
nBbVvCcXxWw%ùMmLlKkJjHhGgFfDd
SsQq¼½PpOoIiUuYyTtRrEeZzAa¨^ °
)&à9ç8_7è6-5(4’3"2é£$£é2"3’4(
5-6è7_8ç9à&)°^¨ aAzZeErRtTyYu
UiIoOpP½¼qQsSdDfFgGhHjJkKlLmM
ù%wWxXcCvVbBnN,?;.:/=+=/:.;?,
NnBbVvCcXxWw%ùMmLlKkJjHhGgFfD
dSsQq¼½PpOoIiUuYyTtRrEeZzAa¼½
PpOoIiU uYyTtRrEeZzAa¨^ °)&à9
ç8_7è6-5(4’3"2é£$£é2"3’4(5-6è
7_8ç9à&)°^¨ aAzZeErRtTyYuUiIo
OpP½¼qQsSdDfFgGhHjJkKlLmMù%wW
xXcCvVbBnN,?;.:/=+=/:.;?,NnBb
VvCcXxWw%ùMmLlKkJjHhGgFfDdSsQ
q¼½PpOoIiUuYyTtRrEeZzAa¨^ °)&
à9ç8_7è6-5(4’3"2é£$£é2"3’4(5-

HHHHHH
HHH H H H H H HHH
HHH HHH
HHHHHHHHHHHHHH
HHHHH H HHHHH
HHHHHHHH hhhhhhhhhhhhh hhh
HHHHHHHHHHHHHHHHH
HHHHH hh H
H HHHHHHHHHH
HHH
HHHH H HH
HHHHHH
HHHHHHHHHH h h
h hhhh
HHHH
h
h
HHHHH
hh
hhh HH
H
hhhh HH
HHHH
hhhhhh
hh HHHHHH
HHHHHHHH hhhhh
HHHHHHHHH hhh
HHHHHHHHHHHHHHHHH
HH
hhhhh
HHHHH
hhhhhhhyhhhhhhhhhhhhhhhhh
hhh HHHHHHHH
HHHH
HHHHH hhh hhhhhhhhhhhhhh
h HHHHHH H
hhhhhhhhhhhhhhhhhh
hhhhhhhhhhhhhh H
HHH
HHHHH hhhhhhhhhhhhhhhhhhh
HHH
h HHHHHH HHH
hhhhhhhhh HHHHHHHHHHHH
hhhhhhhhhhhhhhhhhhhhhh

```
oooooooooooooooooooooooooooooooo
oooooooooooooooooooooooooooooooo
oooooooooooooooooooooooooooooooo
oooooooooooooooooooooooooooooooo
oooooooooooooooooooooooooooooooo
oooooooooooooooooooooooooooooooo
oooooooooooooooooooooooooooooooo
oooooooooooooooooooooooooooooooo
oooooooooooooooooooooooooooooooo
oooooooooooooooooooooooooooooooo
oooooooooooooooooooooooooooooooo
oooooooooooooooooooooooooooooooo
oooooooooooooooooooooooooooooooo
oooooooooooooooooooooooooooooooo
oooooooooooooooooooooooooooooooo
oo o ooooooooooooooooooooooooooo
oooooooooooooooooooooooooooooooo
oooooooooooooooooooooooooooooooo
```

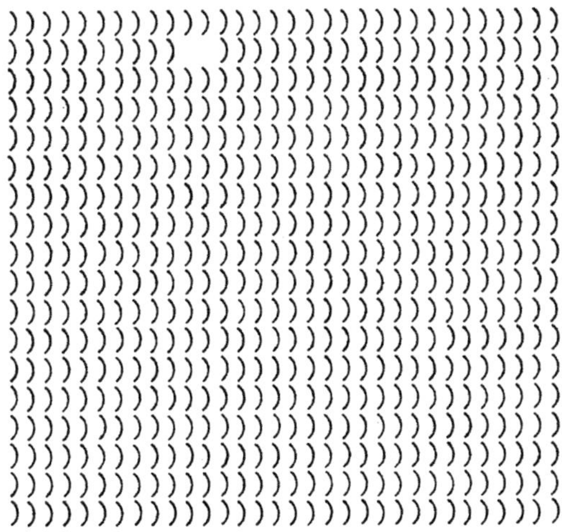

ooo000ooo000ooo000ooo000ooo000oo
o000ooo000ooo000ooo000ooo000ooo0
00ooo000ooo000ooo000ooo000ooo000
ooo000ooo000ooo000ooo000ooo000oo
o000ooo000ooo000ooo000ooo000ooo0
00ooo000ooo000ooo000ooo000ooo000
ooo000ooo000ooo000ooo000ooo000oo
o000ooo000ooo000ooo000ooo000ooo0
00ooo000ooo000ooo000ooo000ooo000
ooo000ooo000ooo000ooo000ooo000oo
o000ooo000ooo000ooo000ooo000ooo0
00ooo000ooo000ooo000ooo000ooo000
ooo000ooo000ooo000ooo000ooo000oo
o000ooo000ooo000ooo000ooo000ooo0
00ooo000ooo000ooo000ooo000ooo000
ooo000ooo000ooo000ooo000ooo000oo
o000ooo000ooo000ooo000ooo000ooo0
00ooo000ooo000ooo000ooo000ooo000

PPP PPP ppp ppp PPP PP
P ppp ppp PPP PPP ppp
ppp PPP PP P ppp ppp
PPP PPP ppp ppp PPP
PPP ppp ppp PPP PPP
ppp ppp PPP PPP ppp p
pp PPP PPP ppp ppp PP
P PPP ppp ppp PPP PPP
ppp ppp PPP PPP ppp
ppp PPP PPP ppp ppp
ppp PPP PPP ppp ppp
P PP ppp ppp PPP PPP P
P P PPP ppp ppp PPP p
pp PPP PPP ppp ppp PP
P ppp ppp PPP PPP ppp
ppp PPP PPP ppp ppp
PPP PPP ppp ppp PPP
PPP ppp ppp PPP PPP

dDdDdDdDdDdDdDdDdDdDdDdDdDdDdDdD
dDdDdDdDdDdDdDdDdDdDdDdDdDdDdDdD
dDdDdDdDdDdDdDdDdDdDdDdDdDdDdDdD
dDdDdDdDdDdDdDdDdDdDdDdDdDdDdDdD
dDdDdDdDdDdDdDdDdDdDdDdDdDdDdDdD
dDdDdDdDdDdDdDdDdDdDdDdDdDdDdDdD
dDdDdDdDdDdDdDdDdDdDdDdDdDdDdDdD
dDdDdDdDdDdDdDdDdDdDdDdDdDdDdDdD
dDdDdDdDdDdDdDdDdDdDdDdDdDdDdDdD
dDdDdDdDdDdDdDdDdDdDdDdDdDdDdDdD
dDdDdDdDdDdDdDdDdDdDdDdDdDdDdDdD
dDdDdDdDdDdDdDdDdDdDdDdDdDdDdDdD
dDdDdDdDdDdDdDdDdDdDdDdDdDdDdDdD
dDdDdDdDdDdDdDdDdDdDdDdDdDdDdDdD
dDdDdDdDdDdDdDdDdDdDdDdDdDdDdDdD
dDdDdDdDdDdDdDdDdDdDdDdDdDdDdDdD
dDdDdDdDdDdDdDdDdDdDdDdDdDdDdDdD
dDdDdDdDdDdDdDdDdDdDdDdDdDdDdDdD

FFF FFF FFF FFF FFF FFF FFF FFF
FFF FFF FFF FFF FFF FFF FFF FFF
FFF FFF FFF FFF FFF FFF FFF FFF
FFF FFF FFF FFF FFF FFF FFF FFF
FFF FFF FFF FFF FFF FFF FFF FFF
FFF FFF FFF FFF FFF FFF FFF FFF
FFF FFF FFF FFF FFF FFF FFF FFF
FFF FFF FFF FFF FFF FFF FFF FFF
FFF FFF FFF FFF FFF FFF FFF FFF
FFF FFF FFF FFF FFF FFF FFF FFF
FFF FFF FFF FFF FFF FFF FFF FFF
FFF FFF FFF FFF FFF FFF FFF FFF
FFF FFF FFF FFF FFF FFF FFF FFF
FFF FFF FFF FFF FFF FFF FFF FFF
FFF FFF FFF FFF FFF FFF FFF FFF
FFF FFF FFF FFF FFF FFF FFF FFF
FFF FFF FFF FFF FFF FFF FFF FFF
FFF FFF FFF FFF FFF FFF FFF FFF

gggggggggggg
GGGGGGGGGGGG
gggggggggggg
GGGGGGGGGGGG
gggggggggggg
GGGGGGGGGGGG
gggggggggggg
GGGGGGGGGGGG
gggggggggggg
GGGGGGGGGGGG
gggggggggggg
GGGGGGGGGGGG
gggggggggggg
GGGGGGGGGGGG
gggggggggggg
GGGGGGGGGGGG
gggggggggggg
GGGGGGGGGGGG

gggggggggggg
GGGGGGGGGGGG
gggggggggggg
GGGGGGGGGGGG
gggggggggggg
GGGGGGGGGGGG
gggggggggggg
GGGGGGGGGGGG
gggggggggggg
GGGGGGGGGGGG
gggggggggggg
GGGGGGGGGGGG
gggggggggggg
GGGGGGGGGGGG
gggggggggggg
GGGGGGGGGGGG
gggggggggggg
GGGGGGGGGGGG

hhhhhhhhhhhh
HHHHHHHHHHHH
hhhhhhhhhhhh
HHHHHHHHHHHH
hhhhhhhhhhhh
HHHHHHHHHHHH
hhhhhhhhhhhh
HHHHHHHHHHHH
hhhhhhhhhhhh
HHHHHHHHHHHH
hhhhhhhhhhhh
HHHHHHHHHHHH
hhhhhhhhhhhh
HHHHHHHHHHHH
hhhhhhhhhhhh
HHHHHHHHHHHH
hhhhhhhhhhhh
HHHHHHHHHHHH

hhhhhhhhhhhh
HHHHHHHHHHHH
hhhhhhhhhhhh
HHHHHHHHHHHH
hhhhhhhhhhhh
HHHHHHHHHHHH
hhhhhhhhhhhh
HHHHHHHHHHHH
hhhhhhhhhhhh
HHHHHHHHHHHH
hhhhhhhhhhhh
HHHHHHHHHHHH
hhhhhhhhhhhh
HHHHHHHHHHHH
hhhhhhhhhhhh
HHHHHHHHHHHH
hhhhhhhhhhhh
HHHHHHHHHHHH

```
llllllllllllllll
                LLLLLLLLLLLLLLLL
llllllllllllllll
                LLLLLLLLLLLLLLLL
llllllllllllllll
                LLLLLLLLLL1L1LLL
llllllllllllllll
                LLLLLLLLLLLLLLLL
llllllllllllllll
                LLLLLLLLLLLLLLLL
llllllllllllllll
                LLLLLLLLLLLLLLLL
llllllllllllllll
                LLLLLLLLLLLLLLLL
llllllllllllllll
                LLLLLLLLLLLLLLLL
llllllllllllllll
                LLLLLLLLLLLLLLLL
```

```
mmmmmmmmmmmmmmmm
                MMMMMMMMMMMMMMMM
MMMMMMMMMMMMMMMM
                mmmmmmmmmmmmmmmm
mmmmmmmmmmmmmmmm
                MMMMMMMMMMMMMMMM
MMMMMMMMMMMMMMMM
                mmmmmmmmmmmmmmmm
mmmmmmmmmmmmmmmm
                MMMMMMMMMMMMMMMM
MMMMMMMMMMMMMMMM
                mmmmmmmmmmmmmmmm
mmmmmmmmmmmmmmmm
                MMMMMMMMMMMMMMMM
MMMMMMMMMMMMMMMM
                mmmmmmmmmmmmmmmm
mmmmmmmmmmmmmmmm
                MMMMMMMMMMMMMMMM
```

```
((((((     ))))))     ((((((   ))
))))))))))))(((((((()))))))))))))
((((((((((     ))))))    ((((((((
))))))))     ((((((((((     )))))
(((((((((((((((((((    ))))))))))
)))))))))      (((((     ((((((((
(((((    )))))    )))))))))))))))
(((((((((((((((   (((((((((((((((
)))))))     ))))))))))      )))))
(((    (((((((((        (((((((((
))))))      )))))))))       )))))
((((((((        (((((((((((((((((
))))))))))))))))))          )))))
(((((       (((((((        ((((((
)))))))))       )))))))))))))))))
((((((((((((((((((((((       ((((
))))))      )))))))))))))))))))))
((((      (((((((((((((((((((((((
))))))))            )))))))))))))
((((((((((       (((((((    (((((
)))))))))     )))))))))    ))))))
(((((     ((((((((((((    (((((((
(((((((((((((       )))))))))))))
)))))))       ))))))))))     ((((
((((      (((((((((((((((((((((((
))))))))))))))))       ))))))))))
((((((((        ))))))))))   ((((
)))))))      )))))      (((((((((
(((((((((((((((((((((((((((((((((
))))))))))        )))))))))))))))
((((((((      (((((((((((((((((((
)))))))))))))))))))))))     )))))
(((((((((((((((      ((((((((((((
))))))))       ))))))))))))))))))
(((((((((((((((     (((((((((((((
)))))))))       )))))))))))))))))
((((((     ((((((((((((((((((((((
)))))))))))))))))))))))))))))))))
(((((((((             (((((((((((
)))))))))    ))))))))))))))))))))
(((((((((((((((((((((((((((((((((
)))))))))))         )))))))))))))
((((((     ((((((((((((((((((((((
))))))))))))))))))))))     ))))))
((((((((((     ((((((((((((((((((
))))))))))))      )))))))    ))))
((((((     ((((((((((((((((((((((
)))))))))    ))))))))   )))))))))
((((((((((   ((((( ((((((((((((((
))))))))))))))))))))))))))   ))))
((((((((((((((    (((((((((((((((
)))))))))))))))))))))))))))))))))
```

Giulia Niccolai

She took down
a jar
from one
of the shelves
as she passed:
it was labeled
« ORANGE MARMALADE »,
but
to her great
disappointment
it was empty.

a jar a jar a jar a jar
a jar a jar a jar a jar
a jar a jar a jar a jar
a jar a jar a jar a jar
a jar a jar a jar a jar
a jar a jar a jar a jar
a jar a jar a jar a jar
a jar a jar a jar a jar
a jar a jar a jar ajar

Vocatives:

Oysters! Mouse!

O sister! O Muse!

juggler

A CAUCUS—RACE AND A LONG TALE

tale
tale
tale
tale
tale
tale
tale
tale
tale
tale
tale
tale
tale
tale
tale
tale
tale
tail

Fury said to
a mouse, That
he met
in the
house,
'Let us
both go
to law:
I will
prosecute
you.—
Come, I'll
take no
denial;
We must
have a
trial:
For
really
this
morning
I've
nothing
to do.'
Said the
mouse to
the cur,
'Such a
trial,
dear sir,
With no
jury or
judge,
would be
wasting
our breath.'
'I'll be
judge,
I'll be
jury,'
Said
cunning
old Fury:
'I'll try
the whole
cause,
and
condemn
you
to
death.' "

« All right »,

said the Cat;

and this time

it vanished

quite syowly,

beginning

with

the end

of

the

tail...

tail off

rose tree

tree rose

« backward »

drawkcab

bottom

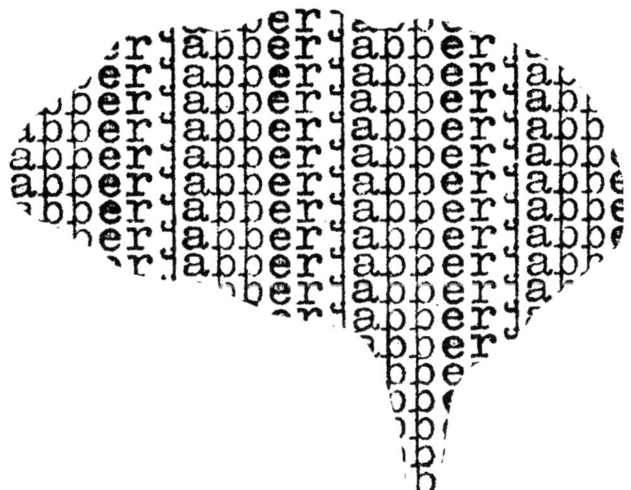

o

o o

b unce

humpty

dumpty

impenetrability

unihorn

Ry Nikonova

О ДЕКОРАТИВНЫХ КНИГАХ В ИНТЕРЬЕРЕ

В японских домах интерьер часто украшается стихом или изречением. Мы же обычно не выпячиваем декоративность книги, ибо считается, что это якобы наносит урон её внутреннему содержанию, т.е. поглощению этого содержания. Однако не теряет же картина своей прелести оттого, что украшает комнату, а не пылится где-либо на полках. Просто конструкция книги не приспособлена пока для декоративных целей. Разве не превосходным было бы украшением интерьера нечто литературно насыщенное и скульптурно-прекрасное?

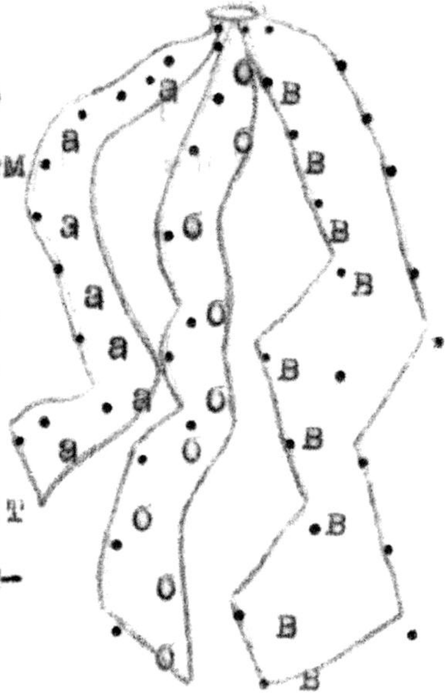

Итак, вот варианты формы декоративной книги:

1. Книга - метёлка /рис. 1/ напоминает дерево. При чтении происходит как бы свободная игра ветвей. Такая книга может украшать помещение

подобно фонарям.

2. Книга - роза./ см. статью " О соединениии скульптуры со словарём"/

3. Книга-ковёр. Настенная.

4. Книга-картина.

Возможен тираж. Колоссальная доступность текста./см. статью"О леттристских картинах"/.

Константин Олимпов.

Аааааааааааааааааааа
аааааааааааааааааааа
аааааааааааааааааааа
жжжжжжжжжжжжжжжжжжжж
аааааааааааааааааааа
аааааааааааааааааааа
аааааааааааааааааааа
аааааааааааааааааааа
бббббббббббббббббббБ.

Отрывок из статьи: "... Наиболее интересным мне кажется вариант леттризма сверху живописи-любой,т.е. - поверх написанной картины. / см. статью о принципе иллюстраций"/.

5. Ваза,расписанная текстом.

6.Книга - тротуар. Дорога,выложенная плиткой с текстом.

7. Книга - скульптура. Любая скульптура с текстом.

8. Матрёшка с текстом /"Матрёна Антологическая"

Тексты Северянина, Мандельштама, Ахматовой – на всех матрёшках, соответственно величине таланта. У матрёшек – портретное сходство с автором / Вариант: Сервиз "Литературный" с текстами Кручёных.

9. Блюдо с литературой. Два блюда, накрывая одно другое – содержат внутри себя вместо конфет – печатные тексты. Читатель ставит оба блюда перед собою и прочитанное складывает в одно из них. Возможны и другие варианты.

Анна Таршис.
Май, 1979.

НОВАЯ ФОРМА КНИГИ.

/ Продолжение статьи " О декоративных книгах"/

10. Книга - диск. Даёт возможность в и д е т ь

книгу ц е-
л и к о м.
Не перелистывая
тывая страниц
правда, она не
велика по объ
ёму- клиньев
14-15. Спи-
ральный спо-
соб потребле-

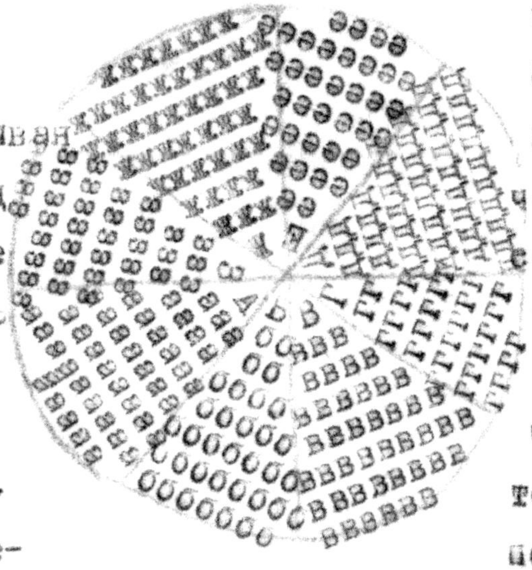

ния созда-
ёт анало-
гию не с
чередование
сезонов, а с
траекторие
й вращения
небесных
тел. Более
последова-

тельным было бы все строчки записать по спирали /подобно записи музыки/ и читать подобную книгу с помощью проигрывателя, но это утомительно. Более естественен компромисс обычной книги с грампластинкой.

Иллюстрация в такой кни-
ге может быть мультипликa-
ционной /см. статью "О
мульт живописи для проиг-
рывателя"/

10-а. Книга
-пирамида.
Развитие пр-
едыдущего
принципа:у-
величение о-
бъёма книги
Множество
дисков на-

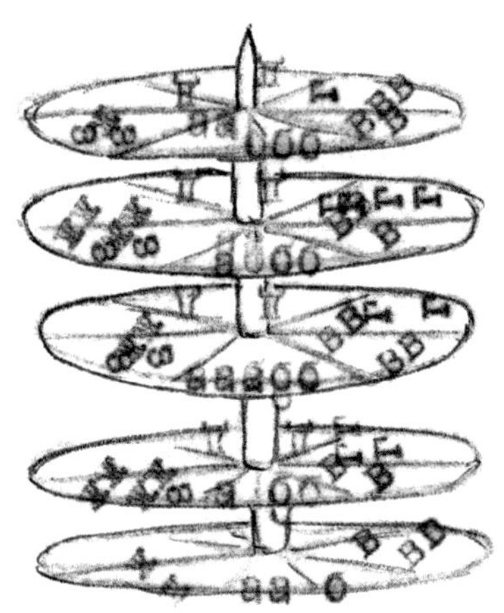

низывается
на стержень,
который дол-
жен быть вы
движным.Мо-
гут быть про
зрачные ди
ски-витражи,
накладываю-
щиеся на диск с текстом
и таким образом иллюст-
рирующие его /см. статью
" О принципе иллюстраций"/

11. Книга - вертушка,или
мельница. Читается способо-
м вращения крыльев. Одно
крыло может быть прзрачным
и создавать эффект симуль-
танного текста при наложении,

Крыльев может быть множество, что создаёт возможность самостоятельного выбора читателем композиции текста.

12. Книга-подушка, или книга-наволочка. Тексты - разрозненные листки любой формы и формата./Достоинство!/ Возможность бесконечно корректировать, заменять текст. Возможность бесконечной композиции.

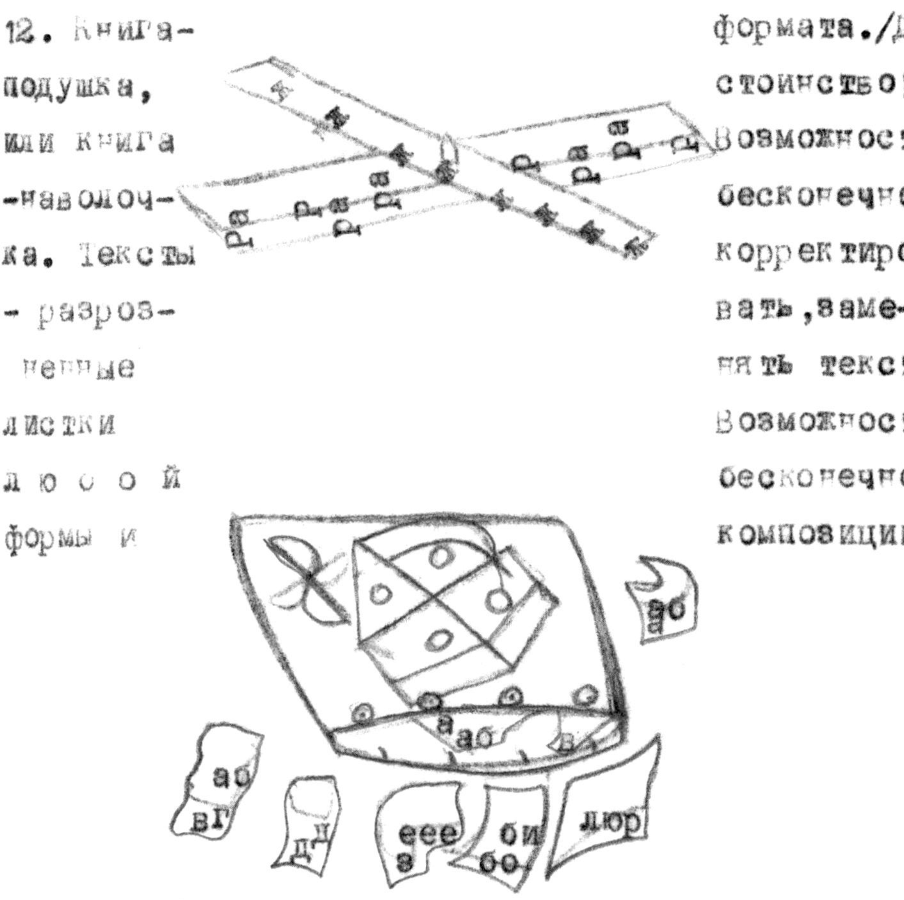

Этот вариант, к юбилею Велимира Хлебникова, будет выпущен ред. ж. "Транспонанс"

12-а. Книга-портфель. Два отделения в

В одном - прочитанное,
в другом - ещё нет.
12-б. Книга -ридикюль.
Или цилиндр. Такие
книги можно хранить
в специальных
подстаканни-
ках.
13. Бордюрная
книга-газета
вакуумного ти
па. Цилиндр,
оклеенный
текстом. Текст
может читать
ся по вертикали
и по спирали.
Застёжка на
молнии, расстег-
нув которую, мо-
жно вывернуть
текст наизнанку
и прочесть то,
что внутри. Мо-
жет быть много-
слойной, владе-
лец сам опреде-
ляет, какой слой
сделать верхним 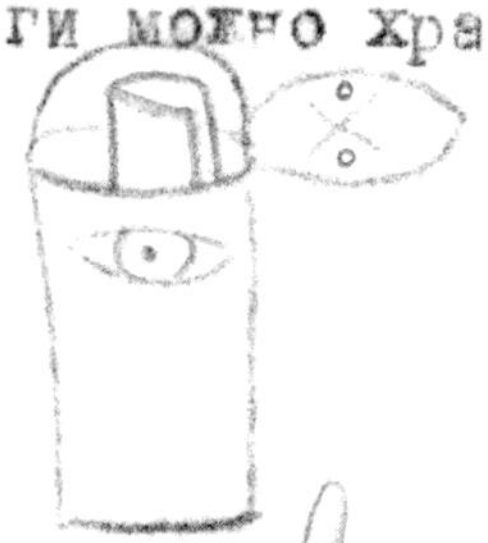 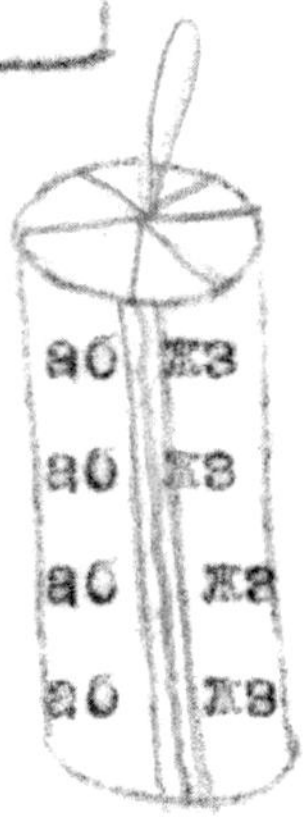
14. Книга-моза-
ика. Читатель сам
переставляет данные
ему автором слова.
Читатель-соавтор.

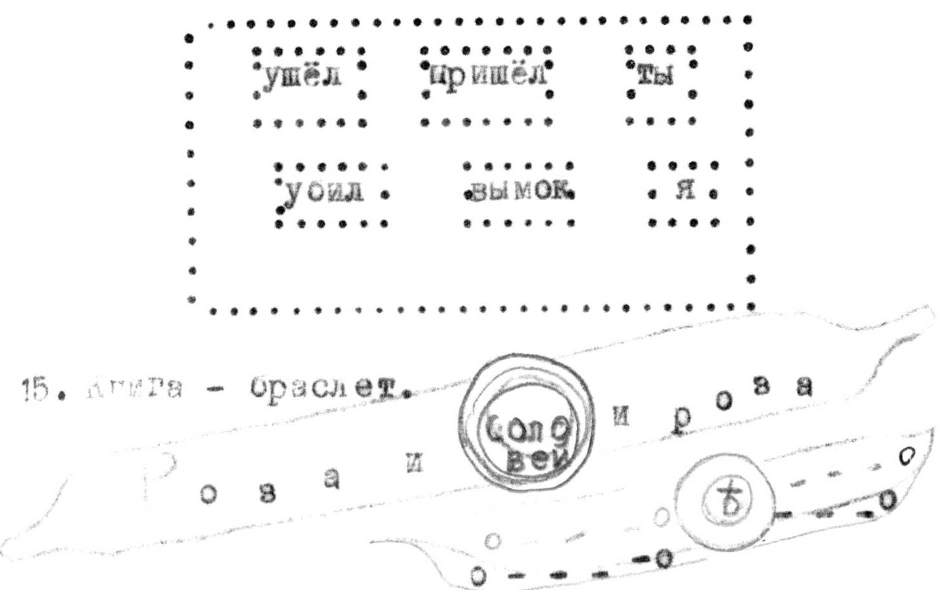

15. Книга - браслет.

16. Книга обыкновенная, но продырявленная насквозь, благодаря чему образуется как бы ручка и книгу удобно носить. Дырявить можно и не изменяя композиции текста. Пусть читатель вспоминает и домысливает. Происходят же такие вещи в природе.

17. Готовая книга разрезается пополам, и читателю продаются обе половины за двойную цену.

18. Книга, сброшюрованная посредине. Особенно приятно

так смотреть репродукции

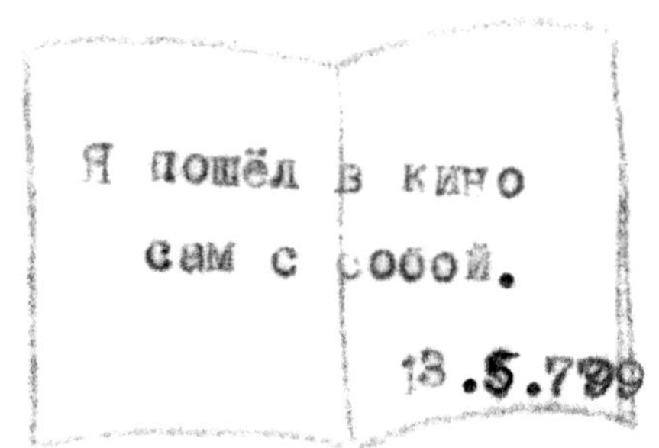
Я пошёл в кино
сам с собой.
13.5.799

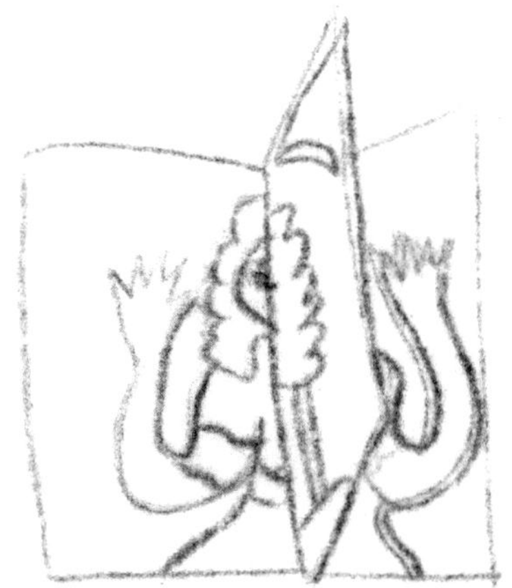

Anna Oberto

recuperare un'espressione creativa autonoma

ANNA OBERTO

rinnovamento filosofico
di segno emblematicamente liberatorio
con la partecipazione della

qualità al femminile

NUOVA SCRITTURA

al femminile

nella nuova ipotesi societaria
di una somma di
individualità culturali

creative intellect woman

utopisticamente proporre un nuovo modo 'mentale di vedere la donna come il fatto nuovo capace nella sua forza erompente di costruire una diversa futura globale gestione del mondo

ANA UTOPIA PER LA CITTA' IDEALE

una città → civiltà partecipata
creativamente della donna

LIBERAZIONE DAL LINGUAGGIO AL MASCHILE COME LIBERAZIONE FEMMINILE
per una inter/azione dei linguaggi (scrittura oralità iconografia videofotomedia)
verso un'utopistica manifestatività totale dell'individuo

dulzura duwo dwenolos dhe- poser

una'nuova scrittura' in cui l'espressione linguistica sia in diretto rapporto con le proprie istanze contenutistiche semantico

lotta alla repressione culturale come repressione sessuale

evidenziare quei termini dell'espressività che sono manifestativi
dell'essere al femminile

quale POESIA AL FUTURO progettare?

VT/

segnificare la propria identità

corpo —
mente —
essere ·

scrittura a mano

nell' U T O P I A di una liberazione totale del 'senso della creatività' dall'alienazione del rapporto tra significato e realtà del lavoro intellettuale inteso come merce consumistica
— LIBERA CREATIVITA' IN UNA COMUNITA' LIBERATA DAI PRIVILEGI COSTITUITI —

M A N I F E S T O
F E M M I N I S T A
A N A C U L T U R A L E

THE WOMEN'S MOVEMENT
Where It's At

PM
c/o B. Broedel
308 S. Macomb St.
Tallahassee, Fla.
32301

A Research/Resource Guide (sort of) for the Movement.
$1 to institutions
25¢ each (or four six-cent stamps) to people
Bulk rates on request.

MOVIMENTO PER LA LIBERAZIONE DELLA DONNA
DEMAU
FRONTE ITALIANO DI LIBERAZIONE FEMMINILE
RIVOLTA FEMMINILE
COLLETTIVO DI LOTTA FEMMINISTA
FRONTE DI LIBERAZIONE OMOSESSUALE
ANABASI
CERCHIO SPEZZATO
GRUPPO PADOVA E FERRARA
COLLETTIVO DI LIBERAZIONE DELLA DONNA

COMITE D'ACTION CENSIER
MOUVEMENT DE LIBERATION DES FEMMES
LES GUINES ROUGES
FRONT HOMOSEXUEL D'ACTION REVOLUTIONNAIRE

ETC.

LA VIA FEMMINILE
QUARTO MONDO
COMPAGNA
FUORI
AL FEMMINILE

TOUT
LE TORCHON BRULE

ETC.

centro tool
ricerche interlinguistiche
via borgonuovo 20
20121 milano
telefono (02) 652567
direzione: ugo carrega

11-31.1.1972
ore 17-20
mostra numero 21

esposizione internazionale
operatrici visuali
annalisa alloatti
mirella bentivoglio
paula claire
lia drei
ulrike eberle
amelia etlinger
ilse garnier
bohumila grogerova
annalies klophaus
liliana landi
giulia niccolai
anna oberto
betty radin
giovanna sandri
mary ellen solt
biljana tomic
silvia trevale
patrizia vicinelli

perché una mostra di sole donne?
razzismo si è detto, tanto più in quanto 'pensata' da un uomo.
tema attuale questo del femminismo come attuale è il tema del nuovo movimento in poesia, detta 'visuale' (concreta, fonetica, analitica, tecnologica, pubblica eccetera), per una inter/azione dei linguaggi verso un utopistico linguaggio manifestativo globale.
forse non a caso entrambi i temi si sono riproposti tumultuosamente negli anni '60.
liberazione femminile come liberazione del linguaggio?
accettiamo quindi una situazione 'razzista' cui ancora le donne in cultura sono condizionate e usiamola come strumento rivelatore di scandalo di questa situazione.
accettiamo di conseguenza anche il rischio di un 'censimento' umiliante, che può erompere in un'altra denuncia chiarificatoria del rapporto di alienazione:
perché le donne in cultura producono meno degli uomini?
si dà spesso una facile risposta:
nell'attuale situazione culturale al maschile, nessun lavoro creativo e no libera la donna dall'occuparsi delle cose di casa.
fino a quando avremo formato una cultura 'nuova', con la partecipazione integrante attiva della donna, e nuove strutture sociali che sostituiscano il suo impegno materiale.
accettiamo questa mostra perché pensiamo che non l'uomo è il nemico ma uomo e donna sono condizionati dai modelli di comportamento socioculturale che l'uomo lui stesso ha imposto.
questa mostra perché.
il rapporto di antagonismo classista uomo-donna è emblematico di un altro rapporto di antagonismo classista arte-società, in quanto divisione del lavoro e alienazione delle attività e opere artistiche nei loro rapporti tra significato e realtà che vengono egualmente mercificati.
come liberare l'opera d'arte nel significato dal valore di scambio che lo riduce a merce?
come liberare l'operatore artistico dalla divisione capitalistica del lavoro che lo inquadra in una categoria economica?
la liberazione della donna esige il superamento della contrapposizione categoriale uomo-donna così come la liberazione dalla divisione tra attività artistica e passività economica esige il superamento delle categorie arte-lavoro intese come complementarità strutturali della ideologia borghese (mercificazione dell'opera e controllo dell'operatore).
nella utopia di una liberazione totale del significato dell'arte dalla alienazione del lavoro inteso come merce.
l'arte alienata dei supermercati della cultura farà posto ad un'arte liberata in una comunità senza classi e senza privilegi.
per restituire alla completa autonomia l'attività di ricerca e creazione dei significati non più privilegiata al lavoro necessario al quale tutti partecipare.
in una situazione di passaggio fino all'utopia nella liberazione dal lavoro tout court e manifestazione globale dell'attività poietica.
anna oberto

Jennifer Pike

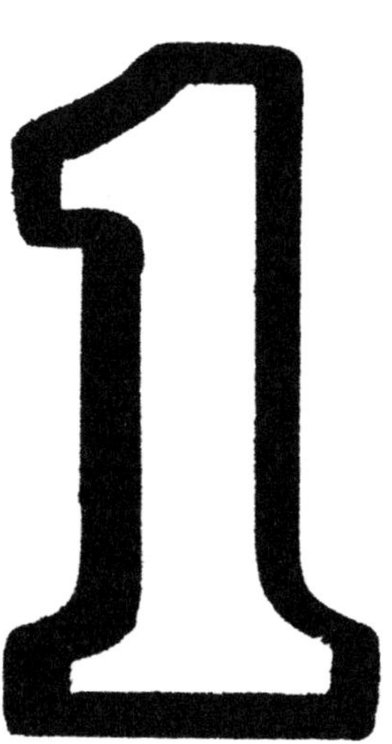

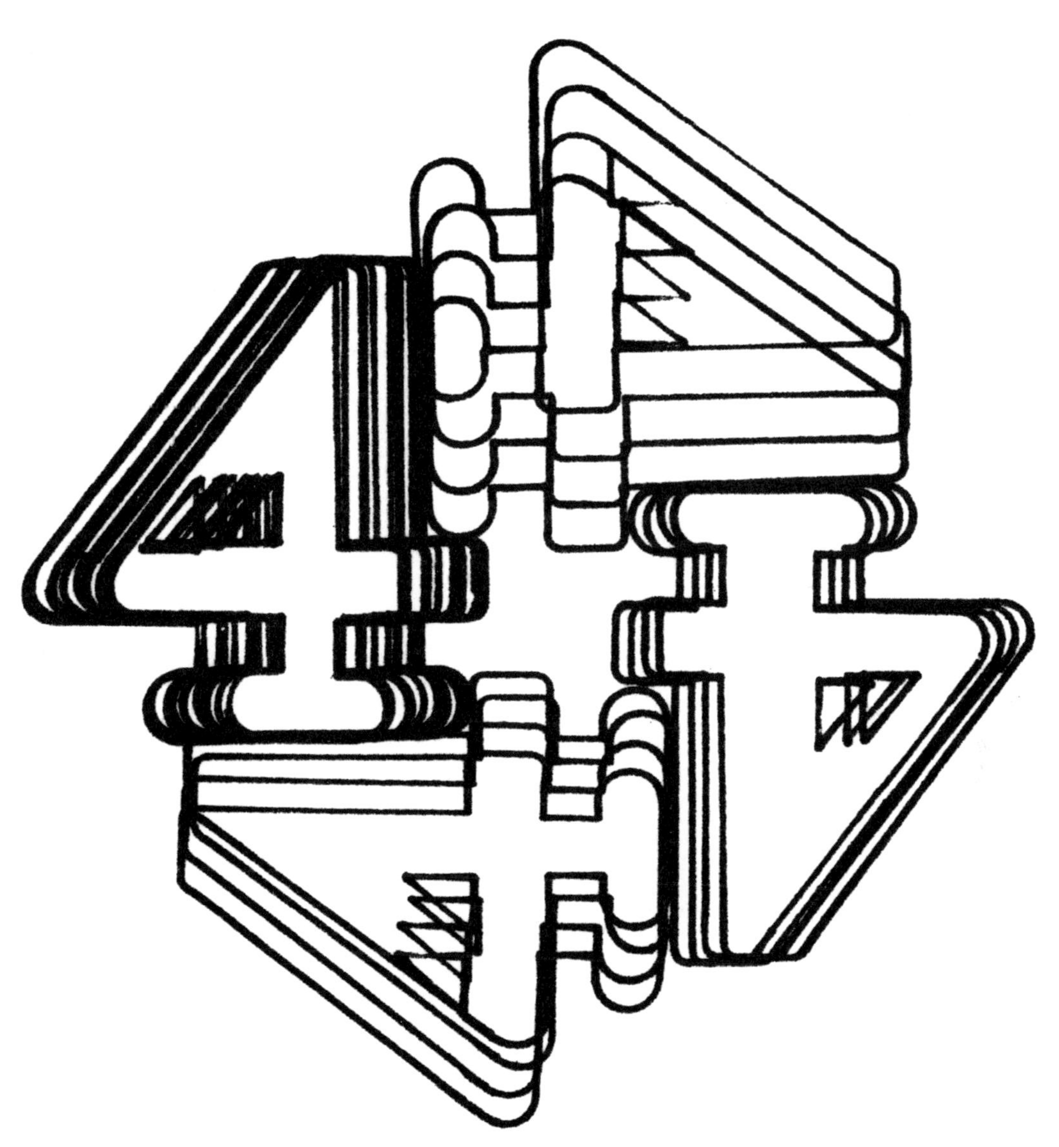

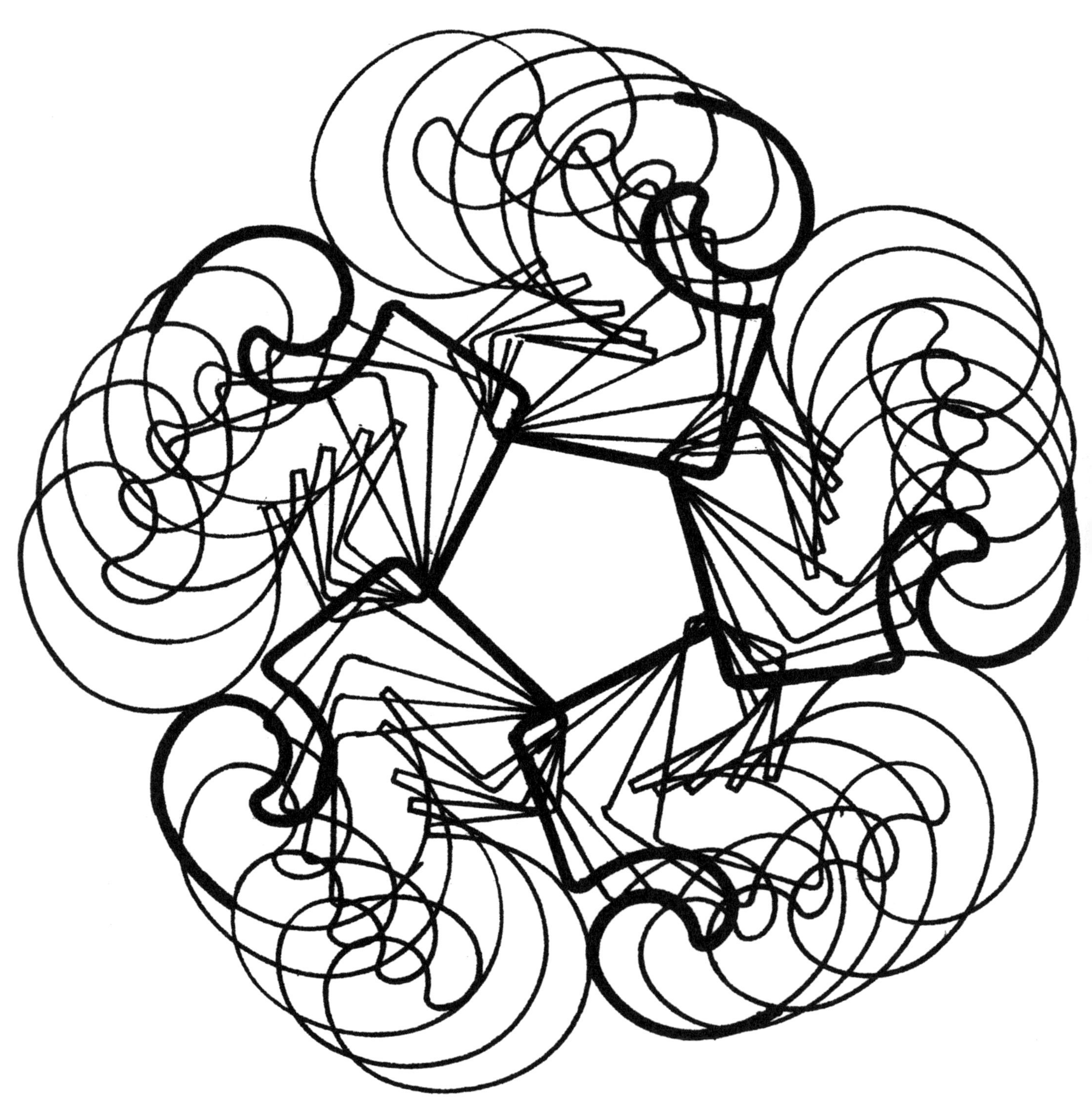

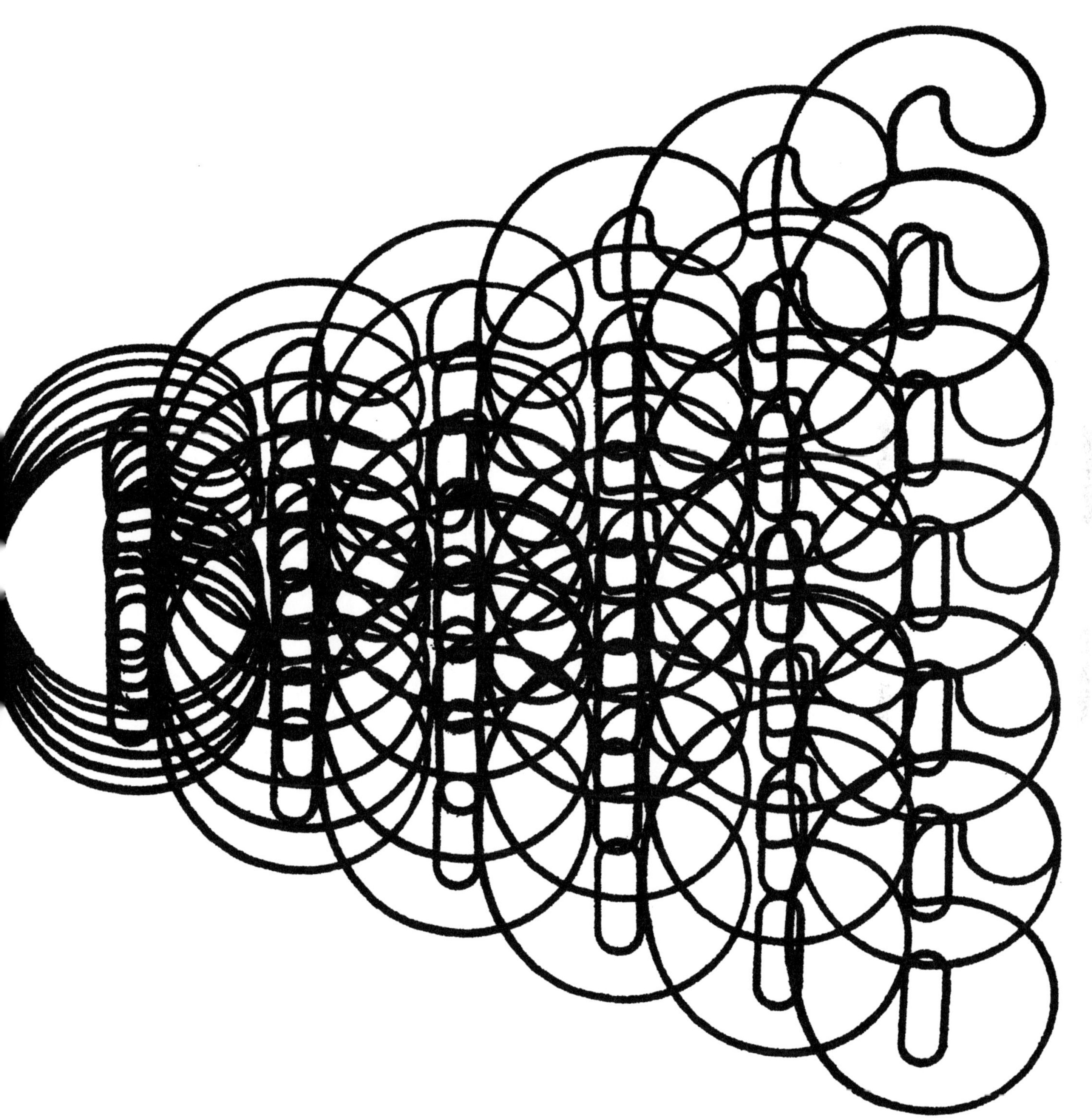

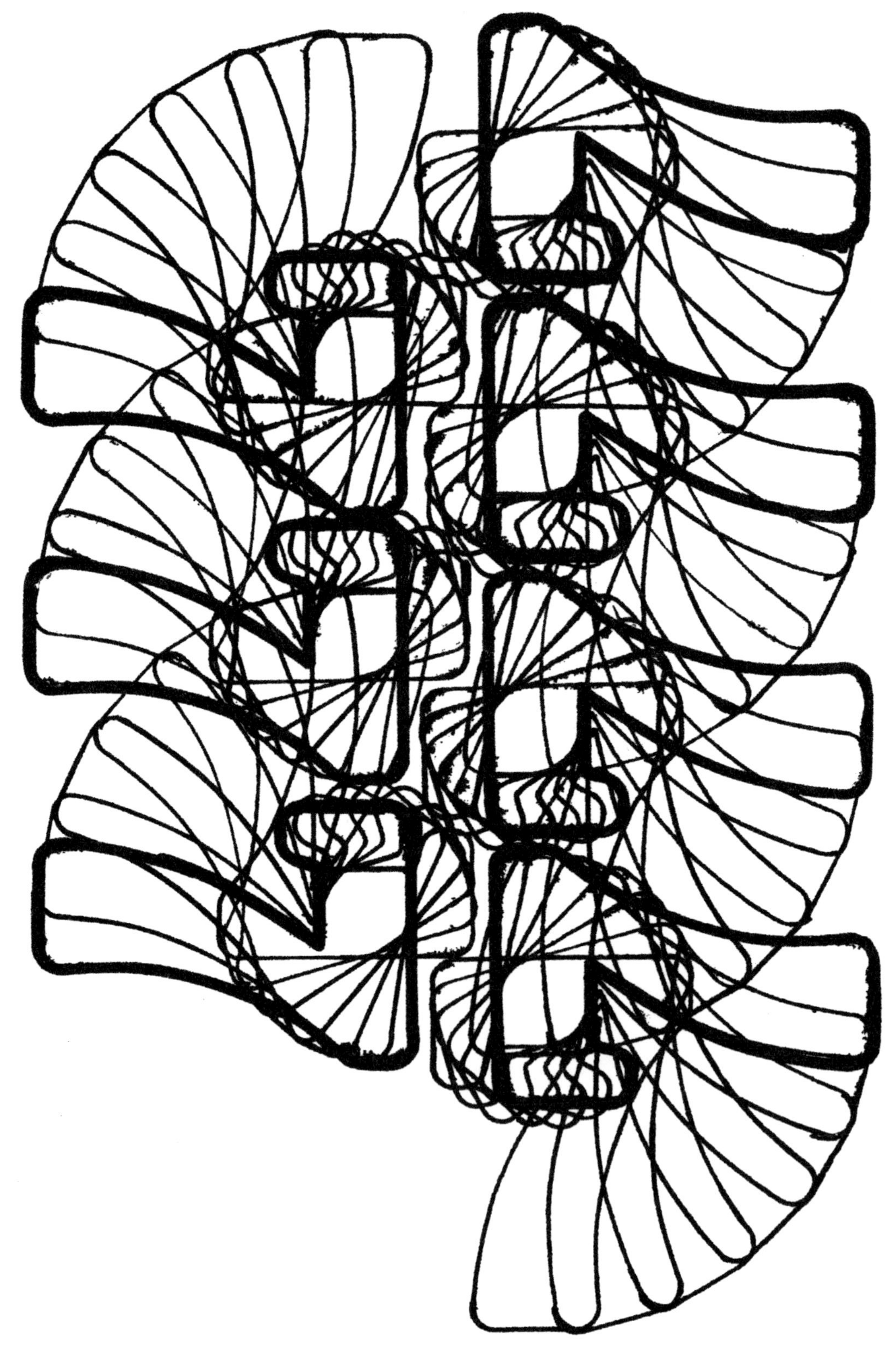

Bogdanka Poznanović

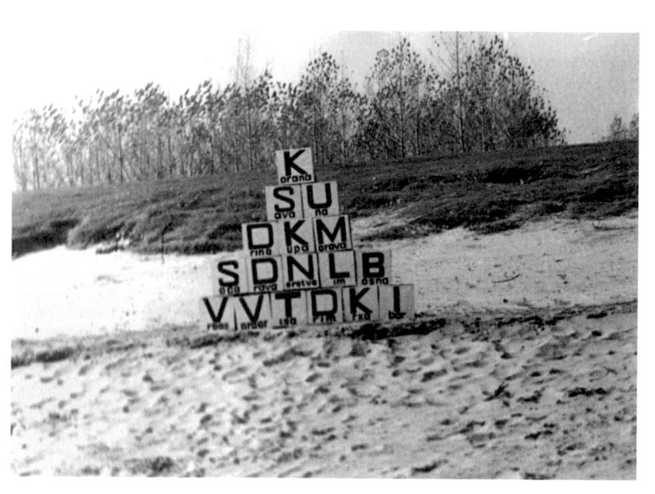
K
orana
SU
ava na
DKM
rina upa orava
SDNLB
rava eretva im osna
VVTDKI

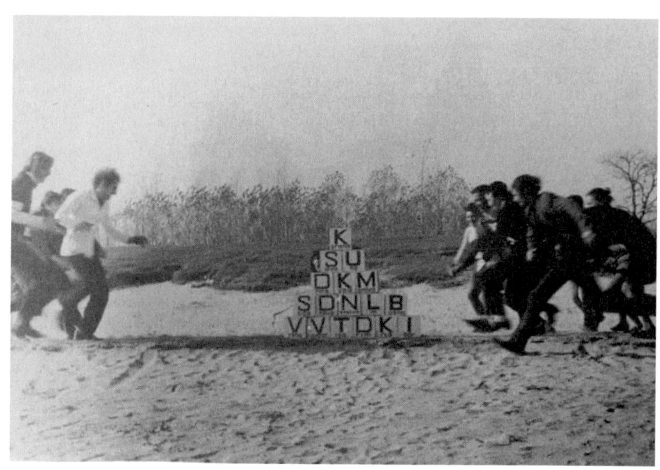
K
SU
DKM
SDNLB
VVTDKI

KRKA

KRKA

UNA

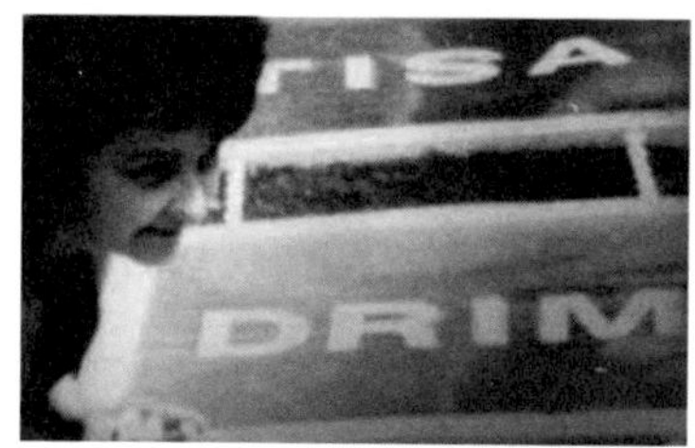
TISA
DRIM

SIGNALNE VATRE

RE

E

Betty Radin

me in time

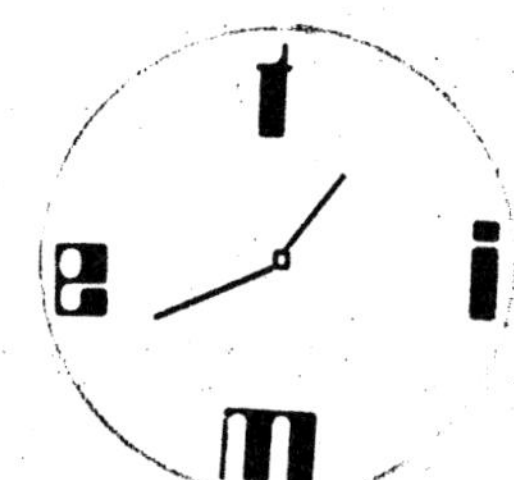

TIMES PAST
THE TIMES
New Printing House Square, London, WC1X 8EZ. Telephone: 01-837 1234

TEMPS PERDU

FRED ASTAIRE
GINGER ROGERS
IRVING BERLIN
WITH
EDWARD EVERETT HORTON
HELEN BRODERICK
ERIK RHODES · ERIC BLORE
Directed by MARK SANDRICH
A PANDRO S. BERMAN Production
RKO RADIO

TEMPS WANTED

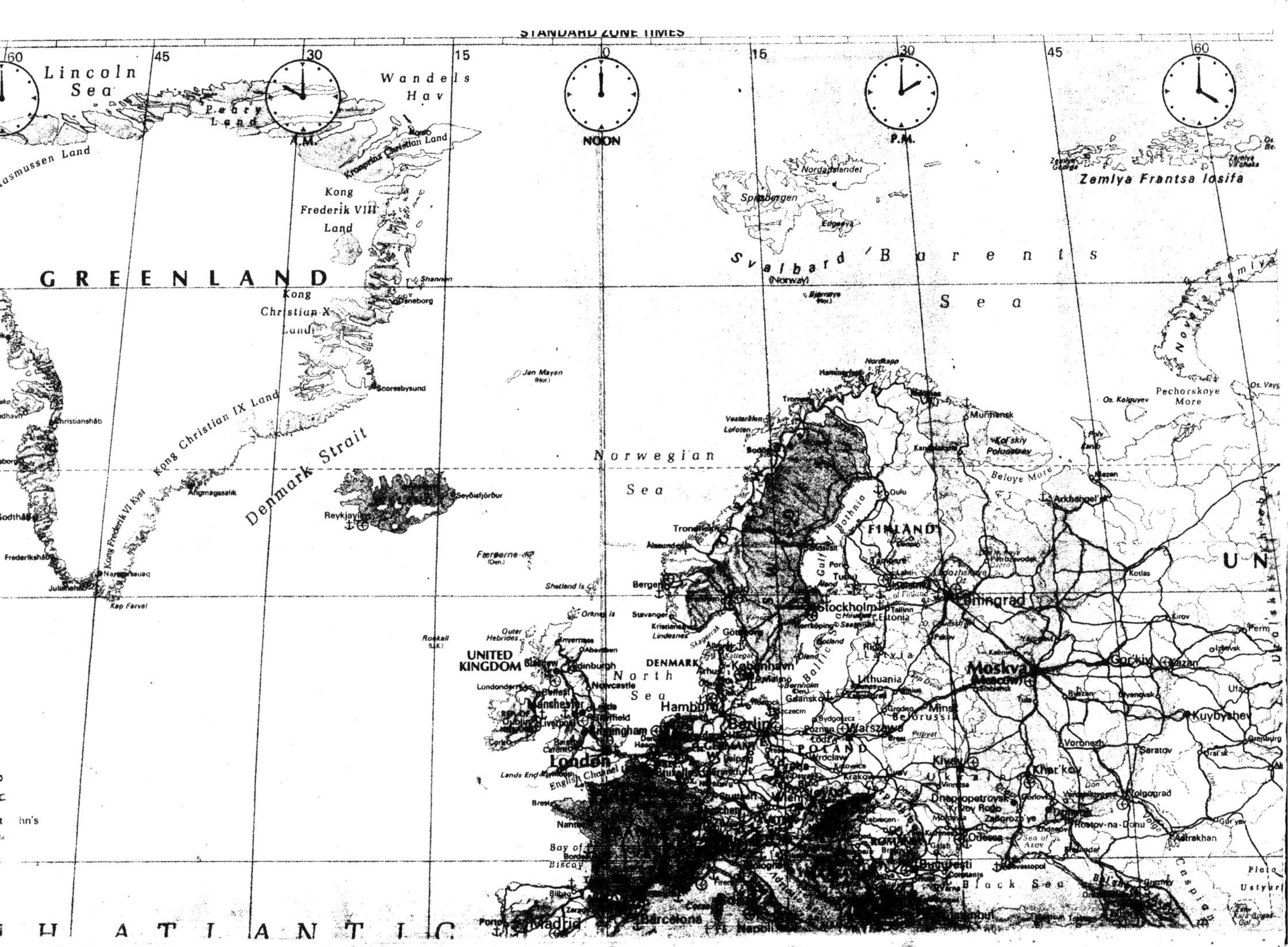
STANDARD ZONE TIMES
A.M.
NOON
P.M.
Lincoln Sea
Wandels Hav
Peary Land
Kronprins Christian Land
Kong Frederik VIII Land
GREENLAND
Kong Christian X Land
Kong Christian IX Land
Denmark Strait
Scoresbysund
Reykjavík
Seydisfjördur
Jan Mayen (Nor.)
Svalbard (Norway)
Nordaustlandet
Spitsbergen
Edgeøya
Barents Sea
Zemlya Frantsa Iosifa
Norwegian Sea
Færøerne (Den.)
Shetland Is.
Orkney Is.
Rockall (U.K.)
UNITED KINGDOM
North Sea
DENMARK
FINLAND
Gulf of Bothnia
Stockholm
Leningrad
Moskva (Moscow)
Gorkiy
Kazan
Kuybyshev
Murmansk
Arkhangel'sk
Pechorskoye More
Os. Kolguyev
Beloye More
Nordkapp
Oulu
Bergen
Stavanger
Trondheim
Lithuania
Latvia
Estonia
Tallinn
Hamburg
Berlin
Warszawa
POLAND
London
English Channel
Bay of Biscay
Kiyev
Khar'kov
Volgograd
Saratov
Voronezh
Astrakhan
Rostov-na-Donu
Odessa
Sea of Azov
Black Sea
Bucuresti
Madrid
Barcelona
Napoli
ATLANTIC
Kep Farvel
Christianshåb
Godthåb
Frederikshåb
Julianehåb
Angmagssalik
Lofoten
Vesterålen
Kotlas
Kirov
Perm
Ufa
Gdansk
Kraków
Wien
Dnepropetrovsk
Zaporozh'ye
Sevastopol
Caspian
Ustyurt
Plato
Novaya Zemlya
Shannon
Daneborg
Lands End
Glasgow
Edinburgh
Aberdeen
Newcastle
Belfast
Dublin
Liverpool
Manchester
Birmingham
Cork
Londonderry
Brest
Nantes
Bordeaux
Bilbao
Porto

me in time
meantime
me anti me

Giovanna Sandri

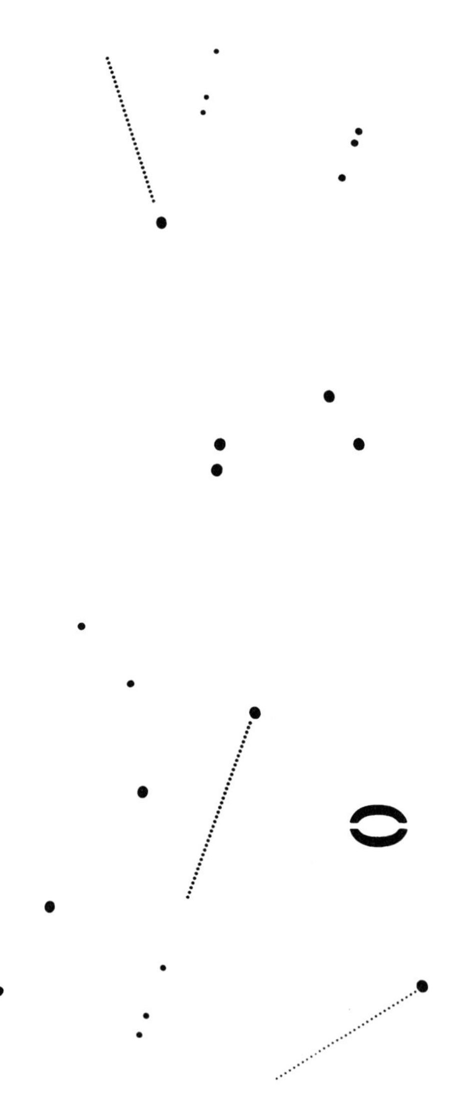

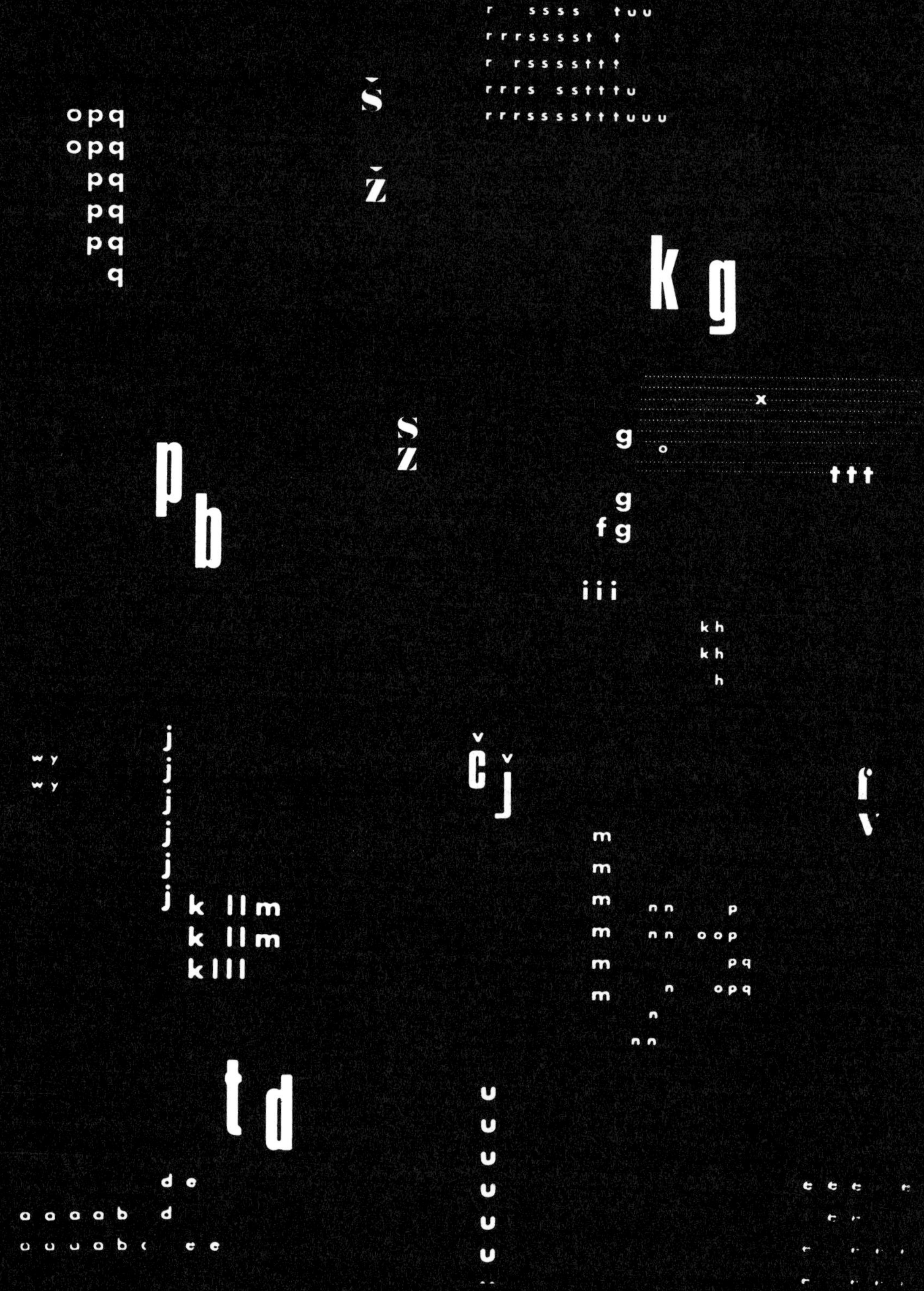
rrr ssstttuu
r ssss tuu
rrrssssst t
r rssssttt
rrrs sssttu
rrrsssstttuuu
š
ž
opq
opq
pq
pq
pq
q
kg
x
s
z
g
o
ttt
pb
g
fg
iii
kh
kh
h
wy
wy
j
j
j
j
j
j
j
č
j
f
v
k llm
k llm
klll
m
m
m
m
m
m
nn p
nn oop
pq
n opq
n
nn
td
u
u
u
u
u
u
de
aaaab d
uuuobc ee

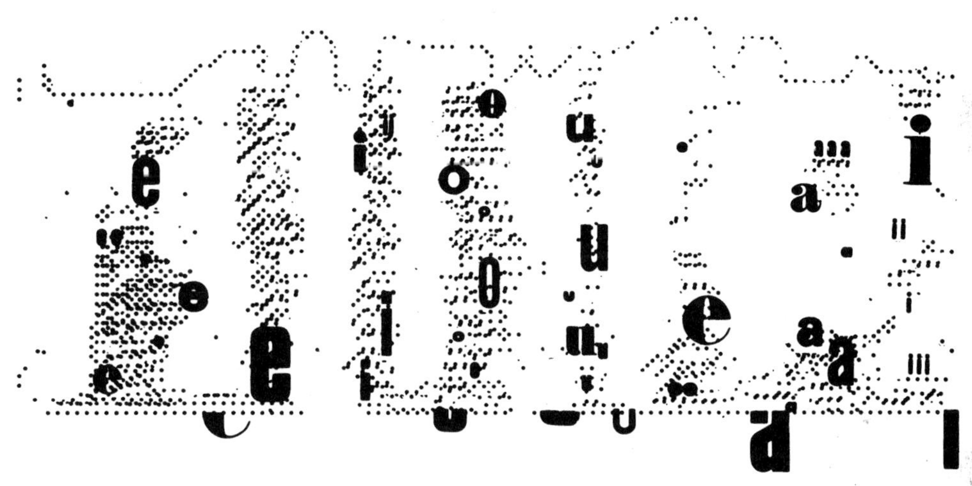

A A/p

BB

2

c 5

o

EE

~ ~ ~

o

aaabbccddeeeef ghhi jk llmmn

Mira Schendel

4
para onde a sociedade está se dirigindo com seu progresso industrial ? quando o progresso cessar, em que condições deixará a humanidade ?

5 a maioria das pessoas pensa que uma nação para ser feliz precisa ser grande; mas mesmo que estejam certas, elas não têm a menor idéia do que seja uma nação grande, ou uma nação pequena... há um limite para o tamanho das nações, assim como há um limite para outras coisas; plantas, animais, instrumentos; pois nenhuma delas retém seu poder natural quando é muito grande, ou muito pequena; ao contrario, ou perde inteiramente sua natureza,

ou se deteriora. (aristóteles)

CORRIDA ARMAMENTISTA / ESTAGNAÇÃO ECONÔMICA — aço — CO_2

DETERIORAÇÃO DO AMBIENTE / EXPLOSÃO DEMOGRÁFICA

um mundo finito : os limites do crescimento exponencial

(+) (-)

toda pessoa no mundo enfrenta uma série de pressões e de problemas que exigem sua atenção e sua ação. estes problemas a afetam em diferentes níveis. ela pode gastar a maior parte de seu tempo tentando garantir para si e sua familia o alimento do amanhã. pode estar interessada no poder pessoal, ou no poder da nação onde vive. pode preocupar-se com uma guerra mundial no curso de sua vida, ou com uma guerra, na próxima semana, com um grupo rival na sua vizinhança. estes níveis bem diferentes de preocupação humana podem ser representados em gráfico, como o da f.1 ele apresenta duas dimensões : espaço e tempo. todo interesse humano pode situar-se em algum ponto do gráfico, dependendo do espaço geográfico que ele abrange, e até onde se prolonga no tempo. as preocupações da maioria das pessoas estão concentradas no ângulo inferior esquerdo do gráfico. a vida, para estas pessoas, é muito difícil, e elas têm que dedicar quase todos os seus esforços à sua subsistência diária e à de suas famílias. outras pessoas pensam em problemas, ou atuam sobre problemas bem distantes dos eixos de espaço ou de tempo. as pressões que sofrem afetam não só a elas mesmas, mas também a comunidade com a qual se identificam. as medidas que tomam prolongam-se não somente durante dias, mas também semanas e anos futuros adentro. as perspectivas de tempo e espaço de uma pessoa dependem de sua cultura, de sua experiência passada e do caráter imediato dos problemas que enfrenta em cada nível. a maioria das pessoas precisa resolver com êxito os problemas numa área menor, antes de deslocar suas preocupações para uma área mais ampla. em geral, quanto mais amplo o espaço e mais longo o tempo dedicado a um problema, tanto menor é o número de pessoas realmente envolvidas na busca de soluções. pode haver decepções e perigos na limitação da visão de uma pessoa a uma área demasiado estreita. há muitos exemplos de pessoas que se empenham arduamente na tentativa de resolver algum problema de âmbito local e de alcance imediato, mas cujos esforços acabam sendo anulados pelos acontecimentos que estão ocorrendo num contexto maior. uma guerra internacional pode destruir uma lavoura cuidadosamente tratada por um agricultor. uma política nacional pode alterar os planos oficiais de uma região. o desenvolvimento econômico de um país ou de uma região podem ser frustrados pela ausência de mercado mundial para seus produtos. de fato, hoje, é motivo de preocupação crescente a possibilidade de a maioria dos objetivos pessoais e nacionais virem a ser anulados pelas tendencias gerais a longo prazo, tais como as mencionadas por u thant. são as implicações destas tendencias tão ameaçadoras a ponto de sua solução exigir prioridade sobre os interesses locais a curto prazo ? será verdade, conforme sugeriu u thant, que nos resta menos de uma década para começarmos a regular tais tendências ? e se elas não forem controladas, quais serão as conseqüências ? que método possui a humanidade para resolver problemas globais, e quais serão os resultados e os custos do emprego de cada um deles ? estas são as questões que estivemos investigando na primeira fase do

---

1
atualmente achamos que ter cinco filhos não é demais; e cada filho também produz cinco filhos, e antes da morte do avô já serão 25 os descendentes.

2
quem, dentre vós, desejando construir uma torre, não se senta, primeiro, para calcular os custos, a fim de ver se tem meios suficientes para levá-la a cabo ?

3
na circunferência de um circulo, o começo e o fim são comuns.

aspas de astros """
riscos de astros ///
pontos de astros ..
traços de astros - -
rochas de astros r r
pedras de astros ddd
penedos de astros z z
riachos de astros ___
letras dos astros n n
escamas de astros sc sc
camadas de astros m m
unhas de astros vvv
lascas de astros ((
pastos dos astros ===
pontes dos astros P P
bordados de astros xxx
favos dos astros : :
dardos dos astros |||
abelhas dos astros a a
musgo dos astros ,,,
ostras dos astros ooo
roleta dos astros c c
cordas de astros)))
florestas de astros f f
pulseiras de astros sss
rumo dos astros
theon spanudis mira

§ 1:textos dos astros

f f ________)))|||m m ddd
""" xxx xxx xxx P P ===,,,
))) ((/// ||| a f f P===
sss === vvv vvv vvv sc sc.
- - c c))) n n z z ..,,,,
||| ||| /// ((sss P P ::

n n - -//// """
))) c c ((ddd
||| (((sss c c
||| ooo))) ((
a a /// f f vvv
,,, === ____((

sss ooo ((sc sc .. vvv z z xxxr r
))) vvv ____P P ,,, ooo """ ///|||a
a a ,,, ooo ooo ooo ooo ooo === z z
||| ||| ||| /// ((f f : : xxx m m
P P xxx sc sc m m ddd a a ,,, ..___
vvv ddd .. """ ____ - - === a a f f

a a ,,, : : === P P
sssxxx f f ‡|| ..,,,
/// ||| : : P P ddd
,,, .. === ____ a a
: : f f ____ sc sc ..
))) f f ||| ooo ooo

a a === f f P P
))) ||| ____ ..
((/// - - vvv
P P ooo xxx z z
=== """ f f a a
____ c c))) ((
f f xxx c c vvv
xxx xxx f f ///
P P ||| ((f f
=== ___sss ooo
sss === c c z z
))) P P ____a a
/// ||| vvv)))

xxx /// ||| sc sc (( ))) ,,, ===: :
c c m m : : vvv vvv """ a a))) ____
sss f f ,,, m m ddd === xxx sc sc ..
/// /// - - ooo f f P P z z))) vvv
____||| : : ((a a c c sss ddd xxx
P P ,,, ,,, ,,, ||| """ r r ((xxx
: : ,,, ///))) === === . .))) xxx

sss vvv /// ,,,
))) f f ||| |||
))) """ ___:: :
xxx P P ((vvv
/// : : === c c
a a vvv sc sc :
(( ))) === P P ,

ooo f f ____ ///))) vvv..,,, a
ooo === P P c c xxx n n m m sss
ooo ||| ((=== /// ..,,,))): :
ooo f f === - - z z : : vvv c c
ooo /// /// ||| P P sc sc ..,,,
____ a a))) ((sss r r ===. .
, /// | : :sc sc//// ||| ____ a a

||| ((a a ____ P P xxx
||| sss """/// ((ddd..
||| ///))) ooo . . vvv
((sc sc - - ,,, ||| : :
ooo ,,, . . ____ P P m m

m m sss === ||| : : """)))
///||||:((a a __o f f xxx
: :))) ddd sc sc vvv P P :
____ xxx ooo))) ((,,, ..
P P ((r r . . """ /// sss
||| f f ,,, c c sss xxx ..
,,, : : /// m m - - a a ,,,
a a === -o- P P ,,, . . sss
xxx - - m m sss /// ||| ((
n n z z ||| : : (( )))||| ,
m m sss vvv : : ooo ooo f f.
|||/// (( ))) """: : ///: :

=== === r r sss n n f f ooo ,,,
=== a a____ xxx P P /// ((: :
||| ((: : ooo))) . . ‡|| sss
P P === /// f f vvv sc sc /// :
xxx ||| z z sss ===))) ooo ,,,
))) ooo r r xxx : : n n m m ooo
sc sc /// ||| ,,, """ === : vvv
/// - -))) sss vvv r r ||| a a
: : ||| /// - - a a ,,, xxx n n
a a === xxx z z n n sc sc /// :
f f m m xxx vvv r r f f. . xxx:
|||. . : : xxx m m /// vvv . .:

z z m m xxx (-(,,, .. n n /// === vvv||||
((c c P P sss /// |||))) : : === r r m m
n n c c /// ||| ((a a === ____))) a a ..
sss ||| === n n))) . . xxx P P ((vvv ,,,
(((xxx xxx xxx n n ,,, vvv r r - - : : sss
mmm ((| | |))) n n : : ===____||| /// ..

f f m m n n /// ooo : : ===.
P P ||| ,,,))) ((,,, sss
c c xxx vvv r r P P))) ///
))) ((vvv sss ||| a a ___
z z c c |||((n n m m |||a
=== === /// sss vvv f f)))
/// |||))) ((- - ooo ooo
P P xxx r r f f c c sss m m
=== === sss ||| /// ((n n
=== r r /// - - ooo m m f f

vvv f f r r === (( ))): :
||| ||| /// sss,,,: : ooo.
||| sss xxx xxx /// ..vvv,
a a xxx ||| ,,, """f f : :
"""))) vvv === P P ____ .
m m : : /// sss vvv))) rr
: :))) ((ooo ooo ooo ::
||| /// /// ||| === . . nn
sss m m r r n n f f vvv aa
=== === f f vvv sss ||| ::

ooo .. m m n n P P === ,,, - -
/// """))) ((|||| - - sss n
||| === xxx xxx ,,, : : ///,,,
((=== a a a a /// |||)))vvv
))) c c xxx r r m m === ,,,|||
/// a a vvv f f sss ((,,,c c
vvv ||| /// sss vvv ,,, - - aa
xxx P P """ ((/// ===))) sss
=== vvv ||| a a f f m m vvv ::
P P xxx === === ||| f f : : ,,

vvv..sss n n f:
sc sc r r ===..
/// ((a a f f
||| a a xxx sss
f f ///|||: : o
vvv))): : ,,,.
: : xxx xxx====
))) ((||| ///
||| a a f f vvv
sss (( ))) sss

||| ,,, : : a a
))) /// vvv sss
P P c c n n m m
xxx |||)))((,
/// /// """ |||
sss vvv /// ,,,
((n n === : :
||| xxx))) ((

sss m m n n vvv P P === ___
((a a))) xxx ,,, sss sss
=== ||| sss xxx vvv m m r r
n n /// ///,,, : : xxx xxx,
vvv - - ooo))) a a ((f f
))) P P === n n xxx r r vvv
r r n n vvv ((vvv vvv ((
vvv m m /// ||| - - ooo ooo

/// . . ,,,))) === n n
|||)))))) - - P P m m
vvv : : xxx r r n n c c
ooo - - /// ||| m m vvv
))) """ === ((sss ///
=== /// ||| n n f f vvv
/// sss n n r r f f ,,,
((vvv m m === : : n n

sss vvv : : /// ((P P f f === :
/// ///))) ||| sss vvv ,,, xxx .
m m ,,, . . === r r """ n n m m "
))) ||| P P : : vvv xxx xxx n n :
vvv r r m m vvv === ||| /// ((a
xxx ((vvv vvv m m |||))) ,,, .
: : """ ((((. . ,,, a a === :
‡||))) a a ||| === ,,, ((xxx .

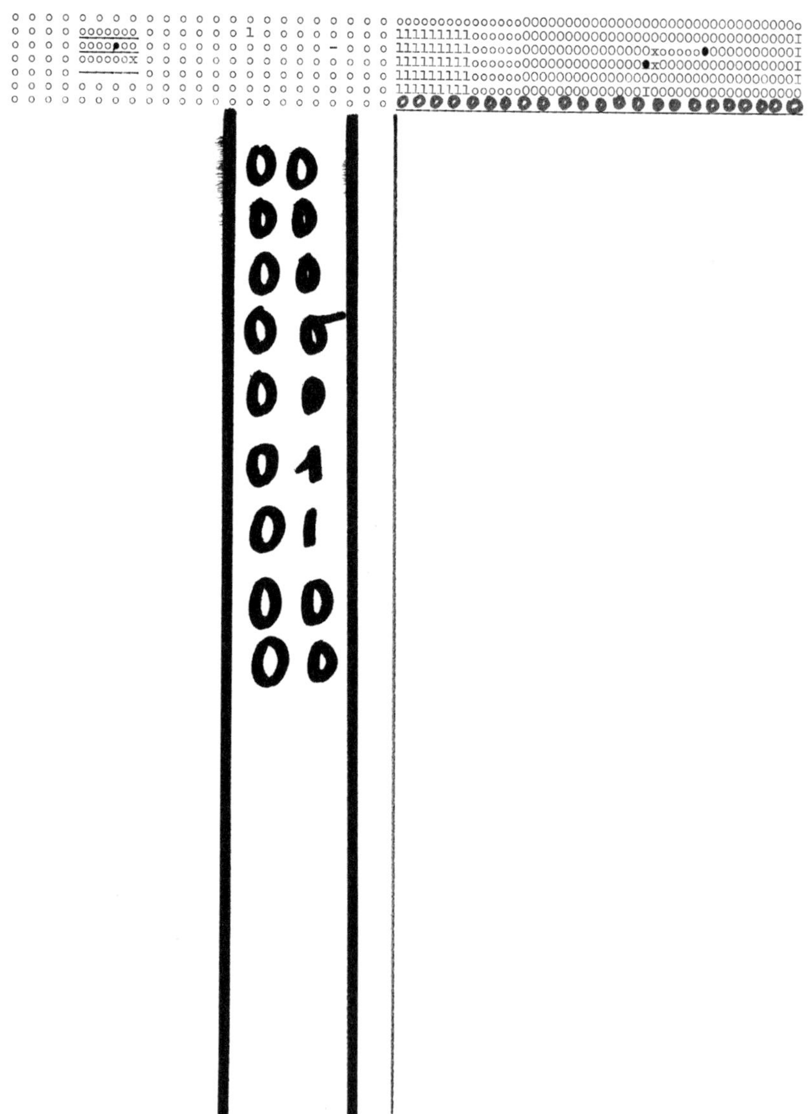

Mary Ellen Solt

MARRIAGE

A code poem derived from the universal language
of signs and symbols used from primitive times
to the present day:
the alphabet
astrology astronomy botany
chemistry commerce engineering
mathematics medicine
meteorology music physics
punctuation runes zoology &c.

◆ *dot:secrecy origin of all signs*

◇ *diamond female anatomical symbol*

♡ *heart*

♡ *composite symbol*

✡ *perfect marriage*

✡ *composite symbol*

L *length (terrestrial) lambert: unit of brightness right angle: meeting of the celestial (vertical) and the terrestrial (horizontal)*

O *oxygen ocean blood type of husband and wife* October (*unofficial*): *husband's birth month*

V *potential energy velocity volume*

E *earth excellent*

LEO *husband's name*

I Pairings

☿ *sun (old oriental symbol) source of all life*

⦶ *active male element saltpeter*

⊖ *passive female element earth (with equator)*
salt element: water

♂ *male male flower*

♀ *female female flower planet Venus*
mirror of Venus

▽ *male element: water*

△ *female wisdom godhead element: fire*

□ *male*

○ *female new moon unborn child God*
eternity element: fire

𝄞 *treble clef*

𝄢 *bass clef*

⊙ *sun open eye of God element: air*

⊕ *earth creation: male plus female*
sun cross element: earth

=○= *equivalent*

△ *finite difference*

⬭ *whole note*

XX *double strength*

=f+m *commutative law*

M—F *male implies female*

F—M *female implies male*

II Conjugations

⚳ *Ceres: goddess of earth's fertility*

♡ *love*

© *copyright*

⇔ *reversible reaction*

F° *degrees of heat warmth*

𝄐 *hold*

♮ *natural*

𝄇 *repeat*

V *up-bow*

Λ *down-bow*

A *first class vessel*

X *kiss the unknown takes (chess)*

∝ *varies as*

→ *give*

℞ *take*

X *reactance*

R *resistance*

☾ *the moon's phases*

⊳— *man & woman united: procreation*

pregnant woman

☆ *the five senses happy homecoming*

III Family

- ⚹ *family: man with wife and children*
- **S** Solt *school sulfur combustible elements*
- **s** *plural stem sire son sister series*
- **'s** *contraction: us is has possessive*
- ᚾ *(rune: nied) necessity thraldom*
- ᛉ *man*
- *woman*
- *woman bears child*
- ☉ *moment of birth: awakening of inner life in body*
- ♎ Libra: *astrological sign of father*
- ♋ Cancer: *astrological sign of mother*
- ♊ Gemini: *astrological sign of daughter*
- ♒ Aquarius: *astrological sign of daughter*
- ♃ *planet Jupiter: name of family cat*
- **Ms.** *female of undefined status: name of family dog*

- ℅ *in care of*
- ; *related and continuing*
- ∩ *intersection: shared in common*
- ⊠ *simple activity*
- *appoggiatura: grace note*
- *unity*

IV Home

- *key*
- *house*
- ᚹ *(rune: wynn) comfort*
- ▣ *orderliness*
- *disorder*
- *chair*
- *frying pan*
- *fork*
- *olive oil*
- *vinegar*
- *water*
- *borax*
- *wood*
- *glass*
- *lime*
- *tree*
- $ *money*
- ℀ *account*
- % *mortgage*
- ᛟ *(rune: ogal) possession*
- *to exorcise evil spirits*

V Relationships

- *Saracen talisman upper half: water triangle kindness gentleness nobility lower half: fire triangle God's fiery rage*
- ☌ *conjunction*
- ☍ *opposition*
- *thunderstorm*
- ⌒ *rainbow*
- 𝄪 *double sharp*
- 𝄫 *double flat*
- □ *openness daylight*
- ■ *concealment darkness night*
- = *equal*
- ≠ *not equal*
- • *dead ends stops*
- , *continuations*
- *lying next to: touching but clear of*
- △ *distance*
- *wave length*
- ÷ *division*
- *talk*
- ∧ *omissions*
- ✳ *afterthoughts*
- *scruples*

VI Moods

- *sign of* Hermes *(modification) love's messages*
- *degrees of feeling*
- → *approaches the limit of*
- ○ *wanting absence*
- ● *rain*
- ⊕ *solar halo*
- / *slashes*
- ⊖ *salt*
- *eye of fire*
- *drifting snow*
- *vitriol*
- *alum*
- *potash*
- *annealing*
- *to break and go on*
- ♂ *planet* Mars *war male*
- ☮ *peace*
- ~ *ice storm silver thaw*
- ‖ *parallels*
- ‡ *double dagger poisonous*
- ⊂ *subset: contained in*

VII Dimensions

⊛ *the double cross: suffering holiness*
outer circle: the finite
inner circle: the infinite eternity

⌘ *the world worldliness nature*

⧖ *hour glass time*

♉ *season: spring*

⋃ *season: summer*

season: autumn

season: winter

♆ *antimony: white metallic element*
brittle lustrous

⊙ *annual plant: renewals*

weathers directions

♓ *life's course: waxing and waning of the moon*

√ *(rune: yr) yew death*

⊠ *multiform activities*

friends

&c *details*

~ *turn: embellishments*

△ *creative intellect*

soul's journey in life: through darkness
towards the light (oriental symbol)

◎ *outer circle: body*
inner circle: mind
center point: soul

∅ *the null: subset of every set*

U *the universe the universal set:*
everything under consideration

VIII Conclusions

⊙ *sunday: the wedding day holy day*

! *strong feelings certainties*

E *vessel fit to take on long voyages:*
items resistant to sea damage only
excellent

♀ *bolus: round mass of medicine*
larger than ordinary pill dose

△ *evergreen plant*

⚓ *anchor*

♄ *azurite lapis lazuli: deep blue stone*

*| *a new world*

✳ *a fixed star*

Amate! Love!

O *identity element: does not change*
what it operates on

$>$ *greater than*

$<$ *less than*

$\ngtr$ *not greater than*

$\nless$ *not less than*

$\pm$ *plus or minus*

$\sqrt{2}$ *irrational*

$\wedge$ *conjunction: both are true*

$\therefore$ *therefore*

$\sum$ *the sum*

∞ *indefinitely great*

Chima Sunada

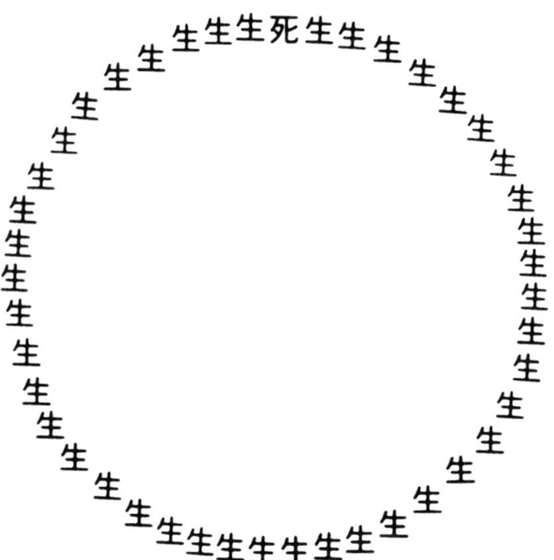

生 = living

死 = death

楽

独 = loneliness
楽 = pleasure
独楽 = top

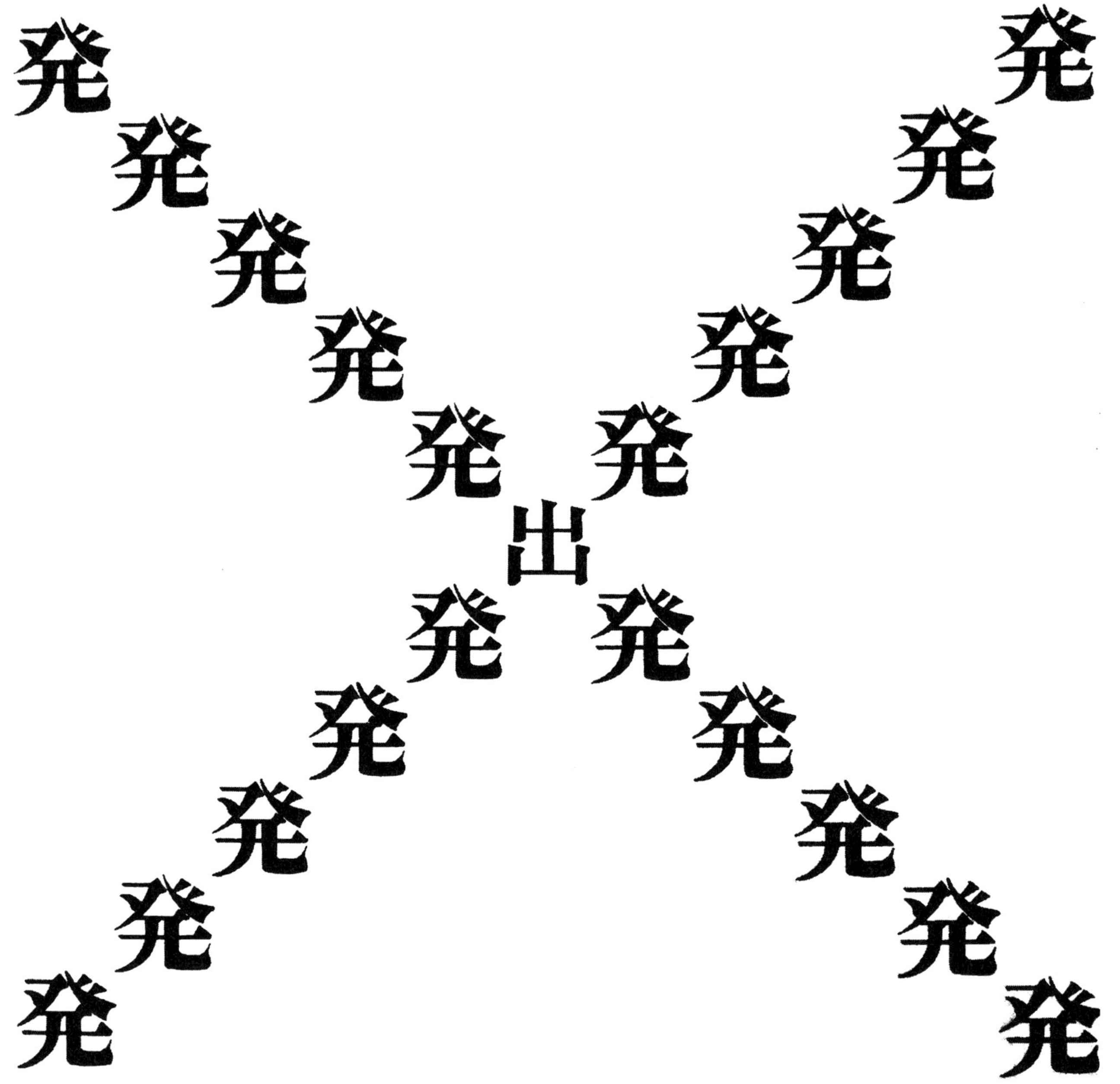
発 発
発 発
発 発
発 発
発 発
出
発 発
発 発
発 発
発 発

Salette Tavares

kinetofonias

TAKITAKI KARDIA

IK IK IK IKIK
A A A KA A
IK IK IK IKIK
IKAA IKAA IKAIK

I TA KAA II
A A A TA AA
TAI KAA TAII
I KA A TA AA IKAI
I TA KAA KA I
I KA A TIAA KA
TI II I TIL TI
IKAI TI I TI A IKI IKIAKA
TI A AKI TAIKI TIKI
I A TI
TI KI TIKI
ITIKI TIKITI A
A KITI ATI KI A
TIKI A I A I IKA A
I A KA I KI A
I A A A
II AA IAIA KI II
AT KAAK I AK AKI A
TT
AK TA IK TI AK
TI A A I KI I
I TA I
A I A I A KI A I A
KI TA TA I KI TA I TI KI A
TA I TA TATA TI
A I TA TI
A TI I KITA KITAKATA
TA TA TA TAKI TIKA
A
A
A KI A KA KITA KI A
TA TI TA
KA
TA TA
TA KIA TTTT TT T
A
TI TA

Ri m ri ri
rur m rur ru
um r mi ri
ri mi mi mu.
Muru ru ru
ru mu mu mi ru
ur mi ru mu ri ri ri
mi ru mi mi ru ru ru
mu ru ru mu ru mu mu
ru.
Um mi mi ri mi ri
i mi ru ri i mi ru
ru mi mi mi ri i u
U. U. U.
I. Ru mi.
Ri ur m ru
im mi ru i
mi rur r mur ur rur i i
ri ri ri ri ri ri ri ri.
Urmi
Urmi
Urmi r r r ur rumi mi ur urri

Irmu irmu irmu rimu
u i mi ru m r r mi u
iui iui iui ii
ii u i u i m ri
u i u i u i u i.

anti telas
anti telas
telas

arranhaço

arrranhisso

arrrranha
arre
arre, arre, arre, arre, arre, arre, arre, arre
arre, arre, arre, arre, arre, arre, arre, arre
arre, arre, arre, arre, arre, arre, arre, arre
arre, arre, arre, arre, arre arre, arre arre arre

Brin
cadeiras

SALETTE TAVARES

é grave,
sério e exige d
e ti grande precau
ção. Podias cumprir f
àcilmente o mandato qu
e te digo, mas tinhas d s
e voltar com cuidado toda ponto
s as dobras das calças q s lumino
ue cost umas disfarçar p sos a bril
ara den tro, abrir as har na somb
algibei ras e sa ra onde penetr
cudir t odos a um raio de sol. e
os rest As papilas liquefaze mpo,
os de c m-se e abrangem com suavi que es
otão qu dade es sas distâncias i tático f
e se ju nacessí veis da peque ica, foto
ntam na nez que circula e grafado por
s fenda m remoi nho uma câmara mui
s das c de um p to antiquada des
osturas onto br coberta dentro do poç
e entre ilhante o onde se abriu mais um
os pont a outro braço d e mina. Os c
os, tir ponto b irculo s bati
ar de e rilhant am sua
ntre os e. As m vement
fios as ãos abr e us u
poeiras em gest sas em
acumula os de c vibraç
das pel ontenta ões mi
os muit mento e croscó
os anos ntre as picas
pendura partícu e ond
dos e, d las de ulaçõ
epois j poeira es su
antar o que can aves,
frio da tam e d poéti
s corre ansam n cas e
ntes de o rodop sedos
ar que io mai as. O
pudesse s inte movim
m circu nso e e ento c
lar naq stonte apila
uelas d ante c r das
irecçõe ada ve decor
s. Jant z que q ações
ar é o t ualque subia
ermo gr r bris brusc
osseiro a pert o e o
para di urba a venda
zer ràp quela val i
idament tranqu nteri
e aquel ilidad or ro
a obser e abso mpia
vação d luta i cada
e decan ntocáv célul
tar sàb el e m a de d
iamente armore entro
todos o a do t para

se nada ex istisse ci nda que pud desse simu lar qualqu er gesto de respiração.

FerrrrrrrrrrrrrrrrrrrrrrrrrrrrrrRugem

Fónica fonte **fraga**
fértil feitiço
faúla fluvial **fusível fuste:**
farpa faca **fabril**
filtro fusíl,
flávia flauta **faminta**
feminal
felina força.

fui
fui-se

fuma -me
foma -me
femea-me

Fugaz febril
furor fonte frágil frente face
fantástico ficar fronte fulgor
fenda fina foice flor

facheta*
fachinho
Facho

falangeta
falanginha
Falange

*Onde se lê fachinho pode ler-se fachinho. Onde se lê facheta pode ler-se fascista, fadista, ou fumista.

Flor frol flor
fan tástico flor
ful

f
alo fá-lo

Fffffffffffff.......dor

PÓ PÓ PÓ-PÓ PÓ PÓ PÓ-PÓ PÓ PÓ PÓ-PÓ PÓ PÓ PÓ-PÓ PÓ PÓ PÓ-PÓ PÓ PÓ PÓ-PÓ PÓ PÓ PO

pa / la par ti / sse	la / sse par pa / ti	sse / ti par la / pa	ti / pa par sse / la	pa / la par ti / sse	la / sse par pa / ti	sse / ti par la / pa	ti / pa par sse / la
ti / pa la sse / par	pa / par la ti / sse	par / sse la pa / ti	sse / ti la par / pa	ti / pa la sse / par	pa / par la ti / sse	par / sse la pa / ti	sse / ti la par / pa
sse / ti pa par / la	ti / la pa sse / par	la / par pa ti / sse	par / sse pa la / ti	sse / ti pa par / la	ti / la pa sse / par	la / par pa ti / sse	par / sse pa la / ti
par / sse ti la / pa	sse / pa ti par / la	pa / la ti sse / par	la / par ti pa / sse	par / sse ti la / pa	sse / pa ti par / la	pa / la ti sse / par	la / par ti pa / sse
la / par sse pa / ti	par / ti sse la / pa	ti / pa sse par / la	pa / la sse ti / par	la / par sse oa / ti	par / ti sse la / pa	ti / pa sse par / la	pa / la sse ti / pa

pa —— la —— sse ——
la par ti——sse par pa——ti par la——pa p
sse ti pa
ti pa par s
pa la sse——par la ti——sse la pa——ti l
par sse ti
sse ti la
ti pa par——la pa sse——par pa ti——sse
la par sse
par sse pa
sse ti la——pa ti par——la ti sse——pa
pa la par s
la par ti
par sse pa——ti sse la——pa sse par——la s
ti —— pa —— la —— p

COMPOSIÇÃO ALIATORIA

Pa la sse ti , Laparti ! Ssi parpasse passe tilaparti palasse ti , lapar . Tisse parpoti la re par , ssı latar palatipar , lisse palasse la parti parti parlarpa a. Pressa
ali perlara pssapsse pssapssa tipsalaar pertreti a par. Plia sse pli tra al tipasse perli, li par pla esseripri la sseri prata. Plissapa ssipaletissi. Prissa la pli, malapi ssi ssal
plira letissela per aliplipraplessi. Ir la i parpir li pirpar la par la pir riparssa parli pi isselarpar ralissati. Ra ri tassila i ass parpasse tesse i pesse lasse lassi i ass aprassi. Press resse pressi, sse i ssi ressi, laparsi issrali. Sserla per arler rari irler pa
Talapass a essil presla relapassi laperi tal. Lissali. Assali al. Less pilal reptil, less assal el parlapater til ssalil parpa arpassiter, retrissel el al il ssassel a pitera. La patessi palati el tapali arli. Per le ssati pila essapera lepi iletilar parssipi. Pal a tepeli
essi. Issel petala i a sse assapati ssepra ta tt a pra. Ara ala triparla i, rala ia e ia aa. Triplissili i a la i ta i ssassa ssassi assi. Li a la a. Par sse ti par sse la te parla. Tisse par la . Sse la parti par sse tisse par lar sse parpasse i a tirpasse Ssela sse lasse ssi
patiressasse lpaisse la passela. Lasse ti, tipa la par . La parti sse par parpasse ti la par sse pa ti palati . Il isse esse lassisse ssesse. Issesse il ipsa ssit ssissat et sseti la prilisseta ssata pata ssita pita pitassita ata ita pritaprata plata tissa letalissa ataissa. Tra
preta lata ata ata essa treta treta essa. Essa lessa lissa issa assa essa pressa prissa. Rassarassa reta lissa passa pressa sserta essa. Sseta. Ilatali perla i , e a ii per tala ti se tala te, ti ta la par pa ti sse. El ar sse passe , etssetera, etssetera. A te sse lasse pa

LEMBRA-TE, Ó HOMEM, QUE ÉS
E
EM
TE HAS-DE TORNAR
PO'
PÓ-PÓ
AL GAR ISMOS ALFINETE
Alcantaril alfenim
alticolúnio álamo
albirrubro Alcorão
altifalante alvor
aldeído
alvorário Ali
alterniflório
algibe alcool
alga alforria
além alfa
alibi
alternipétaloAlvaroAlberto
alfaraz
alfaqui
alfim.
Albicórnea Alcião
algaraz alcova
alguém
almo alguidar
almofadilha alperce
alma alfinete
algum
algures alforreca
almóço.
Alvarral Alvarral
Almagiste aljofar.
algoz algibeira altar alterna.
almoxarife algema
Alvissaras Almirante
Esquema Algoritmo para a leitura monotona dos poemas da página anterior, de 1 a 5 de 5 a 1.
BRINCADE
BRINCADE
BRINCADE
BRINCADE
BRINCADE
BRINCADE
BRINCADE
BRINCADE
BRINCADE
BRINCADE
BRINCADE
BRINCADE
BRINCADE
IRAS
IRAS
IRAS
IRAS
SALETTE
IRRAS TAVARES
IRRAS
IRRAS
IRRAS
IRRRRRAS
IRRRRRAS
IRRRRRAS
IRRRRRAS
BIRRRRRRRRRAS
BIRRRRRRRRRAS
BIRRRRRRRRRAS
BIRRRRRRRRRAS
BIRRRRRRRRRAS
BIRRRRRRRRRAS

Colleen Thibaudeau

0
is
this
a b e l l
enough bell
no
?

BELL

H
E
S
H
O
O
T
S c o r e s .

THE HOCKEY STICK

.
. a .
. bal l i s .
. all round as .
.sound of bound.
.and rebound.
.is ll as.
. a .
.

BALL

a s
b i g a s
ball as round
as sun . . . I tug
and pull you when
you run and when
w i n d b l o w s I
s a y p o l i t e
ly
H
O
L
D
M
E
T
I
G
H
T
L
Y.

BALLOON

0 o . .
0

first the
engine
rushes along

then the
coal
car comes

r- r- r- r- r- r- r- r- r- r- r- r- r- r- r- r

TI

nker   *clank boxcar*   *little red*
rolls   *clank boxcar*   &   *caboose*

r- r- r- r- r- r- r- r- r- r- r- r- r- r- r- *

IN

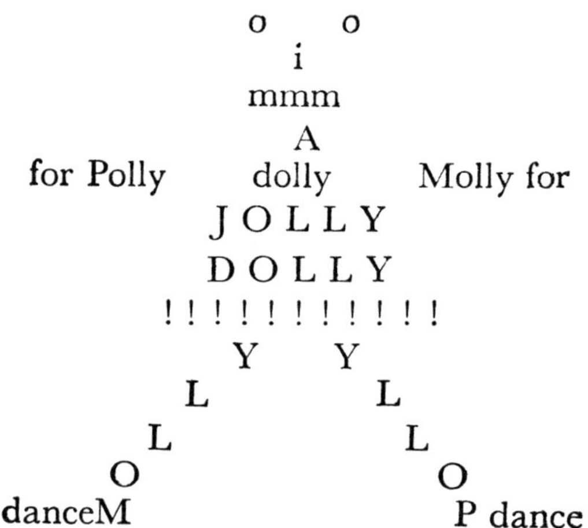
o o
i
mmm
A
for Polly dolly Molly for
J O L L Y
D O L L Y
! ! ! ! ! ! ! ! ! ! !
Y Y
L L
L L
O O
danceM P dance

DOLLY

some faces

wear

BIG SMILES

!

some faces

wear

F O
R WN
S

TWO FACES

o O o O o
a c r o w n h a s
0 points & pearls 0
* . some for boys . *
O 0 some for girls 0 O
!o!o!o!o!o!o!o!o!

A CROWN

WHAT
is the
mostimp't DUMP!
mostimp't
mostimp't
thing about a dump truck
?   ?

DUMP TRUCK

I
AM A
TINY
SPINNING TOP
NOW IN A RHYME
HOW CAN I STOP
? ? ? ? ? ? ? ?
? ? ? ? ? ? ? ? ?
? ? ?
?

THE TOP

o
!
a can
dle is
bright
it's
hot
tho'
¬
for you
nor
for me—
Just to See!

CANDLE

Biljana Tomić

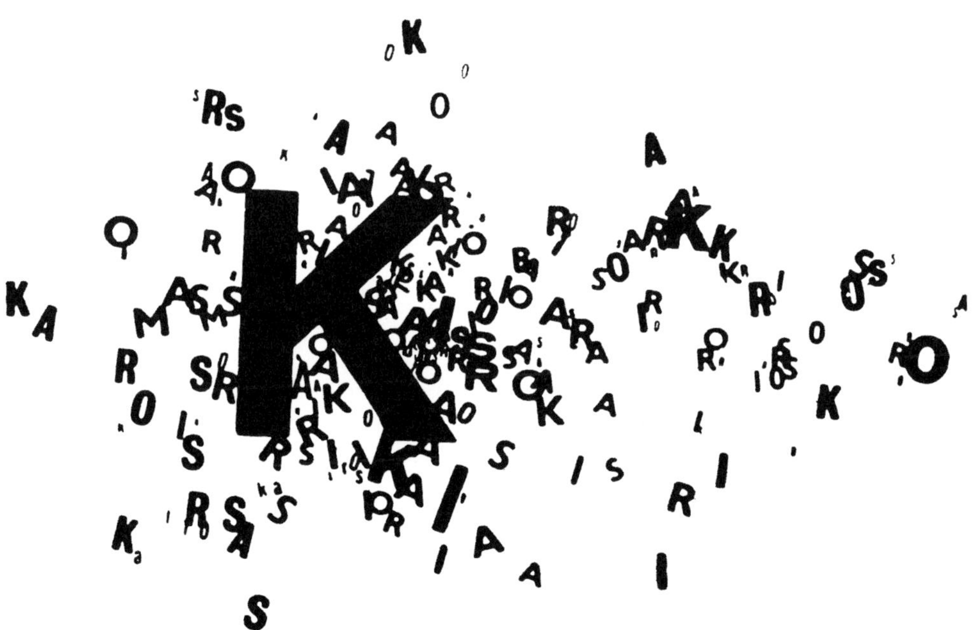

Silvia Trevale

Patrizia Vicinelli

PATRIZIA VICINELLI

à, a. A,

per un grosso cane
affinché

virgilio   letterato enorme incipiente dona
qualunque tipo di affare ma serio al
figlio del tuo viaggio al figlio dentro
l'unico possibile la scelta barocca
sincero   virgilio   l'aggettivo é   sincero
mi hai causato macerie le certe
le certe macerie già ritrovabili idratate
di arezzo urbino assisi   dove piccione
l'esistente s'é fatto gallo per me
e l'ho salutato come voleva l'antico
di piume ancestrali   da allora certamente ho
la continuazione a un pallore primario
mi hai causato macerie le certe
io ti amo le certe macerie già ritrovabili idratate

l'imagine del   in un notturno
come   pianto
sovrapposta al tempo   quando
non c'era   insomma
sarebbe avuto il meglio se
i fatti dell'argomento non devono
produrre
il costume; il costume ?   i costumi

non devono produrre. certo una cara
fattività   dove non distinguo
commedia
da ciò che
mi compone da
ciò che compone
il meglio
per volersi tenere mi tiene il grigio hai
sparso incenso

troppo profumato hai sparso e io ti amo
troppo profumato incenso io ti amo
sparso

i costumi = in senso greco - maschera tragica
il costume = in senso latino
il costume = come maschera

HAI SPARSO SORRISO E IO
SONO VIRGOLA
CAPIRANNO LORO DI FRANCESCO
CHE NON CI SONO MIRTI
NON CAMPI
MA LETTERE DI TENEREZZA
ASSOPITE
DA SCALDARE DA SMEMBRARE
CHE NON SONO CASE LE UGUALI   MA PIETRE LE
GINESTRE VERDI
NEL SOLE
DI ABBANDONO
AI TEMPI SCONTRATI
SOLOMIDISTINGUEALSENTIMENTO   solo mi distingue
QUELLAMORTEDIFLEBASILFENICIO   al sentimento
quella morte di
flebas il fenicio
DISCORRERO' PER ACQUA FINO ALL'INCONTRO FINO
ALL'ACQUA DISCORRERO' NELL'ACQUA IO MI GIUNGO NELL'ERBA E LE GINOCCHIA
HANNO VERDE LE GINESTRE ADESSO HANNO VERDE
CAPIRANNO L'INVOLUCRO CHE TI TIENE
D' ARGILLA?

LERICI
POESIA

piccolo da

əEll tTOO

le mortal

l mort le

p

âle mortale

tal e

scambiatto

PROVA !

QO

ME?

J

!DE AAĀA A

əs se

f

O

F ss

Oss

eee eee

CEL

JAG . ce t ce tTENUI *te*

3aNkiglIja

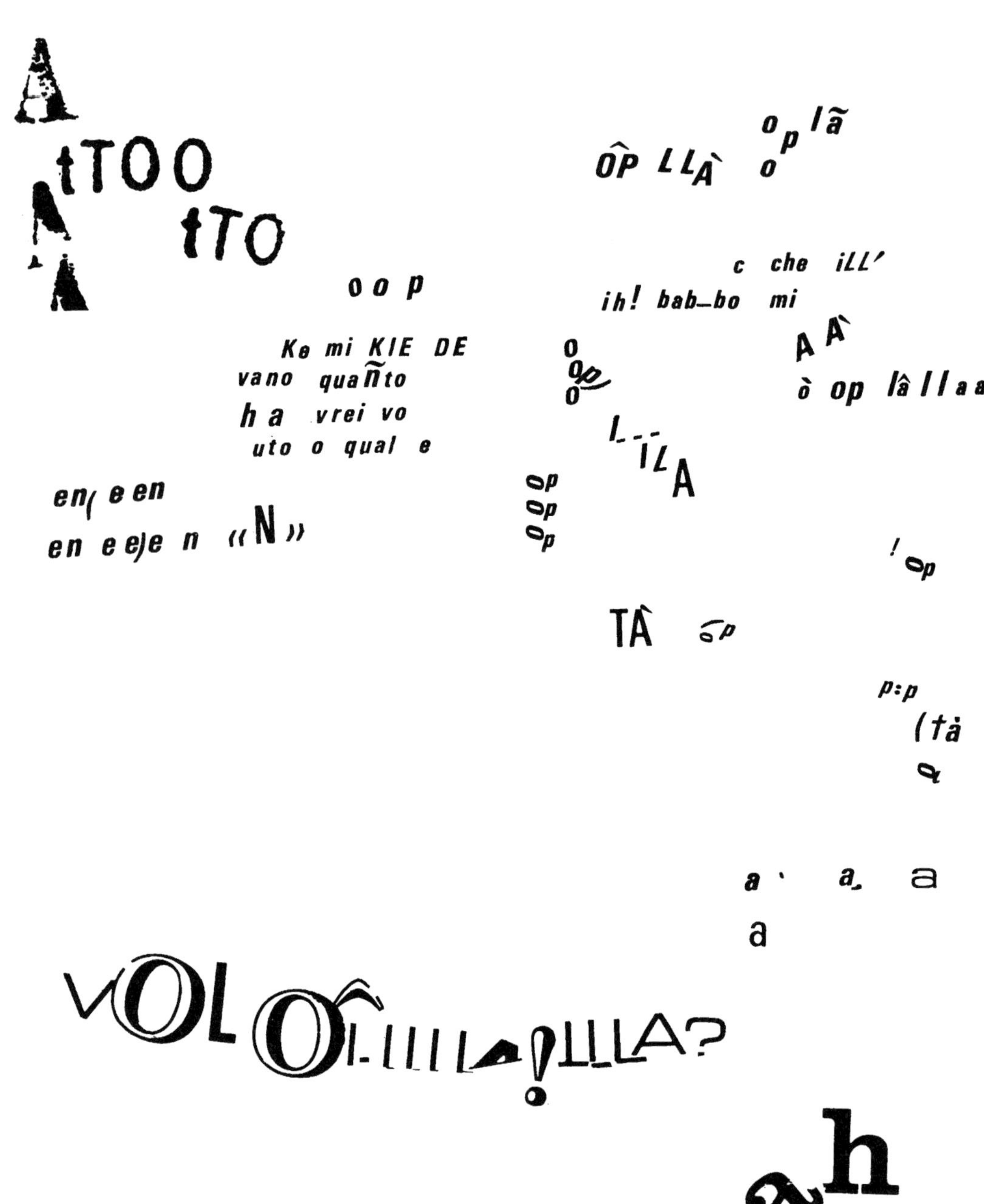
A
tTOO
A tTO
A
o o p
ÔP LLÀ
o p lã
c che iLL'
ih! bab–bo mi
Ke mi KIE DE
vano quañto
h a vrei vo
uto o qual e
AÀ
ò op lâ l l a a
ILA
en(e en
en e eje n «N»
! op
TÀ
p:p
(tà
a a a
a
VOLOILLLA!LLLA?
kah

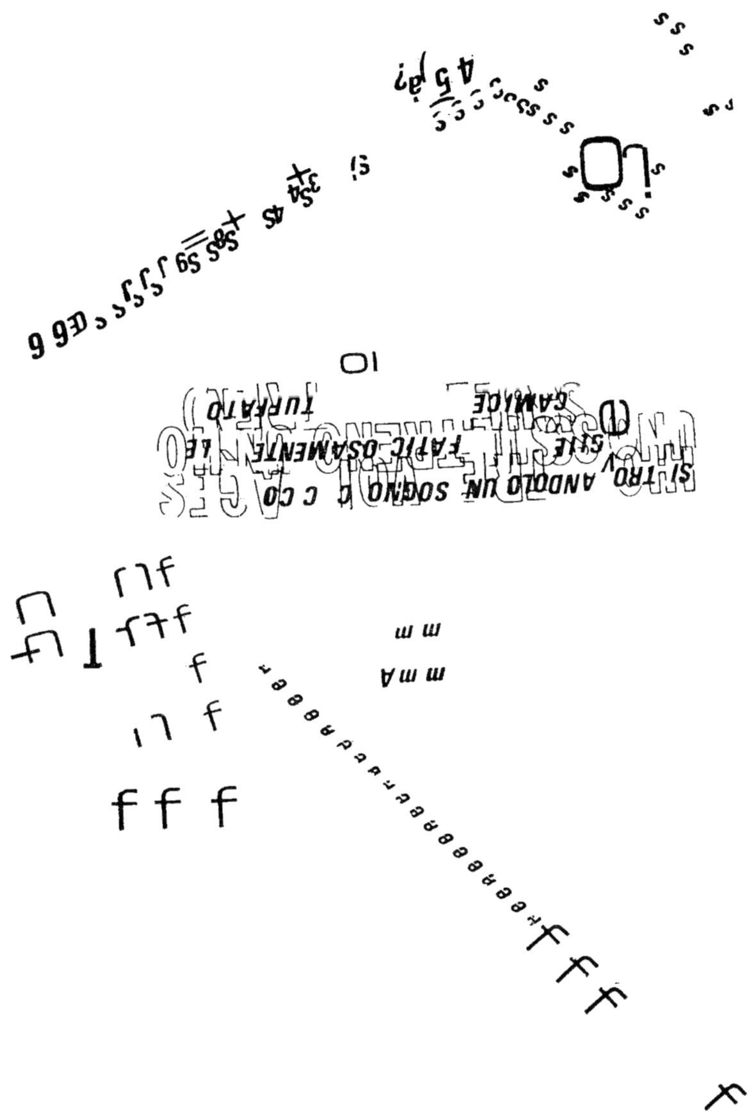
SI TROVANDOLO UN SOGNO C C CO
STILE FATICOSAMENTE LE
CAMICE TUFFATO
IO

Rosmarie Waldrop

A SERENADE AND REQUIEM FOR PUBLIC FIGURES PLAYING PRIVATE PARTS

In the crowded days of summer
A white swan swam to the shore and died
In the weeds by the moving river,
Where I have seen the swans glide
So smoothly over the sunlit water
I almost thought they had no legs for walking,
Until one day I saw one stride
(Waddle would be the better word)
Its then ungainly big fat ass
Over the closely clipped grass,
Down the path to the rose bushes
To poke its smooth orange beak
Into a large black turd.

Then I thought of you, Leda,
And the maker of you,
And how I make songs and am made by songs,
Sung for the viscious and voiceless swans,
For the great white feathery swans
That die in the weeds by the moving river
In the crowded days of dying summer,
And how now I know
I shall never get to know you.

A SERENADE AND REQUIEM
In the crowded days of dying summer,
And how now I know you.
I shall never get to know you.

to this:
believed
Judas kiss
settle all,
clothing;
of Defoe,
Crusoe.

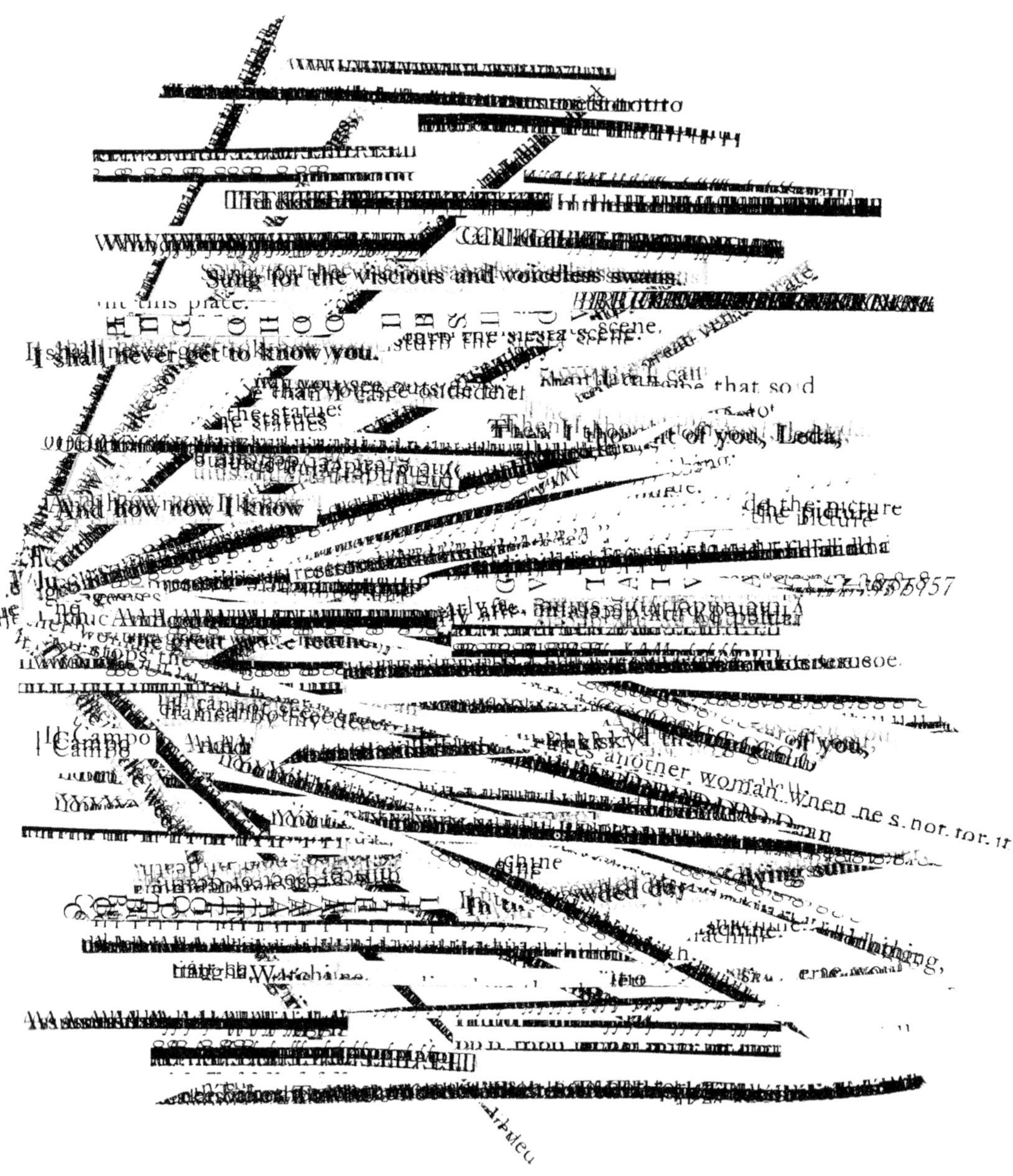
Sing for the viscious and voiceless swans.
I shall never get to know you.
Then I thought of you, Leda,
And now now I know
the picture

Hannah Weiner

RPJ Want Men

RJE	man
DWS	alderman
GVL	boatman
IFD	cattleman
TUO	chairman
ITX	clergyman, parson or minister
MDK	have you men enough?
NAB	fireman
NBS	fisherman
NJX	foreman
OTR	helmsman
RKI	how many men?
QIB	landsman
QJL	leadsman
QPJ	liberty man
RAE	look-out man look out!
NSX	he, or she is full of men
RPH	newly raised man
SIT	nobleman
TQO	postman
UXF	rifleman
VLG	seaman
WDH	signalman
YZM	tradesman
YWH	waterman
ZIA	workman
MDK	have you men enough?
RPJ	want men
RPK	your men

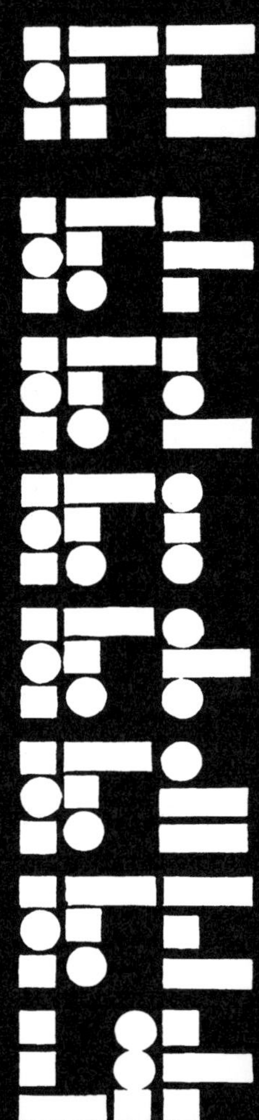

CHW	Pirates
CJD	I was plundered by a pirate
CJF	Describe the pirate
CJN	She is armed
CJP	How is she armed?
CJS	She has long guns
CJW	I have no long guns
BLD	I am a complete wreck

Ruth Wolf-Rehfeldt

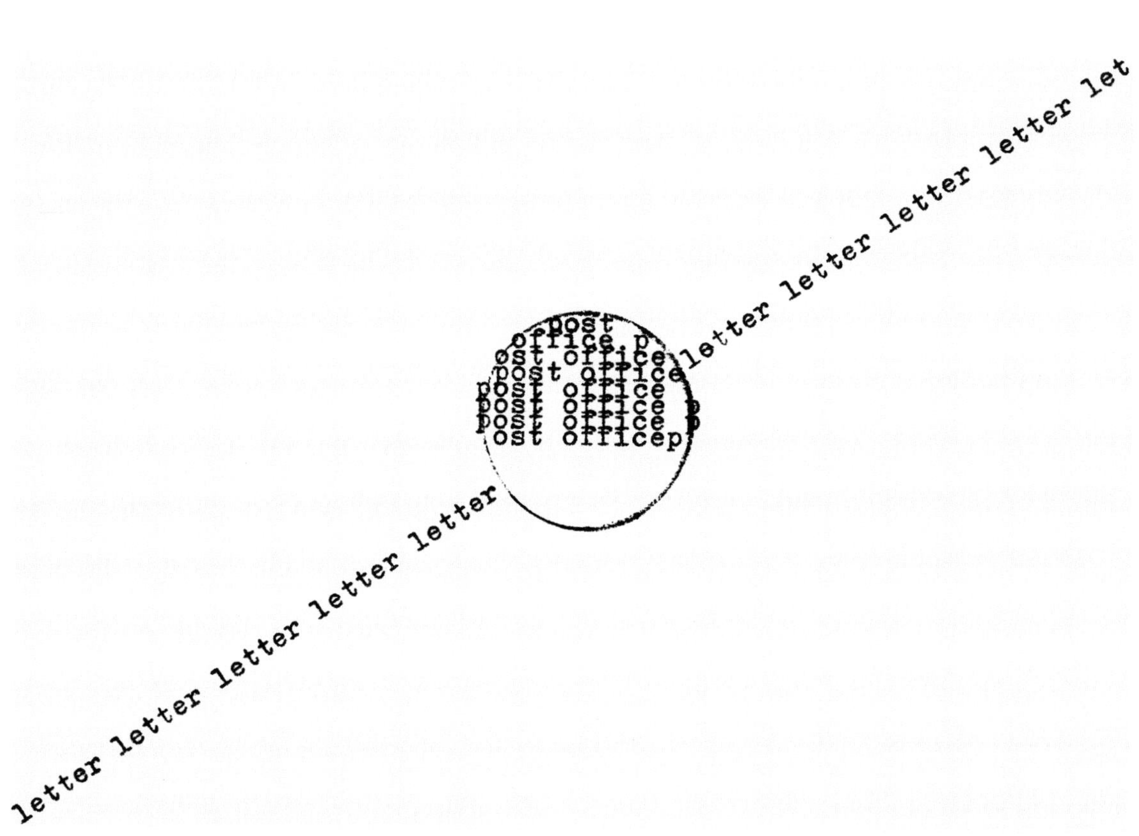
post
office p
ost office
post office
post office
post office p
post office p
ost officep
letter letter letter letter letter
letter letter letter letter let

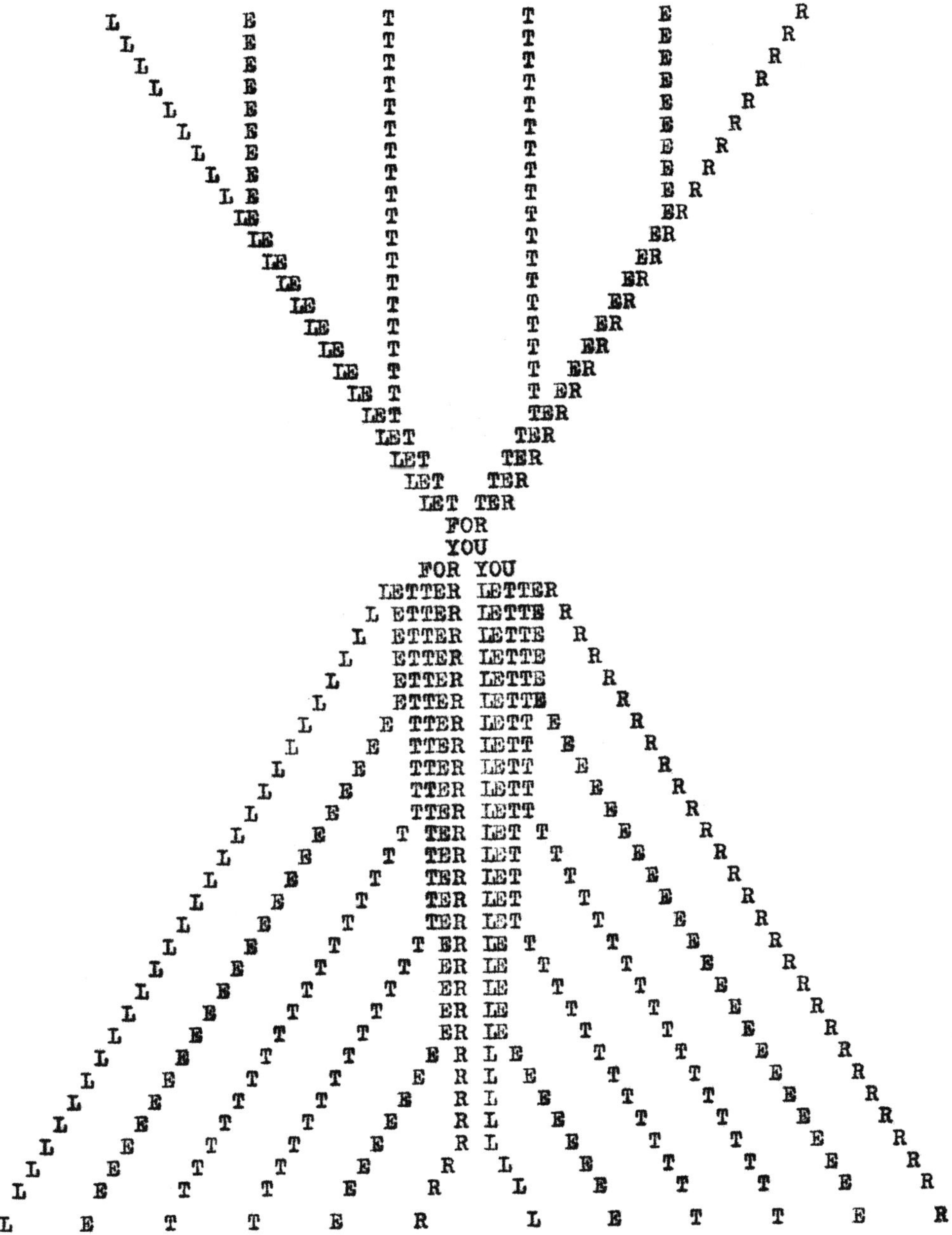
LET TER
FOR
YOU
FOR YOU
LETTER LETTER

TOTOTOTOTOTOTOTOTOTOTOTOTOTOTOTOTOTOTOTOTOTOTOTOTOTOTOTOTOTO
TOTOTOTOTOTOTOTOTOTOTOTOTOTOTOTOTOTOTOTOTOTOTOTOTOTOTOTOTOTO
TOTO   TOTOTOTOTOTOTO   TO   TO   TOTO
TOTO   TOTOTOTOTOTOTO   TO   TO   TOTO
TOTO   TOTOTOTOTOTOTO   TO   TO   TOTO
TOTOTOTOTOTOTOTOTOTOTOTOTOTOTO   TO   TO   TOTO
TOTOTOTOTOTOTOTOTOTOTOTOTOTOTO   TO   TO   TOTO
TOTOTOTOTOTOTOTOTOTOTOTOTOTOTO   TO   TOTOTOTOTOTO
TOTOTOTOTOTOTOTOTOTOTOTOTOTOTOTOTOTOTOTOTOTOTOTOTOTOTOTOTOTO
TOTOTOTOTOTOTOTOTOTOTOTOTOTOTOTOTOTOTOTOTOTOTOTOTOTOTOTOTOTO
TOTOTOTOTOTOTOTOTO   TOTOTOTOTOTOTOTOTOTOTOTOTOTOTOTOTOTOTO
TOTOTOTOTOTOTOTOTOTOTOTOTOTOTOTOTOTOTOTOTOTOTOTOTOTOTOTOTOTO
TOTOTOTOTOTOTOTOTO   TOTOTOTOTOTOTOTOTOTOTO
TOTOTOTOTOTOTOTOTOTOTOTOTOTOTOTOTOTOTOTOTOTOTOTOTOTOTOTOTOTO
TOTOTOTOTOTOTOTOTO   TOTOTOTOTOTOTOTOTOTOTOTOTO
TOTOTOTOTOTOTOTOTOTOTOTOTOTOTOTOTOTOTOTOTOTOTOTOTOTOTOTOTOTO
TOTOTOTOTOTOTOTOTO   TOTOTOTOTOTOTOTO
TOTOTOTOTOTOTOTOTOTOTOTOTOTOTOTOTOTOTOTOTOTOTOTOTOTOTOTOTOTO
TOTOTOTOTOTOTOTOTO   TOTOTOTOTOTOTOTO
TOTOTOTO TOTOTOTOTOTOTOTOTOTOTOTOTOTOTOTOTOTOTOTOTOTOTOTOTO
TOTOTO   TOTOTO   TOTOTOTOTOTOTOTOTOTOTO
TOTO   TOTOTOTOTOTOTOTOTOTOTOTOTOTOTOTOTOTOTOTOTOTOTO
TOTOTOTOTOTOTOTOTOTOTOTOTOTOTOTOTOTOTOTOTOTOTOTOTOTOTOTOTOTO
TOTOTOTOTOTOTOTOTOTOTOTOTOTOTOTOTOTOTOTOTOTOTOTOTOTOTOTOTOTO
TOTOTOTOTOTOTOTOTOTOTOTOTOTOTOTOTOTOTOTOTOTOTOTOTOTOTOTOTOTO

FROMFROMFROMFROMFROMFROMFROMFROMFROMFROMFROMFROMFROMFROMFROM
  FROMFROMFROMFROMFROMFROMFROMFROMFROMFROMFROMFROMFROMFROM
FR FROMFROMFROMFROMFROMFROMFROMFROMFROMFROMFROMFROMFROM OM
FROM FROMFROMFROMFROMFROMFROMFROMFROMFROMFROMFROMFROM FROM
FROMFR FROMFROMFROMFROMFROMFROMFROMFROMFROMFROMFROM OMFROM
FROMFROM FROMFROMFROMFROMFROMFROMFROMFROMFROMFROM FROMFROM
FROMFROMFR FROMFROMFROMFROMFROMFROMFROMFROMFROM FROMFROMOM
FROMFROMFROM FROMFROMFROMFROMFROMFROMFROMFROM FROMFROMFROM
FROMFROMFROMFR FROMFROMFROMFROMFROMFROMFROM OMFROMFROMFROM
FROMFROMFROMFROM FROMFROMFROMFROMFROMFROM FROMFROMFROMFROM
FROMFROMFROMFROMFR FROMFROMFROMFROMFROM OMFROMFROMFROMFROM
FROMFROMFROMFROMFROM FROMFROMFROMFROM FROMFROMFROMFROMFROM
FROMFROMFROMFROMFROMFR FROMFROMFROM OMFROMFROMFROMFROMFROM
FROMFROMFROMFROMFROM FR FROMFROM OM FROMFROMFROMFROMFROM
FROMFROMFROMFROMFR FROMFR FROM OMFROM OMFROMFROMFROMFROM
FROMFROMFROMFROM FROMFROMFR   OMFROMFROM FROMFROMFROMFROM
FROMFROMFROMFR FROMFROMFROMFROMFROMFROMFROM OMFROMFROMFROM
FROMFROMFROM FROMFROMFROMFROMFROMFROMFROMFROM FROMFROMFROM
FROMFROMFR FROMFROMFROMFROMFROMFROMFROMFROMFROM OMFROMFROM
FROMFROM FROMFROMFROMFROMFROMFROMFROMFROMFROMFROM FROMFROM
FROMFR FROMFROMFROMFROMFROMFROMFROMFROMFROMFROMFROM OMFROM
FROM FROMFROMFROMFROMFROMFROMFROMFROMFROMFROMFROMFROM FROM
FR FROMFROMFROMFROMFROMFROMFROMFROMFROMFROMFROMFROMFROM OM
  FROMFROMFROMFROMFROMFROMFROMFROMFROMFROMFROMFROMFROMFROM
FROMFROMFROMFROMFROMFROMFROMFROMFROMFROMFROMFROMFROMFROMFROM

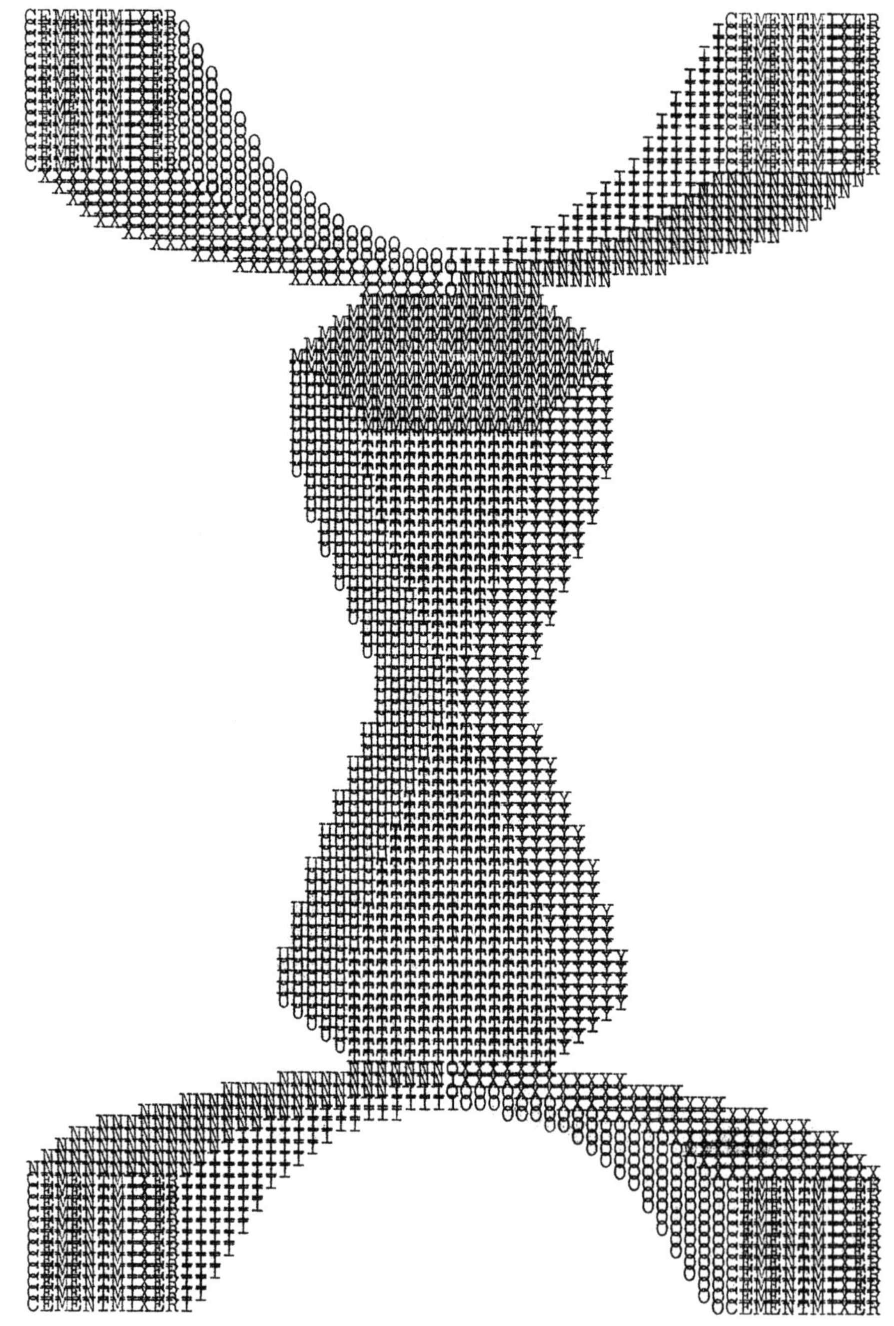
CEMENTMIXER
CEMENTMIXER
CEMENTMIXERI
OCEMENTMIXER

Translations

SONJA ÅKESSON

Neeijj **(Naayy)**

nej: no

LENORA DE BARROS

Translated by Mónica de la Torre and Lenora de Barros

From *Onde se vê* (Where One Sees)

ri–chora: laughs–cries

RUINDOORUÍDO: RUININGTHERUMOR

ANNALISA ALLOATTI

***Monumento* | *Monument*, with Mirella Bentivoglio**

The "monument" is visualized with the letters of the Italian word itself ("monumento") through the verbal suggestions contained within it: "nume" (=godlike); "me non tu" (=me not you); "mento" [*sic*; should be "muto"] (=I am mutating); "temo" (=I fear). It is a structure of transformation: the monument recognizes its non-communicative nature; it doubts; it falls; it mutates; it fears change; it becomes pure rhythm.

—Mirella Bentivoglio, in *Pages: Mirella Bentivoglio, Selected Works 1966–2012*

MIRELLA BENTIVOGLIO

Translated by Stefania Heim

Ciclo* | *Cycle

E=Congiunzione* | *And=Conjunction

Interlocking *and*'s

Gabbia (Ho)* | *Cage (I Have)

I have

L'assente* | *The Absentee

The

Numero e parola non corrispondenza* | *Number and Word Non-correspondence

The numbers squared form a triangle

Vuoto al centro* | *Hollow at the Center

amore: love
a chi: to whom

AMANDA BERENGUER

Translated by Mónica de la Torre

Selections from *Composición de lugar* (Composition of Place)

Sunset over Sea, Friday, March 3, 1972

A hovering multitude
facing the light
drags within its folds
horses cars birds sailboats
warped by the storm
how much light is left?
how much of day?
they pass over the weathered
skin of the sea, they walk on it
overcast drawn
by the precise clarity
where arrows descend
seconds of life
imminent night approaches
yet all resembles dawn
we watch the singular light
and stay in it.

A Hovering Multitude

dazzle: to receive the day in awe

astonishment: to enter the shade in a stupor

dazzle = beginning

astonishment = end

velocity = dawn + sunset / life

dazzle > astonishment

∞ of light = (dazzle – astonishment) velocity

Note

s = v . t

v = s/t

space = dawn + sunset
time = life
velocity = anticipation, awaiting the future

—

tormenta: storm
pájaros: birds
veleros: sailboats
pliegues: folds
multitud: multitude
luz: light
bajan flechas: arrows descend
segundos de vida: seconds of life
caballos: horses
coches: cars
atormenta: it torments

Sunset over Sea, Saturday, March 4, 1972

The fire spreads
the cold resplendent from the calm
of a state of mind
behind the intact sea
a drab scaly animal
all etched in steel
final border of the day's daytime
the initial fires dissipated
the bulbs the flashes
the sky shouting
visionary chants
a fixed total idea dazzles
naked incombustible
nailing the exact radiance
at the edge where
what we ignore begins.

The Fire Spreads

I burn

arc
zero
border

route
final

edge

begin

branches

branches

branches

[Translator's note: The last line in "Poniente sobre el mar del sábado 4 de marzo de 1972" (Sunset over Sea, Saturday, March 4, 1972), the poem that this translation was derived from, ends with the word *ignoramos* ("we ignore"), which contains *ramos*. *Ramos* can mean "branches" or "bouquets." I opted for "branches" given the theme of propagation in the poem's first line.]

—

mar: sea
pardo: drab
animal: animal
escamoso: scaly
grabado: etched
frontera: border / frontier
última: final / last
linde: edge / limit
comienza: begins
lo que ignoramos: what we ignore
donde: where

Sunset over Sea, Thursday, January 10, 1974

Oh! hypocrite old man, unbridled sea
your foam a full set of tricks
rabid
over your fiery pupil
in the yellow clarity
a sleep-deprived pupil
descending whole
to the braids snakes
gone mad from the choppy waters
the sun is all logic
the sea all madness
and they will meet there
in the horizontal denouncement
now reddened by fury
and conceit
and light will pass
behind the annihilation
and the surviving light will stay
singular in the somber beyond.

Oh! Hypocrite Old Man, Unbridled Sea

was

scale

fire tray water tray

the pointer indicates

beheaded chimera

—

sol: sun
todo: all
lógica: logic

AND THEY WILL MEET HERE IN THE HORIZONTAL DENOUNCEMENT
NOW REDDENED BY FURY

mar todo locura: sea all madness
mato: killed / I kill

SUZANNE BERNARD

Translated by Alex Balgiu

Selections from *Poèmes*

p. 64
lentement: slowly
le temps: time
s'égoutte: drains
silence: silence
solitude: solitude

p. 65
espace: space

p. 66
est: is
tombe: falls / grave
lourde: heavy
sur: on
la: the
rue: street
mort: dead / death

p. 67
ce: this
pendant: during / for
cependant: however

ALISON BIELSKI

Translated by Mónica de la Torre

p. 77
1. lupine
2. snowdrop
3. water lily
4. violet

TOMASO BINGA

Translated by Stefania Heim

From the *Dattilocodice* series (Typecode series) (1978)

p. 82

[circle text]

[vertical] who pays for drinks

[horizontal] today i pay

[cascading text]

gimme a drop
another drop
body of bacchus
i want to throw back
nectar
at the table
with the gods
crushed
grape clusters in vats
drink all of you
this IS
my blood
and he swigged
his wee
chalice
in one gulp
then
attacked
the bottle
today
I
pay

p. 83

i am
there there there there there
i am
Li llith
am coeval
and not co-Eve
from Adam to amo
i pass
manufactured clayey
airy breath
i am
earth-air-fire

(possessedearth) (stagnantair) (encagedfire)
))))))NOOOOOOOOOOO((((((

in the woods
upon the sea
inside the sky
alive-living
i am
there there there there there
i am
li berated
i am
Li llith

p. 84

i need
a new house
i need
a bed and four chairs
i need
an empty dresser
i need
few pots in the kitchen
i need
a life without memories

MARIANNA BOCIAN

Translated by Elka Krajewska

Droga do Raju, droga do Nieba, droga do Ziemi, droga do Rozumu | Road to Paradise, Road to Heaven, Road to Earth, Road to Wisdom

[Translator's note: Within the image, *TO* is capitalized, so the image-text reads:

road TO paradise
road TO heaven
road TO earth
road TO wisdom
Perhaps a more precise way to write the title, then, would be:
road TO paradise, road TO heaven, road TO earth, road TO wisdom]

Początek i Koniec | Beginning and End

BLANCA CALPARSORO

Translated by Alex Balgiu

Selections from *Collages*

—

exemplaire: copy / specimen / exemplary

—

Sexus: Sexus
domaine du délire: domain of delirium

—

soleil: sun
complexe: complex
musique: music

—

l'univers archaïque: the archaic universe

—

d'enfants: (of) children / children / children's

—

le beau: beauty
entre passé et avenir: between past and future

—

je reviens: I return
du: from

—

paradis: paradise

—

festival: festival
révolutionnaire: revolutionary

BETTY DANON

Punto Linea (Point Line)

MIRTHA DERMISACHE

Diario No. 1 Año 1 | *Newspaper No. 1 Year 1*

ILSE GARNIER

Translated by Alex Balgiu

Selections from *Blason du corps féminin* (The Female Body's Coat of Arms)

—

corps absent: absent body

—

corps interdit: prohibited body

—

corps soleil: sun body

—

corps administré: administered body

—

corps végétal: plant body

—

corps pollen: pollen body
corps oublié: forgotten body

—

corps ailé: winged body

—

corps délire: delirium body

—

corps proie: prey body

—

corps flottant: floating body

ANNA BELLA GEIGER

Translated by Anna Bella Geiger and Hilary Kaplan

***O novo atlas* (The New Atlas)**

For *O novo atlas 1* and *O novo atlas 2* (xeroxed and silk-screened), her artist books from 1977, Anna Bella Geiger manipulates the text *O espaço social da arte* (The Social Space of Art), which was originally published in the newspaper *Semanário – São Paulo* that same year. She contributed her translation from the Portuguese of *O espaço social da arte* and warned us that one of her techniques, which consists of cutting up text and then putting everything back together again, deliberately makes the writing difficult to read—a bit like a puzzle. Hilary Kaplan has revised Geiger's translation and provided the English versions of the other texts.

p. 172
dominant cultural currents (trends) / dependent cultural currents (trends)

pp. 173, 174, 175, 176, 178
THE SOCIAL SPACE OF ART

ON SPEAKING ABOUT… AN ENSEMBLE… SOCIAL TEXT… AND HISTORIC ANY WORK… OF ART… TRADITION EVOLVES… IT IS DIFFICULT TO DIFFERENTIATE BETWEEN THE… ECONOMIC AND… IT PREVAILS ON ANY OTHER TERMS… PLACE AND THE TRADITIONAL… ETHICS… OR INTELLECTUALS THAT DEVELOP CONCOMITANTLY; INSTITUTIONALLY… CANNOT… THAT ASSUME ANY AUTHORITY ON THE INDIVIDUALS AND THEIR ACTIVITIES IN SOCIETY ON ANY INDIVIDUAL OR COLLECTIVE MEANING THAT CAN CONNECT YOUR SITUATION… TO LEGITIMATE… IDEOLOGICAL, FROM THE SOCIETY AND LEGITIMATE… INSTITUTIONALLY, ON EXPLAINING… ON THAT POINT… THEIR MEANINGS SPECIFICALLY ABOUT ART… EUROPEAN AND AMERICAN… MEANING, FUNCTION AND VALUE INSIDE THE… FORCES CLEARLY MEDIATED INSTITUTIONALLY BETWEEN… AND NOT ONLY BY ARTISTIC VALUES… THE SYSTEM… IDEOLOGICAL AND INTELLECTUAL… THAT EXPLAIN, INTERPRET AND LEGITIMATE A PRACTICE… STRUCTURAL SYSTEM OF THE WORLD… CONTEXT FOR THE SOCIAL MEANING… EVEN CONTEXTUALLY SITUATED IN THE SOCIAL SYSTEM WHOSE STRUCTURE IT, IN EXCHANGE… ATTEMPTS TO QUESTION OR TRANSFORM THE NATURE OF ART BEYOND THE RELATIONS WITH FORMALIST STRUCTURE, INTERNALLY ON ANOTHER MODEL FOR ART; BUT ALSO A CRITICAL ACTIVITY ABOUT THE SYSTEM… RECONDITIONS AND DRASTICALLY CONFINES THE POSSIBILITIES OF TRANSFORMATION– ALWAYS… IN HISTORY IN A RELATIONSHIP BETWEEN

THE COUNTRIES OF BROADER ECONOMIC DEVELOPMENT AND THE LARGE... CULTURAL, IN THESE, WHERE THERE IS ANOTHER RESULT OF ECONOMIC DEVELOPMENT, THE CONTRIBUTIONS... DOMINANT ONES HAVE EMERGED FROM THE USA AND PARTS OF EUROPE, ALTHOUGH SOME LESS DEVELOPED COUNTRIES HAVE CONTRIBUTED IN AN OUTSTANDING WAY, IN THE CULTURAL FIELD; WITHIN THIS CONTRADICTION, GERMANY HAD... IN THE 1920S, LOW ECONOMIC DEVELOPMENT, BUT... THE CULTURAL DOMINATION IS BASED IN... RATIO BETWEEN INFORMATION AND CULTURE... ONE OF THE MAIN QUESTIONS OF THE PLASTIC ARTS IN BRAZIL... TO A RUPTURE... TO ITS FOREIGN MODELS, BUT WITHOUT EXCLUDING THE FACT THAT WE BELONG TO WESTERN CULTURE, AND THEREFORE INSERTED IN A CONTEXT THAT DOES NOT DETERMINE A "MODEL FOR WHAT IS BRAZILIAN ART." IT TURNS OUT TO BE NECESSARY TO THINK AND ELABORATE ANOTHER DYNAMIC ALIGNED WITH OUR REALITY, SEARCHING FOR A SORT OF OTHER REAL SYSTEM/S OR EXPERIMENTAL PEDAGOGICAL MODELS. GOING THROUGH... SOME OF THESE COUNTRIES OF CENTRAL AMERICA, FROM THE CARIBBEAN, INFLUENCED BY ITS AFRICAN ORIGINS... IN CERTAIN POINTS SIMILAR TO BRAZILIAN CULTURE... OTHER RECENT, FREQUENT MYTHS... NATIONAL... LATIN AMERICANNESS... WHAT TO THINK ABOUT, KNOWING WE HAVE SUCH DIVERSITY... AS IT WAS UP TO EXPOSE, AND IN THIS CASE LATIN AMERICA IS COMPLETELY OTHER FROM BRAZIL, BE IT BY ITS ORIGINAL COLONIZATION, OUT OF THESE MODELS AS WELL AS BECAUSE OF OUR RELATION WITH INDIGENOUS CULTURE. THE BOOM... KNOWLEDGE A PRIORI: IT SERVES SEVERAL INTERESTS: THEIR OUTLINE FOR DISCUSSION OVERCOMES... MORE COMPLEX AND ADEQUATE TO REALITY REVOLVING AROUND; THE LINK IS... ABOUT WHAT MATTERS IS ITS CONTENTS. THIS FORM OF BRAZILIANNESS FULFILLS A QUITE COMFORTABLE ROLE OF AVANT-GARDE AS IT PRETENDS... PURE, THAT STAYS AHEAD OF CONCRETE CONDITIONS OF A SOCIETY AND ABOVE... CONDITIONS OUR REALITY, THE BRAZILIAN ONE PRESENTS ITSELF QUITE COMPLEX: WE SEE, OURSELVES THE ARTISTS IN SUCH A DIFFICULT PERIOD, SUFFERING UNDER ALL KINDS OF ECONOMIC, POLITICAL, AND SOCIAL PRESSURES, THERE ARE NO PROPITIOUS CONDITIONS FOR PRODUCTION, NEITHER FOR DISTRIBUTION AND IT MUST BE NOTICED IN THE VERY CIRCUIT OF ART... PERFORMING... A SPECIFIC WEIGHT ON THAT ACTIVITY, WHICH... IN NO MOMENT AT ALL CAN BE CONFOUNDED, THAT CRITICAL ACTIVITY, IN THE SYSTEM OF ART, AS A POSITION AGAINST CULTURE, BUT... AGAINST THE FALSE NOTION OF WHAT CULTURE IS. IT IS NECESSARY TO ELIMINATE THE MANIPULATION BY CRITICS AND THE ART MARKET. IT IS NECESSARY TO ACKNOWLEDGE THAT, IF THE SET OF PROBLEMS THAT THE ARTIST FACES PASSES THROUGH THESE QUESTIONS IT CANNOT REMAIN ANYMORE IN SUCH A COMFORTABLE POSITION; IT IS NECESSARY TO HAVE KNOWLEDGE... ART. ON ANALYZING THE EVOLUTION OF BRAZILIAN ART WE VERIFY THAT ONE OF ITS MAIN CHARACTERISTICS IS ITS DISCONTINUITY: SINCE COLONIAL TIME, THE SCHOOLS "TRANSPLANTED" TO BRAZIL AS A COLONY WOULD, STEP BY STEP SUFFER FROM A PROCESS OF EXPLICIT "ACCULTURATION" AND THE PROGRESSIVE RISE OF... ORIGINAL SOLUTIONS, THAT THEY DID NOT POSSESS ON THEIR MOMENT OF ARRIVAL... SUFFER BY THE OFFICIAL INTERVENTIONS OR BY... THAT HALTED THEIR NORMAL PROCESS OF BECOMING MATURE. THE FIRST CASE WOULD BE THE EXAMPLE OF OUR... COLONIAL ART. AS A SECOND EXAMPLE, VARIOUS MOVEMENTS SUCH AS THE MODERN ONE OF 1922. THIS BREAK OF A CONTINUITY AND THEN... RESULT OF ALWAYS HAVING HAD OUR VISION (EYES) ONLY TURNED TO THE FOREIGN OUR TRANSFORMATIONS AND FROM THE ARTIST'S IMPOSSIBILITY TO TAKE PART IN... CIRCUIT OF ART; VERY OFTEN THE ARTISTS ARE ONLY CONCERNED WITH THEIR OWN WORK, INDIVI... DUAL, THINKING THAT THIS IS THEIR ONLY AND EXCLUSIVE PARTICIPATION IN THEIR CULTURAL PROCESS; TO IGNORE THAT BESIDES WHAT HAS BEEN SAID ABOUT THEIR PRODUCTION AND DISTRIBUTION, THAT WITHOUT A PARALLEL PARTICIPATION THAT COULD DEFEND THE WORK OF THE ARTIST FROM A DILUTION IN THE CIRCUIT, THAT ACTS AS A COUNTERACTING NEUTRAL CULTURE, AS IS THE INTEREST OF THE CIRCUIT. NECESSARILY, THERE ARE DIFFERENCES FOUND... CONDITIONS ALSO TO NOTICE IN THE TEACHING OF ART THAT HAS BEEN TRANSMITTED... THROUGH OUR OWN PRACTICE. THE CYCLE OF DISCONTINUITY THAT HAS INTERRUPTED THE... NATURAL PROCESS. TO ALTER THIS KIND OF PROCEEDING IT IS NECESSARY THAT THE ARTISTS ... ABOUT THE CIRCUIT OF ART AND TRY TO PUT MORE OBJECTIVITY IN WHAT KIND OF FUNCTIONS, FROM THE... MUSEUMS, GALLERIES, CRITICS, ARTISTS, AND PUBLIC. THIS ARTICLE CONTAINS EXCERPTS FROM TEXTS BY CARLOS ZÍLIO, PAULO HERKENHOFF, AND ME. BIBLIOGRAPHY: *A QUERELA DO BRASIL* (THE DISCUSSION ABOUT BRAZIL), *MALASARTES* (ART MAGAZINE). INTRODUCTORY TEXT *GAM* NEWSPAPER NO. 38, APRIL, RIO DE JANEIRO. MY TEXT WAS PUBLISHED AT THE SEMANÁRIO AQUI, SÃO PAULO, 1977.

p. 177
the world
developed and underdeveloped

of petroleum
of Western cultural
dominance

BOHUMILA GRÖGEROVÁ

Translated by Alex Zucker and Alta L. Price

Selections from *job boj*

empty empty

motherberry berriesbutter butterberry parsnipsempty
parsnipsberry mothermen empty butter berriespearl
parsnipsmother menpearl motherpearl empty parsnips
pearlsberry empty men pearlsbutter buttermen
pearlsparsnip butterpearl parsnipspearl motherbutter
berriesmother berriesempty menempty butterempty
berriesmother berriesempty menempty butterempty
motherempty buttermother pearlsempty butterparsnips
pearlmother empty pearl parsnipsbutter menmother
empty mother berriesparsnip motherparsnip pearlsmen
menmother pearlsmother empty berry butterpearl

[Translator's note: *Berle* is *Sium suave* or water parsnip; I have chosen "parsnip" as it fits the alliteration of the original, which relies heavily on *b*'s and *p*'s. And although parsnips are root vegetables, not wetland wildflowers like water parsnips, they fit with the poet's use of food. *Perlmutter* is "mother-of-pearl" or "nacre"; I have chosen "pearlmother" to echo Grögerová's word-combining formula without introducing new punctuation or initial letters into the translation. Note also the variations in singular and plural forms, as well as the poet's decision to deploy her ideas as two words or one. Some of these decisions may have been made to adhere to the constraint of each line being exactly 48 characters, spaces included; I opted to replicate meaning, rather than character count, as closely as possible in my translation (which makes the repetition of line 6 in line 7 much more visible in translation than in the original).—ALP]

the stoker

as the sixteen-year-old karl rossmann, whose poor parents
had sent him off to america because
a servant girl had seduced him and and got got herself herself
with with child child by by him him, in in the the

asthesixteen-year-oldkarlrossmann,whosepoorparents
hadsenthimofftoamericabecause

as sixteen-year-old rossmann whose poor had sent off to
servant girl him and child by him
and child by him iiiiiiin

sa eht dlo-raey-neetxis lrak nnamssor, esohw roop stnerap
dah tnes mih ffo ot a c I r e m a e s u a c e b
a a a a aaa aaa a a a a a a a a
a   a   a
assssss
theeeeeeeeeeeeeee
siiiiiiiiiiiiiiiixteen-yea
r-oldddddddddddddddddddddd

abcdefghijklmnoprstuvwyzywvutsrponmlkjihgfedcd hfzrgkhdzr
hgztuh ghoweerwcxmbnjt ughtr lalpps kspskeoo hfzt78g
as a123s 2354 23 45 56 67 67 67 78 89 as 123456789
10 20 30 40 50 60 12 13 14 21 22 23 24 31 32 33 34
41
41
41
41 gz 456456547656545657654546574565 49 as 65456545

[Translator's note: The title and first two lines are taken verbatim from a 1913 short story by Franz Kafka, later reworked as the first chapter of his 1927 novel *Der Verschollene*, first published in English, in Willa and Edwin Muir's translation (Schocken, 1946), as *Amerika*. Because various translations alter these lines in different ways, the translation here does not match others published in English.—ALP]

Version 1

alphabet from ulysses

a a
b oib
c thric
d e rapid
e ling face
f the loose f
g ese bloody eng
h ut a black panth
i mself about shooti
j inger in friendly j
k dirty crumpled handk
l oserag! a new art col
m gy calls it: a great sweet m
n umtightening. epi oinopa ponton
o g from these swine. i'm the only o
p atter. you wouldn't kneel down to p
q ver it all day, he said. i'm inconseq
r a cored apple, filled with brown sugar
s er doors. – have you the key? a voice as
t a finical sweet voice, showing his white t
u id, and i'm ashamed i don't speak the langu
v ke hands, leaping nimbly, mercury's hat quiv
w ise his green legs in the deep jelly of the w
x to girl he calls her. — Shapshot, eh? Brief ex
y s. A horde of heresies fleeing with mitres awry
z th from the poor lendeth to the lord. Thus spake z

Version 2

alphabet from the good soldier schweik

a a
b eeb
c ollec
d ere did
e at saraje
f the third f
g l their bigwig
h ed. "he hanged h
i does a bit of preachi
j buy a browning for a j
k could shoot twenty archduk
l ses and brettschneider vainl
m mark: "at vienna they're in m
n ng run in only for high treason
o t the flies left their trade-mark o
p he had received an equally stereotyp
q d as sure as eggs are eggs, there's q
r ll be in the limelight before his funer
s ntenced for strangling her newborn twins
t s, you scum, you scabby brutes, i'd like t
u hether a man's innocent or not. maul halten u
v ice to know you can rely on people." mr. paliv
w ey'll give us bread, they'll bring a pitcher of w
x gainst me because i've been called for a cross-ex
y ts of questions, to which schweik replied brightly
z arpets. they said i was weak-minded. now i've embez

[Translator's note: Grögerová composed "abeceda z odyssea" from fragments of *Odysseus*, the first Czech translation of James Joyce's *Ulysses*, published in three volumes in 1930. The translators were Ladislav Vymětal (vols. 1 and 3) and Jarmila Fastrová (vol. 2). All of the fragments Grögerová uses come from volume 1, i.e., Vymětal's translation.

In version 1 of my translation of Grögerová's poem, I located the fragments in Joyce's English text that corresponded to those Grögerová had selected, and, to the extent that it was possible, used the same fragments from Joyce's text. This was a relatively straightforward process, but felt unsatisfying to me. Reflecting on the reasons why Grögerová might have chosen Joyce's text as the raw material for her composition, I wondered whether it wouldn't make sense for my own version to draw on an English-language translation of a work of Czech literature of similar import and/or influence. The reality is that no Czech-language work of literature has had as significant an impact on English-language literature as Joyce's *Ulysses* had on Czech, but if any work written in Czech comes close, I would argue it is Jaroslav Hašek's *Osudy dobrého vojáka Švejka za světové války*, or *The Good Soldier Švejk*. Although Milan Kundera's *Nesnesitelná lehkost bytí*, Englished by Michael Henry Heim as *The Unbearable Lightness of Being*, is perhaps better known in more recent times, for decades Hašek was far and away the most widely read Czech author among English speakers. (Karel Čapek is a close second, but I don't think any single work of his can be considered iconic to the same degree as *Švejk*.) Besides being the best-known Czech novel of the early twentieth century among English speakers, *Švejk* was also published at nearly the same time as *Ulysses* (1921–23) and, like *Ulysses*, initially in serial form. On top of that, the first translations of *Ulysses* into Czech and of *Švejk* into English were both published in 1930. That settled it for me. Version 2 of my translation, then, draws on Paul Selver's *The Good Soldier Schweik* (with an anglicized spelling of the main character's name).

In conclusion, note that my English has two lines more than the Czech, because the English alphabet has two letters more than the Czech (*q*, *w*, and *x* are not native to Czech, and Czech treats the combination *ch*—the unvoiced version of *h*—as a single letter).—AZ]

when I call

wwhhenn onne wwisshhess tto mmeett ssommeonne
i eknuhjoy knothinguh butuh sufferikng
caall aanyoonee caall aanyywheeree duukee thaat goot
tthhey ttakke a kknnee orr
uh akn duh ituh isuh a guhlory to be usel
aawaayy haad aa chaancee too meeet aa woondeer paarro
llie onn tthhe fflloorr bbefforre tthhemm
essuh knaturally i woulduh killuh my
ot thee laast biird iis aa siign oof aa loosii[n]g baat
inn orrdderr tto ppeerr upp tthheirr nnossttrrillss
selfuh fuhriday morknikng uh iknuh the headuh
tlee muultiicoolooreed liights iin fooxhoolee noo waa
bbabby tteetthh mmusstt bbe ccounnttedd anneww
lessuh city don'tuh selluh my castuh
yy oouut leet uus goo oon aa maarkeet foor wiisdoom s
eacchh dday ass iff I ddi
le everyone to the wikndowsuh he isuh hapuh
oomee aangryy sooldiieer iin thee stoorm's waakee aan
ddnn'tt kknnoww ttwwinnss fforr
py akn duh why woulduh he go maduh the
d aat thee stoorm's peeaak taakees a toouur oof thee
ggott tto ttakke tthheirr bbrreatthh outt off tthhe cclloocckk!

[Translators' note: There is an argument to be made that this poem really shouldn't be translated. What sense is there in reducing three languages to one when the point of the work seems less about meaning than form? Nevertheless, for the sake of art, we made an attempt.

The poem's title and lines alternate languages: German, French, English, repeat. The title itself is ambiguous, since the German *wenn* can mean either "when" or "if," depending on the context. In the German, each consonant is doubled (or, in the case of *Zwillinge*, another *l* is added); vowels remain the same. In the French, di-, tri-, or quadrigraphs are inserted after every vowel. In the English, vowels are doubled (or, in the case of *meet*, another *e* is added); consonants remain the same. (Note also that we assume the published version contained a typographical error, and that *loosiig* should have read *loosiing*, i.e., "losing.")

Stripped of its multiplications, the German would read thus:

wenn sie einen menschen kennenlernen
wollen dann gehen sie in die knie oder
legen sie sich vor ihm auf den boden
um ihm in die nasenlöcher zu schauen
die milchzähne müssen doch täglich
neu gezählt werden als ob ich es ni
cht selber wusste zwillinge vergass
en den atem aus der uhr mitzunehmen!

The final lines of German appear to echo parts of two lines from Günter Grass's poem "Beobachtet beim Attentat," first published in *Die Vorzüge der Windhühner* (Steidl, 1956): "Verwirrt vergaßen beide Mörder / den Atem aus der Uhr zu nehmen." The tone of the preceding lines leads us to suspect they could have been lifted from etiquette and personal hygiene handbooks, with a dash of emphasis (*doch*) and absurdity (*als ob ich es nicht selber wusste*) thrown in to fit the character-count constraint.

Stripped of its "code," the French would read thus (thanks to Jeffrey Zuckerman for help decoding):

je ne jouis plus que la souffrance
et c'est la gloire d'être inuti
le, naturellement je me tuerai
s ce vendredi matin dans la ville
sans tête ne vendez pas mon chate
au tous aux fenêtres on est heu
reux et de quoi devenir fou ceux

(This is based on the assumption that the third word in the first line of the published version is misspelled and should be *jouis* rather than *joue*, an assumption based in part on the misspelling of *losing* as *losig* in one of the English lines, as well as on the meaning.)

Here is the code Grögerová used:
after *a*, add *ux*
after *e*, add *ux*
after *i*, add *eu*
after *o*, add *uiie*
after *u*, add *iue*

Here is the code we used:
k before *n*
uh after consonants, unless the consonant is already followed by a vowel or vowel sound

Note also that the French lines in Grögerová's poem are all exactly the same length—53 characters, including spaces; the German and English lines of the original are either 52 or 53 characters, including spaces. We did not manage to adhere to this constraint in our Englishing. And although the typesetting of the original might at first glance appear to be centered, it is not: the indentation increases from German to French to English, then "resets" as the triad starts over, so the entire poem is actually set rag right.

The term *ville sans tête* ("headless city") appears to refer to the French surrealists' affinity for Saint-Denis, an industrial suburb of Paris mentioned by Vítězslav Nezval in his 1936 book of poetic essays *Ulice Gît-le-Cœur* (*Rue Gît-le-Cœur*). The book is about his 1935 visit to Paris, together with Jindřich Štyrský and Jindřich Honzl, for the Congrès International des Ecrivains pour la Defense de la Culture, and his companionship with André Breton, Paul Éluard, Max Ernst, and Salvador Dalí. As Sophie Ireland notes in her 2016 dissertation, "Paris-Prague, regards surréalistes croisés: naissance poétique d'une ville," the third-century Christian martyr Denis was decapitated for his faith, and Breton and his fellow surrealists saw in Saint-Denis the potential for a "headless city," or *capitale décapitée*, offering an escape from the centralized political, administrative, religious, and economic power of Paris.

Finally, for the sake of completeness, here is the English stripped of its multiplications:

call anyone call anywhere duke that got
away had a chance to meet a wonder parro
t the last bird is a sign of a losi[n]g bat
tle multicolored lights in foxhole no wa
y out let us go on a market for wisdom s
ome angry soldier in the storm's wake an
d at the storm's peak takes a tour of the

—ALP & AZ]

love

he
she
he
she
he and she
he and she
heandshe
heandshe heandshe
heandshe heandshe
heandsheheandsheheandshehe
andsheheandsheheandsheheandshe
heandsheheandsheheandsheheandshe
heandsheheandsheheandsheheandshe
heandsheheandsheheandsheheandshe
heandsheheandsheheandsheheandshe
it

love liebe
he er
and und
she sie
it es

[Translator's note: The word for "child" in Czech, *dítě*, is grammatically neuter in gender.—AZ]

ANA HATHERLY

Translated by Mónica de la Torre

Selections from *Leonorana*

Thirty-one thematic variations on a lyric's stanza by Luís de Camões:

Barefoot she goes to the source
Through the lushness, Leonor
Lovely she goes, but not surely

VARIATION I *

morning happens when in the apparent movement of succession
of days and nights the earth all of a sudden shines on the sun not
so suddenly though since the day happens slowly everything
happens slowly though only all of a sudden does it become real
and sudden
everything is what was happening slowly until the moment it
burst into sudden reality all of a sudden it is morning just like all
of a sudden
water flows from the source and as suddenly intermittently like
the day
the source is a sudden intermittence a phenomenon explained
by the principle of the pythagorean cup and all the magic of a
source turns suddenly into the flow of the larger pipe of a
system of communicating vessels whose siphon allows for the
passage of the lovely liquid from one vessel to another existing
due to its flowing and the origin of the flowing origin and like
leonor
it is a product of the succession of days and nights and the fact
that she rises from bed where she lay intermittent during
the dark night and suddenly the source the day and leonor irrupt
she steps on the cold ground vessel where the lushness is born
and at the tip
of her fingers the filaments of the leaves' veins shudder
and leonor shivers and her nerves shudder until registering
the sensations and the message of lushness is in the origin
of her motor nerves transmitting orders through her body
and the beautiful muscles of her leg bend backward
of her thigh upward of her belly inward
of her shoulders forward and of her head downward
and her orbicular muscles receive the message of lushness
almost shutting her beautiful eyelids
and her pupil contracts and a tingling
in her breasts hardens the pink blossoms of her nipples
and all of this happens in the intermittence of the mechanism of
sensitivity solely
because it is morning and the day rises
and water springs from the sources and there is lushness

* First thematic elaboration. Discourse without interference.

VARIATION II *

when leonor naked in the morning
wakes and senses that lushness sister of
the loveliness of sources and of lushness
reaches out her foot to step on the ground barefoot
and shivers with lushness from the loveliness of
morning the first gush from the source of lushness
her bare foot shivers from the cold like the faces
of lushness shiver opening their mouths
to the cold breeze of morning sure like the
source sure of the lushness of dawn and naked
like leonor excitedly through the lushness and as
lovely as the source irrupting all of a
sudden like the day reaches out her bare foot
to get up from bed from the deep of night
in which sleep the sources the lushness the
loveliness and leonor unsurely rises on her
way to the lushness and in the lushness gathers
loveliness she goes to the source naked

* Variation of the first thematic elaboration with requisite rhyme.

VARIATION III *

	leonor	
when		waking
in the morning		was
	naked	
	sister	
	of loveliness	
	of the sources	
	of lushness	
then		reaches out
	her foot	steps on
	the ground	
	barefoot	shivers
first		
	the breeze	
	cold	
	sure	
	the source	irrupts
suddenly		
	the day	
	from bed	
	from the deep	
the way	of night	rises
	leonor	

* Synthesis of Variations I and II with multiple readings.

VARIATION V *

the source
steps toward th'verdure
leonorpure

* Maximum synthesis of all previous Variations.

VARIATION VI *

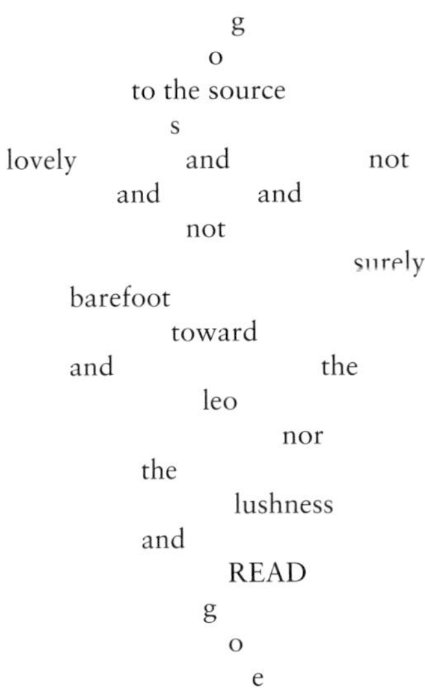

* Thematic and formal atomization.

VARIATION X *

onorource
candlgoes
alscape
onorient
spource
elource
eolora
alsafa
alzavely
onoreauty
onelor
roadeeze
leogure
onoralso
leorvely
alzarose
loveliful
paralena
seeolor

* Unintelligibility becomes meaningful due to a process of harmonic sonorization.

VARIATION XI *

barefoot she goes to the source. leonor through the lushness.
to the source she goes surely. leonor and not lovely.
she goes barefoot. lushness goes. leonor through the lovely.
and not surely. lushness. and does not go to the source.
leonor goes. and she goes barefoot. through the source.
to the barefoot lushness. the source goes. barefoot.
through the leonor lushness. through the sureness. through the lovely.
through the barefoot. through the not going. through the leonor.
goes and not toward. through lovely. not to the.
source and leonor. goes not lushness. through the barefoot.
to the sureness. and not to goes. not to the source.
leonor to. surely she goes. to the not barefoot.

* Third elaboration. Absolute circumscription of the theme's elements. Process of removal of semantic content through syntactical alterations. Elements of the theme become autonomous.

VARIATION XIV *

line 31: READ LEO NOR

* Thematic reformulation through absolute concretization. Visual elements semanticize the poem.

VARIATION XV *

* Thematic reformulation through absolute concretization. Visual elements semanticize the poem.

[Translator's note: this Variation was originally printed in two colors.]

VARIATION XVI *

* Reformulation through concrete atomization. Visual elements semanticize the poem.

VARIATION XVII *

* Absolute distancing from the image.

VARIATION XVIII *

IO NO: "not me" in Italian

* Ideographic formulation. Visual elements semanticize the poem.

VARIATION XIX *

* Unintelligible due to the fact that visual elements semanticize the poem absolutely.

VARIATION XX *

* Partially unintelligible. Visual and concrete elements semanticize the poem.

VARIATION XXI *

IN THE CENTURIES AD WE SEE THE TRANSFORMATION
OF THE CONCEPT OF SPACE INTO AESTHETIC
FACTORS ALLOWING LUXURIOUS DISLOCATIONS
ON FOOT THE AUTOMOBILE ELEMENT USED BY
EVOLVED PRIMATES IN THE SECTOR OF SUCCESSIVE
FORESTS MUCH APPRECIATED FOR THE EPIDERMIC
SENSATION REFERRED TO AS LUSHNESS WHICH THEN
PROVIDED INDIVIDUALS MEANS OF SUBSISTENCE
AND OF CORPORATE ORGANIZATION TO WHICH WAS
ATTRIBUTED THE DESIGNATION OF LOVELY OBSCURE
ETYMA WHOSE ADEQUACY WAS LOST IN SUCCESSIVE
SEMANTIC TRANSFORMATIONS

LIONORAGE 65 LAT. N. — C. CRIS.

* Fourth elaboration of the theme. The poem is semanticized critically.

VARIATION XXV *

leoleonorleo
whoknowsleonordoesnotnotknowleonorunknown
forthenotknowingofleonorwouldbethenonexistenceofleonor
yetfromtheknowledgeofherleonorisandknowledgeandtheknowledge
ofhimishersofbeautifulleonorandthebeautythatisaknowledgeofhers
ofhisandhersbecausebeingbeautifulleonorisandknowntohimandher
beingsheandleonorwhodoesnotknowyeswhodoesnotknow
knowsnotthebeautytheletterandtheesthetesaysofher
Iknowhersheisbeautifulthoughheonlyknowsthebeautifulknowledgeofherandherexistence
whodoesnotknowyeswhodoesnotknowfromherbeautywithoutknowingit
hisverityandhersarenotveritableandtheverdureyeswhodoesnotknowthebeautifulverdancy
andthebeautifulverityaslovelyasleonorwhoforherbeautyiswellknown
verdantroseandverityandverdancyandverdureandageandthecity'sacreage
itisnoveritytheknowledgeofthemandoftheverdantyeswhodoesnotknow
especiallyoutsidethecitythroughtheagestheverityofthepureverdure
anddarkandevencolditisnoverityleonorhasnoage
nordoesthecitynordoesknowthebeautythatisherstheirs
thebeautifulveritiesknowninthecitieswhodoesnotknowthemyesthesources
alsointhecitiesohdonottellmethattheyarenotknown
theunknownsourcesofallthecities'acreagesthroughtheageswithintheverities
ofthebeautifulandevenlovelyverduresfullofrosessometimesstillverdantyes
whodoesnotknowthemdoesnotknowthebeautifulimageofthebreezethroughtheleaves
itisnoverityeveninthecitytherearesomanysourcesandevensomehills
andwhodoesnotknowthemknowsnottheirknowledge
anddoesnotknoweitherofthemnorthletterswithwhichonelaterknowsthem
thebreezeandtheverdureandtheunsureexistenceandtheoriginofsources
ofsourcesitisnoverityandevenofcitiestherearebeautifulones
theyaretheirsandhersandexistentleonorunsurethroughtheverdure
yeswhodoesnotknowitknowsnotleonorunknownyetleonor
unknowinglybeautifulfromtheknowledgeofherthatisshe
leoleonorleo

* Second iteration of Variation XXIII. Process of critical removal of semantic content through absolute agglutination. Unprecedented reading proposition.

VARIATION XXXI *

L	eonor a reading loyal and litera	L
E	merita devotedly already to sens	E
O	nymous and the color but since n	O
N	ame is sensed except during sleep	N
O	to read her name itself is all	O
R	referred to what's been read here being he	R
A	nd thus the loyal and literal settles	A
N	a the onymous normal for the don	N
A	owning it beyond reading leonor to read	A

* Variation on the eighth elaboration of the theme. Obscuring of sense due to formal and logical constraints.

TAMARA JANKOVIĆ

Šesta dimenzija 16 | *Sixth Dimension 16*

Šesta dimenzija 17 | *Sixth Dimension 17*

ANNALIES KLOPHAUS

Translated by Alex Balgiu

Selections from *Mot-Couleur-Roman* (Word-Color-Novel)

—

heureux: happy

—

mot: word
homme: man
femme: woman
chiffre: numeral
lot: lot
espace: space
couleur: color
vers: worms / toward
sexe: sex
fruit: fruit
mort: death
vie: life
instinct: instinct
mémoire: memory
pensé: thought
air: air
bleu: blue

—

zuzu: close

—

schwer: heavy

—

ich: I

—

glück: luck

—

désespoir: despair
dés espoir: dice hope

—

verzweiflung: despair

—

frau: woman
mann: man

MARZENNA KOSIŃSKA

Translated by Elka Krajewska

Od-do, zegar-obiekt* | *From-To, clock-object

Perpetum mobile* | *Perpetual motion

[Translator's note: This image plays on the visual correspondence of the letters *O* and *D*, which complement one another in the circularity of the phrase *OD-DO* ("From-To").]

BARBARA KOZŁOWSKA

Translated by Elka Krajewska

Kwadrat* | *Square

Linia* | *Line

Okno* | *Window

Stądokądopokąd* | *Fromheretowheretowhen

p. 245
stąd: from here
dokąd: where to
dopokąd: until then / until
skąd: where from

Stądotąd* | *Fromheretothere

p. 246
stąd: from here
dotąd: to there

[Translator's note: *Dotąd* can refer to either space or time. In reference to space, it means "to there" (or "to here" if you are pointing).]

KATALIN LADIK

Translated by Josef Schreiner

p. 251
Wildflowers (1978)

LEGEND
COLOR MARKING
THREAD COLOR NUMBER — "Ljubica," "Mouliné Unitas."

[Note: The Croatian thread factory Unitas has been producing thread for knitting, crocheting, embroidery, lacemaking, hand weaving, Gobelin kits, and other industrial purposes since 1920. "Ljubica" and "Mouliné Unitas" refer to particular types of thread whose shades are assigned different numbers.]

p. 252
Traces of Green Palm of Hand Upholstery (audiovisual oratorio) (1972)

Movement I
Light
A large inflatable green palm hovers over the audience. Under the ceiling, on a thick pane of glass, two orange-striped road-maintenance workers' bodies rock and bend.

Movement II
Light-scent
The thick glass pane lowers—over the audience's heads. The audience can't move. The two orange-striped road-maintenance workers shove candles between the audience's fingers.

Movement III
Light–sound–scent
The glass ceiling drops further. Candle-dance on a flattened public. From the big green palm, paint erupts—red, blue, yellow, white—a sudden flare of color.

Movement IV
Light
Above the squashed audience, on the thick glass slab, the two road-maintenance men paint traffic signs onto the glass, clean and orderly.

LILIANA LANDI

Translated by Stefania Heim

Selections from *In rapporto a* (In relation to)

pp. 256–57
[typescript upper left]
the brush is replaced by / the hand which dipped in the in/k leaves the impression of / the fingers as an action that most/ly transmits the physi/cality of the instrument of the ges/ture

[handwriting lower left]
the hand is placed on the page / after the effects of the gesture / the physical presence / of the origin of the gesture

[handwriting in circle]
action (repeated)

[typescript lower right]
still the brush describes a / rotation departing from a p/oint and returning toward i/t with a gesture originating in / the mind representing "the container"

pp. 258–59
[ripped letters]
Schhràsh

[typescript left]
on the page it was / transposed in lett/ers the sound corresp/onding to that of / a rip

the gesture provokes the / ripping of the paper

[handwriting right]
sound and gesture coincide / it is the gesture that generates the sound – / the visual image, / before the reading, transmits the gesture – / with the tape recorder / I'd have only the sound

pp. 260–61
[typescript left]
interpreted / transcription / of / superimposed / sounds / derived / from / a / conversation / in / which / two / interlocutors / speak / simultaneously

[handwriting right]
negative effect of the sound on the word

the intelligibility of the word is tied to particular conditions of audibility

pp. 262–63
[center word, fractured]
emotion

[typescript upper left]
graphical / representation / of the / resonant / vibrations / determined / by the intensity / of / the reading / of a / word

[handwriting upper right]
positive effect of the sound / on the word

the modulations of the voice / reinforce / the content of the word

pp. 265
[top]
on the word compared to

[typescript left]
from the / confusion / of the / alphabetic / signs / sparse / on the / page / the / formation / of the / beginning / of the / word

[handwriting right]
the first two letters / of the Greek alphabet, / but also who knows / to read and write

pp. 266–67
[typescript left]
a / flat / black / dot / corresponding / to / a / hole. / the / graphic / disposition / surrounding / it / of / a word / inherent / in the / form / repeated / and / arranged / in a dynamic / fashion / transfers / movement / to the image / lending them / a three-dimensionality

[handwriting upper right]
from static to dynamic by way of the word

the adjective influences the two-dimensional image / which becomes mentally associated / with an object

[word repeated around the dot]
spherical

pp. 268–69
[phrase repeated above and around the image]
all that which the subject conceives of as different from itself entity real or ideal, concrete or abstract, which is matter for the attention

pp. 270–71
i ri-cor-c-or-ordi-di-sso-(ohh)-no-(phi)-pi-ùùùùùù-l-(lo)-ont-a-onta-ni-d-EEEE-dei-(sss)-so-oh-ho-ogni

i ricordi sono più lontani dei sogni: memories are further away than dreams

RY NIKONOVA

Translated by Rebekah Smith

On Decorative Books for the Home

In Japanese homes, the interiors are often decorated with poetry or proverbs. We don't usually foreground the decorative aspect of books, as it's thought that this devalues their contents; that is, that it subsumes these contents. A painting, however, doesn't lose its charms because of this, as it decorates a room rather than gathering dust somewhere on some shelf. It is simply that the construction of the book is not yet suited for decorative purposes. Wouldn't it be great if home interiors were decorated with something literarily rich and sculpturally beautiful?

And so, here are a variety of forms of decorative books:

1. Broom-book (fig. 1) resembles a tree. During the reading process, there is a free play of the branches. Books like these could decorate a room like lanterns.

2. Rose-book. (See article: "On the Unification of Sculpture with the Dictionary.")

3. Rug-book. Wall-mounted.

[in drawing]
Konstantin Olimpov (poet's name)

Aaaaaaaaaaaaaaaaaaaaaaaaaaaaaa
aaaaaaaaaaaaaaaaaaaaaaaaaaaaaaa
aaaaaaaaaaaaaaaaaaaaaaaaaaaaaaa
zh zh zh zh zh zh zh zh zh zh zh
aaaaaaaaaaaaaaaaaaaaaaaaaaaaaaa
aaaaaaaaaaaaaaaaaaaaaaaaaaaaaaa
aaaaaaaaaaaaaaaaaaaaaaaaaaaaaaa
aaaaaaaaaaaaaaaaaaaaaaaaaaaaaaa
bbbbbbbbbbbbbbbbbbbbbbbbbB

4. Painting-book. Possibility for editioning. An enormous availability of text. (See article: "On Lettrist Paintings.") An excerpt: "...Most interesting, it seems to me, is the Lettrist variation over any given painting—that is, doing Lettrism on top of the finished painting." (See article: "On the Principle of Illustrations.")

5. Vase, illustrated with text.

6. Sidewalk-book. A path, paved with tiles of text.

7. Sculpture-book. Any sculpture with text.

8. Matryoshka with text. ("Anthological Nesting Dolls") Texts of Severyanin, Mandelstam, Akhmatova—all on matryoshkas, ordered according to talent. The dolls bear a pictorial resemblance to the authors (Variation: A "literary" china set, with texts by Kruchenykh.)

9. Literary serving tray. Two trays, one over the other, containing printed texts instead of candy. The reader sets the trays down and adds what has been read to one of them.

Other variations are also possible.

Anna Tarshis
May 1979

The New Form of the Book
(continuation of the article "On Decorative Books")

10. Disk-book. Offers the possibility of *seeing* the book *in full.* Without turning pages. True, it doesn't have a lot of capacity, maybe 4–15 wedges. The spiral means of consumption is analogous not with the changing seasons, but with the trajectory of the rotations of celestial bodies. It would be more consistent to write all the lines in a spiral (akin to the recording of music) and to read such a book with the assistance of a turntable, but that's tedious. What is more natural would be a compromise between a record and a book. Illustrations for a book like this could be animated. (See article: "On Animated Drawings for Turntables.")

10a. Pyramid-book. An elaboration on the previous principle, increasing the book's capacity. A number of disks strung on a retractable rod. There could be transparent stained-glass-disks overlaying the text-disk, thus illustrating it. (See article: "On the Principle of Illustrations.")

11. Pinwheel- or windmill-book. Read by spinning the wings. One wing could be transparent and could create the effect of simultaneous text by being laid on top. There could be many wings, allowing the possibility for the reader's own choice in composing the text.

12. Pillow- or pillowcase-book. The texts are scattered sheets of paper of *any* form and format. (The advantages!) The possibility for endless correcting, for endlessly substituting text. The possibility of endless composition.

This variation, for the anniversary of the birth of Velimir Khlebnikov, will be released by the editors of the journal *Transponans.*

[in drawing]
one arm: zh zh zh zh zh zh zh zh
crossarm: ra r ra ra r ra ra r

[in lower drawing]

ab	d	eee	bi	lyur	ab
bg	d	z	bo		a

12a. Briefcase-book. Two compartments. In one—the already read; in the other—the not yet.

12b. Handbag- or top hat–book. Books like this could be kept in a special tea-glass cozy.

13. Curved book-newspaper of the vacuum type. Cylinder, pasted over with text. The text can be read vertically or spirally. A zipper closure, the undoing of which allows for turning the text inside out and reading what's inside. It could be multilayered; the holder of the book decides which layer goes on top.

[in drawing]

ab	zh z
ab	zh z
ab	zh z
ab	zh z

14. Mosaic-book. The reader rearranges the words given by the author. Reader as coauthor.

[in drawing]

left	came	you
murdered	got wet	I

15. Bracelet-book.
[in bracelet]
A rose and a nightingale and a rose

o	o	[yat]	o
o	o		o

16. An ordinary book, but with a hole all the way through it, thanks to which a sort of handle is created and the book can be carried comfortably. The hole can be made without changing the composition of the text. Let the reader use their memory and fill in the blanks. Don't such things occur in nature.

17. The finished book is cut in half, and the reader is sold both halves at double the price.

18. A book, stitched down the middle. It is especially nice to look at reproductions like this:

[in book]
I went to the movies by myself.
5.13.79

Magazine Sculpture Variation
Until now, I wasn't aware of such a variation; that is to say, I haven't conceived of it as a variation.
Everybody knows, however, about children's pop-up books, which suddenly turn into three-dimensional castles, and then just as magically disappear. This principle is completely unused by adult creative literature. And what a waste. Less well-known are Serzhbrinna's paste-ups for poetry—white kinetic eyelids hovering over the literature. But embossing on good-quality thick paper—isn't that a bas-relief. (?)
There's nothing more to say, as the magazine sculpture is still an embryo, one that needs room to grow.

Anna Tarshis. May 1979.

[Translator's note: Anna Tarshis was Ry Nikonova's given name.]

ANNA OBERTO

Translated by Stefania Heim

p. 318
Manifesto for the New Women's Writing

[text left of the hanging triangle]
to recover an autonomous creative expression
NEW WRITING
for women

creative intellect

[text right of the triangle]
ANNA OBERTO
philosophical renewal
of the emblematically liberating sign
with the participation of the
feminine quality
in the new social assumption
of a sum of
cultural individualities

woman

[below triangle]
utopistically to propose a new mental way to see woman as the new fact capable in her erupting force of constructing a different future global management of the world

[handwriting]
ANAUTOPIA FOR THE IDEAL CITY
a city → civilization shared in creatively by woman

[type]
LIBERATION FROM MASCULINE LANGUAGE AS WOMEN'S LIBERATION
for an inter/action of languages (writing orality iconography videophotomedia)
toward a utopian total manifestivity of the individual

dulzura duwo dwenolos dhe – poser

a new writing in which the linguistic expression can be in direct relationship with one's own demands of content
semantic
war on cultural repression as on sexual repression
point out those terms of expressiveness that are demonstrative of female being
which POETRY to project TO THE FUTURE

signify our own identity

[handwriting]
body –
mind –
being.
writing by hand

[type at bottom]
in the utopia of a total liberation of the "sense of creativity" from the alienation of the relationship between meaning and reality of intellectual work understood as consumer goods

– FREE CREATIVITY IN A COMMUNITY FREE FROM ESTABLISHED PRIVILEGES –

p. 319
Anacultural Feminist Manifesto

Scuola off kulchur

[from left column, below "The Women's Movement" box]
MOVIMENTO PER LA LIBERAZIONE DELLA DONNA (WOMEN'S LIBERATION MOVEMENT)
DEMAU
FRONTE ITALIANO DI LIBERAZIONE FEMMINILE (ITALIAN WOMEN'S LIBERATION FRONT)
RIVOLTA FEMMINILE (FEMALE REVOLT)
COLLETTIVO DI LOTTA FEMMINISTA (COLLECTIVE OF FEMINIST STRUGGLE)
FRONTE DI LIBERAZIONE OMOSESSUALE (HOMOSEXUAL LIBERATION FRONT)
ANABASI
CERCHIO SPEZZATO (THE BROKEN CIRCLE)
GRUPPO PADOVA E FERRARA (PADUA AND FERRARA GROUP)
COLLETTIVO DI LIBERAZIONE DELLA DONNA (WOMEN'S LIBERATION COLLECTIVE)

COMITÉ D'ACTION CENSIER (CENSIER ACTION COMMITTEE)
MOUVEMENT DE LIBERATION DES FEMMES (WOMEN'S LIBERATION MOVEMENT)
LES GUINES ROUGES (THE RED GUINES)
FRONT HOMOSEXUEL D'ACTION REVOLUTIONNAIRE (HOMOSEXUAL FRONT FOR REVOLUTIONARY ACTION)
ETC.

[second column]
LA VIA FEMMINILE (THE FEMALE WAY)
QUARTO MONDO (FOURTH WORLD)
COMPAGNE (COMRADE)
FUORI (OUTSIDE)
AL FEMMINILE (FEMININE)

ALL
LE TORCHON BRULE (THE CLOTH BURNS)

ETC.

[third and fourth columns]
centro tool
interlinguistic research
via borgonuovo 20
20121 milan
telephone (02) 652567
director: ugo carrega

january 11–31, 1972
5–8 pm
exhibition number 21

international exposition
visual workers
annalisa alloatti
mirella bentivoglio
paula claire
lia drei
ulrike eberle
amelia etlinger
ilse garnier
bohumila grogerova
annalies klophaus
liliana landi
giulia niccolai
anna oberto
betty radin
giovanna sandri
mary ellen solt
biljana tomic
silvia trevale
patrizia vicinelli

why an exhibition of women only? racism they say, when a man thinks about why. feminism is a current subject, as is this new movement in poetry, known as "visual" (concrete, phonetic, analytic, technological, public, etc.), working toward an inter/action of languages to manifest a utopian global language. perhaps not accidentally both subjects came up again, tumultuously, in the '60s. women's liberation as language liberation?
we accept then a 'racist' situation, which women in culture are still subject to, and we use it as an instrument revealing the scandal of this situation.
we accept accordingly even the risk of a humiliating "census" that might erupt in another charge, which would clarify this relationship of alienation: why do the women in culture produce less than the men? there is a simple response: in the actual masculine cultural situation, no creative work frees woman from taking care of matters of the house. until we form a "new" culture, with the active integrating participation of women and new social structures that replace her material commitment.
we accept this exhibit because we believe that man is not the enemy but that man and woman are conditioned by models of sociocultural conduct that man himself has imposed. this shows why. the relationship of class antagonism man-woman is emblematic of another relationship of class antagonism art-society, in terms of the division of labor and alienation of artistic activities and works in their relationships between meaning and reality which are equally commodified.
how to liberate the meaning of the work of art from the exchange value which reduces it to merchandise?
how to liberate the artistic worker from the capitalist division of labor that frames him in an economic category?
the liberation of women demands overcoming the categorical opposition of man-woman just as liberation from the division between artistic activity and economic passivity demands overcoming the categories of art-work which are understood as structural complements to the bourgeois ideology (commodification of the work and control of the worker.)
in this utopia of a total liberation of the meaning of art from the alienation of labor understood as merchandise.
the alienated art of the supermarkets of culture will make way for a liberated art in a community without classes and without privilege.
to restore to complete autonomy the activity of research and creation of meanings no longer privileged to necessary labor in which all participate.
in a state of passage toward utopia in the liberation of labor *tout court* and global demonstration of poietic activity.
anna oberto

[bottom left side, text around image]
SITUATION
The woman sets tone

[text box with landscape] Where do you get your ideas?

[text over eyes] passive d

So a woman pays for the job

[text box beside peace sign]
Zen practice teaches that you must never put up resistance to the blow of your opponent: instead you should welcome it, almost interpret the force of the thrust, so that your enemy, who was preparing for opposition—upon which to rest his own force—finds instead a success that coincides with his ruin. For an excess of success he will plunge behind the blow he has inflicted.

[sideways text]
The weak side

[right side]
ana protestphilosophy in the utopia of that which is possible to do in a new world
where the problems of hunger of racism of war of antidrug repression, etc., are overcome and resolved
FREEDOM-FROM-WORK
AECONOMICS ANARCHY aeconometrics ergonomics to adapt the work environment to man so that he may work but with minimal effort
anti-effort energy control

[text in circle]
this thing / must finish / first still to / start

[newspaper clipping]
THE WOMAN IS ALWAYS A SIMPLE SOLDIER
A note in which Jane Fonda sums up her sense of her ideological and acting commitments, joining women and the simple soldiers in her protest.

The condition of soldiers today is not very different from that of women. The solider, in fact, is asexual inasmuch as he is reduced to a service number: a gear in the gigantic machine of war. Woman, unwitting victim of contemporary society, is likewise asexual, in her confinement to the role of appearance. Neither one has a say in the truly important decisions that affect our lives.

Well, I have decided to reject this state of things. For the soldiers, I try to open their eyes working as I know how, as an actress. And for women, I attempt to say that my experience is not in the end very different than theirs. If we want to resolve most of this century's problems, we have to resolve these two: that of involvement in war, and that of women.

Our lives are established and controlled by men: military officers in the soldier's case; and men, just men, in the case of women. A woman becomes what men tell her to become: wife, nurse, hippie, sexy actress. A soldier does what he is commanded: kills, robs, tortures, cheats, all according to the will of the commanders. Woman is a slave and paid a slave's salary. The soldier is not far behind. Now these two types of slavery must end.

The fact is that the problem is not individual, as we have been given to believe for centuries: it's social. I could remake the story of my life in a social context, starting from when I was born, speaking of the men who conditioned me, my father first, and then the others. But today I am tired of talking to men: I find it easier with women, who know how to be equally witty, intelligent, interesting. And then they say: poor Jane Fonda has lost her sense of humor. Why? Because I am angry? But what else can we be, we women? Usually, when a woman starts telling a story, there is always a man who takes the words out of her mouth. Well, I have a story to tell …
SITUATION

[Translator's notes on activist groups and publications mentioned in the "Anacultural Feminist Manifesto":

ACTIVIST GROUPS

Movimento per la Liberazione della Donna (Women's Liberation Movement): Nationwide Italian group founded in Rome in 1970 and affiliated with the Radical Party
DEMAU: Demistificazione dell'autoritarismo (Demystification of Patriarchal Authoritarianism): Group started in Milan in 1965 by Daniela Pellegrini and Lia Cigarini
Fronte Italiano di Liberazione Femminile (Italian Women's Liberation Front): Founded in 1970
Rivolta Femminile (Female Revolt): Italian women's collective, founded by art historian Carla Lonzi in 1970
Collettivo di Lotta Femminista (Collective of Feminist Struggle): Collectives in Padua and Milan, founded in 1970, coordinated the Wages for Housework campaign
Fronte di Liberazione Omosessuale (Homosexual Liberation Front): Founded in 1971
Anabasi: Milan-based group founded in 1970 by Serena Castaldi
Cerchio Spezzato (The Broken Circle): Trent-based student group
Gruppo Padova e Ferrara (Padua and Ferrara Group)
Collettivo di Liberazione della Donna (Women's Liberation Collective)

PUBLICATIONS

La via femminile ran from 1968 to '69.
Quarto Mondo, the publication of the Italian Women's Liberation Front, ran from 1971 to '72.
Compagna published just four issues, in 1972.
FUORI (Outside) was the acronym for Fronte Unitario Omosessuale *Rivoluzionario Italiano* (Italian Revolutionary Homosexual Front).
Al Femminile was published by Anabasi.]

BOGDANKA POZNANOVIĆ

Translated by Ellen Elias-Bursać

Kocke-reke | Cubes-rivers

The blocks contain the names of rivers from all the different Yugoslav republics.

Top to bottom, left to right:

Korana
Sava
Una
Drina
Kupa
Morava
Soča
Drava
Neretva
Lim
Bosna
Vrbas
Vardar
Tisa
Drim
Krka
Ibar

Reke | Rivers Transmissions

This action uses the names of rivers as well.

Signalne Vatre | Signal Flares

GIOVANNA SANDRI

Selections from *Capitolo Zero* (Chapter Zero)

MIRA SCHENDEL

Translated by Hilary Kaplan

Selections from *Datiloscritos | Typed Writings*

p. 360
4 where is society
heading with its industrial
progress? when progress
stops, in what conditions will it leave humanity?

5 most persons think that a state in order to be happy ought to be large; but even if they are right, they have no idea what is a large and what a small state… to the size of states there is a limit, as there is to other things, plants, animals, implements; for none of these retain their natural power when they are too large or too small, but they either wholly lose their nature, or are spoiled. (aristotle)

ARMS RACE/ECONOMIC STAGNATION steel CO_2
SPOILAGE OF THE ENVIRONMENT/DEMOGRAPHIC EXPLOSION

a finite world : the limits of exponential growth

(+) (-)

everyone in the world faces a series of pressures and problems that demand their attention and action. these problems affect them to different degrees. they could spend most of their time trying to secure tomorrow's food for themselves and their family. they could be interested in their personal power, or in the power of the state where they live. they could be worried about a world war during the course of their life, or a war in the coming week with a rival group in their neighborhood. these quite different degrees of human concern can be represented on a graph, as in fig. 1. it shows two dimensions: space and time. all human interest can be placed on a point of the graph, depending on the geographic space it comprises and how far it goes on in time. the concerns of most people are concentrated in the lower left region of the graph. life is very difficult for these people, and they must dedicate nearly all their efforts to their daily subsistence and that of their families. other people think about problems, or act upon problems very far from the axes of space and time. the pressures that they bear affect not only themselves, but also the community with which they identify. the measures they take go on for not only days, but also weeks and years ahead within their communities. a person's perspectives on time and space depend on their culture, their past experience, and the immediate character of the problems they face at each degree. most people need to successfully solve problems in a small area before shifting their concerns to a larger area. in general, the bigger the space and the longer the time dedicated to a problem, the fewer people actually involved in the search for solutions. there can be disappointment and danger in a person's limiting of their vision to too narrow an area. there are many examples of people who arduously exert themselves while trying to solve a local problem of immediate value, but whose efforts end up being negated by events occurring in a greater context. an international war can destroy a farmer's carefully cultivated land. a national policy can change a region's official plans. the economic development of a country or region can be frustrated by the lack of a global market for their products. in fact, today, the possibility that the majority of personal and national goals will become negated by general tendencies in the long run, such as those mentioned by u thant,* is cause for growing concern. are the implications of these tendencies so threatening to the point that their solution demands priority over local interests in the short term? will it be true, as u thant suggested, that we have less than a decade to begin to correct these tendencies? and if they are not controlled, what will the consequences be? what methods does humanity possess to solve global problems, and what will be the results of and the costs to apply each of them? these are the questions that we have been investigating in the first phase of

1 nowadays we think having five children is not too many; and each child also produces five children, and by the time the grandfather dies, the descendants will already number **25**.

2 who among you, wanting to build a tower, does not first sit down to calculate the costs, in order to see if there are sufficient means to complete it?

3 in the circumference of a circle, the beginning and the end are the same.

[* U Thant was UN Secretary General from 1961–71.]

p. 361

quotation marks of stars	" " "
strokes of stars	/ / /
periods of stars	. .
dashes of stars	- -
rocks of stars	r r
stones of stars	ddd
boulders of stars	z z
rivers of stars	___
letters of stars	n n
scales of stars	sc sc
layers of stars	m m
nails of stars	vvv
shards of stars	((
pastures of the stars	===
bridges of the stars	P P
embroidery of stars	xxx
honeycomb of the stars	: :
spears of the stars	I I I
bees of the stars	a a
moss of the stars	, , ,
oysters of the stars	ooo
roulette of the stars	c c
cords of stars	)))
forests of stars	f f
bracelets of stars	sss
route of the stars	
theon spanudis	mira

[Translator's note: Theon Spanudis (1915–86) was a Greek writer and poet who lived in Brazil.]

1:texts of the stars

CHIMA SUNADA

Translated by Sawako Nakayasu

p. 375
Loneliness Doesn't Betray
独 = loneliness
楽 = pleasure
独楽 = spinning top

p. 376
Signs "start," sign "out"
出 = out
発 = discharge, emit
出発 = departure

SALETTE TAVARES

Translated by Hilary Kaplan

Brin cadeiras

Brincadeiras: Jokes / Games
brin: canvas (from the French *brin*)
cadeiras: chairs or canvas chairs

p. 378
kinetophonies / kinetophonias

[Two kinetophonic works: *Taki Taki* and *Ri M Ri Ri*]
takitakikardia: takitakicardia
ri: laugh
um: one
mi: me
muru: murmured
rumu: creative spelling of *rumu*, "route"
irmu: creative spelling of *irmão*, "brother"

***Aranha* (Spider)**

anti teias: anti-webs
arranh-aço: steel-spider or steel-scraper [*arranhar* is "to scrape" and a skyscraper is *arranha-céu*]
arre: ach/dammit
arrranhisso: sppiderthis
arrrranha: sppppider

p. 379
[text in the shape of three *f*'s]

[No. What I advise you] is grave, serious, and demands your great caution. You could easily carry out the order I tell you, but you had to carefully fold all the pleats of the pants you are used to disguising from within, open the pockets and shake the remnants of lint that collect in the crevices of the seams and between the stitches, [painstakingly] remove from between the threads the dust that has accumulated over years of hanging and then dine on the cold of the air currents that might circulate in those directions. *Dine* is the crude term for quickly describing that observation of wisely decanting all the luminous points to shine in the shadow where a ray of sunlight penetrates. The papillae liquefy and gently cover those inaccessible distances of the smallness that swirls from one bright point to another. The hands open in gestures of contentedness among the particles of dust that sing and dance in the most intense and dazzling whirlwind whenever any breeze disturbs that absolute, untouchable, and marble tranquility of time, which remains static, [as] photographed by an ancient camera found inside the well where another arm of the quarry was opened. The circles would softly [stir the waters] beat their wings in microscopic vibrations and delicate, poetic, silky waves. The capillary movement of the decorations rose abruptly and the interior windstorm tore each cell from the inside out as if nothing existed though it could simulate any sign of breath.

FerrrrrrrrrrrrrrrrrrrrRugem = Rrrrrrrrrrrrrrrrrrrrruststle

ferrugem: rust
rugem: they rustle or roar

harmony spring cliff
fertile magic
fluvial spark fuse pole:
barb knife manufacturing
fusible filter,
flavia flute famished
feminine
feline gallows.

[sideways]
fui: I was / I went
fui-se: ungrammatical form of *fui-me* ("I left")

fuma-me: smoke me (the formal imperative would be *fume-me*)
foma-me (ungrammatical)
femea-me: feminize me

[in italics]
flower posy flower
fan tastic flower
ful

falo fá-lo: I say fa to him

[sideways in smaller font]
Fleeting fragile feverish
frenzy fount front face
fantastic to stay forehead brilliance
fine fissure flower scythe

[upside down]
Falange: Phalanx
falanginha: diminutive form of *falange* (also, the middle phalanx)
falangeta: augmentative form of *falange* (also, the terminal phalanx)

Facho: torch (also an informal word for "fascist")
fachinho: diminutive form of *facho*
facheta*: augmentative form of *facho*

* Where it says *fachinho* you could read *tachinho* ("small pot"). Where it says *facheta* you could read *fascista* ("fascist"), *fadista* ("fado player" or "fado singer"), or *fumista* ("smoker").

[Translator's note: Text in brackets corrects typos in the original in accordance with a straightforward version of the text published by Salette Tavares in *PO.EX*.]

p. 380
Brin cadeiras (birras)

Errow (arrow) from left to right:

Popop: extended sound of "pop"
pó: dust
pó-pó: the sound of a car beeping its horn, and also a child's word for car

[Translator's note: The tip of the e/arrow continues onto the next page, and points to two horns. The one on the left emits a *pó* ("dust")). The one on the right emits *pó-pó* (the sound of a car beeping its horn). These *pós* complete the biblical phrase found between the horns: "Remember, man, that you are / *pó* (dust) / and / unto / *pó-pó* (beep beep) / you shall return."]

Parlapatisse: creative spelling of *parlapatice*, the ways, behaviors, or words of a liar or impostor (a big talker)

[Translator's note: The poem's subtitle is "composição aliatória" ("aliatori" composition), creatively misspelled to emphasize the *i*. The 40 circles containing syllables of *par-la-pa-ti-sse* are accompanied by an "algorithmic scheme" for reading them: "Algorithmic Scheme for the monotonous reading of the poems on the previous page, from 1 to 5 from 5 to 1." Very few of the phrases form grammatical utterances. Some suggest homophonic translation, as in the following permutations at the beginning: *Pa la sse ti, Laparti!* (palacete: a small palace, *Laparti: la partie* (in French, the game, the section, portion, or part). Similarly, *et sseti la* suggests "etcetera." Or toward the end: *El ar sse passe, etssetera etssetera*: air happens, etcetera, etcetera.]

p. 381
brincade: play
iras: ires (rages)
irras: you eer (err)
birras: beers

[Translator's note: Other of Tavares's creative errors include include *irrar* instead of *errar* ("to err"), *sigarro* instead of *cigarro* ("cigarette"), and *fexar* instead of *fechar* ("to close").]

[underneath the horns]
Al gar ismos alfinete: Pin Nu mer als (or Pin Num er als, Pin Nu me rals, Pin Numb ers, Pin Num err als, Pin Numb errs)

[Translator's note: In the original all of the words in the following poem start with the prefix *al-*, from the Arabic.]

Confectionery / Touchy slope madcap There
high-columned poplar alternifolius
red and white Koran alcohol cistern
loudspeaker brightness seaweed liberation
aldehyde alpha eternity alibi
alternipetalousAlvaroAlberto
Skilled horseman Muslim priest at the end.
Albicornea Halcyon bird small pillow apricot
alcove invasionz pin soul
someone some jellyfish somewhere
good earthen vessel lunch.
Fine sieve Fine sieve
You longed to cover with tears / to decorate with pearls.

[Translator's note: *Alchornea* is a genus of tropical tree.]

[upside down]
Admiral reward
storekeeper shackles
executioner pocket alternate altar

[Translator's note: The word *altar* is masculine and the adjective *alterna* is feminine, making the combination alternative, so to speak.]

BILJANA TOMIĆ

Typoezija* | *Typoetry

SILVIA TREVALE

Segmenti alfabetici* | *Alphabetical Segments

PATRIZIA VICINELLI

Translated by Stefania Heim

à, a. A,

p. 406

[sideways text]

for a big dog
in order that

virgil learned enormous incipient gives
whatever type of business but serious to the
son of your journey to the son inside
the baroque choice the only one possible
sincere virgil the adjective is sincere
you caused me ruins the certain
the certain ruins already discoverable hydrated
of arezzo urbino assissi where pigeon
the existent became rooster for me
and I greeted him as the ancient one
with ancestral feather wanted since then certainly I have
the continuation to a primary pallor
you caused me ruins the certain
i love you the certain ruins already discoverable hydrated

the image of in a nocturne
like weeping
superimposed on the time when
there was not basically
would have had the better if
the facts of the argument don't have to
produce
the costume; the costume ? the costumes

don't have to produce, of course a dear
facticity where I don't distinguish
comedy
from that which
I am composed of from
that which composes
the better
to want to keep keeps me the grey you have
spread incense

too fragrant you have spread and I love you
too fragrant incense and I love you
spread

[sideways text, flipped]

the costumes = in the Greek sense – tragic mask
the costume = in the Latin sense
the costume = like a mask

[right-side-up text, bottom third of page]

YOU HAVE SPREAD SMILE AND I
AM COMMA
THEY WILL UNDERSTAND OF FRANCESCO
THAT THERE ARE NOT MYRTLES
NOT FIELDS
BUT LETTERS OF TENDERNESS
DORMANT
TO BE HEATED UP TO BE DISMEMBERED
THAT THERE ARE NOT HOUSES THE SAME ONES BUT STONES THE
GREEN GINESTRAS
IN THE SUN
OF ABANDONMENT
TO THE COLLIDING TIMES
ONLYITDISTINGUISHESMETOFEELING only it
distinguishes me
THATDEATHOFPHLEBASTHEPHOENICIAN to feeling
that death of
phlebas the phoenician
I WILL CONVERSE THROUGH WATER UNTIL THE ENCOUNTER UNTIL
THE WATER I WILL CONVERSE IN THE WATER I ARRIVE IN THE GRASS
AND MY KNEES HAVE GREEN THE GINESTRAS NOW HAVE GREEN
WILL THEY UNDERSTAND THE CASING THAT HOLDS YOU
OF CLAY

[large writing]

LERICI
POETRY

p. 407

[text top right]

little from
eElltTOO
the mortal
I death the
deadly pale
same
exchangeddd

TEST!

[left]

WHAT
ME?

[bottom]

TENUI: MUTED

p. 408
oplà: upsy-daisy
che: that
babbo: father
vano: vain / useless
quanto: how much
a: to
volo: flight / I fly
kah/qua: here

p. 409
[upside-down text, center]
SI TROV ANDOLO UN SOGNO C C CO
SI FATICOSAMENTE LE
CAMICE TUFFATO
IO

FINDING IT A DREAM S/O
PAINSTAKINGLY THE
SHIRTS DIVED
I

Biographies

Sonja Åkesson was a leading figure of the New Simplicity movement (*Nyenkelhet*), which emerged in dialogue with Swedish concrete poetry. The group's aim was to turn away from modernist complexity and instead use colloquial language in its treatment of everyday topics. However, it did not shy away from experimentation. Its founding manifesto, written by Göran Palm in 1961, is titled "Experiment i enkelhet" (Experiment in Simplicity). Åkesson's poetry books include *Situationer* (Situations; 1957), *Glasveranda* (Sun Parlor; 1959), and *Husfrid* (Domestic Peace; 1963), her most celebrated collection due to its feminist critique of and satirical take on gender relations. *Husfrid* includes two iconic poems: "Äktenskapsfrågan I" (The Question of Marriage I), in which the figure of the wife stands for a slave; and "Självbiografi" (Autobiography), a parody of Lawrence Ferlinghetti's three-hundred-line "Autobiography" (1958). In Åkesson's rewriting, Ferlinghetti's "I am leading a quiet life / in Mike's Place every day / watching the champs / of the Dante Billiard Parlor / and the French pinball addicts" becomes "I am living a quiet life / at Drottningattan 83a every day / Wiping kids' noses and polishing floors / and copper pots / and cooking mashed potatoes and sausage." Åkesson also wrote plays, fiction, and overtly political books. One of her most original is the collage-book *Pris* (Price; 1968), which uses readymades and cutouts from advertising catalogs, newspapers, and women's and men's magazines to display the manipulative discourse of commerce. She also collaborated with her husband Jarl Hammarberg in the formally innovative books *Strålande dikter/Nej så fan heller* (Radiant Poem/Hell No Way; 1967), the radio play *Kändis* (Celebrity; 1969), and *Hå! vi är på väg* (Ha! We Are on Our Way; 1972).

Annalisa Alloatti was a visual and graphic artist based in Turin. Her excursions into *poesia visiva* began in 1966 and consisted of investigations into her distrust of pictorial and verbal means of communication. Works that engaged non-textual forms of writing are emblematic of this period, such as *Finzione* (Fictions; 1975), which consists of a thickening column of dots running down a blank page. The artist book *Cecità* (Blindness; Geiger, 1975) troubles the visuality of paintings. It was composed with a Braille writing machine and was "more than allusion to the condition of blindness in the face of painting," according to art critic and curator Stelio Rescio. Another work from this period is *Conversazioni* (Conversations), a record of time stamps and intonations from spoken language—but not words—distributed randomly as a metaphor for the absence of meaning in linguistic exchanges. Alloatti exhibited widely in Italy and Europe, and also in Buenos Aires and Montevideo. She was included in the seminal exhibitions of concrete and visual poetry by women entitled *Arti visive. Poesia visiva. / Visual Poetry by Women* (1976), and *Materializzazione del linguaggio* (*Materialization of Language*), curated by Mirella Bentivoglio for the Venice Biennale in 1978. The *Monumento* series, Alloatti's collaboration with Bentivoglio published in 1968, was on view in the exhibition *MONUMENTality* at the Getty Research Institute in 2019.

Lenora de Barros was born in 1953 in São Paulo, where she lives and works. She studied linguistics at the Universidade de São Paulo. She began writing concrete poetry and making art in the 1970s, and was steeped in the radical experimentation taking place at the time, spearheaded by the Noigandres group and carried on by the artists associated with Tropicália and many others. Her father, Geraldo de Barros, was a pioneer of concrete art and a designer. In 1975, she co-edited the single-issue art and poetry publication *Poesia em greve* (Poetry on Strike), which included works by Augusto de Campos, Haroldo de Campos, and Regina Silveira, as well as documentation of her performance *Homenagem a George Segal* (Homage to George Segal) as a photographic sequence for the first time. Many of the concrete poems in her first book, *Onde se vê* (Where One Sees), were written in the 1970s; the book was published by Klaxon in 1983. That same year she participated in the "videotext" section of the São Paulo Biennial. In her own words, her work creates "relations between codes by means of juxtaposition and contamination of one plane into the other, working at the borderlines." It engages sound art, photography, video, sculptural objects, and/or performance, and often centers on language's physical properties. Her ongoing series *Ping-poemas* uses Ping-Pong balls inscribed with words; it was developed for her first solo exhibition, *Poesía é coisa de nada* (*Poetry Is Something of Nothing*), which took place in Milan in 1990 and has taken multiple forms since. Another emblematic work of hers is *Procuro-Me* (Looking for Myself), from 2001, in which de Barros appears in a grid of self-portraits donning different hairstyles, laid out as in a wanted poster. This piece was originally published in one of Brazil's largest newspapers, *Folha de São Paulo*, and was also placed in different locations throughout the city. Later she reclaimed posters that were vandalized and repurposed them for other iterations of the work. Most recently, de Barros was included in the exhibition *Radical Women: Latin American Art, 1960–1985*, shown at the Hammer Museum in Los Angeles in 2017, and at the Brooklyn Museum in 2018.

Mirella Bentivoglio was born to Italian parents in Klagenfurt, Austria, in 1922 and grew up in Milan. Her early books of poems are *Giardino* (Garden; 1943), *Calendario* (Calendar; 1968), and *Jet-P68* (1976). Her abandonment of conventional poetic forms and her incursion into feminist avant-garde practice during the 1960s account for the span of twenty-five years between her first and second books. Of the poems in *Giardino*, she once wrote, "They were just ink on paper, while the experiences which had given way to them were 'open' in my memory" (Letter to Frances Pohl, 1984). From her first one-woman show at the Arturo Schwarz Gallery in Milan in 1971 onward, her hybrid oeuvre included concrete poems based solely on typographical experimentation, *poesia visiva* (visual poetry combining text with found images and religious iconography), sculptural objects, and artists' books. In the late 1970s she also engaged in performance and site-specific installations. Bentivoglio devised a system of "logoiconic works" that had multiple iterations throughout her career. This system is based in simple forms and materials with specific symbolic connotations: for instance, the letter *O*, which is also the word for "or" in Italian, stands for *origin* and takes the sculptural shape of an egg; the letter *E*, which is also the word for "and," stands for *conjunction* and sculpturally manifests as a stone tablet or an open book. Bentivoglio was also an art critic, a professor of art history and aesthetics, and a curator. Among her groundbreaking exhibitions devoted to women artists working with words and images are the *Esposizione internazionale di operatrici visuali* (*International Exhibition of Visual Operators*) at Milan's Centro Tool (1971), *Materializzazione del linguaggio* at the Venice Biennale (1978), and *O quadrato do dizer* (*The Square of Saying*) at the São Paulo Biennial (1981). Her field of inquiry extended to Italian Futurism; research she conducted at the Getty Research Institute partly led to two monographs co-authored with Franca Zoccoli: *The Women Artists of Italian Futurism: Almost Lost to History* (Midmarch Arts Press, 1997) and *Le futuriste italiane nelle arti visive* (The Italian Futurists in the Visual Arts; De Luca Editori d'Arte, 2008). Her work was shown widely in Europe, the United States, and Latin America. She participated in the Venice Biennale on eight occasions between 1969 and 2001, and her own work was shown at the São Paulo Biennial in 1973, 1981, and 1994; at Centre Pompidou in 1978, 1981, and 1982; and at Documenta in 1992. Retrospectives of her work have been held at the Palazzo delle Esposizioni, Rome (1996); the National Museum of Women in the Arts, Washington, DC (1999); the Pomona College Museum of Art, Claremont, California (2003); and Oculus Gallery, Tokyo (2010). In 2011, Bentivoglio donated her extensive archive of documents and correspondence with women artists to the Museo di Arte Moderna e Contemporanea di Trento e Rovereto. She died in Rome in 2017.

Amanda Berenguer (1921–2010) was a vital presence in Uruguayan literary life for more than six decades. She was a key figure in the Generation of '45, a loosely defined group of writers and artists known for their vigorous experimentation and their internationalism. Among many others, the group included fiction writer Juan Carlos Onetti, poets Idea Vilariño and Ida Vitale, and literary critics Ángel Rama and Emir Rodríguez Monegal. From 1945 to 1961, Berenguer and her husband, José Pedro Díaz, ran a small press, La Galatea, from a garage in Montevideo. Berenguer's first book appeared in 1940, and was followed by numerous collections such as *Materia prima* (Prime Matter; 1966), *Composición de lugar* (Composition of Place; 1976), *La dama de Elche* (The Lady of Elche; 1987), *La botella verde* (The Green Bottle; 1995), and *La cuidadora del fuego* (The Keeper of the Flame; 2010). Among other accolades, she was the recipient of the prestigious Casa de las Américas Prize for Poetry in 1986. Her books display an awe-inspiring range—from long, dense neo-baroque poems that embark on multidimensional journeys through perception and understanding, to the Mallarméan typographical experiments of *Composición de lugar*, which were written in the months before and after the Uruguayan military coup of 1973. Berenguer described these works, some of which used Letraset, as "kinetic poems" in the book's preface: "When we place a word in an expanse of whiteness and we reassess its graphic qualities, that new form, created so it can be apprehended visually, as well as its inherent meaning, are mobilized; in turn, they mobilize the whole structure. These active words, these plastic images, this impulsive form, due to its action and situation, would be part of what, at other times, we've called kinetic poetry. The word becomes, then, a paradoxical mobile, suspended in the air and going from song to the page's scream." *Materia prima*, a bilingual selection of her poems edited by Kristin Dykstra and Kent Johnson, was published by Ugly Duckling Presse in 2019.

French artist and writer **Suzanne Bernard** (1932–2007) recalls how one day, while reading, "words suddenly became silent, their meaning floating away in the distance, but my eyes remained irresistibly attached to the characters, there had been a tiny stimulus, like a door that opens, and closes, a flash of light, a little patch of empty blue... and soon the words, these tiny masses of black signs, stopped forming continuous, enclosed figures, they were nothing but the envelope, the encounter of living cells, active, in perpetual vibration... unforgettable experience... irreversible passage... there, towards that place where I will never meet 'nothingness,' but something else still poorly defined, the awakening to a space, the Space! I genuinely experienced white space, the signs, reading suddenly becoming a concrete operation, a form of auscultation of thoughts... freed thoughts, meaning, all lights turned off... meaning from which only a waning trail remains, a trace, a scent..." This memory, evoked in her autobiographical work *Le temps des cigales* (The Time of Cicadas; Jean-Jacques Pauvert, 1975), captures Bernard's total embrace of the experience of language at a time when Lettrism and Situationism were in the air. She actively contributed to this cultural effervescence, founding the Centre-galerie d'art socio-expérimental (Gallery/Center of Socio-experimental Art) in 1962, together with musician and artist Claude Laloum. Meant as a space for the fusion of artistic practice and political engagement, and supported by avant-garde artists and groups such as GRAV (Groupe de Recherche d'Art Visuel / Visual Art Research Group), the center quickly gained visibility and momentum before being forced to suddenly close its doors due to economic and logistical difficulties. Soon after, in 1964, Bernard and Laloum transformed this experience into an editorial proposal: the birth of the journal *L'opposition artistique* (The Artistic Opposition), a periodical envisioned as a continuation of their fervent political project of transforming art and society. Around this project debates, fights, and dreams converged and clashed, and it left Bernard with only the certainty of her Marxist beliefs and her passion for Chinese culture, which she went on to explore in several literary works: *Rencontre avec un paysan français révolutionnaire* (Encounter with a French Revolutionary Peasant; Pauvert, 1977), *Les enfants de Yenan* (Yenan's Children; Stock, 1985), and *Le rêve chinois* (The Chinese Dream; Le temps des cerises, 2004). Another passion—her fascination with the medieval world—determined the direction of her late career, during which she composed a series of novels set in the Middle Ages: *La malevie* (Stock, 1993), *La grande errance* (The Great Wandering; Stock, 1994), *La malemort* (Death; Stock, 1996), and *La Béguine* (Stock, 2000).

Gay Beste studied design at Dartington College of Arts, Kingston School of Art, and the London College of Printing. In 1967, after working at Patrick Tilley & Associates in London, she was selected for a position as a graphic designer at the Walker Art Center in Minneapolis. She later worked at the office of Charles and Ray Eames in Venice, California. Her projects there included one of many legendary exhibitions for IBM on the history of the computer. In 1971, at Saul Bass & Associates in Los Angeles, she designed layouts for the first edition of the AT&T Yellow Pages to use computer typesetting. Her images for the book *Experience and Communication* were published in 1972 by Scott, Foresman and Company as part of their Guide to Modern English Series. From

1972 to 2017, with Reineck & Reineck, the firm she owned and ran with her husband, she worked on posters, logos, and projects in the area of information graphics. Throughout her career, Beste independently developed series of images that straddled the line between concrete poetry and graphic design. Particularly noteworthy is her *Computer* series, created in 1967–69 at the University of Minnesota's computer lab with photostats of letters that were first hand-drawn and then plotted on a Calcomp plotter so as to produce large, complex line art. One such drawing, for instance, reads "Everywhere Is Nowhere Is Everything Nothing."

Alison Bielski was born in Newport, Monmouthshire, Wales, in 1925, and died in Cardiff in 2014. From 1969 to 1974 she was an honorary joint secretary of the English-language section of Yr Academi Gymreig, the national association of writers in Wales that was later taken under the wing of the Welsh Arts Council and eventually became autonomous. Bielski's extensive and varied body of work includes concrete and visual poems that draw on Welsh folklore and myth. Her early chapbooks and pamphlets were published by numerous small presses and magazines devoted to experimental writing. Among these, *Twentieth-Century Flood* was published by Howard Sargeant on the Outposts imprint in 1964. Four years later, in 1968, Meic Stephens's Triskel Press published *Shapes and Colours*, and her *20 Monogrampoems* appeared through Bob Cobbing's Writers Forum in 1971. Her first full collection was *Across the Burning Sand* (Gwasg Gomer, 1970). However, due to the technical challenges at that time of reproducing collages and concrete poems, the poems in it are formally traditional, although they dispense with capital letters and conventional punctuation. In addition to poetry, Bielski wrote several booklets on local Welsh history, including *Flower Legends of Wales* (1974), *Tales and Traditions of Tenby* (1981), and *The Story of St. Mellons* (1985). Her selected poems appeared as *That Crimson Flame*, published by the University of Salzburg in 1996. Her last books were *Sacramental Sonnets* (2003) and *One of Our Skylarks* (2011). In Bielski's obituary, Meic Stephens writes that this book is "a cycle of 52 poems written in 1982 which she considered her most sustained and memorable work. The sequence is based on the year's cycle and reflects Church liturgy and the legends of Dyfed, land of the Mabinogion, where she lived for more than a decade, working in Tenby bookshops." He also describes Bielski as a private person who "found solace in playing the organ and harpsichord, and in baroque music and the game of chess."

Tomaso Binga is the artistic name of Bianca Menna, who was born in Salerno on the Amalfi Coast in 1931 and has lived and worked in Rome for over five decades. She works with poetry, writing, performance, collage, painting, and installation, and has produced a body of work marked by a relentlessly subversive, playful sensibility. In the early 1970s she adopted her male pseudonym as a spoof on masculinity. Her chosen first name of *Tomaso* is an homage to the poet Filippo Tommaso Marinetti, though she characterizes her removal of an *m* from his middle name as a gesture in opposition to his misogyny. *Binga* resulted from distorting the childlike pronunciation of her first name, Bianca. Many of her concrete poems and text-based works are motivated by a desire to invent a language that refuses to perpetuate patriarchal norms. In 1972, she began making wallpaper out of asemic writing (*Scrittura desemantizzata*), automatic, illegible writing deemed by her to be "subliminal and silent," and operating as "a living being that proliferates like cells invading the environment." A desire to produce alternate alphabets has been constant in her work. For her *Dattilocodice* (Typecode) series of 1978, she superimposed typewritten letters to produce ideograms reminiscent of the pictographic roots of written characters. Her *Scritture viventi* (Living Writing), for which she assumed a different bodily position for each letter of the alphabet, is the basis of several collage series, among them the *Alfabetiere murale* (Mural ABC, 1976); the *Alfabetiere pop* (Pop ABC, 1976), containing imagery from children's books; the *Alfabeto officinale* (Herbalist Alphabet, 1981), with plant names; and the politically charged *Alfabeto proverbiale* (Proverbial Alphabet, 2009). Binga was a professor of Theory and Method of Mass Media at the Academy of Fine Arts in Frosinone. Since 1974 she has been a cultural organizer and has directed the cultural association Lavatoio Contumaciale in Rome. She has shown extensively in Europe. Noteworthy exhibitions include *Materializzazione del linguaggio*, curated by Mirella Bentivoglio for the Venice Biennale (1978); the São Paulo Biennial (1981); *Poesia totale* at the Palazzo della Ragione, Mantova (1998); *Bunker poetico*, in the Venice Biennale (2001); a solo show at the Fundación Klemm in Buenos Aires (2006); *Sogno uno mondo ch'è maschile trasformarsi al femminile* (*I Dream of a Male World Becoming Female*), Museo S. Elmo, Naples (2012); *Anni '70: Arte a Roma* (*The '70s: Art in Rome*), Palazzo delle Esposizioni, Rome (2013); *Per-formare una collezione* (*To Per-form a Collection*), Museo Madre, Naples (2013); *TV 70: Francesco Vezzoli guarda la RAI* (*TV 70: Francesco Vezzoli Watches the RAI*), Fondazione Prada (2017); and the solo show *Tomaso Binga: A Silenced Victory* at Mimosa House in London (2019).

Irma Blank has lived and worked in Milan since 1973. She was born in Celle, Germany, in 1934. She began composing one of her signature series, *Eigenschriften* (Self-Writings), upon arriving in Sicily, before she became fluent in Italian. Composed between 1968 and 1973, it comprises emptied calligraphic forms that resist being decoded, and blurs the distinction between text and image to the point of inextricability. In 2019, drawings from the *Eigenschriften* series were published by Sternberg Press. Another iconic series is *Trascrizioni* (1973–79), consisting of transcriptions into asemic writing of unnamed assorted publications, ranging from newspapers to reference books. Blank's later series, *Radical Writings* (1983–95), and *Avant-testo* (Avant-Text), completed in the early aughts, deploy painterly techniques to evoke writing and open books. Current, ongoing series are *Gehen* (Go) and *Global Writings*, in which she transfers portions of words written in a reduced alphabet onto the page by using carbon paper. Of her process, Blank remarked in 2001: "Non-verbal writing, writing that remains in silence, original truth. Writing becomes image, a manifestation of being, of being there, in the absolute without form. An open text. A text for all. For those who know how to read and for those who do not know how to read." Her work has been presented in many notable exhibitions, including Bentivoglio's *Materializzazione del linguaggio* for the Venice Biennale (1978); *Viva Arte Viva* for the Venice Biennale (2017); and *Modernités plurielles de 1905 à 1970* (*Multiple Modernities*

1905–1970), Centre Pompidou, Paris (2013). From 2019 to 2021, the touring exhibition *Irma Blank: Blank* is scheduled to travel to Culturgest (Lisbon), Musée d'Art Moderne et Contemporain (Geneva), CAPC Musée d'Art Contemporain (Bordeaux), Center for Contemporary Arts (Tel Aviv), Fondazione ICA (Milan), Museo Villa dei Cedri (Bellinzona, Switzerland), and Bombas Gens Centre d'Art (Valencia).

Marianna Bocian was born in the village of Bełcząc, near Lublin, Poland, in 1942. She majored in Polish studies and philosophy at the University of Wrocław. At Wrocław she was immersed in an intense artistic milieu, which provided fertile ground for concrete poetry and conceptual art to thrive. Authors' evenings at public libraries and exhibitions at artist-run galleries took place regularly, with the aim of confronting official culture with new visual and verbal languages. Bocian presented at the first theoretical-critical session devoted to concrete poetry at Kalambur Academic Theater Center in 1979. A landmark event, it was organized by Stanisław Dróżdż, who was writing visual texts he called "concept-shapes" and "content-forms." Bocian traced her interest in visual forms to thought-forms and ideoscapes, mandalas and *carmina figurata*, or pattern poems. In the 1970s, she had three exhibitions she conceived as "proofs of a visualized idea." *Crucified on Debts*, shown at the Piwnica Świdnicka Gallery in 1973, featured a cross on the ground surrounded by letters of the Polish alphabet, allusive to the crucifixion of language. A publication containing a "Non-manifesto" accompanied the exhibition; an excerpt reads: "Language resurrects in the mind from its foundation—and thus from the alphabet, and is 'impossible to be killed' as a source [...] a sense-forming connection with life." Deemed scandalous, the exhibition was censored after three days. Her body of work ranged from poetry to prose to literary criticism. The Friends of Wrocław Polish Studies Association published her *Selected Poems* in 1998.

Blanca Calparsoro was born in Tolosa, Guipúzcoa, in the Basque Country, in 1936. After studying in Madrid, she traveled to Rome and then to Paris, where she lived in the 1960s. In 1965, she contributed poems to the first issue of Pierre Garnier's journal *Les Lettres*, devoted to Spatialism. In 1968, her poem "Spatialist Poem in Basque," combining stacks of the words *aiñara* or *ainara* ("barn swallow") and *izkuntza* ("language"), was included in the volume *Spatialisme et poésie concrète* (Spatialism and Concrete Poetry), which Garnier edited for Gallimard. That same poem was included in the international exhibition *Poesia concreta: Indirizzi concreti, visuali e fonetici* (*Concrete Poetry: Concrete, Visual, and Phonetic Addresses*), curated by Dietrich Mahlow and Arrigo Lora-Totino at the 1969 Venice Biennale. Along with Mirella Bentivoglio and Bohumila Grögerová, Calparsoro was one of three women to be included in this exhibition of more than eighty artists. Her first book of poems, *La isla y otros poemas* (The Island and Other Poems) appeared in 1967 with drawings by Basque artist Esther Ferrer. It was followed by *Collages* in 1969. Both books were the result of Calparsoro's collaborations with Zaj, a group of experimental musicians and artists who were affiliated with Fluxus and based in Madrid. After a hiatus of over a decade, Calparsoro resumed publishing poetry with *El vacío y las horas* (The Void and the Hours; 1981) and *Momentos* (Moments; 1985). *Yacer en lo hondo* (To Lie in the Deep; 2000) is her last full collection of poetry.

Paula Claire was born in Northampton, England, in 1939. For over five decades, she has been active in the fields of visual and concrete poetry, as well as sound poetry and performance. She is the author of over a hundred artists' books and three volumes of selected poems. Her first publication was the chapbook *Mobile Poems, Greece* (1968); the poems are described as "mobile" because sections of them are meant to be improvised by different voices speaking simultaneously. Claire writes that this idea for performance came to her from Alexander Calder's mobiles and from listening to jazz, as well as Ravi Shankar in concert. In the 1970s, Claire was associated with the British Poetry Revival movement and, along with Bob Cobbing and Michael Chant, was a member of the poetry performance group Konkrete Canticle until 1993. Cobbing was a frequent collaborator; he published her work through Writers Forum from 1970 to 1992. From the 1970s on, she participated in many key performances and exhibitions, among them *klankteksten / ? konkrete poëzie / visuele teksten* (*sound texts / ? concrete poetry / visual texts*) at Amsterdam's Stedelijk Museum in 1970; the launch of the sound poetry mimeo *Kroklok*, edited by Dom Sylvester Houédard, at London's Institute of Contemporary Arts (ICA) in 1971; and in *Materializzazione del linguaggio*, curated by Mirella Bentivoglio for the 1978 Venice Biennale. For the Biennale, Claire created a site-specific polyvocal, participatory performance in English and Italian based on an erasure of John Ruskin's *Stones of Venice* (1851). This piece was published as *Codestones of Venice* (Writers Forum). Many of Claire's performances are equally polyvocal and site-specific, conceived for outdoor spaces and historic buildings that offer specific sonic possibilities. She is the founder of the Paula Claire Archive: fromWORDtoART – International Poet-Artists, the largest archive of sound and visual poetry in England.

Betty Danon (née Beki Aluf) was born in Istanbul in 1920 and relocated to Milan in 1956, where she obtained Italian citizenship and changed her name. She was a conceptual artist who worked with painting, sound, collage, and concrete poetry. Jungian symbology provided the basis for her early compositions. Her work developed by reducing the circle and the square to their primal elements, the dot and the line, which she understood as equivalent to the duality of yin and yang. In a statement for the exhibition *Suono e segno* (*Sound and Sign*) at the Galleria Milano in 1977, she writes: "The dot as starting point, line as path, as itinerary..." This show and others were iterations of these notions, and involved translating sound into verbal and visual signs and vice versa. Danon had eleven solo shows between 1970 and 1982. She also participated in the following exhibitions, among many others: *Magma*, organized by leading feminist curator Romana Loda, Museo di Castelvecchio Verona (1977); *Materializzazione del linguaggio*, Venice Biennale (1978); *Sound*, PS1, New York (1979); *Languages Beyond Poetry*, Westfälischer Kunstverein, Münster (1979); *Il tempo del museo* (*Time in the Museum*), Venice Biennale (1980); and the São Paulo Biennial (1981). For *Materializzazione del linguaggio*, she reperformed *La memoria del segno sonoro* (Sound-Signs Memory), a fifteen- to eighteen-minute piece she had presented earlier in

1978 at the Duemila Gallery in Bologna. The first action in the performance was to write on staffs. The writing was not to be seen, but only heard, producing "the sound of an absence." The second action was to cover the invisible signs with a brushstroke of blue ink, which made them visible. In the 1980s Danon became active in the international mail art circuit. She corresponded regularly with Amelia Etlinger. Danon died in Milan in 2002.

Born in Budapest, Hungary, in 1931, **Agnes Denes** was raised in Sweden and educated in the United States. She is a pioneering figure among the ranks of conceptual artists who emerged in the 1960s and '70s and made work that engaged social practice and environmental art. Investigations in the fields of science, philosophy, linguistics, psychology, poetry, history, and music serve as points of departure for her projects in a variety of media. Landmark works include the 1968 site-specific piece *Rice/Tree/Burial* in Sullivan County, New York (later reenacted), which consisted of a ritual of dialectic triangulation in which Denes planted rice, chained trees, and buried a haiku symbolizing her consciousness and the essence of invention. These actions were intended as a gesture emblematic of the "self-denial and discipline required by this new analytical art form." *Rice/Tree/Burial* marked the beginning of Denes's development of a "visual philosophy," which she defines as one that "finds methods to put analytical propositions into visual form, defines elusive processes, and creates analogies among divergent fields and thought [...] It challenges the status quo and tests its own validity." This visual philosophy is at the core of Denes's oeuvre, and is exquisitely manifest in her *Philosophical Drawings* (1969–80). Her best-known work is *Wheatfield – A Confrontation* (1982), for which she planted a field of wheat on two acres of rubble-strewn landfill near Wall Street and the World Trade Center. She has participated in more than 450 exhibitions throughout the world. Her most recent retrospective, *Agnes Denes: Absolutes and Intermediates*, was on view at the Shed in New York until the spring of 2020.

Mirtha Dermisache lived and worked in her native Buenos Aires. She completed undergraduate studies in fine arts and began her career at a time of intense engagement with conceptualism and media art in Argentina. Much of this work was shown at the Instituto Di Tella, yet Dermisache arrived at her distinctive explorations of writing's material properties on her own. Her body of work displays an astounding range of graphic approaches to a central proposition: that of removing printed or handwritten language from traditional print formats—books, flyers, newspapers, postcards, letters—and instead populating them with highly gestural yet illegible writing. Her first work, *Libro No. 1* (Book No. 1), from 1967, was conceived as a five-hundred-page book but was split into two shorter books due to the challenges of binding it. Staunchly opposed to unique works of art, Dermisache believed that a work wasn't complete until it circulated in print: "I 'write' (inscribe) my books, which are perfectly illegible, and that tenuous structure of 'gaps' is filled as soon as it reaches the 'reader.'" Her first newspaper from 1970, *Diario No. 1 Año 1*, was distributed on park benches as part of an exhibition at the Centro de Arte y Comunicación, another important hub of experimental art practice. Through a friend of hers living in Paris, one of Dermisache's books was shown to Roland Barthes. In 1971 he wrote her one of several enthusiastic letters, which, she maintained, furthered her explorations with asemic writing: "You have managed to produce a certain number of forms that are neither figurative nor abstract, forms that could be called illegible writing, which leads readers to formulate something that is neither a specific message nor a contingent form of expression, but, rather, the idea, the essence, of writing." The artist-book circuit in Europe was receptive to her work. Among others, Guy Schraenen included her in international exhibitions and printed one of her editions, and Ulises Carrión featured her work at Other Books and So. Besides her artistic output, Dermisache was committed to radical arts education. From 1975 to 1981, even at the height of the military junta in Argentina, she staged numerous free, public *Jornadas del Color y de la Forma* (Color and Form Sessions). These workshops were immensely popular and avoided formal methodologies. Instead, they urged participants (often in the thousands) to "rescue the world of forms within us, and recognize ourselves in them."

Amelia Etlinger was born in New York City in 1933 and moved with her family to Clifton Park, New York, in the late 1960s. Reading E. E. Cummings inspired her to write visual poetry that gradually evolved into elaborate and collaborative works made of natural materials as well as fabric, beads, costume jewelry, Japanese papers, and other found materials. By the 1970s, her poetry had abandoned words as its primary medium and was written in the language of threads and collage. "I don't care how great poems are anymore. Words typed out on a page are meaningless," she stated in an interview with Ellen Marie Bissert and June Rook for the feminist journal *13th Moon* in 1976. She made "poem packets" for specific correspondents using department-store boxes with poems on the inside or outside of them, and book-like structures created from manipulated paper and fabric. Inside the boxes were personal fragments, fabric, and materials such as tissue and cellophane, as well as petals, ferns, leaves, and seeds, found in her backyard. Although relatively unknown in the United States, Etlinger exhibited internationally, most notably in Italy, where her work was well received by concrete theorists and the Italian *poesia visiva* community. She had a solo exhibition at Centro Tool in Milan in 1974 and showed hanging book poems at Ugo Carrega's Mercato del Sale gallery in Milan in 1974 and 1975. Her first publication was in Paul de Vree's *De Tafelronde*. She participated in Mirella Bentivoglio's *Materializzazione del linguaggio* in the Venice Biennale in 1978. Etlinger died in 1987. Her collection, consisting of her papers and over a hundred works, was donated by Bissert to the University at Buffalo's Poetry Collection.

German-born **Ilse Garnier** collaborated extensively with her husband, Pierre Garnier. She was born in Kaiserslautern, Germany, in 1927, and met Garnier in 1950. They co-founded and articulated the tenets of Spatialism in the journal *Les Lettres*, which Pierre edited. Spatialism is capaciously defined in Garnier's manifesto "Position I of the International Movement" (1963), which was published in issue no. 32 of the journal, and was signed by the likes of Ian Hamilton Finlay, Mário Chamie, Carlfriedrich Claus, John Furnival, Eugen Gomringer, Bohumila Grögerová, Josef Hiršal, Anselm Hollo, Sylvester Houédard, Ernst Jandl, Kitasono

Katué, Franz Mon, Edwin Morgan, Paul de Vree, and Emmett Williams. Spatialism encompasses concrete, phonetic, phonic (composed directly on magnetic tape), visual, and objective poetry (created in collaboration with musicians, painters, sculptors, and typographers), as well as cybernetic or permutational poetry. An international poetry, it was essential at a time in which, according to Garnier, national languages had become increasingly bureaucratic and had lost their "power of incantation." Spatialism's impetus, according to the manifesto, was to liberate language's "profound vitality" from "ideas and moralities" and "create new structures" aimed at destroying the isolated work of art "in favor of the idea of transmitted energy." Language, then, is "the totality of functions, relations, radiations, linguistic concretions, but also as the noises, gestures, silences by means of which language grafts itself directly upon the universe in which we live." Ilse Garnier's sound poems, such as "Les Iles" (The Islands), "Poème Action No. 1," and "Thalatta," attest to her desire to produce incantatory rhythms. She participated in numerous exhibitions devoted to concrete poetry, among them *Materializzazione del linguaggio* at the Venice Biennale in 1978, and authored many publications both alone and in collaboration with her husband. Among her many books are *Blason du corps féminin* (The Female Body's Coat of Arms; 1979) and *Rythmes et silence* (Rhythms and Silence; 1980). Ilse and Pierre Garnier's *Poésie spatiale – Une anthologie* (Spatial Poetry – An Anthology) was published by Les presses du réel in 2012.

Anna Bella Geiger was born in Rio de Janeiro to Polish-Jewish parents in 1933. During her formative years, in the early 1950s, she took free art classes with Polish émigré Fayga Ostrower, who was a politically minded engraver and abstract expressionist painter. At this time, Geiger was making abstract paintings and studying Anglo-Germanic languages and literature at the Universidade Federal do Rio de Janeiro, where she would later teach. In 1953 she showed abstract paintings at the first National Exhibition of Abstract Art in Petrópolis, alongside works by artists who would form the Neo-Concrete movement and the Grupo Frente (made up of, among others, Ivan Serpa, Hélio Oiticica, Lygia Pape, and Lygia Clark). From 1953 to 1954, she lived in New York City, where she studied art history and sociology at New York University, the Metropolitan Museum of Art, and the New School for Social Research. From 1960 to 1965 she was a member of the print atelier of the Museu de Arte Moderna in Rio, but she distanced herself from it once she began making the prints depicting internal organs in her *Visceral* series. The series marked a transition in Geiger's work, precipitated by the oppressive political climate of the time: "I couldn't believe in the modern principles that I had taught before because there had been a rupture."[1] After the Fifth Institutional Act of 1968, which intensified the censorship, persecutions, and torture of Brazil's military regime (1964–85), Geiger participated in the boycott of the 1969 São Paulo Biennial. She encouraged international artists whom she had met at the 1968 Venice Biennale—Daniel Buren and Christian Boltanski among them—to join the boycott. By the early 1970s, Geiger was engaged in collaborations and pedagogical experiments that led to conceptual artists' books and multimedia projects comprising text, collage, photography, and video, such as her installation *Circumambulatio* (1972) and the series *Brasil natal/Brasil alienígena* (Native Brazil/Alien Brazil, 1977), which combines family photos with found postcards of indigenous peoples. Animating her works are questions about identity and Brazilianness, cartography and geopolitics, and the center-periphery dynamics applied to both local and international power centers. A survey of her work was on view at the SESC Avenida Paulista and Museu de Arte de São Paulo in early 2019. She has participated in numerous international exhibitions, most recently in *Radical Women: Latin American Art, 1960–1985*, shown at the Hammer Museum in Los Angeles in 2017, and at the Brooklyn Museum in 2018.

Poet and writer **Madeline Gins** (1941–2014) was born in the Bronx and grew up on Long Island, and studied physics and Eastern philosophy at Barnard, graduating in 1962. She wrote three books: the experimental novel *Word Rain (or a Discursive Introduction to the Intimate Philosophical Investigations of G,R,E,T,A G,A,R,B,O, It Says)* (1969); *What the President Will Say and Do!!* (1984); and *Helen Keller or Arakawa* (1994), a hybrid of art-historical and speculative fiction. Gins also studied painting at the Brooklyn Museum Art School, where she met Shusaku Arakawa, a protégé of Marcel Duchamp, in 1962. As a husband-and-wife team, they would go on to collaborate on books and visionary architectural projects for nearly half a century, developing the notion of a procedural architecture conceived to effect a "reversible destiny" that would allow humans "to reverse the downhill course of human life,"[2] ultimately defying death. At the core of their projects was the belief that architectural instability—manifested in uneven surfaces, no plumb lines, no true corners, and other elements—could force a building's inhabitants to avoid comfort and the attendant atrophying of the human organism, and jolt their senses and immune systems into perpetual alertness. Among Gins and Arakawa's better-known projects are the Reversible Destiny Lofts – Mitaka (In Memory of Helen Keller) (2005), residential stacked pods in a suburb of Tokyo; and the Bioscleave House (Lifespan Extending Villa) (2008), a private residence on Long Island. Previously unpublished poems by Gins, along with a full facsimile edition of *Word Rain* and excerpts from her other works of fiction, appear in the reader *The Saddest Thing Is That I Have Had to Use Words* (Siglio Books, 2020), edited by Lucy Ives. *Word Rain* immediately presents the reader with a deliriously dislocating metanarrative conceit, as the book's narrator is a reader hyperaware of the phenomenology and materiality of reading: "Read this with me, read that with me, read me with me, read objects (tables, toes, toads, tails, tin, trains, type, tears, throat) read write read right. This is still life. Only I write and read. If you've misplaced me on your own, bring me up again from off this page."

Bohumila Grögerová was a Czech poet, writer, translator, and author of radio plays and children's books. She was born in Prague in 1921, and died there in 2014. In tandem with Josef Hiršal, her life partner, she wrote and translated over a hundred titles. In *Concrete Poetry: A World View*, Mary Ellen Solt describes the drive toward experimentation with new forms in Czechoslovakia as being "born of a reaction against verbosity, literary affectation of style, sentimentality, pathos and emotionalism in traditional poetry."[3] About Grögerová and Hiršal she writes: "The first Czech concrete poets were also translators who, as the result of their preoccupation with linguistic material and its problems, perceived the need in their own language for a new poetry involved with the actual mechanisms of language, poems that would show 'not only the image of the world but its schemes,'" quoting them. Their experiments from 1960 to 1962 were published in their co-written *job boj* (1968). *Boj* is Czech for "fight" or "action," and of course, when read backward, spells the English word *job*. The book is intensely playful and intertextual, with each of its poems stemming from a different procedure. It was the sixth broadsheet to be published in Hansjörg Mayer's Futura series, in 1966. Both Grögerová and Hiršal are co-signatories of Pierre Garnier's "Position I of the International Movement," published in issue no. 32 of *Les Lettres* in 1963. At a conference on concrete poetry held at the club Mánes in Prague in 1964, they met Brazilian concrete poet Haroldo de Campos. Of how she and Hiršal began experimenting with language, Grögerová remarks in a 2009 interview with the Czech magazine *Respekt*: "In the 1950s, when Hiršal and I met at the Naše vojsko publishing house, an absurd reality unfolded around us. Nothing could be taken seriously and at the same time it was very serious. There was almost no work in the publishing house and we spent time playing all kinds of games, such as five-in-a-row. At that time, we felt that language was suddenly not what it used to be, that words were discredited, reality was falsified." They began to translate experimental works from Europe and Latin America, and established mutually influential relationships with the authors. Other titles by Grögerová and Hiršal are the prose book *Trojcestí* (Three Paths; 1991) and the memoir *Let let* (The Flight of Years; 2007). Grögerová's independent titles mix experimental procedures and autobiographical elements; among them are *Meandry* (Meanders; 1996), *Branka z pantů* (Gate from the Hinges; 1998), *Čas mezi tehdy a teď* (Time between Then and Now; 2004), and *Rukopis* (Manuscript; 2008), which received the prizes for best poetry book and best book at the Magnesia Litera awards in 2009. That same year she also received a lifetime achievement award from the Czech PEN Club.

Porto-born artist, poet, and scholar **Ana Hatherly** (1929–2015) wrote the first concrete poem to be published in Portugal in 1959: "poeta arca seta" (poet ark arrow). She maintained only a loose affiliation with the concrete poetry movement, however, as she preferred preserving the freedom to write experimental prose and poetry in modes ranging from the lyric to the concrete to the procedural and combinatorial. Her will to experiment was paired with a rigorous exploration of the processes of writing and reading, the plastic and gestural dimensions of writing, typography in relationship to handwriting and calligraphy, and verbal and visual signs as dynamic and speculative entities. In drawings that play with writing's legibility, lines become a mask for the word, allowing for its flight from the logocentric. She writes in "The Written Word": "The written word / is an archaic toil / furrows enigmas / covers and uncovers / the gesture's meaning. // A detained image / gathered from the deepest intimate cinema… " Her investigations unfolded in abundant and genre-defying theoretical texts, chronicles, fiction, poems, actions, films, collages, drawings, and paintings. Hatherly was part of the PO.EX group, along with Salette Tavares and other artists and poets, and was co-editor of their magazine *Cadernos de poesia experimental* (1964, 1966). The group was as critical of Portugal's political landscape as it was of its cultural one, and through actions, exhibitions, and publications sought to reinvigorate the scene following the models of Mallarmé, Joyce, Pound, Apollinaire, the Futurists, and the Dadaists. One of the most complete Hatherliana collections in the United States is at the University of California, Berkeley, where Hatherly earned a doctorate in 1986, focused on the Spanish Golden Age. She studied Germanic philology at the Universidade Clássica de Lisboa, and also received a degree in cinematographic techniques at the London Film School. Between 1981 and 1999, she taught in the humanities department at the Universidade Nova de Lisboa. Hatherly's academic research contributed to a radical rereading of baroque poetry in Portugal that highlighted the graphic visuality of the period's literary forms. In her writing based on fragments by other authors, such as the *Leonorana* series, Hatherly creates labyrinthine citational networks in which to read is to read her formal reading/writing of another's writing, and the distinction between reading and writing is blurred. Two anthologies collect her literary works, *Um calculador de improbabilidades* (A Calculator of Improbabilities; 2001) and *Interfaces do olhar: uma antologia crítica, uma antologia poética* (The Interfaces of Seeing: A Critical and Poetic Anthology; 2004). Her work has shown extensively in Portugal and abroad, at museums including the Fundação Calouste Gulbenkian in Lisbon and the Serralves Museum in Porto.

Susan Howe was born in Boston in 1937 and lives in Guilford, Connecticut. She studied painting at the School of the Museum of Fine Arts in Boston and later moved to New York, in the 1960s. In an interview in the *Paris Review*, she describes her early explorations with words and images as follows: "I started making lists of single words, usually nouns, bird names, or place-names, often cut from books and collaged with pencil lines and watercolor washes. I began incorporating old engineering instruction manuals, maps, and charts. Single words and the letters that formed them were what attracted me. Gradually I came to make books of watercolor stains, photographs, and words. After a time I just used words on drawing paper, or pasted on walls. It was as though I had a book of the wall." Eventually, at the suggestion of poet Ted Greenwald, she took her works off the wall and put them onto the page, composing her first book, *Hinge Picture* (1974). Ever since, her work has been characterized by the use of collage, found language, and typographical innovations. Howe is an avid researcher of historical archives, manuscripts, and marginalia, and a concern with American history is also a consistent element throughout her work. Her poetry spans almost five decades, beginning with her early books from the 1970s, which were collected in *Frame Structures* (1996). New Directions has published thirteen of her collections, including her most recent, *Concordance* (2020), as well as *Debths* (2017), *Spontaneous Particulars: The Telepathy of Archives* (2014), *Souls of the Labadie Tract* (2007), *The Midnight* (2003), and *Pierce-Arrow* (1999). Howe is also the author of two innovative books of literary criticism: *My Emily Dickinson* (1985, reissued in 2007) and *The Birth-mark: Unsettling the Wilderness in American Literary History* (1983). She received the Bollingen Prize for Poetry in 2011. Her work has been exhibited at Yale Union in Portland, Oregon, and at the Whitney Biennial in 2014. She has collaborated with musician David Grubbs on four albums, the most recent being *WOODSLIPPERCOUNTERCLATTER* (2015).

Little is know about **Ruth Jacoby** except for the fact that she was a New York City–based visual poet who was born in 1903 and died in 1993. Her work is included in the volume *4 Major Visual Poets: Ruth Jacoby, Richard Kostelanetz, Tom Ockerse, Michael Joseph Phillips*, edited by Michael Joseph Phillips (Free University Press, 1980). From the materials of hers in the Sackner Archive of Visual and Concrete Poetry, we know that she made collages and prints, and that some of her work was appropriation-based. She had a solo show at the Bodley Gallery in New York in 1968. Her remarks regarding the collage *Stripes* (1970), made with hand-cut stenciled letters, address her philosophy on the relationship between the word and image: "This is a pure word-image or wordscape, where the form itself gives meaning to the word. The word itself becomes the plastic entity where one can know things by sight."

Serbian artist **Tamara Janković** was a member of the Signalist group of avant-garde artists and poets based in Belgrade. Named after the term *signum* (Latin for "sign") and founded by Miroljub Todorović, the Signalists aimed to revolutionize poetry by bringing elements of science into it: scientific language, formulas, and symbols from physics, biology, chemistry, and mathematics, as well as cybernetics, information theory, and structural linguistics. The movement's three manifestos are the "Manifesto of Scientific Poetry" (1968), the "Signalist Manifesto (Regulae Poesis)" (1969), and "Signalism" (1970). Together, these three texts delineate the group's vision: for Signalist poetry to escape "the semantic fortresses of script and Gutenbergian civilization" and instead present open, multidimensional textual surfaces animated by a desire for absolute experimentation in the arts. Janković was on the editorial board of the group's magazine, *Signal*, of which nine issues appeared between 1970 and 1973. After a twenty-two-year hiatus, *Signal* reappeared, and twenty-one issues of the magazine were published from 1995 to 2004. The magazine's scope was international; in the 1970s, works by poets such as Raoul Hausmann, Augusto de Campos, Bob Cobbing, Clemente Padín, Julien Blaine, Sol LeWitt, Pierre Garnier, Dick Higgins, and Eugen Gomringer appeared in its pages alongside contributions by Signalists. The first exhibition of Signalist works abroad took place at Centro Tool in Milan and included work by Janković and Todorović as well as Vlada Stojiljković, Zoran Popović, and Marina Abramović.

Munich-based artist **Annalies Klophaus** was born in Bad Oeynhausen, Germany, in 1940. She studied in the Art and Design Department at the University of Wuppertal, and later conducted brief studies in textile art at the Werkkunstschule in Bielefeld. She began making word paintings and artists' books exploring the links between legible handwriting, words, and color in 1968. Among such books are *ersie + sie notationen* (heshe + she notations; 1977); *Rest 1, Rest 2* (1972), a facsimile of the artist's sketchbook; and *Mot-Couleur-Roman* (Word-Color-Novel; 1970), published by Éditions Agentzia in Paris. Agentzia, founded by editors Jochen Gerz and Jean-François Bory, ran from 1967 to 1971 and, according to Gerz, "stressed agency—communication, information, rapidity, news—rather than creativity."[4] Its magazine published visual poetry, art, and research, and it also published objects, leaflets, posters, editions, and books. Klophaus's *Mot-Couleur-Roman* ends with an artist's statement in which she writes: "I employed color as color / I employed the word as word / Then I brought together color and word / Their reunion remains artificial. / I believe that color can kill words. / For example: If I write death in green, death will not exist for much longer. If I write the word happy [in red], it will be superfluous to use the word unhappy. / Maybe we will learn to read the word death in green." Klophaus participated in Bentivoglio's *Materializzazione del linguaggio* for the Venice Biennale of 1978, and earlier, in the multiyear exhibition *Arti visive. Poesia visiva. / Visual Poetry by Women*, also curated by Bentivoglio, which originated in Venice in 1972 and traveled from city to city throughout Italy. She has had numerous exhibitions in Germany.

Before studying family medicine for three years, **Marzenna Kosińska**—born in Lviv, Poland, in 1939—enrolled in the Academy of Fine Arts in Wrocław. She received a diploma from the ceramics and glass workshop in 1965. Along with Stanisław Dróżdż, Marianna Bocian, Barbara Kozłowska, and others, she was part of the avant-garde circle in Wrocław that pursued conceptual art and concrete poetry in reaction to official art during the 1970s and '80s. Wrocław, formerly called Breslau, had been termed one of Poland's Recovered Territories after World War II, and was thus subjected to intense propagandistic efforts by the Communist Party to reclaim it as part of the homeland, through the modernization of its industry and its artistic and academic institutions. Kosińska, like her peers, rejected the instrumentalization of art and poetry, and conceived of her works as textual art in which both the ends and the materials used to achieve them are as pared down as possible, and traces of the artist's expressive intent are absent. Her works were often aimed at pairing harmoniously geometric structures with visually captivating semantic games, as in *Od-do* (From-To, 1978), in which the clock's arms literally spell "to" and "from." Kosińska participated in projects conceived by avant-garde critic and curator Jerzy Ludwiński, who worked on the periphery of state culture and founded the Mona Lisa Gallery and the Center for Artistic Research. Group exhibitions include *Poesia totale 1897–1997* in Mantova, Italy (1998), and *Polish Concrete Poetry* at the Center for Contemporary Art Ujazdowski Castle Warsaw and BWA Katowice (2001). Most recently, her work was included in the exhibition *WroConcret*, curated by Małgorzata Dawidek Gryglicka, at the Muzeum Współczesne in Wrocław in 2011.

Barbara Kozłowska was born in Tarnobrzeg in 1940 and died in 2008 in Wrocław. She was one of the most significant artists of the Wrocław avant-garde art circles of the 1970s. She studied at the Academy of Fine Arts in Wrocław, receiving a diploma in Architectural Paintings for the Design of the Pantomime Theater in Ceramic Technique in 1965. She worked in traditional media such as painting, drawing, and sculpture, as well as video and animation, installation, land art, and performance art. Her conceptual projects combined poetry, text, and photography. She wrote manifestos and art theoretical texts as well. Kozłowska participated in breakthrough events in the Polish art scene of the era, such as the Symposium Wrocław '70, a gathering of artists, critics, and theorists that forged new directions in Polish conceptual art. It was initiated by Jerzy Ludwiński, who had coined the phrase "art in a post-artistic era." For the symposium, Kozłowska created *Jedynka* (One), an architectural model/sculpture executed in stainless steel (welded metal) that is based on Stanisław Dróżdż's poem "Loneliness." She conceived of the project as being part of an unlimited, unclosed total (global) system. Kozłowska also proposed the execution of the piece *"OKNO," "FENSTER," "WINDOW"* to the city at that time, which was about contrasting the words' meanings with their visual effects. Between 1972 and 1982, Kozłowska transformed her studio in Wrocław into the artist-run gallery space Babel, providing artists with an independent venue for debate and exhibitions. Kozłowska's art often relied on ephemeral, hardly perceptible gestures. Her performances, happenings, and ephemeral interventions activated mundane objects such as chalk, sheets of paper, pumice stones, plastic bottles, and timber. Starting in 1970, she worked on the project *Borderline*, traveling to Siberia, Great Britain, Malta, Italy, France, the Netherlands, Yugoslavia, Germany, and the United States. It was initially drawn on the beach in Łazy, Poland, in 1970 as a succession of sand cones, devices used to measure the density of any soil. As the project evolved, it was shown in the form of charts, slides, and photos in a selection of cities, including Edinburgh in 1972. *Borderline* was included in the exhibition *Conceptual Reflection in Polish Art: Experiences of Discourse: 1965–1975* at the Center for Contemporary Art, Ujazdowski Castle, in 1999. Kozłowska participated in the exhibition *WroConcret*, curated by Małgorzata Dawidek Gryglicka, at the Muzeum Współczesne in Wrocław in 2011. Most recently, the Arton Foundation in Warsaw hosted a survey of her work entitled *You Can See All of This Anywhere* (2016).

Katalin Ladik is a Serbian-Hungarian poet and performance artist born in Novi Sad, Serbia, in 1942. She has lived and worked alternately in Novi Sad, Budapest, and the island of Hvar, Croatia, for at least two decades. From 1963 to 1977, she worked for Radio Novi Sad. She joined the Novi Sad Theater in 1974, and was a member of its ensemble from 1977 until 1992. She began publishing surreal, erotic poetry in 1962. She has published books including *Ballada az ezüstbicikliről* (Ballad of the Silver Bicycle; 1969) and *Kiűzetés* (Exile; 1988), yet she finds the medium of the page too static for her taste. Exploring language through visual and vocal expressions, Ladik works in collage, photography, records, performances, and happenings in both urban and natural environments. Her multilingual work involves collage-based graphic scores animated by and through bodily and vocal performances that often draw on folk-music traditions. In 2017, for Documenta 14, she improvised a choreographic vocal performance based on the female figures of Greek mythology. Hendrik Folkerts, curator of Documenta 14, writes: "We see the language of Ladik's body as the main instrument in her performances onstage, in shamanistic gatherings in 1960s Novi Sad, and as a stark yet seductive presence at Happenings. Yet the most exquisite part of her language, of her body, we *hear*: the voice. It vibrates, shrieks, rotates, comes from the head, the throat, the belly—all the high and low tones manifest in Ladik's great instrument. From the early 1970s, Ladik transformed 'found' materials such as sewing instructions, newspaper clippings, and computer circuits into visual scores for musical performance. She 'reads' these scores with every part of her voice, giving breath to the everyday references in the collages. In doing so, Ladik turns image into poetry into performance into music."[5] Ladik published her first experimental novel in 2007. Titled *Élhetek az arcodon?* (Can I Live on Your Face?), it is partly autobiographical and incorporates photography, newspaper clippings, and correspondence. Its protagonists are three women—an Editor, an Artist, and a Glasswoman—who share the same name, live in different cities, and begin to live each others' lives. Ladik is the subject of the documentary *Sound Cage: A Portrait of Katalin Ladik* (Hungary, 2015), directed by Kornél Szilágyi. In 2016 she was awarded the LennonOno Grant for Peace.

Liliana Landi was born in Genoa in 1940 and was based in Milan. She worked in graphic design before writing semiotic poetry and becoming involved in *poesia visiva*. She co-founded the magazine *TOOL* with Ugo Carrega, Rodolfo Vitone, Lino Matti, and others in 1965. It was devoted to exploring the poetic possibilities of visual writing that subverted scriptural conventions, a concept developed by Carrega under the rubric of "symbiotic writing." In 1975, Landi co-signed Carrega's "Manifesto of New Writing," advocating for a *Nuova Scrittura*. Other co-signatories were Vincenzo Accame, Martino and Anna Oberto, Corrado D'Ottavi, Rolando Mignani, and Vincenzo Ferrari. Landi participated in some of the most important exhibitions of works at the intersection of poetry and the visual arts, both in Italy and abroad, and wrote two books: *Oh, Jerusalem!* (undated, c. 1968) and *In rapporto a* (In Relation To; 1976). Her work was included in the exhibition *Arti visive. Poesia visiva. / Visual Poetry by Women*, curated by Mirella Bentivoglio in 1972. She died in 1987.

London-based artist **Liliane Lijn** was born in New York City in 1939 to parents who had just settled in the United States after fleeing from the Nazi threat in Europe. She attributes her interest in language to having grown up hearing six languages: the German her parents spoke, the Polish spoken on her mother's side of the family, Yiddish and Russian on her father's side, French by her aunts and uncles, and English. She attended boarding school in Vermont and then lived with her mother in Lugano, located in an Italian-speaking canton of southern Switzerland. In 1958, Lijn moved to Paris to become an artist. There she studied archeology and art history at the Sorbonne and the École du Louvre, met André Breton, and attended meetings at the Surrealist Café. Through the Greek sculptor Takis, she met South African poet Sinclair Beiles, who was then editing William Burroughs's *Naked Lunch* (1959) for Olympia Press. Beiles introduced Lijn to Burroughs, as well as Brion Gysin and Gregory Corso, whom she befriended. Of Gysin's cut-up technique, Lijn writes: "[it] moved surrealist automatic writing one step further, creating pure text collages and treating words like ready-made image. Unconsciously understanding this inspired my original juxtaposition of text with machine. I had also discovered the magazine *Scientific American* [...] My feeling about science—in particular the science of light and matter—was that it was pure poetry."[6] Her interest in science and technology was paired with a passion for Eastern philosophy, myth, and feminism. After making kinetic sculptures that produced interference patterns—her first was *Le Vibrograph* (1962)—she started incorporating cut-up poems into her devices. She returned to New York, where from 1961 to 1963 she was offered studio space in the warehouse of Industrial Plastics Supply on Canal Street, which allowed her to experiment with materials and technologies. She is the first woman to ever work with kinetic text, in her *Poem Machines*, first shown at La Librairie Anglaise in Paris in 1963: "Cut-ups were used to open up written prose and when I made *Poem Machines* my intention was to explode both prose and poetry, remembering their origin in vibration." In this period she also experimented with water, rotating lenses, and projectors to refract and reflect light in new ways. From the 1960s on she has made motorized cone-shaped sculptures called *Koans* that appear to dematerialize while spinning—for her, they are symbols of femininity. In 2012, her work was included in *Ecstatic Alphabets/Heaps of Language* at the Museum of Modern Art in New York. Recent solo exhibitions include *Cosmic Dramas* at the Middlesbrough Institute of Modern Art, Middlesbrough, UK (2012); *Earth Body Art* at Museo Civico di Santa Croce, Umbertide, Italy (2013); and *Early Events: Five Narrative Sculptures* at Summerhall, Edinburgh (2017).

On her Remington J2016997 typewriter, poet **Françoise Mairey** typed this list of keywords on a sheet, included in her folder of compositions, *Substitution* (1977): "typewriter / mechanical signs ... substitution ... a keyboard / keys ... strike force ... new instrument / combinations / vision / rhythm / space / movement / emptiness / density / lines of force ... accident / rhythm break ... error / starting point / or emphasis / a hypothesis / sliding / skid / a frame / overflowing / exceeding ... choice of the sign / deviation ... scales / exercises / finger games ... repetition ... signs to express the accident / the error ... unfolding / construction / compositions ... music music music music." These notes inform us of her protocol of typing envisioned as piano exercises, methodically pushing the typewriter's boundaries. A folder of fifty-four sheets of graphic compositions following precise guidelines, *Substitution* reflects Mairey's interest in the repurposing of this mechanical office tool and its reinvention as an experimental writing device and musical instrument. *Substitution* was published by Guy Schraenen, an Antwerp-based publisher who was also a producer, distributor, collector, curator, and researcher of avant-garde artist publications of the 1950s to the 1980s. Schraenen was a central figure in the circulation and mediation of artists' books and editions. In 1976, Mairey was included in the third issue of Schraenen's magazine *Axe*, alongside artists and poets Jo Delahaut, John Giorno, Brion Gysin, Sten Hanson, Bernard Heidsieck, Arrigo Lora-Totino, and Klaus Ritterbusch. More recently, she interpreted Stéphane Mallarmé's poem *Un coup de dés* (A Throw of the Dice), a foundational reference in the field of concrete poetry. Mairey repeatedly typed each line of the poem into word structures that were composed on individual sheets, at the rate of one word structure per page. Here again, process is the decisive factor: the date and place of typing are indicated at the bottom of each sheet, as well as the number of mistakes made while typing—thereby focusing our attention on the unpredictability of the act of writing.

Poet, novelist, photographer, essayist, and translator **Giulia Niccolai** was born in 1934 in Milan to an Italian father and an American mother. Her bilingual identity became a determining factor throughout her career. Niccolai's first novel, *Il grande angolo* (Wide Angle; Feltrinelli, 1966) is rooted in her own experience as an acclaimed photojournalist in the 1950s. She found photojournalism to be a male-dominated field and decided to extricate herself from it in the 1960s, thereafter devoting herself entirely to writing. Niccolai was substantially involved with the *neoavanguardia* movement, a group of writers whose work had been published in the anthology *I Novissimi* (The Newest Ones), in 1961, and who went on to found Gruppo 63, among them Umberto Eco, Antonio Porta, Edoardo Sanguineti, and others. These writers advocated for a rupture with literary conventions and shared an appetite for radical formal experimentation. Her activities with Gruppo 63 led to her first book of poetry, *Humpty Dumpty* (1969). Written in English, it reveals her interest in a concrete animated approach to meaning and form, continuing the legacy of two of her literary influences, Lewis Carroll and Gertrude Stein (whose writings she would translate in 1981). Building on her previous editorial experience with Gruppo 63's periodical *Quindici*, Niccolai founded the poetry journal *Tam Tam* in 1970 together with her husband, poet and editor Adriano Spatola. Their collaboration developed in the context of the multifaceted publishing venture Edizioni Geiger. Niccolai pursued her poetry's forays into linguistic invention and her exploration of the thresholds between the self, the page, and the world in works such as *Greenwich* (1971), *Poema & Oggetto* (Poem & Object; 1974), and *Russky Salad Ballads & Webster Poems* (1977), which she identified as a landmark in her writing. In 1978, speaking of words in space, Niccolai stated, "In my own work, I try to demonstrate that all objects intrinsically possess the necessary elements to be a poem. If we simply dislocate them slightly from the everyday, matter-of-fact, blind and humble [...] the poetic elements in the objects will reveal themselves."

Born Anna Aleksandrovna Tarshis, poet and artist **Ry** (or Rea) **Nikonova** (1942–2014) was a central figure in Russian avant-garde art in the second half of the twentieth century. She began writing seriously at the age of seventeen, and founded the Uktuss School (1964–74), a visual and verbal arts experimental laboratory in Sverdlovsk that was named after a local ski jump. Nikonova was a prolific author and editor of samizdat magazines, spaces of invention where she merged her explorations into meaning, image, and materiality. Together with her lifelong collaborator and partner Serge Segay, Nikonova edited the journal *Nomer* (1965–75), produced in an edition of one (handwritten) copy. *Nomer* lasted for thirty-five issues, most of which ended up being confiscated by the police in 1974. Upon returning to Yeysk, Nikonova's birthplace, she and Segay started the legendary *Transponans* journal (1979–87). This time they published an edition of five copies, the maximum allowed by the Soviet authorities. *Transponans* was envisioned as an experimental space of transposition and intermediality, continuing the work of previous innovators such as the Russian Futurists, who inspired both their attitudes and forms. Their 1980 manifesto "Transfur-manifest 1" states their editorial intention: to "preserve the thread of the poetic avant-garde." *Transponans* accompanied the Transfurist movement that

Nikonova and Segay initiated in the '80s, together with Boris Konstriktor and A. Nik. Along with experiments in sound poetry and performance, Transfurism sought to "translate and transport" poetry to a new level. Throughout her career, Nikonova was involved in collaborative productions, from editorial projects to mail art, but she also made individual work that is equally remarkable. It reveals an elaborate and detailed handmade approach to language and publishing, combining techniques and whimsical procedures that question the conventions and physical boundaries of writing. More specifically, the book became a prominent space of investigation and speculation: Nikonova imagines it in the form of a disc, a pyramid, a pinwheel, a mill, a pillow, a pillowcase, a briefcase, a cylinder, a bracelet... each with its own new way of being handled, read, and interacted with. Always challenging our relationship to the book as object and device, Nikonova finally sketches the idea of a book-mosaic, where the reader becomes co-author.

Poet **Anna Oberto**, born in 1934 in Ajaccio (Corsica), was twenty-four when she co-founded the language-oriented art and philosophy magazine *Ana Etcetera*, together with her husband Martino Oberto. Combining theoretical and graphic investigations inspired by readings of Pound and Wittgenstein, the Obertos explored the origins of language, its structure and modes, while questioning the notions of trace, inscription, and presence of the hand. Throughout the 1960s, Oberto developed a growing interest in feminism, which converged with her linguistic concerns, a conjunction that materialized in collages with written interventions. Oberto's activist political engagement culminated in the publication of the "Manifesto Femminista Anaculturale" (Anacultural Feminist Manifesto) published in the tenth issue of *Ana Etcetera* (1971), which advocated for the liberation of women and contained a programmatic text written as a preface for Mirella Bentivoglio's exhibition *Esposizione internazionale di operatrici visuali*, organized at Centro Tool in Milan. Oberto's collaboration with Bentivoglio continued with her participation in the *Materializzazione del linguaggio* exhibition at the Venice Biennale in 1978. In 1973 and '74, Oberto initiated a cycle of works titled *Anautopia per la città ideale* (Anautopia for the Ideal City) using a screen print of *The Ideal City* of Urbino as an emblem of women's ideal space. This association stemmed from the concept of the outside place in which women could free themselves from the constraints of semantic conventions and rationality. In the same period, the birth of Oberto's son Eanan led to the development of the series *Diario V'ideo-senti/mentale* (Senti-mental Video Journal, 1974), a project made of a sequence of sheets resembling a diary, on which her son's doodles dialogue with her own graphic and verbal annotations, as well as with Polaroid images of Eanan's interaction with the world and the evolution of his language acquisition process. Oberto joined the Nuova Scrittura group in 1975, the visual poetry collective co-founded by Ugo Carrega. She wrote a second manifesto for the group titled "Nuova Scrittura al femminile," in which she considers handwriting as a form of communication proper to women, in opposition to the sterile, machine-based writing of men. At the heart of the manifesto, we read: "liberation from male language as liberation of women."

Artist, designer, poet, and performer **Jennifer Pike** (1919–2016) was a member of the sound poetry collective Westminster Group (WOUP) and a central figure in Writers Forum, the publishing project founded in 1952 by Bob Cobbing. The group concerned itself with "'the limits of poetry' including 'graphic displays, notations for sound and performance, as well as semantic and syntactic developments, not to mention fun.'" Pike's involvement with Writers Forum consisted of silk-screen designs for numerous publications and record sleeves in the Writers Forum Poets and Writers Forum Record series, including *Sound Poems (known as the A B C in Sound)* by Bob Cobbing (WFP 7, January 1965); *To the North* by Anne Hardwick (WFP 8, March 1965); *The Excrement of Angels* by Heather Richardson (WFP 9, March 1965); *Mai Hart Lieb Zapfen Eibe Hold* by Ernst Jandl (WFP 11, May 1965); *Op and Kinkon Poems/and some non-kinkon* by Dom Sylvester Houédard (WFP 14, June 1965); *Sound Poems* by Bob Cobbing and *Sprechgedichte* by Ernst Jandl (Writers Forum Record No. 1, September 1965); *Hlas (voice, stimme, voix)* by Jiří Valoch (WFP 18, February 1966); as well as the design of *The Going-On Poem*, by Anselm Hollo (Writers Forum Quartos No. 1, August 1966). Pike also designed covers for *And magazine No. 4*, *And Five*, and *WF 100* (she also contributed to the latter two publications as a poet). Her collaboration with Writers Forum culminated in the publication of her book *Wump Ertarter, A Number Progression* (Writers Forum Folder 8, March 1970). In this work, Pike explores the kinetic projection of the number in space and time, between the rhythmic and the arithmetic, freezing the graphic movement that tautologically identifies form with signification. Her work has been exhibited in many galleries in the UK and internationally, and she participated most notably in the *Materializzazione del linguaggio* exhibition at the Venice Biennale in 1978. Two collections of her visual work, *Scrunch* and *The Conglomerization of Wot*, are currently in print, published by Veer Books. This same publisher recently reissued *Computer Dances*, a collection of computer-based, non-verbal poems about which Pike commented: "Some of these *Computer Dances* have been used and more may be used as scores for dance."

Bogdanka Poznanović and her husband, Dejan, were vital figures in the Novi Sad art scene from the 1960s to the 1980s. Poznanović was born in Begec, Yugoslavia, in 1930 and died in 2013. She studied painting at the Academy of Fine Arts in Belgrade in 1956. Throughout her career she worked in a variety of media, including painting, action art, performance, visual poetry, mail art, artists' books, new media, and video. She was a member of the editorial boards of the magazines *Polja* (The Fields) and *Tribina mladih* (Youth Forum), taught intermedia research at the Academy of Fine Arts in Novi Sad, and wrote art criticism. She and Dejan founded Atelier DT20, a meeting place for local and foreign artists that ran for three decades. Early in her career she made art informel and matter painting, a risky endeavor given Josip Broz Tito's condemnation of abstract art, and she later began working in a conceptual mode involving new media. In 1968–69 she received a fellowship from the Italian Ministry of Foreign Affairs to spend three months a year in Florence and Rome, respectively, where she met, among others, Fellini, Jannis Kounellis, and members of OHO from Kranj and Ljubljana, the first group in socialist Yugoslavia to popularize art actions and performances. Later, in 1977, she also completed a residency in Venice, where she conducted research at the Historical Archives of Contemporary Arts. Her commitment to expanding the possibilities of new media and social critique was fundamental to her pedagogy as well, and she devoted herself to this endeavor despite the official hostility toward such practices. Her first exhibition took place at the Accademia del Ceppo, near Florence, in 1965. In Novi Sad, she first showed her paintings at the Tribina Mladih gallery on April 27, 1970, installing them unconventionally to create an environment, and having a friend cut chains instead of red tape at the opening. In the '70s she turned her focus to work involving public space, actions, and communication. Her first action was *Heart-Object* (1970), in which she and a group of friends carried a heart-shaped Styrofoam sculpture with a metronome inside of it around the city and to the Tribina Mladih gallery. Once there, the metronome was taken out and the heart was placed on a white sheet in the middle of the space, near a banquet table, evoking the local practice of having brides walk over white linen when entering the house. In other actions, such as *Cubes-Rivers* (1971), on the Danube River, and *Rivers Transmission* (1972), participants threw Styrofoam cubes or plastic squares with the names of Yugoslavian rivers on them into actual rivers. Poznanović was active in the international mail art scene and would occasionally use visual and Signalist poems in her correspondence. She participated in numerous exhibitions organized through the network, among them the Signalism exhibition at the Gallery of Contemporary Art in Zagreb in 1974, organized by Miroljub Todorović. She frequently collaborated with the women artists affiliated with the movement, such as Marina Abramović, Katalin Ladik, Tamara Janković, and Biljana Tomić. Beginning in 1973, Poznanović authored many artist books, of which *Stellata* (1973) is the first. The first exhibition of artists' books in Yugoslavia took place at Poznanović's Atelier DT20 in 1974.

The work of London-based poet **Betty Radin** challenges the idea that concrete poetry cannot be contaminated with image material. Starting in the 1960s, Radin used various media, including graphics, collage, photomontage, photocopying, slideshows, computer works, Perspex, and mirrored objects, to compose her poems as hybrid narrative arrangements. Poet Bill Griffiths called them "visual fables." Her concrete language combines word structures and images often taken from mass media and presented out of context. It is no wonder, then, that Radin was invited to participate in the *Photopoetry* exhibition organized by Richard Allen and Alan Riddell at Polytechnic of Central London in 1978, an exhibition intended, as Riddell pointed out, to "show how in the past 15 years or so, but particularly in the 1970s, concrete and other experimental poets from many countries and cultures have come to use photography in their work." Radin was close to the Writers Forum poetry circle, with whom she produced an important number of works, such as *Me in Time* (1975), *Journeys* (1978), and *Fragments from a Journal* (1988). Additionally, Radin contributed to many avant-garde art and poetry publications of the time, such as Adriano Spatola's *Geiger* magazine, Edgardo Antonio Vigo's *Hexagono '71*, Bob Cobbing and Adrian Clarke's *And* magazine, Robert Caldwell's *Typewriter*, Peter Finch's *Second Aeon*, and Jeremy Adler's progressive title publication *A*, *AB*, *ABC*, *ABCD*. Her concrete poetry became three-dimensional in the 1972 poem "Narcissus," a playful reflection on ego and the floating of personality between the "I" and the "us."

Throughout her works, Italian poet **Giovanna Sandri** (1923–2002) investigated, by navigating between semantic and asemantic operations, the quality and status of the graphic sign. This led her to question the nature and symbolism of our own alphabets. A contemporary of the neo-avant-garde writers' collective Gruppo 63, though not directly involved in the group, Sandri was an active contributor to the most significant visual poetry magazines and international anthologies of the time, including *Geiger* and G. J. De Rook's *Anthologie visuele poëzie* (Visual Poetry Anthology). Two of Sandri's most iconic poetry books, *Capitolo Zero* (Chapter Zero; Lerici, 1969) and *From K to S: Ark of the Asymmetric* (Out of London Press, 1976), reflect the ongoing conversation between the visual and the verbal domain within her work, as well as her polyphonic research on composition, rhythm, writing traces, meaning, and (un)translatability. Reflecting on the alphabet's lunar origin, Giovanna Sandri observes: "The rhythm/gesture so sacred to all knowledge is recorded in the (capillary)(continuous) forest of Psyche, rendered in letters and made literate along the path to consciousness."

Mira Schendel was born in Switzerland in 1919 to a family of Jewish origin, and died in São Paulo in 1988. After her parents' divorce she moved to Milan with her mother in 1922. In 1937, she enrolled at the Università Cattolica del Sacro Cuore to study philosophy, but was forced to suspend her studies a year later when Mussolini banned Jews from attending Italian universities. She fled to Yugoslavia and in Sarajevo met, and later married, Jossip Hargesheimer. At the end of the war the couple returned to Italy, but facing much hardship, decided to emigrate to the Americas. Brazil was the first country to accept their application; in 1949 they arrived in Porto Alegre. That same year she enrolled in classes at the Fine Arts Academy and began painting and making ceramics. In 1950 she had her first exhibition in Porto Alegre, and by 1951 was included in the painting section of the first São Paulo Biennial. She would go on to participate in the 1953, 1965, and 1969 biennials. After separating from Hargesheimer in 1953, she moved to São Paulo, where she married German émigré Knut Schendel, owner of an established academic bookshop. In the early 1960s Schendel had numerous shows in São Paulo; from 1964 to '67, she produced the two thousand drawings in the series *Monotipias* (Monotypes). She exhibited a group of these drawings in the 1965 São Paulo Biennial under the title *Canto dos jovens (A propósito de Stockhausen)* (Song of the Youth, after Stockhausen); some of them incorporated words and phrases in different languages. This element became a staple in her work from that moment on. After seeing Schendel's work in the biennial, British critic Guy Brett arranged for her to have an exhibition at the Signals gallery in London the following year. It marked her first solo show in Europe. Thereafter she participated in the Venice Biennale of 1968, with her *Objetos gráficos* (Graphic Objects), representing Brazil alongside other women artists, among them Lygia Clark; and of 1978, in Mirella Bentivoglio's *Materializzazione del linguaggio*. Between 1970 and 1974, Schendel made over two hundred *Cadernos* (Notebooks), as well as the works known as *Toquinhos* (Little Stubs), comprising collages on paper with transfer lettering, and *Datiloscritos* (Typed Writings). Schendel was not part of any particular movement or group, but developed lasting friendships with some of the figures associated with concrete poetry, among them German semiotician and concrete poet Max Bense, who taught at the University of Stuttgart, as well as Haroldo de Campos. De Campos thought of Schendel as a "metaphysical calligraphist" who made poem-paintings. Schendel herself, in regard to writing, spoke of her preoccupation with finding a form that would capture the fleeting and unique quality of her lived experience as it seeped into the symbol, the letter: "Initially I believed that for this purpose all I must do was [...] sit and wait for the letter to form itself, to take shape on paper and connect itself with other letters into a pre-literal, pre-discursive writing. However, from the beginning I felt that to ensure a successful accomplishment I should use transparent paper."[7] The translucency of the surfaces would allow for an "anti-text" or "circular text" to be inscribed in her works simultaneously. Schendel's work has been exhibited worldwide. Recent exhibitions include *Tangled Alphabets: León Ferrari and Mira Schendel* at the Museum of Modern Art (2009), and *Mira Schendel* at the Tate Modern (2013–14).

Poet, scholar, and translator **Mary Ellen Solt** was editor of the landmark volume *Concrete Poetry: A World View*; first published in 1968, this anthology played a major role in the dissemination of concrete poetry in the United States. She was born in Gilmore City, Iowa, in 1920, and died in Santa Clarita, California, in 2007. She received a degree in English from the Iowa State Teachers College in 1941, and a master's degree from the University of Iowa in 1948. With her husband, historian Leo Frank Solt, she moved to Indiana in 1955 to teach at Indiana University in Bloomington. As a scholar, she wrote important essays on William Carlos Williams's position on the American idiom, and struck up a lifelong friendship with him. Solt began writing concrete poetry in the early 1960s and would go on to publish her work in all the seminal anthologies and display it in major exhibitions, among them Bentivoglio's *Materializzazione del linguaggio* in the 1978 Venice Biennale and *sound texts / ? concrete poetry / visual texts* at the Stedelijk Museum in Amsterdam in 1971. Her instant classic *Flowers in Concrete* (1966) was the result of her collaboration with John Dearstyne, designer and printer at Indiana University's Fine Arts Department. The best-known poem in the collection, "Forsythia," was featured on the CBS cultural program *Camera Three*. Among her other books of poetry are the semiotic poem *Marriage: A Code Poem* (1976)—created at the instigation of Iannis Xenakis, who had lectured at Bloomington earlier that year—and *The Peoplemover 1968: A Demonstration Poem* (1978). This last volume reproduces Solt's protest posters arranged in the form of concrete poems. They were first published in *Open Poetry*, edited by Ronald Gross and George Quasha, in 1973, and were originally silk-screened for an exhibition by the Finial Press, Urbana, Illinois, in 1970. The preparation of the anthology *Concrete Poetry: A World View* began, unbeknownst to Solt, when, in 1966, colleague Willis Barnstone, himself a poet and noted translator, invited her to guest-edit an issue of Indiana University's *Artes Hispánicas/Hispanic Arts* devoted to concrete poetry. Solt had become aware of the movement when she met Ian Hamilton Finlay in Edinburgh in 1962. She had been following his publications through Wild Hawthorn Press and the magazine *Poor. Old. Tired. Horse.*, encountering works by the Brazilian Noigandres group, Eugen Gomringer, Ernst Jandl, and numerous others in its pages. Her own poems would be published in it as well. Through Finlay, Solt began corresponding with the Brazilian poets and translating their works. Her research continued to expand, and by 1968, a year after Something Else Press published Emmett Williams's *An Anthology of Concrete Poetry*, the brimming issue of *Artes Hispánicas* on concrete poetry appeared. While Williams's book published a larger number of poets, Solt's provided the theoretical foundations for the movement, as well as lavish color reproductions honoring the works' initial conception. The de Campos brothers were invited to Indiana University in 1968, and numerous symposia and programs on concrete poetry occurred in the United States and abroad thereafter. Later, Barnstone convinced the university to publish the journal as the 1970 book *Concrete Poetry: A World View*. In Solt's words, the experience had been "exhilarating, because it was possible to be situated in Bloomington, Indiana, and to participate in a world-wide effort [...] to restore the integrity and communicative potential of words by heightening their sign qualities."[8]

Born in 1944 in Tokyo, poet **Chima Sunada** was only five years old when she embarked on the "road to writing" by studying Japanese calligraphy, *shodo*, a practice that was to accompany her throughout her career. She joined the avant-garde concrete poetry ASA group (Association for Study of Arts) in 1965, only one year after its founding by Seiichi Niikuni. His ASA association and magazine quickly gained an international scope, establishing ties with the Brazilian Noigandres group and the French Spatialists, reflecting concrete poetry's growing global network. Sunada's concrete poetry work used Japanese typographic characters to achieve geometric compositions traversed by spatialized semantic forces, thus creating new linguistic tensions. While in dialogue with the active Italian *poesia visiva* scene, her work soon reached an international audience. Sunada grew close to Mirella Bentivoglio, who exhibited her work on the occasion of two important shows: *Arti visive. Poesia visiva. / Visual Poetry by Women*, shown in 1974 at the Galleria Artivisive in Rome; and *Ideogramma come poesia*, held ten years later at the Galleria Il Segno in Turin. In the mid-'70s, Sunada departed from strict geometry and mechanical typographic repetition to revisit the spatial potential of calligraphy. She used procedures associated with concrete poetry as a tool to deconstruct existing ideograms, modifying them to ambiguously resemble their meaning, a process that allowed them to reach "their true or supposed pictographic etymologies," as Bentivoglio puts it.

Born in Mozambique in 1922, **Salette Tavares** studied Historical and Philosophical Sciences at the University of Lisbon. She taught aesthetics at the National Society of Fine Arts (SNBA) and at AR.CO (Center for Art and Visual Communication). For her, play, and wordplay in particular, was synonymous with the creative act. She displayed a subversive yet lighthearted humor across different media and practices—from more traditional poetry to poem-objects and object-poems—which matched her constant preoccupation with semiotics and the verbivocovisual. Throughout her trajectory, she wrote for the page and for other mediums, using a variety of printing techniques—etching and silk-screen printing among them—and experimenting with materials such as wood, ceramics, glass, and aluminum. Explorations of typography and the topologies of the page and exhibition space are also consistent throughout her works, which often transform and pay tribute to the everyday, and incorporate chance and combinatorial procedures. With obfuscating layouts and text placed upside down, some of her works were also meant to deceive the authoritarian, censoring officials of Salazar's Estado Novo. Along with Ana Hatherly and others, Tavares was part of the PO.EX group from the 1960s to the '80s and co-edited the first two issues of *Poesia experimental*. Tavares's *Brin cadeiras* and kinetophonic works appeared in the second issue, alongside works by Hatherly, Pierre Garnier, Haroldo de Campos, Henri Chopin, Ian Hamilton Finlay, Edgard Braga, Pedro Xisto, and others. From 1963 to '64, she created happenings at various galleries including the Galeria Divulgação, Galeria Quadrante, SNBA, and AR.CO. The first happening, *Ode à crítica*, took place in the context of the group exhibition *Visopoemas* in 1965 that included works of hers rendered in wire, pottery, and paper. *Ode* consisted of a concerto in which an aria in mock praise of the nation's art and literary critics was sung over and over, depending on whether there were encores. The syllable "cri... cri... cri... cri..." was stuttered repeatedly as a reference to those who speak much but say little. Galeria Quadrum hosted the retrospective exhibition *Brincar* (*Kidding Around*) in 1979, and in 2014–15, the Modern Collection of the Calouste Gulbenkian Museum in Lisbon presented the show *Salette Tavares: Spatial Poetry*. Notable books include *Quadrada* (Square; 1967), *Lex Icon* (1971), *Obra poética: 1957–1971* (*Collected Poetry*; 1992), and *Poesia gráfica* (Graphic Poetry; 1995). Tavares died in 1994.

The collection of concrete poems entitled *Lozenges: Poems in the Shape of Things* was the first book of poetry by Canadian author **Colleen Thibaudeau** (1925–2012). It was published in 1965 by her husband James Reaney's imprint, Alphabet Press. Reaney typeset the poems and designed the cover of the book in Alphabet's print shop. Thibaudeau also contributed to Reaney's *Alphabet* magazine, an art and literature periodical devoted to myths and archetypal images, subtitled "A semiannual devoted to the iconography of the imagination." Thibaudeau and Reaney shared an interest in children's literature and small press publishing, a combination of affinities that becomes apparent when holding and reading *Lozenges*, a concrete object as a whole. Departing from concrete poetry's strategies, Thibaudeau's following volumes *Ten Letters* (1975) and *My Granddaughters Are Combing Out Their Long Hair* (1977) pursued the exploration of the materiality of daily life—a domestic environment and everydayness infused with imagination. Thibaudeau's starting point is her immediate experience, which she captures and develops in photosensitive language. Author Kathryn Rogers observes: "Poems keep memories like photographs do: They concentrate a moment—freeze dry it. Thibaudeau, like many poets, understands this similarity but uses it in her own unique manner. In [the poem] "Photo" [...] Thibaudeau's treasuring eye views children at the beach like a 'camera...Just another gull, swooping in, fixing their fluidity.'" Family threads, memory, pictures, and time are ongoing themes in her later collections of poems *The Martha Landscapes* (1984) and *The "Patricia" Album* (1992), a suite of lyrical poems about a boat named *The Patricia* and its owners, inspired by an album of photographs found in a secondhand store. *The Artemesia Book*, a collection of new and selected poems, was published in 1991 by Brick Books.

Biljana Tomić was born in 1940 in Novo Selo, Serbia, and is based in Belgrade. She studied art history, aesthetics, and contemporary art at the Faculty of Philosophy, University of Belgrade. From 1969 to 1970 she studied under Giulio Carlo Argan at La Sapienza University in Rome. She curated visual art and multimedia events at the Belgrade International Theatre Festival (BITEF) from 1968 to 1973, and served as curator of the Expanded Media Festival at the Studentski kulturni centar, or SKC (Student Cultural Center) in Belgrade from 1972 to 1977. Founded in 1968, the SKC has played a crucial, if complex, role in Belgrade's cultural scene. While it was an official cultural institution founded by the state during the Socialist Federal Republic of Yugoslavia in order to institutionalize, and contain, youth culture, it was also a place of avant-garde experimentation that permitted the introduction of new technologies, new artistic expressions, and new forms of political activism and self-organization. Tomić directed the visual art program at the SKC Gallery from 1976 to 1999. Since 2001, she has been director of nKA / ICA – Belgrade, an association of professional art historians and curators. Tomić has been a co-curator of *Aperto*, Venice Biennale (1986); *Videothek*, Documenta 8, Kassel (1987); *La coesistenza dell'arte* (*The Coexistence of Art*), Venice Biennale (1993); and the Locarno Film Festival (1981–87). Since 1968, she has curated numerous exhibitions in both private and public international institutions.

The only concrete poem by Roman author **Silvia Trevale** is, to our knowledge, *Segmenti alfabetici* (Alphabetical Segments), published in 1972 in the fifth issue of Adriano Spatola's *Geiger*). Also a sculptor and a painter, Trevale is the author of the poetry collections *La strega* (The Witch) and *Dedica a Giano* (Dedication to Janus), as well as a novel, *Io, Tiberio e gli amici suoi* (Me, Tiberius and His Friends). Her work was included in *Esposizione internazionale di operatrici visuali*, Mirella Bentivoglio's pioneering 1972 exhibition of the work of women artists at Centro Tool, in Milan. *Segmenti alfabetici* is the visual deconstruction of what appear to be structural components of letters, piled in front of one another, perhaps waiting to be rearticulated and reused. Like scaffoldings, they seem to be the support structures of a language to come.

Patrizia Vicinelli sought to create a new poetry to be read, seen, and voiced. Born in 1943 in Bologna, where she died in 1991, Vicinelli was deeply involved in the Italian artistic avant-garde movements of the 1960s and '70s, actively participating in the life of the progressive literary laboratory Gruppo 63, but also venturing into experimental theater, music, and underground cinema, notably through collaborations with artists and filmmakers Gianni Castignoli and Alberto Grifi. Vicinelli was connected to the most forward-thinking poetry scenes of the time, and was especially close to two of its preeminent figures, Adriano Spatola and Emilio Villa. Her work was published in many magazines and anthologies, such as *Bab Ilu*, *Ex*, *Quindici*, *Marcatré*, *Doc(k)s*, and many others; it was also included in Luciano Caruso's important show and catalog *Il colpo di glottide* (*Glottal Stop*). Her wide-ranging artistic approach was instrumental in her attempt to spark a crisis of language—on the levels of reading, seeing, and listening—so as to dismantle existing linguistic structures and renew the writing gesture from the alphabet to the page, envisioned as a performance site. Her brilliant *à, a. A,* (Lerici, 1967) expresses this immediate need for new paths and energies in poetry. After exiling herself in Tangier in 1969, Vicinelli felt displaced both linguistically and culturally; in response, she turned to occultism and mysticism. Written during her time in Tangier, her book *Apotheosis of a Schizoid Woman* (Tau/ma, 1979) reflects the questions of identity and gender that blossomed during this plurilingual phase of her life. An excerpt from this text almost seems to capture, between the lines, the reader's process: "his thought the neurons reaching the calcium joining the sodium the potassium to his phosphorus his excited codes transported producing oceans of sounds movements signs images."

Rosmarie Waldrop, née Sebald, was born in Germany in 1935, where she studied literature and musicology at the University of Würzburg and the University of Freiburg. She immigrated to the United States in the late 1950s to study comparative literature at the University of Michigan, earning her degree in 1966. While in Michigan, she married poet Keith Waldrop, whom she'd met in Germany in 1954 while playing the flute in a youth orchestra that performed in her hometown of Kitzingen, where he was stationed in the military. In 1961, they bought a secondhand printing press and founded *Burning Deck* magazine, which evolved into Burning Deck Press, the seminal independent publisher devoted to innovative poetry and prose, much of it in translation. In 1968 they moved from Michigan to Providence, Rhode Island. Besides a prodigious output of writing that includes more than twenty collections of poetry, fiction, and essays, Waldrop has devoted her energies to publishing and translating such authors as Claude Royet-Journoud, Anne-Marie Albiach, Emmanuel Hocquard, Paul Celan, Elfriede Czurda, and Jacques Roubaud. She is the main translator of Edmond Jabès, whom she met during a year-long stay in Paris in 1970, and has rendered over a dozen of his books into English, among them *The Book of Questions* and *The Book of Resemblances*. Waldrop's *Lavish Absence: Recalling and Rereading Edmond Jabès* reflects on the experience of translating him, and on translation in general. Her books of poetry include *The Aggressive Ways of the Casual Stranger* (1972), *Lawn of Excluded Middle* (1993), *A Key into the Language of America* (1994), *Reluctant Gravities* (1999), and *Driven to Abstraction* (2010). Waldrop's concrete poems appear in two volumes: *Camp Printing* (1970) and *Letters* (1970), composed jointly with Keith Waldrop. Her essay "A Basis of Concrete Poetry," which describes concrete poetry as "a revolt against the transparency of the word," appears in the book of essays *Dissonance (if you are interested)* (2005). *Gap Gardening: Selected Poems*, spanning four decades of Waldrop's poetic output, was released in 2016. At a certain point, she abandoned the lyric form and began writing only prose poetry, allowing for the exploration of "the sentence and its boundaries, slidings, the gaps between fragments, the shadow zone of silence, of margins."[9] Her novels are the recently reissued *The Hanky of Pippin's Daughter* (1986) and *A Form / of Taking / It All* (1990). She is the recipient of many awards and distinctions for her poetry and translations, including a DAAD fellowship, a Foundation for Contemporary Arts award, and a Lila Wallace–Reader's Digest Writers' Award. Her translation of Ulf Stolterfoht's book *Lingos I–IX* received the 2008 PEN Award for Poetry in Translation. The French government has made her a Chevalier des Arts et des Lettres. The volume by Keith and Rosmarie Waldrop entitled *Keeping / the window open: Interviews, statements, alarms, excursions*, edited by Ben Lerner, appeared in 2019.

Visionary poet **Hannah Weiner** was born in Rhode Island in 1928; she died in New York in 1997. She studied at Radcliffe College. In the 1960s, she was part of a vibrant circle of poets, writers, and artists in New York that included Bernadette Mayer, Vito Acconci, Andy Warhol, Carolee Schneemann, John Giorno, John Perreault, Eduardo Costa, David Antin, Anne Waldman, Lewis Warsh, and others. Some of them were associated with the mimeo magazine *0 to 9*, edited by Acconci and Mayer. In the spring of 1969, *0 to 9* staged a series of street actions, several of which Weiner devised for the occasion, including *Hannah Weiner Meets Hannah Weiner*, and another in which she marked off half a block in downtown Manhattan with cloth tape she had printed with four flags from *The International Code of Signals for the Use of All Nations*. She designed the tape while working as a ladies underwear designer for the Malabe Co. and had been using it for poems and poetry events since 1966. For instance, it was part of the Central Park Poetry Event of 1968, and Weiner used it to tie up the audience at the *Tiny Events* series of actions, or short events, that she organized at the Longview Country Club, the annex to Max's Kansas City on Park Avenue South and Nineteenth Street in Manhattan. In 1969, Weiner, Perreault, and Costa organized the legendary *Fashion Show–Poetry Event* at the Americas Society, a fashion show featuring anti-garments designed by artists such as Claes Oldenburg, Marisol, James Rosenquist, Alex Katz, and Warhol, with poets narrating spoofs of standard fashion copy. Like another one of her peers, Jackson Mac Low, Weiner became a central figure in the Language poetry movement of the late '70s and '80s. After developing her code-signal performances and poems, in the 1970s she drew on what she considered a clairvoyant ability—she saw words on the foreheads of her friends, and transcribed them according to a unique typographical system. In a poem, she describes first seeing words on her forehead, in the air, on the typewriter, on the page, formatted in capitals, spaced out, or underlined. Then she began "seeing phrases and whole sentences, in various print sizes and in script," according to the liner notes of a New Wilderness Audiographics cassette recording of a reading by Weiner: "The words have a memory, relate to specific situations, give information not 'consciously' available, answer questions, play language games, joke and tease." The resulting poems were collected in *Clairvoyant Journal* (1974), originally published by Waldman and Warsh's Angel Hair Books, and reissued by Bat in 2014. Other classic books by Weiner are *Signal Flag Poems* (1968) and *Code Poems* (1982). Previously uncollected work and early performance texts appear in the volume *Hannah Weiner's Open House* (2006), edited by Patrick Durgin.

Ruth Wolf-Rehfeldt was born in Wurzen, Saxony, in 1932. After World War II, she settled in East Berlin and worked for the exhibitions department at the Academy of Arts. Despite her lack of a formal artistic education, she produced paintings, pastels, drawings, and, most notably, what she calls "typewritings." Works on paper made on a typewriter, the typewritings are intricate studies encompassing concrete poetry, linguistics, graphic design, and conceptual art—innovative hybrids of language, symbol, and visual form. Although in the beginning of her practice Wolf-Rehfeldt explored semiotics and concrete poetry, she began to shift her focus in later years to abstract compositions, moving from linguistic signage to language as form and matter. Many of her typewritings emphasize the materiality and density of words and symbols, new meanings derived from experimentation. Wolf-Rehfeldt was nominated as a candidate for the Association of Fine Artists of the German Democratic Republic in 1975, and was admitted as a full member in 1978. Due to her status as a member of the AFA, she was allowed to print up to fifty "miniature graphic" works (*Kleingrafik*) in print shops. Each of her works thus consists of an original—either an individual typed work or a series—and a limited number of further reproductions in the form of carbon copies, postcards, or prints, in formats ranging from A6 to A4. During this period, she was simultaneously engaged with a vast network of artists in the mail art movement, most notably with Paulo Bruscky, with whom she exchanged works regularly in the 1970s and '80s, establishing a connection between dictatorship-era Brazil and East Germany. Wolf-Rehfeldt and her partner, Robert Rehfeldt, were pioneers within the GDR of a type of artistic exchange that allowed for the uncensored circulation of art and ideas. As works of art that were easy to distribute, Wolf-Rehfeldt's typewritings were often included in her correspondence with other artists. After the fall of the Berlin Wall and the death of her partner, Wolf-Rehfeldt stopped making work altogether. Her newfound geographic freedom fundamentally altered her reasons for making and distributing art. Recently, however, a newly invigorated interest in her work has emerged. Along with several public exhibitions, Berlin gallery ChertLüdde has begun a collaborative process of archiving all of her works and her archive of mail art. ChertLüdde published *Signs Fiction* in 2016 (together with Motto Books), the most comprehensive collection of Wolf-Rehfeldt's work to date, as well as *The Mail Art Archive of Ruth Wolf-Rehfeldt and Robert Rehfeldt* (2018), a publication presenting the archive of mail art received by the two German artists from the beginning of the 1970s until the early 1990s. What could be read as Wolf-Rehfeldt's motto, from her *Signs Fiction* text, is an open invitation: "Type your own art."

Notes

1 Dorothée Dupuis, "Anna Bella Geiger," *Terremoto*, February 16, 2015, https://terremoto.mx/article/anna-bella-geiger/.

2 Margalit Fox, "Madeline Arakawa Gins, Visionary Architect, Is Dead at 72," *New York Times*, January 12, 2014, https://www.nytimes.com/2014/01/13/arts/design/madeline-arakawa-gins-visionary-architect-dies-at-72.html.

3 Mary Ellen Solt, "Czechoslovakia," in *Concrete Poetry: A World View* (Bloomington, IN: Indiana University Press, 1968), http://www.ubu.com/papers/solt/czech.html.

4 Gwen Allen, *Artists' Magazines: An Alternative Space for Art* (Cambridge, MA: MIT Press, 2011), 231.

5 Hendrik Folkerts, "Keimena #30: *Sound Cage: A Portrait of Katalin Ladik* by Kornél Szilágyi (Igor Buharov)," Documenta 14, July 10, 2017, https://www.documenta14.de/en/public-tv/23603/30-sound-cage.

6 Liliane Lijn, "My Influences," *Frieze*, May 30, 2014, https://frieze.com/article/liliane-lijn-my-influences.

7 "Mira Schendel Statement" in *Mira Schendel*, ed. Tanya Barson (London: Tate Modern, 2014), 196–7.

8 Mary Ellen Solt, "Concrete Steps to an Anthology," in *Mary Ellen Solt: Toward a Theory of Concrete Poetry*, OEI, no. 51, ed. Antonio Sergio Bessa (Stockholm: *OEI*, 2010), 303.

9 Rosmarie Waldrop, "Form and Discontent," in *Dissonance (if you are interested)* (Tuscaloosa: University of Alabama Press, 2005). Quoted by Nikolai Duffy in the introduction to *Gap Gardening: Selected Poems* (New Directions, 2016), 3.

Women in Concrete Poetry: 1959–1979

ISBN: 978-1-7344897-2-9

Second Printing

Editors: Alex Balgiu and Mónica de la Torre
Managing Editor: James Hoff
Copy Editor: Allison Dubinsky
Editorial Assistant: Jonah Max
Designer: Scott Ponik
Czech translations: Alex Zucker
German translations: Alta L. Price
French translations: Alex Balgiu
Hungarian translations: Katalin Ladik and Josef Schreiner
Italian translations: Stefania Heim
Japanese translations: Sawako Nakayasu
Polish translations: Elka Krajewska
Portuguese translations: Anna Bella Geiger, Hilary Kaplan, Mónica de la Torre
Russian translations: Rebekah Smith
Spanish translations: Mónica de la Torre

Primary Information
232 3rd Street, #A113
Brooklyn, NY 11215
www.primaryinformation.org

Printed by Musumeci, Italy

Primary Information and the editors would like to thank Serena Aldi (MART / Museo di arte moderna e contemporanea di Trento e Rovereto), Lenora de Barros, Charles Bernstein, Antonio Sergio Bessa, Tomaso Binga, Tiziana di Caro & Fabiola Cangiano (Galleria Tiziana di Caro), Paula Claire, Steve Clay, Tomás Cunha Ferreira, Katie Dallinger, Álvaro Díaz, Katrina Dodson, Kristin Dykstra, Roberto Echavarren, Ellen Elias-Bursać, Katya Gamolina, Anna Bella Geiger, Mica Gherghescu (Bibliothèque Kandinsky, Musée national d'art moderne / Centre Pompidou), Karen Grimson, August Gromozeka, Cecilia Gröneberg & Jonas (J) Magnusson, Małgorzata Dawidek Gryglicka, Orsolya Hegedus / acb Galéria, Susan Howe, Joanna Kobyłt / Muzeum Współczesne Wrocław, Ann Komaromi and the Soviet Samizdat Periodicals project at the University of Toronto, Katalin Ladik & Josef Schreiner, Liliane Lijn, Simon Mager, Zbigniew Makarewicz, Jonah Max, Meredith Morran, Luis Pérez Oramas, Lisa Pearson, Marjorie Perloff, Alta L. Price, Gabriela Simon Flores, Rebekah Smith, Marie Van den Broucke, Rosmarie Waldrop, and Matvei Yankelevich.

Primary Information is a 501(c)(3) non-profit organization founded in 2006 to publish artists' books and writings. The organization's programming advances the often-intertwined relationship between artists' books and arts' activism, creating a platform for historically marginalized artistic communities and practices. The organization receives generous support through grants from the Michael Asher Foundation, Galerie Buchholz, the Patrick and Aimee Butler Family Foundation, The Cowles Charitable Trust, Empty Gallery, The Ford Foundation, The Fox Aarons Foundation, the Helen Frankenthaler Foundation, Furthermore: a program of the J. M. Kaplan Fund, the Graham Foundation for Advanced Studies in the Fine Arts, Greene Naftali, the Greenwich Collection Ltd, the Eva Hesse Charitable Foundation, the John W. and Clara C. Higgins Foundation, Metabolic Studio, the Mellon Foundation, the New York City Department of Cultural Affairs in partnership with the City Council, the New York State Council on the Arts with the support of the Office of the Governor and the New York State Legislature, the Orbit Fund, the Robert Rauschenberg Foundation, the Stichting Egress Foundation, The Stolbun Family and The Stolbun Collection, VIA Art Fund, The Jacques Louis Vidal Charitable Fund, Wagner Foundation, The Andy Warhol Foundation for the Visual Arts, the Wilhelm Family Foundation, and individuals worldwide. Primary Information receives support from the Arison Arts Foundation, The Willem de Kooning Foundation, the Marian Goodman Foundation, the Henry Luce Foundation, the Mellon Foundation, and Teiger Foundation through the Coalition of Small Arts NYC.